The Oxford Dictionary of

Pragmatics

For my daughter, Elizabeth, my wife, Lihua Li, and my father, and in loving memory of my mother, Hexia Feng (1921–2010)

Also by Yan Huang

Anaphora
published in Oxford Studies in Typology and Linguistic Theory

Pragmatics
published in Oxford Textbooks in Linguistics

The Oxford Dictionary of

Pragmatics

YAN HUANG

OXFORD
UNIVERSITY PRESS

OXFORD
UNIVERSITY PRESS

Great Clarendon Street, Oxford, OX2 6DP,
United Kingdom

Oxford University Press is a department of the University of Oxford.
It furthers the University's objective of excellence in research, scholarship,
and education by publishing worldwide. Oxford is a registered trade mark of
Oxford University Press in the UK and in certain other countries

First published 2012
First published in paperback 2015

Impression: 1

Published in the United States of America by Oxford University Press
198 Madison Avenue, New York, NY 10016, United States of America

British Library Cataloguing in Publication Data
Data available

ISBN 978–0–19–953980–2 (Hbk.)
ISBN 978–0–19–871281–7 (Pbk.)

Contents

Preface

The aim of this dictionary is to provide an authoritative, comprehensive, and up-to-date explanation of the terms which are likely to be encountered in contemporary linguistic pragmatics.

Pragmatics is one of the most vibrant and rapidly growing fields in contemporary linguistics and the philosophy of language. In recent years it has also become increasingly a central topic in cognitive science, artificial intelligence, informatics, neuroscience, language pathology, anthropology, and sociology. As a result, pragmatics has become one of the few branches of linguistics which has sprawled and is still sprawling in many directions, embracing or interfacing with a highly diverse range of subjects both within and outside linguistics. Given this rapid development and the high diversity of the field, it is not surprising that numerous new theories and sub-branches have appeared in the last two decades or so, engendering many new terms. In addition, the advent of pragmatics has, for many linguists, caused a reassessment of the general boundaries round linguistics, since some traditional terms must necessarily be redefined. However, many of the terms (including some of the new ones) are formulated at such an intimidating level of technicality that they are not easily accessible to the student.

The dictionary contains over 2480 terms grouped into over 2400 entries across the whole field of pragmatics. The main body of the dictionary is organized around entries alphabetically presented. It covers approaches, concepts, schools of thought, terms, theories, and important figures that are derived not only from the central canon of pragmatics such as implicature, presupposition, speech acts, deixis, reference, and politeness/impoliteness but also from recently emerged sub-branches of pragmatics such as clinical pragmatics, historical pragmatics, and literary pragmatics. Notice that entries for important figures are restricted to deceased scholars. Given that the central topics of inquiry of pragmatics have their origin in the philosophy of language and that pragmatics is still being heavily influenced by it, I have included related terms in the philosophy of language. Since some areas of pragmatics are intimately interwoven with its sister field of semantics, there is also overlap here too.

In writing the definition of a first-level entry, I have tried to avoid circularity, i.e. not to use the headword or some derivative of it as part of a concise statement of the meaning and/or usage of the term, so that the definition does not itself include what is to be defined. But there are cases where this is difficult to avoid. In these cases, the aim of the opening definition of the term is not intended to be a full non-circular one but a functional guide to the precise usage of the term, aimed at a reader who is either sufficiently well informed in the subject to be able to use it or sufficiently well motivated to navigate through other entries.

The organization and style of the dictionary are largely in line with Peter Matthews' *Concise Oxford Dictionary of Linguistics*. But the style of the dictionary is slightly more technical than that of Matthews' dictionary, given the more specialized scope and target readership of the present undertaking. In addition, I have also adopted some of the good practices found in David Crystal's *A Dictionary of Linguistics and Phonetics* (6th edition).

In line with Matthews' dictionary and other Oxford dictionaries, I have used an asterisk to point to related entries. Although its uses in linguistics are for other purposes, I do not think that confusion will arise. I have also adopted a light formula to give reference to relevant seminal and most recent work for further reading, using the simple direction 'see' rather than 'see e.g.'.

The dictionary is of interest primarily to undergraduate and postgraduate students specializing in linguistics with little or no prior background in or knowledge of pragmatics. It will be suitable for students taking linguistics option as part of a language, humanities, or social science degree, and for researchers in the philosophy of language, the sociology and psychology of interaction, anthropology, cognitive science, artificial intelligence, neuroscience, and language pathology, as well as linguistics. It will also be of interest to anyone with an interest in language, especially the study of linguistic meaning.

The dictionary can be used in two ways. The most obvious one is as a simple reference work. When as a reader you come across an unfamiliar term in a book or journal article, you can use the dictionary to look up what the term means and how it is used by various writers, sometimes with reference to related terms. But the dictionary is also carefully constructed so that it can be used for systematic browsing, in a way that is increasingly familiar from the use of browsers on the internet. For these purposes, the cross-references and suggestions for further reading have been kept to the most effective number—neither too few nor too many—for browsing to be both easier and more reliable than on the internet. If, for example, you wish to learn something about the concept of implicature, you can first go to the entry for that term. This entry will then direct you in turn to the entries on conversational implicature and on conventional implicature, and from there you will be guided to the one on conventionality, and so on, with alternative routes depending on your particular interests and concerns. The system of cross-referencing deployed in the dictionary is extensive enough that you will be directed to not only a list of properties for conversational implicature and conventional implicature, but eventually to a network of more distantly related terms such as *conversational implicature*$_O$, *conversational implicature*$_F$, *generalized conversational implicature (GCI)*, *particularized conversational implicature (PCI)*, *standard conversational implicature*, *additive implicature*, *subtractive implicature*, *audience implicature*, *utterer implicature, near-implicature, direct implicature, indirect implicature, sentence implicature, speaker implicature, politeness implicature, impoliteness implicature, embedded implicature, nonce implicature, short-circuited implicature, actual implicature, potential implicature, im-plicature, meta-implicature, F-implicature, impliciture, explicature, scalar implicature, non-conventional implicature, conventionalized implicature, 'live' implicature, Q-implicature, I-implicature, M-implicature, R-implicature*, and *r-implicature*. You will also be led to the entry on the originator of the notion of implicature, the British philosopher H. P. Grice. For many beginning students, gathering information systematically in this way proves more efficient, and more comfortable, than reading through a conventionally constructed textbook.

No person can be a specialist in the whole of pragmatics. I alone am responsible for any remaining errors in the dictionary. Therefore, I sincerely and warmly welcome comments from readers drawing my attention to these errors.

In a few cases, I was unable to trace copyright material holders, and would be grateful for any help that would enable me to do so.

Yan Huang 黃衍
January 2012
Auckland, New Zealand

Acknowledgements

I owe my greatest debt of gratitude to Peter Matthews. It was his excellent *Concise Oxford Dictionary of Linguistics* that inspired me to write this book. His encouragement, advice, and support have improved the dictionary significantly. I wish particularly to thank David Cram, who, acting as a referee for Oxford University Press, read through a complete draft and made many invaluable comments in his typical erudite fashion. He has also taught me a few rules of thumb for how to compile a specialized vocabulary dictionary like this. My thanks go to Louise Cummings and Mante Nieuwland, who helped with entries in clinical and experimental pragmatics respectively. For reading portions of the manuscript and offering useful comments at an early stage of this project, I should like to thank five anonymous Oxford University Press referees. I am grateful to Natsuko Shintani for her assistance with the alphabetic ordering of entries and references. I would like to thank John Davey of Oxford University Press for his encouragement, advice, and patience, and Sarah Barrett for her professionalism shown in copy-editing this dictionary. Last but not least, the dictionary also owes a great deal to my family. My wife and daughter have been a continual source of encouragement, support, and love. I dedicate this book to them and my father, and in loving memory of my mother.

Introduction: what is pragmatics?

Pragmatics is one of the most vibrant and rapidly growing fields in linguistics and the philosophy of language. In recent years it has also become increasingly a central topic in cognitive science, artificial intelligence, informatics, neuroscience, language pathology, anthropology, and sociology. But what is pragmatics? It can be broadly defined as the study of language in use. However, such a definition may be too general and vague to be of much use. This is because pragmatics is a particularly complex subject, with all kinds of disciplinary influence and few, if any, clear boundaries.[1] The aim of this introduction is to survey the representative research areas in contemporary pragmatics and present an authoritative and up-to-date description of the contemporary landscape of pragmatics, in the hope that it will help the reader make a better use of the dictionary.

1 Anglo-American pragmatics

1.1 Anglo-American, component, view of pragmatics

Since at least Levinson (1983), the study of pragmatics has been acknowledged as being split between two schools of thought: the Anglo-American and (European) Continental traditions. Within the Anglo-American conception of linguistics and the philosophy of language, pragmatics may be defined as the systematic study of meaning by virtue of, or dependent on, the use of language. The central topics of inquiry include implicature, presupposition, speech acts, deixis, and reference, all of which originate in 20th-century analytic(al) philosophy (e.g. Huang 2007: 2). This is known as the component view of pragmatics. On this view, a linguistic theory consists of a number of core components: phonetics, phonology, morphology, syntax, and semantics. Each of these core components has a relatively properly demarcated domain of inquiry. Pragmatics, then, is just another core component placed in the same contrast set within a linguistic theory. By contrast, other 'hyphenated' branches of linguistics such as anthropological linguistics, educational linguistics, and sociolinguistics lie outside this set of core components. The component view of pragmatics is to some extent a reflection of the modular conception of the human mind: the claim that the mental architecture of *homo sapiens* is divided roughly

[1] Ariel (2010) coined the metaphor 'big-tent pragmatics' to refer to the heterogeneous nature of pragmatics. Under big-tent pragmatics, there are two groups of pragmaticists: what she called 'problem-solvers' and 'border-seekers'.

into a central processor and a number of distinctive, specialized mental systems known as modules (e.g. Fodor 1983; Huang 2007: 198–201).[2] Inspired by this Fodorian modularity of mind thesis, an area of research in pragmatics called 'modular pragmatics' has emerged. Modular pragmatics considers the question of whether or not there is a pragmatic module in the human mind. Although it is generally accepted that pragmatics does not constitute a modular system, there are scholars such as the Israeli philosopher Asa Kasher who are of the view that certain parts of pragmatics are modular. On his view, modular pragmatics consists of a pragmatic central system of pragmatic knowledge, by which conversational implicature, for example, is generated. It also has pragmatic modules. One such module is claimed to be the cognitive system which governs both the production and comprehension of speech acts, and especially indirect speech acts. Kasher called this cognitive system the 'modular speech act theory' (e.g. Kasher 2010a). Within relevance theory, Sperber and Wilson have abandoned their earlier position of treating pragmatics or utterance comprehension as a Fodorian central, inferential process. Instead, they now take the view that utterance comprehension involves a more modular ability for mind-reading or 'theory of mind', which involves the more general metapsychological ability to inferentially attribute mental states or intentions to others on the basis of their behaviour. Furthermore, Sperber and Wilson argued that, contrary to the popular assumption that a sub-module is not needed to handle pragmatic abilities in mind-reading, utterance comprehension is subject to a distinct interpretation sub-module of the 'theory of mind', i.e. a specialized, automatic computational device, with its own special principles and mechanisms (e.g. Wilson and Sperber 2004; Huang 2007: 200–201).

[2] A particular version of the American cognitive scientist Jerry Fodor's modularity of mind thesis is the massive modularity of mind thesis. The term 'massive modularity' was introduced by the French social and cognitive scientist Dan Sperber. According to this view, the human mind is largely, if not entirely, composed of modules. Two forms of the massive modularity of mind thesis can then be identified: strong and weak. On the authority of the strong massive modularity of mind thesis, the human mind does not contain any overarching general-purpose mechanism. In other words, every central process is modular. By contrast, the weak massive modularity of mind thesis maintains that while central processes are largely modular, there are also non-modular, general-purpose processes. The massive modularity of mind thesis is not, however, espoused by Fodor (e.g. Meini 2010). Furthermore, in the opinion of the British philosopher Gabriel Segal, modularity can be divided into diachronic and synchronic modularity. The former is a cognitive module that follows a genetically and developmentally determined pattern of growth. By comparison, synchronic modularity refers to a module that is static. Finally, there are competence and performance modules. A competence module, also referred to as a 'Chomskyan' or 'information module', is one that constitutes a system of mental representation. It is said to contain linguistic, biological, psychological, physical, and mathematical knowledge. It runs in contrast with a performance module, also termed a 'computational module'. A performance module is one that functions as a computational mechanism. In other words, it is a device that processes mental representations (e.g. Carston 2010a).

1.2 Contextualism vs. semantic minimalism in the contemporary philosophy of language

Currently there is an ongoing, heated debate between contextualism and semantic minimalism in the philosophy of language. As a broad school of thought in the contemporary philosophy of language and linguistics, contextualism (also known as 'contextualist semantics' in opposition to 'minimal(ist) semantics') endeavours to provide an account of contextual variations in semantic content in terms of a criterion of contextual best fit. According to this view, pragmatically enriched entities such as speech acts are the primary bearers of truth-conditional content. Only in the context of an utterance does a sentence express a determinate semantic content. In other words, semantics goes only part of the way towards the computation of utterance meaning; it is pragmatic enrichment that completes the process as a whole. Two versions of contextualism can be identified: moderate and radical or full-fledged contextualism. While the former acknowledges limited pragmatic influence on semantic content, the latter holds the view that pragmatic processes such as free enrichment play a central role in explaining contextual variations in semantic content (e.g. Recanati 2005). For some scholars, the contextualist position can be distinguished from a 'pragmatist' position. One main, though subtle, difference between the two positions is that while the former appeals primarily to facts about linguistic meaning, the latter involves pragmatic principles or maxims (e.g. Carston 2010b). Closely associated with contextualism is the position known as 'truth-conditional pragmatics': the view that various pragmatic processes influence and determine the truth-condition of an utterance (e.g. Recanati 2010). Contextualism is represented by the work of the French philosopher François Recanati, neo-Gricean pragmatics, and relevance theory.

By contrast, the central thesis of semantic minimalism or literalism is that context is allowed to have only a very limited or minimal effect on the semantic content of an utterance. In addition, semantic minimalism holds that semantic content is entirely determined by syntax, that semantic context-sensitivity is grammatically triggered, and that it is not the job of semantic content to capture one's intuitive judgement of what a speaker says when he or she utters a sentence. Consequently, the object of study of semantics should be strictly separated from pragmatic intrusion (e.g. Borg 2007; 2010). Currently there are a number of variants of semantic minimalism. These include the British philosopher Emma Borg's minimal semantics, the Norwegian philosopher Herman Cappelen and the American philosopher Ernest Lepore's insensitive semantics, and the American philosopher Kent Bach's radical semantic minimalism. For Borg, semantics should operate independently of, and prior to, the actual use of a linguistic expression by a speaker to communicate. The role of semantics is simply to explain formal linguistic meaning, but not to give a full account of the nature of meaning or indeed to explain communication (e.g. Borg 2004). Insensitive semantics takes the view that apart from a very specific and limited set of linguistic expressions such as *I*, *foreigner*, and *local*, which are context-sensitive, all other linguistic expressions have constant meanings. The semantic meaning of a sentence expresses a complete truth-conditional proposition independently of contexts of use. In other words, semantics is 'insensitive' in that it operates independently of, or is not sensitive to, any features of contexts of utterance. This 'insensitive' view of semantics is supplemented by Cappelen and Lepore's speech act pluralism. Speech act pluralism is of the view that what is said may express more than one proposition, or that an utterance in its context can carry out more than one speech act. In other words, each minimal representation may correspond to a wide variety of speech acts which it is capable of conveying, hence the name. What is said depends on a wide range of factors other than the proposition semantically expressed. It depends on a potential infinitude of features of the context of utterance and of the context of those who report on or think about what was said (e.g. Cappelen and Lepore 2005). Finally Bach's radical semantic minimalism maintains that the semantic properties of a sentence should be taken as on a par with the sentence's syntactic and phonological properties. There is no pragmatic intrusion into what is said, because certain aspects of communicative content do not need to be recognized as either part of what is said or part of what is implicated. Rather, they constitute a middle ground between what is said and what is implicated. Bach called this middle level of speaker-meaning 'impliciture' (e.g. Bach 2004; Huang 2007: 223; 2010e).

Next, there is semantic relativism. Semantic relativism is an approach in the contemporary philosophy of language and linguistics that falls largely in the semantic minimalist camp. While acknowledging that varying standards have a semantic role to play, proponents of semantic relativism reject the contextualist claim that the role in question is relevant to the determination of what is said by an utterance. Rather, the role played by varying standards is relevant to determining whether what is said is true or false. Some semantic relativists distinguish a context of use from a context of assessment, and insist that epistemic standards, for example, are features of the context of assessment. For instance, according to semantic relativism, the proposition expressed by the sentence *John knows that there was a network outage yesterday* does not vary across different contexts (specifically in relation to the meaning of *know*), but its truth value is relative to, or varies with, a standard of knowledge (e.g. Garcia-Carpintero and Kölbel 2008).

Finally, of some interest is what Recanati (2005) called indexicalism. This is the position in the contemporary philosophy of language and linguistics that assumes that there is a role for speaker's meaning to play in the determination of the truth-conditional content of a sentence, but only when a slot is set up by the sentence itself to be pragmatically filled in its logical form. To this end, a range of 'covert' or 'hidden' indexicals is posited to provide syntactic triggers for the additional context-sensitivity demanded by indexicalists, thus also referred to as 'hidden indexicalism'. No top-down pragmatic influence is allowed to affect the truth-conditional content of the sentence. This position is represented by the work of the American philosopher Jason Stanley and his colleagues (e.g. Stanley 2000; Recanati 2004). Interestingly enough, indexicalism is considered to be a version of moderate contextualism by semantic minimalists, and a variety of semantic minimalism by contextulists. An alternative view is that contrary to indexicalists, context-sensitivity called for by contextualists lies in the circumstances of evaluation rather than a truly indexical content for a sentence. This position is termed 'non-indexical contextualism' (e.g. McFarlane 2007).

1.3 Central topics in Anglo-American pragmatics

With this philosophical background in place, let me move to the central topics of inquiry of Anglo-American pragmatics (also variously called 'hardcore', 'pure', 'micro-', 'philosophical', and 'theoretical pragmatics').

The notion of implicature (both conversational and conventional) was put forward by the British philosopher H. P. Grice (e.g. Grice 1989). Conversational implicature is any element of meaning implied by a speaker and inferred by an addressee which goes beyond what is said in the strict sense. It is derived from the speaker's saying of what is said by virtue of the co-operative principle and its attendant maxims of conversation (e.g. Grice 1989; Horn 2004; Huang 2007; 2010a; 2010d; 2010f; 2010i). Since its inception, the classical Gricean theory of conversational implicature has remained one of the two foundation stones of current pragmatic theorizing. Furthermore, it has provided a starting point for a staggering amount of research, giving rise to neo-Gricean pragmatics (e.g. Levinson 2000; Huang 2004; 2006c/2009; 2007; Horn 2007; 2009), relevance theory (a reductionist revision of the classical Gricean programme, e.g. Sperber and Wilson 1995; see also Huang 2007: 201–5; 2012 for a comparison between neo-Gricean pragmatics and relevance theory), novel concepts like impliciture (e.g. Bach 2004; Huang 2007; 2010e) and pragmatically enriched said (Recanati 2004), and interesting work in experimental pragmatics (e.g. Noveck and Sperber 2004; Sauerland and Yatsushiro 2009; Meibauer and Steinbach 2011).

In addition, classical and neo-Gricean pragmatics has been integrated with other current linguistic theories to bring about optimality-theoretic pragmatics (Blutner and Zeevat 2004) and game- and decision-theoretic pragmatics (Benz, Jäger, and van Rooij 2006). Optimality-theoretic pragmatics is a recently developed formal pragmatic theory of pragmatic competence combining the insights from both optimality theory and neo-Gricean pragmatics. From the perspective of optimality theory, pragmatics is taken to be characterized by defaults and preferences, and utterance interpretation, to present an optimization problem. Although the concept of optimization was developed in pragmatics right from the very beginning, the application of optimality theory to pragmatics makes it possible for pragmatics to be formalized utilizing a system of ranked constraints to achieve both expressive and interpretive optimality. A particular version of optimality-theoretic pragmatics is bidirectional optimality-theoretic pragmatics. What takes centre stage in bidirectional optimality-theoretic pragmatics is the insight that in communication, not only does the addressee need to determine the optimal interpretation of a given form, but the speaker also needs to express the meaning by selecting the optimal form. Consequently, one needs a two-dimensional search for both interpretative and expressive optimality in terms of form–meaning pairs. This bidirectional approach was partially motivated by the American linguist Laurence Horn's reduction of Grice's maxims of conversation to the addressee-oriented Q- and speaker-oriented R-principles and the British linguist Stephen Levinson's, to the Q- and I-principles. In these principles, the perspective of the speaker and that of the addressee are conditioned on each other (e.g. Blutner and Zeevat 2004).

Another formal pragmatic approach to language in use, which is closely related to optimality-theoretic pragmatics, is game- and decision-theoretic pragmatics. Although its roots can be traced back to the late 1960s, game- and decision-theoretic pragmatics is also a newly emerged theory. It attempts to combine some of the central ideas of both game and decision theory and classical and neo-Gricean pragmatic theory and to apply them to the pragmatic use of language. At the heart of game- and decision-theoretic pragmatics lie two basic assumptions. First, utterance interpretation is treated as a game. Secondly, there is a decision problem in an utterance game. The success of utterance interpretation relies on how the utterance game is played by its speaker and addressee, and on the overall preference made by the players over the ultimate outcomes of the game. In addition, insights from evolutionary game theory—a branch of game and decision theory—are borrowed to explain the emergence of regularities or conventions of language use (e.g. Benz, Jäger, and van Rooij 2006). Construed thus, game- and decision-theoretical pragmatics can be seen as a variety of normative pragmatics. Normative pragmatics is a form of pragmatics that assumes that language is a kind of game, and as such it has rules. These rules are of crucial importance for the use of language and should be the primary pursuit of pragmatics. This view of pragmatics was put forward especially by the American philosopher Wilfrid Sellars and advanced by the American philosopher Robert Brandom (e.g. Peregrin 2010). In contrast to conversational implicature, conventional implicature is a non-truth-conditional meaning that is not derived in any general, natural way from the saying of what is said, but arises solely from the conventional features attached to particular lexical items and/or linguistic constructions (e.g. Grice 1989; Huang 2010d).

Presupposition is a proposition whose truth is taken for granted in the utterance of a sentence. The main function of presupposition is to act as a precondition of some sort for the appropriate use of the sentence. This background assumption remains equally valid when the sentence that contains it is negated. Presupposition has long been considered a linguistic phenomenon that is balanced on the edge between semantics and pragmatics, but how much is semantics and how much is pragmatics is debatable (e.g. Huang 2007; 2010i).

The notion of a speech act, introduced by the British philosopher J. L. Austin, refers to the uttering of a linguistic expression whose function is not just to say things but actively to do things or to perform actions as well. Speech act theory was established in the 1960s (e.g. Austin 1962; Searle 1969), and has remained to date another cornerstone of pragmatics. Cultural and interlanguage variations in speech acts have been major pursuits of cross-cultural and interlanguage pragmatics (e.g. Huang 2006a/2009/2010; 2007). From a more formal perspective, the integration of speech acts with intentional logic has given rise to what is called illocutionary logic in formal pragmatics. Various aspects of speech act theory have also been formalized in artificial intelligence and computational pragmatics.

Deixis is the phenomenon whereby features of context of utterance or speech event are encoded by lexical and/or grammatical means in a language. There are three major categories of deixis: person, space, and time deixis. Person deixis is concerned with the identification of the interlocutors or participant roles in a speech event. Space deixis is the specification of location relative to that of the participants at utterance time in a speech event. Finally, time deixis is concerned with the encoding of temporal points and spans relative to the moment at which an utterance is produced in a speech event. Two minor categories of deixis can further be identified: social and discourse deixis. Social deixis is the codification of the social status of the speaker, the addressee, and/or a third person or entity referred to, and of the social relationships holding between them. Discourse, text, or textual deixis is concerned with the use of a linguistic expression within an utterance to point to the current, preceding, or following utterances in the same spoken or written discourse (e.g. Huang 2007).

Finally, reference is the relationship between a linguistic expression and an entity, activity, property, relationship, etc. or a set of entities, activities, properties, relationships, etc. in the external world, to which it refers. In other words, referring is an act of a speaker picking out a particular entity or a particular set of entities, denoted by a linguistic expression, in the external world. It is performed through the speaker's utterance of that linguistic expression on some occasion. Defined thus, reference is essentially a context-dependent aspect of utterance meaning and it therefore falls broadly within the domain of pragmatics (e.g. Abbott 2010).

2 Continental pragmatics

Within the European Continental conception of linguistics, pragmatics is taken to present a functional perspective on all core components and 'hyphenated' areas of linguistics and beyond. Verschueren (1999: 7, 11), for example, claimed that pragmatics constitutes 'a general functional (i.e. cognitive, social and cultural) perspective on linguistic phenomena in relation to their usage in forms of behaviour'. Elsewhere, he elaborated by saying: 'Pragmatics should be seen ... as a specific perspective ... on whatever phonologists, morphologists, syntacticians, semanticists, psycholinguists, sociolinguists, etc. deal with' (Verschueren 1995: 12). This represents the perspective view of pragmatics. Consequently, within the wider Continental tradition, the empirical orbit of pragmatics has been considerably widened, encompassing not only much that goes under the rubric of non-core branches of linguistics such as sociolinguistics, psycholinguistics, and discourse analysis, but also some that fall in the province of neighbouring social sciences.

However, there has recently been some convergence between the two traditions. On the one hand, important work has been done on micro-pragmatic topics such as implicature, speech acts, and presupposition from the Continental perspective. On the other hand, research within the Anglo-American conception has been extended not only to some core topics in formal syntax such as anaphora (e.g. Huang 1991; 1994/2007; 2000a; 2000b; 2004; 2006b/2009; 2010b; 2010g; Chiou and Huang 2010; Levinson 2000) and the lexicon in lexical pragmatics (the systematic study of aspects of meaning-related properties of lexical items that are dependent on and modified in language use, i.e. that part of lexical meaning which is parasitic on what is coded but is not part of what is coded: Huang 2009; see also Blutner 2004; Wilson and Carston 2007; Horn 2007), but also to certain 'hyphenated' domains of linguistics such as computational linguistics, historical linguistics, and clinical linguistics, giving rise to computational pragmatics, historical pragmatics, and clinical pragmatics (see below). This is also true in relation to cognitive science—an interdisciplinary amalgam of philosophy, psychology, linguistics, anthropology, computer science, artificial intelligence, and neuroscience. One case in point is relevance theory, which has taken over many insights from cognitive psychology. Another case is the recent emergence of experimental pragmatics.

Each side of the Anglo-American/Continental divide complements, and has much to learn from, the other. Whereas the strength of the Anglo-American branch lies mainly in theory and in philosophical, cognitive, and formal pragmatics, the Continental camp has much to offer in empirical work (empirical pragmatics), and socio- (or social, societal), cross- (or inter-) cultural, and interpersonal pragmatics (e.g. Huang 2010c).

3 Macro-pragmatics (I): cognitively oriented

Computational, experimental, and socio- (or societal) pragmatics, for example, can be taken to be branches of what may be called macro-pragmatics—the study of the use of language in all aspects. Current topics of inquiry in macro-pragmatics can roughly be divided into two groups: cognitively and socially and/or culturally oriented. The former includes cognitive pragmatics, psycho- or psycholinguistic pragmatics (including both developmental and experimental pragmatics), (part of) interlanguage pragmatics, computational pragmatics, clinical pragmatics, and neuropragmatics. The latter includes socio- (or societal) pragmatics, cultural, cross- (or inter-) cultural pragmatics, and interpersonal pragmatics.

Cognitive pragmatics has its roots in the emergence of modern cognitive science in the 1970s. A typical example of cognitive pragmatics (and inferential pragmatics) is relevance theory. Grounded in a general view of human cognition, the central tenet of relevance theory is that the human cognitive system works in such a way as to tend to maximize relevance with respect to cognition and communication. Thus, the communicative principle of relevance is responsible for the recovery of both the explicit and implicit content of an utterance. Furthermore, as mentioned above, it is hypothesized that pragmatics, which incorporates the relevance-theoretic comprehension procedure, is a sub-module of 'theory of mind', i.e. a variety of mind-reading (e.g. Sperber and Wilson 1995; Wilson and Sperber 2004; Huang 2007). Another significant cognitive approach to pragmatics is cognitive pragmatics theory developed by the Italian cognitive scientist Bruno Bara. Cognitive pragmatics theory offers an explanation of the cognitive processes that are involved in intentional verbal and non-verbal communication. The practitioners of the theory contend that a 'partner' (addressee) in communication establishes the communicative intention of an 'actor' (speaker) by identifying the behaviour game that the actor intends him or her to play. Pragmatic phenomena are accounted for in terms of the complexity of the inferential steps (the 'inferential load') needed to refer an utterance to a particular behaviour game and the complexity of the underlying mental representations. Cognitive pragmatics theory has been applied to studies of developmental pragmatics in children, the comprehension of pragmatic phenomena in head-injured subjects, and pragmatic decay in subjects with Alzheimer's disease (e.g. Bara 2010). In these cases, cognitive pragmatics theory overlaps with clinical and neuropragmatics.

Psycho- or psycholinguistic pragmatics is the psycholinguistic study of aspects of language in use and mind. It is primarily concerned with the issue of how human beings acquire, store, produce, and understand the use of language from the vantage point of psychology. Within psycho-pragmatics, developmental or acquisitional pragmatics studies the empirical development of pragmatic competence in children, utilizing both observation and experiments. Topics been discussed in developmental pragmatics include the acquisition of scalar implicature, metaphor, and irony. Using both psycholinguistic and neurolinguistic methods, experimental pragmatics investigates, through carefully controlled experiments, such important pragmatic issues and theories as scalar implicature, felicity conditions on speech acts, reference, metaphor, neo-Gricean pragmatic theory, and relevance theory (e.g. Noveck and Sperber 2004; Sauerland and Yatsushiro 2009; Meibauer and Steinbach 2011).[3] One point to note here is that the majority of work in experimental pragmatics has been carried out from the perspective of relevance theory. The importance of psycho-pragmatics, as pointed out by Cummings (2005), is that it has a crucial role to play not only in the formulation and development of pragmatic theories but also in the testing and revision of these theories.

Next, we have interlanguage pragmatics. What, then, is an interlanguage? Simply put, it is a stage on a continuum within a ruled-governed language system that is developed by second or foreign language (L2) learners on their path to acquiring the target language. This language system is intermediate between the learner's native language and his or her target language. It gives rise to the phenomenon of what the American psycholinguist Dan Slobin called 'first language thinking in second language speaking'. The notion of interlanguage was introduced by the American linguist Laurence Selinker. Interlanguage pragmatics is at the interface between pragmatics and second language acquisition. It studies how non-native speakers of a language acquire and develop their ability to understand and produce pragmatic features in a second language, i.e. an interlanguage. Central research topics include pragmatic awareness, pragmatic transfer, the development of pragmatic competence, speech act comprehension and production, and the relationship between second language grammar and pragmatics. The sub-branch of interlanguage pragmatics that investigates the empirical acquisition and development of pragmatic competence in children is called 'developmental interlanguage pragmatics'. The best-studied interlanguage is that developed by speakers of English as a second language. Other interlanguages that have been investigated include

[3] Notice the experimental paradox—a well-known dilemma in experimental psycholinguistics including experimental pragmatics. The dilemma is that the more perfect an experiment, the less like the real speech situation it is, and the more likely that subjects of the experiment will produce unnatural responses. On the other hand, the more like the real speech situation the experiment, the less easy for the experimenters to control the external factors that may interfere with the experiment. The consequence of this paradox is that it is almost impossible to design a perfect experiment (e.g. Aitchison 2003).

Chinese, German, Hebrew, Japanese, and Spanish (e.g. Kasper and Blum-Kulke 1993; Achiba 2003; Barron 2003; Kasper 2010).

Computational pragmatics is the systematic study of the relation between utterances and context from an explicitly computational point of view. This includes the relation between utterances and action, between utterances and discourse, and between utterances and their uttering time, place, and environment. Two sides to the question of how to compute the relation between linguistic aspects and contextual aspects can be identified. On the one hand, given a linguistic expression, one needs to work out how to compute the relevant properties of context. In this respect, local pragmatics tackles problems which are posed within the scope of an individual sentence, though their solutions generally require greater contextual and real-world knowledge. Typical examples include resolving syntactic and lexical ambiguity, interpreting metaphor and metonymy, and determining reference. On the other hand, in the case of language generation, the task is to construct a linguistic expression that encodes the contextual information a speaker intends to convey. Given the relevant properties of the context, one needs to work out how to compute the relevant properties of the linguistic expression. This study of the relation between linguistic aspects and contextual aspects requires the building up of explicit computational representations at either side of the relation. A particularly important topic of inquiry in computational pragmatics is inference. Abduction, the resolution of reference, the generation and interpretation of speech acts, and the production and comprehension of discourse structure and coherence relations have figured prominently in computational pragmatics (e.g. Bunt and Black 2000; Hobbs 2004; Jurafsky 2004). Note next that computational pragmatics is different from cyberpragmatics. Cyberpragmatics refers to a newly emerged research area in which internet-mediated interactions are analysed mainly from a cognitive pragmatic point of view. A wide variety of interactions on the internet are dealt with in cyberpragmatics. These include emails, web pages, chat rooms, social networking sites, blogs, 3D virtual worlds, instant messaging, and video-conferencing (e.g. Yus 2011).

Clinical pragmatics involves the application of pragmatic concepts, theories, and findings to the assessment, diagnosis, and treatment of pragmatic aspects of language disorders. It studies such pragmatic concepts and phenomena as Grice's co-operative principle and its attendant maxims, conversational implicature, speech acts, inferences, context, non-literal meaning, deixis, and conversation and discourse from a clinical perspective. Pragmatic deficits have been examined in a variety of clinical groups including children and/or adults with developmental language disorder, autism spectrum disorder, learning disability, left- or right-hemisphere damage of the brain, closed head injury, Alzheimer's disease, and schizophrenia (e.g. Cummings 2009; Perkins 2007). Insofar as most of these clinical groups are defined by an underlying neurological condition, and a large amount of research involves children, clinical pragmatics overlaps to some degree with developmental pragmatics, and with neuropragmatics, to which I now turn.

Neuropragmatics is a recently developed branch of pragmatics that examines the neuro-anatomical basis of language in use. It is concerned with the relationship between the human brain/mind and pragmatics. It investigates how the human brain/mind uses language, i.e. how it produces and comprehends pragmatic phenomena in healthy as well as neurologically impaired language users. Pragmatic phenomena that have been studied include speech acts, implicature, discourse, metaphor, and sarcasm. The majority of neuropragmatic research has focused on aspects of pragmatics in adults with identifiable clinical disorders and brain pathology. The brain-damaged populations include patients with left- and right-hemisphere damage, traumatic brain injury, neuro-degenerative disorders like Parkinson's disease and dementia, and schizophrenia (e.g. Bara and Tirassa 2000; Stemmer and Schönle 2000; Cummings 2010). This field of inquiry overlaps in particular with clinical and experimental pragmatics.

4 Macro-pragmatics (II): socially and/or culturally oriented

I come next to the second group of branches of macro-pragmatics. These branches constitute what is sometimes called 'soft pragmatics'. This is in contrast to so-called 'hard pragmatics'—a trend in pragmatics that studies language in use from a philosophical, logical, and (formal) linguistic perspective.

Socio- (or societal) pragmatics sits at the interface between sociolinguistics and pragmatics and studies the use of language in relation to society. One topic that has long been the focus of sociopragmatic research is politeness. Broadly defined so as to encompass both polite friendliness and polite formality, politeness is concerned with the actions people take to maintain their own face and that of the people they are interacting with. Defined in this way, politeness functions as a precondition of human communication. On the other hand, more recently, impoliteness has also become a central topic of inquiry in sociopragmatics. By impoliteness is meant any face-aggravating behaviour relevant to a particular context. For some scholars, impoliteness has to be intentional (on the part of the speaker) and has to be perceived or constructed as intentional (on the part of the addressee). For others, intentions play no part in impoliteness. If intentions and recognition of intentions are involved, then rudeness rather than impoliteness occurs (e.g. Bousfield 2008; Bousfield and Locher 2008). In Culpeper (2011), impoliteness has been classified into three types: (i) affective, (ii) coercive, and (iii) entertaining impoliteness. Other topics that have attracted attention in sociopragmatics include social deixis, social conventions on the performance of speech acts, and social factors which constrain language in use, such as the overriding of conversational implicature by the Malagasy taboo on exact identification (e.g. Huang 2007). From a macro point of view, the hand of societal pragmatics can be detected in any area that pertains in any way to society, dealing with topics as diverse as language in education, pragmatics and social struggle, and what is called 'critical pragmatics'. Critical pragmatics is the work done in sociopragmatics that follows the tradition of critical linguistics, particularly critical discourse analysis. Critical discourse analysis deals with the relationship between language and power in society, especially the way in which discourse is ideologically influenced by, and can itself have an impact on, social power. As in critical discourse analysis, in critical pragmatics great emphasis is also put on the relationship between language and social power and between language and ideology (e.g. Mey 2001). Notice that the term 'critical pragmatics' has a totally different sense in the philosophy of language and formal pragmatics. It is the term employed by the American philosopher John Perry and the Basque philosopher Kepa Korta to refer to the philosophical position that takes the contents of an utterance as central and critical to both pragmatics and semantics. According to critical pragmatics, language is a way of doing things with words, meanings of linguistic expressions and contents of utterances derive ultimately from intentions, and language combines with other factors to allow human beings to achieve communicative goals (e.g. Korta and Perry 2011).

Institutional pragmatics refers to an area of research in pragmatics which investigates the use of language in social institutions and in an institutionalized context, such as courtroom interaction, job interviews, and police interrogation (e.g. Roberts 2010).

Cultural pragmatics, sometimes also known as 'anthropological' or 'ethnographic pragmatics', is the systematic study of language in use and its place in the functioning of human communities and institutions from a cultural or anthropological view, especially but not exclusively focusing on a non-Western culture or cultures. It overlaps with the ethnography of communication and ethnography of speaking. A particular variety of cultural pragmatics is ethnopragmatics. Ethnopragmatics is an approach to language in use that is semantically grounded in natural semantic metalanguage developed by the Polish-born Australian linguist Anna Wierzbicka and her colleagues. Utilizing cultural scripts and semantic or reductive paraphrase explications as analytical tools, practitioners of ethnopragmatics aim to find out more about speech practices and language use of particular, local cultures, contextualized and understood in terms of the beliefs, norms, and values of speakers themselves. In other words, the emphasis of ethnopragmatics is on culturally anchored analyses and explanations, thus rejecting what the ethnopragmaticists labelled 'universal(ist) pragmatics', namely, any pragmatic theory that views human communication as governed largely by a rich inventory of universal pragmatic principles, with variations between cultures being accounted for in terms of local adjustments to and local construals of these universals (e.g. Goddard 2006).

Somewhat similar to ethnopragmatics, described above, is ethnographic pragmatics, defined in its narrow sense. It refers to the ethnographically oriented approach to context-sensitive language use associated particularly with the work of the American linguist Michael Silverstein and his students. Influenced by his teacher, the Russian-born linguist Roman Jakobson, research conducted in Silverstein's ethnographic pragmatics has focused largely on non-Western cultures, societies, and languages.

A third variety of cultural pragmatics is emancipatory pragmatics. A recently emerged research framework in pragmatics, emancipatory pragmatics attempts to free the study of language in use from the confines of the theoretical and methodological orthodoxies grounded in the dominant thought and practice derived from Anglo-American and European languages and ways of speaking, with the attendant premises of individualism, rationality, and market economy. The focus of emancipatory pragmatics is also placed on non-Western languages and ways of speaking, and on describing a language and/or culture strictly in its own terms (e.g. Hanks, Ide, and Katagiri 2009).

Somewhat overlapping with socio- and cultural pragmatics is interpersonal pragmatics. Interpersonal pragmatics is a research arena that concentrates on the interpersonal and relational aspects of language in use, especially of how interlocutors utilize language to establish and maintain social relations, and how interactions between interlocutors both affect and are affected by their own and others' understanding of culture, society, etc. Central topics of inquiry include face, politeness/impoliteness, respect/deference, identity, gender and mitigation (e.g. Locher and Graham 2010).

Cross- (or inter-) cultural pragmatics is the systematic study of the use of language across different cultures and languages. Since 1980s, a principal concern of cross-cultural pragmatics has been the issue of how particular kinds of speech acts, especially such face-threatening acts as requests, apologies, and complaints, are realized across different cultures and languages. One of the most influential investigations is the large-scale Cross-Cultural Speech Act Realization Project carried out in the 1980s. In this project, the realization patterns of requesting and apologizing in German, Hebrew, Danish, Canadian French, Argentinean Spanish, and British, American, and Australian English were compared and contrasted (e.g. Blum-Kulka et al. 1989). Since then, strategies for the performance of a variety of face-threatening acts in a much wider range of languages have been examined. These languages include Catalan, Chinese, Danish, Dutch, German, Greek, Hebrew, Japanese, Javanese, Polish, Russian, Thai, Turkish, four varieties of English (British, American, Australian, and New Zealand), two varieties of French (Canadian and French), and eight varieties of Spanish (Argentinean, Ecuadorian, Mexican, Peninsular, Peruvian, Puerto Rican,

Uruguayan, and Venezuelan). As a result of these studies, it has now been established that there is indeed extensive cross-cultural/linguistic variation in directness/indirectness in the expression of speech acts, especially in face-threatening acts, and that these differences are generally associated with the different means that different languages utilize to realize speech acts. These findings have undoubtedly contributed to our greater understanding of cross-cultural/linguistic similarities and differences in face-redressive strategies for face-threatening acts (e.g. Huang 2007). A sub-branch of cross- or intercultural pragmatics is postcolonial pragmatics, which studies the use of language of the colonizers in a postcolonial society or postcolonial societies. In a postcolonial society, a second (as opposed to a foreign) language is sometimes used in interaction, as in the use of English in contemporary India (e.g. Anchimbe and Janney 2011).

Another recently emerged branch of pragmatics that has a close affinity with socio- and cross-/intercultural pragmatics is variational pragmatics. It endeavours to study and determine the influence or impact of macro-social factors such as region, social class, ethnicity, gender, and age, and the interplay of these factors on language use, especially pragmatic variation, in interaction. Construed thus, variational pragmatics also represents a research domain at the intersection of pragmatics and sociolinguistics, in particular dialectology (e.g. Barron and Schneider 2010).

Mention should be made of conversation(al) analysis (CA), sometimes also called 'conversation(al) pragmatics'. Since Levinson (1983), conversation analysis has become a branch of macro-pragmatics. Grown out of a breakaway group of sociologists known as ethnomethodologists within micro-sociology, conversation analysis represents an empirical, procedural, and inductive approach to the analysis of (audio and/or video recordings of) naturally occurring, spontaneous conversations, or 'talks in (face-to-face) interaction'. It is concerned with the discovery and description of the methods and procedures that participants employ systematically to display their understanding of the structure of naturally occurring, spontaneous conversations in face-to-face interaction. In conversation, there are rules governing sequential organization such as the turn-taking system, the formulation of adjacency pairs, and the mechanism for opening or closing a conversation. There are also norms regulating participation in a conversation, such as those for how to hold the 'floor', how to interrupt, and how to remain silent. Other interesting structural devices of conversation include the preference organization, the pre-sequence system, and the repair mechanism (e.g. Sacks 1992; Sidnell 2011). Given that conversation is the most important spoken manifestation of language, conversation analysis has to be closely linked to prosodic pragmatics—a study of how prosody, like intonation, can affect the interpretation of a variety of linguistic phenomena in relation to context (e.g. Hirschberg 2004). Furthermore, since rules, norms, and regulations for conversational interaction may vary from culture to culture, society to society, and language to language, conversation(al) pragmatics may overlap with the ethnography of speaking and cross-cultural pragmatics. Conversation analysis can further be divided into pure conversation(al) analysis (pure CA) and applied conversation (al) analysis (applied CA). By 'pure conversation analysis' is meant the type of conversation analysis that collects data from naturally occurring conversations. In other words, in pure conversation analysis the data is not arranged or provoked by the analyst, as in a psycholinguistic experiment or a sociolinguistic interview. Used in contrast to pure conversation analysis, 'applied conversation analysis' is a term employed with reference to the type of conversation analysis that studies specific types of conversational situation (e.g. ten Have 2010). For some scholars, CA is opposed to discourse analysis (DA).

5 Macro-pragmatics (III)

I turn finally to a group of branches and research areas of macro-pragmatics that are not easily and/or neatly placed in the above two categories.

Historical pragmatics is a branch of macro-pragmatics that emerged in the 1990s. It is concerned with the investigation of language change between two given points in time in individual languages and in language generally from a pragmatic perspective. Two main research trends correspond roughly to the distinction between 'external' and 'internal' language change. The first, 'external' research strand, is called 'pragmaphilology'. Pragmaphilology represents primarily a 'macro'-approach to the study of the pragmatics of historical texts at a particular point of time. The focus is on the wider changing social and cognitive contexts of the texts in which pragmatic change occurs. It is closely related to 'historical discourse analysis proper' in historical discourse analysis. The second, 'internal' research trend is diachronic pragmatics in its narrow sense. Diachronic pragmatics in this sense represents a 'micro'-approach to change in pragmatic phenomena over time, concentrating on the interface between a linguistic structure and its communicative use across different historical stages of the same language. Furthermore, a methodological distinction is made between the 'form-to-function' and 'function-to-form' modes. The former, called 'pragmalinguistic diachronic pragmatics', is semasiological and the emphasis is on how a particular linguistic form has undergone functional changes; the latter, termed 'sociopragmatic diachronic pragmatics', is onomasiological and the focus is on how a particular pragmatic function has changed the form it uses. Diachronic pragmatics in the sense being described here is closely related to 'diachronically oriented discourse analysis' in historical discourse analysis. Since the boundary between pragmaphilology and diachronic pragmatics is sometimes not clear-cut, an intermediate category, dubbed 'diachronic pragmaphilology', has also been proposed. In addition to the two main approaches, there is a third research strand, labelled 'pragma-historical linguistics'. Given that textual data is heavily used in both historical pragmatics and historical discourse analysis, there is a considerable overlap between the two fields. At the early stage of its development, historical pragmatics was called 'new philology' or 'diachronic textlinguistics' (e.g. Traugott 2004; Culpeper 2010; Jucker and Taavitsainen 2010).

Next, historical sociopragmatics involves the interaction between historical pragmatics and sociopragmatics. According to some scholars, historical sociopragmatics is more closely related to the pragmaphilology research trend in historical pragmatics. It constitutes a systematic study of interaction between aspects of social context and particular historical language uses that give rise to pragmatic meanings. Historical sociopragmatics can be either synchronic or diachronic. Synchronic historical sociopragmatics studies how language use shapes and is shaped by social context at a certain moment of time in the past. By contrast, diachronic historical sociopragmatics traces how changes in language use shape social context, changes in social context shape language use, and/or changes take place in the relationship between language use and social context (e.g. Culpeper 2009/2011).

Directly opposed to historical pragmatics is synchronic pragmatics. Synchronic pragmatics is a subfield of pragmatics that studies language use in general or in a particular language as it is, or was, at a particular point in time. In other words, synchronic pragmatics is concerned with the pragmatics of what the Swiss linguist Ferdinand de Saussure called an '*état de langue*', i.e. the pragmatics of the state of language at a particular point in time, regardless of its previous or subsequent history.

The term 'applied pragmatics' has two senses. In its broad sense, applied pragmatics makes reference to any application of the concepts and findings of theoretical pragmatics to practical tasks such as the diagnosis, assessment, and treatment of pragmatic disorders, human–computer interaction, and the teaching and learning of a second and foreign language. In the last connection, the field is often called 'second and foreign language (L2) pragmatics'. 'Second and foreign language pragmatics' is a term that is interchangeable with applied pragmatics in its narrow sense. It is part of instructional pragmatics, i.e. pragmatics that is concerned with how to teach and learn pragmatics in language, especially second and/or foreign language, instruction (e.g. Ishihara and Cohen 2010). Applied pragmatics should not be confused with applying pragmatics. The latter is a term that is used within the Continental tradition of pragmatics for any dynamic, user-oriented, problem-solving activity employing pragmatic knowledge in the real-world context, especially of the social struggle. Described thus, applying pragmatics has an overlap with critical pragmatics in its sociological sense.

'Corpus' is a systematic collection of naturally occurring spoken or written language or a variety of such a language, which can be searchable online. When it is accessible on a computer, it is called 'computer corpus' or 'corpora'. By corpus pragmatics is meant the investigation of language use on the basis of the analysis of corpora. Corpus pragmatics forms part of empirical pragmatics. It can be divided into two types: corpus-based pragmatics and corpus-driven pragmatics. In the former, researchers approach the corpora with a set of assumptions and expected findings. By contrast, the latter investigates linguistic forms and pragmatic functions that emerge from the corpora in order to discover things that have not been recognized. Much of the current research in corpus pragmatics is corpus-based rather than corpus-driven. From a methodological point of view, corpus pragmatics can be either form-based (i.e. it takes a linguistic structure as its starting point and examines the range of pragmatic functions the form serves in a corpus) or function-based (i.e. it takes a particular pragmatic function as a point of departure and studies how such a function is actually realized). Finally, corpus-based or driven research in pragmatics can be either qualitative (treating corpora primarily as a source of natural data) or quantitative (studying patterns of frequency, distribution, and collocation using statistical techniques) (e.g. Andersen 2011; Rühlemann 2011).

Literary pragmatics can be best described as covering an area of research rather than a well-defined unified theory. It represents a domain at the intersection of pragmatics, literary theory, and the philosophy of literature. It is the study of the use of linguistic forms in a literary text and the relationship between author, text, and reader in a sociocultural context from a pragmatic perspective, focusing on the question of what and how a literary text communicates. Two complementary aspects of literary pragmatics can be identified. On the one hand, how can the insights of pragmatic theories be employed for the study of literature? On the other, how can the insights of literary pragmatics contribute to general pragmatic theories? Literary pragmatics can further be divided into two sub-branches: formalist and historical literary pragmatics. Formalist literary pragmatics seeks to characterize literariness in terms of the pragmatic properties of literary texts, concentrating on formal analyses which are based on formal systems or pragmatic processes. Key research themes include speech acts in literary communication and free indirect discourse or speech. In contrast with formalist literary pragmatics is historical literary pragmatics. Interdisciplinary in nature, historical literary pragmatics places an emphasis on the interconnections between literary studies, history studies, sociocultural studies, and pragmatic studies. For example, it uses the insights of the American linguist Penelope Brown and the British linguist Stephen Levinson's face-saving model of politeness to characterize the relationship between language users, i.e. writers and readers, in a literary context (e.g. Pilkington 2010). Next, somewhat related to literary pragmatics is pragmatic stylistics or pragmastylistics. 'Pragmatic stylistics' refers to the application of the findings and methodologies of theoretical pragmatics to the study of the concept of style in language, i.e. systematic variations in usage in written or spoken language including those in literary texts among individual writers, genres, and periods (e.g. Black 2006).

Originating in part from the work of the British philosopher J. L. Austin, legal pragmatics is concerned mainly with the study of legal documents and spoken legal discourse in the courtroom from a pragmatic point of view. Pragmatic features in written legal texts and spoken legal discourses that have been analysed include speech acts such as legal performatives, presuppositions, turn-taking, question–answer adjacency pairs, and silence. The sociopragmatic concepts of power and politeness and impoliteness have also been used in these studies (e.g. Kurzon 2010).

Finally, feminist pragmatics represents an approach to the study of gender and language in use incorporating insights from both feminism and pragmatics. Within this approach, it is assumed that on the one hand, if pragmatics is to provide a theoretical framework for the investigation of gender and use of language, it has to be informed by the findings of feminist scholarship. On the other hand, pragmatics can inform feminist research on gender and language in a wide range of contexts (e.g. Christie 2000).

Directory of symbols and abbreviations

*	indicates a separate entry on the term
&	conjunction
$\vee$	disjunction
$\sim$	negation
$\rightarrow$	implication
$\leftrightarrow$	mutual implication/equivalence
$\forall$	universal quantifier
$\exists$	existential quantifier
=	identity relation
$< >$	Q- or Horn scale
[ ]	I-scale
{ }	M-scale
$<< >>$	rank order
iff	if and only if
t	'true'
f	'false'
p, *q*, *r*...	propositional or sentential variables
x	individual variables
U	utterer
E	empathy
LOG	logophoric
NP	noun phrase
VP	verb phrase
Ø	zero anaphor or gap

A

A-first analysis (of anaphora) A version of the *neo-Gricean pragmatic theory of anaphora developed by the British linguist Stephen Levinson. In this account, the American linguist Noam Chomsky's binding condition A is accepted as a basic rule of grammar. Binding conditions B and C are then reduced to pragmatics by the systemic interaction of the *Q and *M-principles. See Levinson (2000); Huang (2004). *See also* B-first analysis (of anaphora); B-then-A analysis (of anaphora).

A-first plus B-first analysis (of anaphora) *See* B-then-A analysis (of anaphora).

***a posteriori* proposition** A *proposition that is derivative from experience of the senses. Contrasted with an ***a priori* proposition**.

***a priori* proposition** A *proposition that is not derived from experience of the senses, but is independent of and prior to observation of reality in the external world. Contrasted with an ***a posteriori* proposition**.

AAC = augmentative and assisted communication, augmentative or alternative communication.

abbreviation *See* law of abbreviation.

abduction, abductive A term introduced by the American philosopher Charles Sanders Peirce, though the notion can be traced back to the English scientist Sir Isaac Newton and the German philosopher Christian Wolff. Abduction is a process of *reasoning or *inference from available evidence to a wider conclusion on the grounds that the conclusion explains the evidence best. A representative case of **abductive reasoning** or **abductive inference** is an inferential pattern that is sometimes referred to as *inference to the best explanation. E.g. if one sees water on the kitchen floor, one may infer that the dishwasher has broken down. Pierce was of the view that while abduction is a creative process, the results are susceptible to rational evaluation and revision, which means that abduction is non-demonstrative. Non-demonstrative inferences like abduction play a central role in pragmatics. In recent years, abduction has figured especially prominently in computational pragmatics, and some novel ideas have been developed out of it and artificial intelligence. See Hobbs (2004). *See also* deduction; induction.

aboutness *See* intentionality, representation.

aboutness condition (on topic–comment constructions) A well-formedness condition on *topic–comment constructions, which states that in a topic–comment construction, some constituent of the comment clause or the comment clause as a whole must say something about the topic. See Huang (2000).

abrogation The British linguist Derek Bousfield's term for a linguistic defensive counter strategy. In this strategy, by switching his or her social and/or discourse role, a speaker endeavours to deny personal responsibility for the initial offending situation he or she has caused, which may trigger a *face-threatening act against him or her by the person who has been offended. E.g. a parking warden says *Well you see I'm just doing my job* when confronted by the owner of the vehicle to which he has wrongly issued a parking ticket. See Bousfield (2008).

absolute frame (of spatial reference) A linguistic frame of reference to express a spatial relation between a *figure and a ground. An absolute frame is a coordinate system that is based on absolute coordinates like north/south/east/west. E.g. in *The dog is (to the) east of the car*, the fixed bearing 'east' is used to specify the spatial relationship between the figure ('the dog'); the ground ('the car'). See Levinson (2003). *See also* intrinsic frame (of spatial reference); relative frame (of spatial reference).

absolute homonymy, absolute homonym *See* homonymy, homonym.

absolute politeness *Politeness independent of a context of use or a speech event. Used in contrast to **relative politeness**, by which is meant politeness dependent of a context or a speech situation. Thus, in the absolute sense, *Could you please turn the TV down a bit?* is more polite than *Just turn the TV down*. But there are occasions where the former might be interpreted as less polite than the latter. On the British linguist Geoffrey Leech's view, it is only in the relative sense that one can speak of concepts such as over- and under-politeness. More recently, Leech has replaced 'absolute politeness' with 'semantic politeness' and 'relative politeness' with 'pragmatic politeness'. See Leech (2007).

absolute social deixis The codification of the social status of the speaker, the addressee, or a third person or entity referred to, as well as the social relationship holding between them by linguistic forms that are reserved for authorized speakers, addressees, or other recipients. E.g. in imperial China, there was a form *zhen* that was reserved specially for the emperor to refer to himself. See Huang (2007). Contrasts with **relational social deixis**.

absolute synonymy, absolute synonym *See* synonymy, synonym.

abuse A term introduced by the British philosopher J. L. Austin to refer to a category of *speech act infelicity or unhappiness. An abuse arises from a violation of the *felicity conditions that require a performer of a certain performative or speech act to have certain attitudes or actions. E.g. if one makes a promise without any intention to do what one has promised to do, an abuse is committed. In this case, the speech act of promising is indeed accomplished, but in an insincere way. See Austin (1962). *See also* misfire; misexecution; misinvocation; sincerity condition.

acceptability, acceptable The extent to which a linguistic construction is judged by native speakers of a language to be possible, natural and appropriate in that language. Acceptability is related to a speaker's performance, i.e. the actual use of his or her language in a specific context, and is hence particularly relevant to pragmatics. **Grammaticality** or **well-formedness**, by contrast, is the extent to which a string of words conforms to the set of given rules defined by a particular grammar of the language. It is therefore considered to be related to a speaker's competence. According to the American linguist Noam Chomsky, acceptability and grammaticality should not be confused. On the one hand, a sentence may be grammatical but nevertheless unacceptable, either because it does not make any sense or does not appear to be normal or appropriate in a given context. On the other, a sentence may be slightly ungrammatical but nevertheless acceptable in an appropriate context.

accessibility A measure of the ease or difficulty with which a speaker can retrieve a piece of information or a linguistic form from his or her memory or construct a piece of information on the basis of a stimulus by processing it. It is a concept used especially in relevance theory.

accidental face damage **1.** Any *face attack that is not intended by a speaker, but is perceived or construed by the addressee as intentional on the part of the speaker. Contrasted with **incidental face damage** and **intentional face damage**. **2.** = **incidental face damage**.

accommodation A concept generally attributed to the American philosopher David Lewis, but which in fact originated with the British philosopher Peter Strawson. In pragmatic usage, accommodation provides an explanation for how a missing proposition required by what a speaker has said is supplied by the addressee so that what has been said can be accepted. In other words, the addressee accommodates to the speaker. Thus, in the case of *presupposition, accommodation provides a dynamic process of repair in discourse, whereby a tacit extension is made by the addressee to the discourse context to allow update with otherwise unfulfilled propositions. Put slightly differently, accommodation results in the acceptance by the addressee of a presupposition made by the speaker that is not previously part of their *common ground, e.g. if someone who is late for a meeting says *I'm sorry I'm late. My car broke down*. Even if no one in the audience previously knew that the speaker has a car and came by car, he or she will accommodate the non-explicitly stated presupposition and let it carry through unblocked. What happens here is that the presupposition is simply added to the discourse context as if it had been there all along. For some scholars, accommodation can be divided into **local**, **intermediate**, and **global accommodation**. See Huang (2007).

accommodation analysis (of presupposition) A particular version of the *filtering-satisfaction model advanced by the German-born American linguist Irene Heim, couched in her dynamic semantic theory of context change. Central to this approach is Heim's belief that the meaning of an expression, including the *presupposition of a sentence, is its *context change potential. The context change potential of a sentence is the intersection of any context set in a common ground together with the proposition expressed by the sentence. In this analysis, two types of context are identified, corresponding to two types of accommodation: (i) global context generating global accommodation and (ii) local context yielding local accommodation. The former is preferred over the latter. Presupposition is accounted for in terms of accommodation. See Huang (2007). *See also* filtering-satisfaction analysis (of presupposition); cancellation analysis (of presupposition); neo-Gricean analysis (of presupposition).

acknowledgement A type of *communicative illocutionary act proposed by the American philosophers Kent Bach and Robert Harnish, which is broadly equivalent to the British philosopher J. L. Austin's speech act type of *behabitive and the American philosopher J. R. Searle's speech act type of *expressive. Paradigmatic cases include apologizing, condoling, congratulating, greeting, and thanking. E.g. *We thank you for your hospitality*. *See also* constative (2); effective.

acquired pragmatic disorder A type of pragmatic impairment, which has an onset in adulthood, i.e. after the period in which pragmatic skills have been fully acquired, e.g. when an adult with previously intact pragmatic skills sustains a traumatic brain injury and cannot process non-literal aspects of language. In this case, he or she has an acquired pragmatic disorder. See Cummings (2009). Contrasted with a **developmental pragmatic disorder**.

acquisitional pragmatics *See* developmental pragmatics.

act of identity A view put forward by the British sociolinguist Robert LePage that the performance of any *speech act by an individual constitutes an act of identity, i.e. an act performed to project the speaker's social identity.

act of predicating/predication *See* propositional act.

act of referring/reference *See* propositional act.

actional level (of pragmatic analysis) *See* pragmatic analysis level.

activity type A term used by the British linguist Stephen Levinson for an event which is goal defined, socially constituted, and culturally recognized, e.g. a lecture, a buffet lunch, and a job interview. For Levinson, this term is preferable to the term 'speech event', since the latter may imply that all the acts that make up a speech event are acts of speaking.

actual implicature *See* im-plicature.

actual presupposition *See* pre-supposition.

actual world *See* possible world(s).

***ad hoc* concept** A notion introduced by the American psychologist Laurence Barsalou, which refers to the pragmatic adjustment of a lexical concept in the linguistically decoded logical form of a sentence uttered. E.g. in *The children stood in a circle around the Christmas tree*, the circle is likely to be only approximately circular; hence what is expressed is not the encoded concept CIRCLE but a broadened or loosened concept CIRCLE*, where the asterisk is conventionally used to mark an *ad hoc* concept. The notion is widely employed in relevance theory to account for e.g. metaphor, hyperbole and loose use. *Ad hoc* is Latin for 'to this'. See Carston (2002); Huang (2007). *See also* lexical narrowing; lexical broadening.

adaptability A term encountered in the European Continental tradition of pragmatics for the property of language that enables people to make negotiable choices from a variable range of options in such a way as to approach points of satisfaction for communicative needs. Also called **adaptation**. See Verschueren (1999). *See also* negotiability; variability.

additive implicature A *conversational implicature that builds pragmatic content into the semantic content of a sentence uttered. E.g. the implicature 'together' arising from the uttering of the sentence *John and Mary danced last night*. See Levinson (2000). Contrasts with **subtractive implicature**.

address A type of *vocative. Addresses can occur wherever other *parentheticals can. E.g. *Dean* in *My view, Dean, is that we should set up a new research centre.* All addresses can be used as a call. *See also* call.

address form *See* forms of address.

addressee Occasionally also called an **allocutor**. A person who is the recipient of a message, especially one to whom the speaker speaks or addresses an utterance in a speech event. Often contrasted with **addresser**. *See also* bystander; eavesdropper; hearer; overhearer; attributive addressee; indefinite addressee; speech event participant; ratified participant.

addressee honorific A type of *relational social deixis that holds between speakers and addressees. Addressee honorifics are linguistic forms used by a speaker to signify respect towards an addressee. In this type of honorific, respect or honour can be conveyed without a direct reference to the target of the respect being necessary. E.g. the use of *ma'am* in *Yes, ma'am*. Addressee honorific is less common than *referent honorific. Also called **addressee-controlled honorific**. *See also* bystander honorific.

addressee('s) maxim *See* speaker's maxim.

addresser A person who is the sender of a message, especially a **speaker** or writer who speaks or writes in a speech event. Often contrasted with **addressee**. *See also* bystander; eavesdropper; hearer; overhearer; speech event participant; ratified participant.

adjacency pair In a conversation, a sequence of two structurally successive utterances or *turns produced by two different speakers and ordered as a *first pair part (FPP); a *second pair part (SPP). The second pair part is of a type required or expected by the first pair part. E.g. a question is normally followed by an answer, as in A: *Where's John?* B: *He's in his office*. If there is no detectable gap between the end of the first pair part and the start of the second pair part, the two turns are said to be latched.

adverb of space *See* demonstrative.

adverbial demonstrative *See* demonstrative.

affective impoliteness A term used by the British linguist Jonathan Culpeper to refer to the type of *impoliteness that displays a speaker's heightened emotional state, typically anger, towards the addressee or a third party for creating the negative emotional state for the speaker. E.g. *You'll drive me mad*. *See also* coercive impoliteness; entertaining impoliteness.

affective meaning *See* expressive meaning.

affirmative proposition Any *proposition that asserts what is the case. E.g. the proposition expressed by the sentence *After seven years of marriage, they had grown apart*. Contrasts with **negative proposition**, namely, any proposition that denies what is the case. E.g. the proposition expressed by the sentence *Professor Smith is not on sabbatical*. From a strictly philosophical or logical point of view, there does not seem to be a good way of making such a distinction.

afterthought *See* antitopic.

'afterward' pragmatics *See* 'beforehand' pragmatics.

agreement maxim One of a set of *maxims of politeness proposed by the British linguist Geoffrey Leech, which is addressee-oriented. What the principle basically says is: maximize agreement but minimize disagreement between self and others. More recently Leech has preferred to use the term 'pragmatic constraint' over the term 'maxim'. See Leech (2007). *See also* approbation maxim; generosity maxim; modesty maxim; sympathy maxim; tact maxim.

AI = artificial intelligence.

aizuchi A Japanese device for *back-channelling, ranging from short utterances like *hai* 'yes', *ee* 'yes', and *soo* 'I see' to a great variety of vocalic and consonantal sounds including grunts. See Mey (2001).

algebra semantics A formal approach to natural language semantics applying notions and techniques of Boolean algebra. Also called **Boolean semantics**.

algorithm *See* heuristic.

alienable possession implicature A *conversational implicature that arises from the use of an indefinite expression which denotes alienable possession. E.g. the uttering of *John saw a dog yesterday* gives rise to the conversational implicature that the dog in question was not John's own dog. This is because dogs are alienable possessions of a person. Contrasted with an **inalienable possession implicature**.

allocutor *See* addressee.

allopract A term introduced by the Danish linguist Jacob Mey for a concrete realization of a particular instantiation of a given *pragmeme. An important class of allopract is *indirect speech acts. See Mey (2001).

alternative style *See* avoidance style.

ambiguity, ambiguous The property that a word (in the sense of word form) or a sentence has two or more different meanings assigned by the language system. E.g. *John was looking for his glasses* is ambiguous, because *glasses* can mean either spectacles or drinking containers. Ambiguity is usually divided into various types such as **lexical ambiguity**, **syntactic ambiguity**, **semantic scope ambiguity**, and **pragmatic ambiguity**. Lexical and syntactic ambiguity can also be combined to form **lexico-syntactic ambiguity**. Other categories of ambiguity that have been identified include ambiguity by level, ambiguity by tense, ***de dicto/de re* ambiguity/opaque-transparent ambiguity, referential ambiguity**, and **type-token ambiguity**. *See also* vagueness (2).

ambiguity by level *See* token.

ambiguity by tense *Ambiguity arising from a linguistic expression which can encode two or more tenses. Thus, *The guards hit the prisoners* is ambiguous between present and past tense.

American pragmatism A term that is often found in the history of pragmatics for *pragmatism (1). The development of American pragmatism has influenced in one way or another all European traditions of pragmatic theorizing. Contrasts with the **Anglo-Saxon approach** (to pragmatics), **French approach** (to pragmatics), **German approach** (to pragmatics), and **British contextualism and functionalism**.

ampliative inference A term deployed by the British linguist Stephen Levinson to refer to any *inference that expands the information given. E.g. an inference from *John has had a shower* to *John has had a shower this morning*. Also known as **ampliative reasoning**.

analytic(al) philosophy The term is best seen as one that covers a diverse collection of philosophical methods, techniques, and tendencies rather than a philosophical doctrine or school. Analytic(al) philosophy takes the process of analysis to be central to philosophical method and relies heavily on logical and linguistic analysis, from which it derives its name. It has been the dominant academic philosophical tradition in the English-speaking world. Prominent figures include the philosophers Gottlob *Frege, Bertrand Russell, George Moore, Ludwig *Wittgenstein, and Rudolf Canap. Analytic(al) philosophy has given rise to many central topics in pragmatics. Sometimes also known rather misleadingly as **linguistic philosophy (2)** or **Oxford philosophy**. *See also* logical positivism; philosophy of language; linguistic philosophy (2).

analytic/synthetic distinction A contrast originated with the German philosopher Immanuel Kant. An **analytic proposition** is one in which the concept of the predicate is contained in the concept of the subject. E.g. since the idea 'red' is contained in the idea of 'red roses', *All red roses are red* is then **analytic** or **analytically true**. An analytic proposition which is true by virtue of its logical form is known as a *tautology. By contrast, a **synthetic proposition** is one where the concept contained in the predicate is not contained in the subject. *All roses are red* is **synthetic** or **synthetically true**, because the idea 'red' is not contained in the idea of 'roses'. The truth of a synthetic proposition depends on the relation between its meaning and the way the world is. The entire distinction was called into question by the American philosopher W. V. O. Quine.

anaphor Also called an **anaphoric expression**. A linguistic expression that derives its interpretation from its antecedent (1). E.g. *himself* in *Gordon despised himself.*

anaphora, anaphoric **1.** A relation between two or more linguistic elements, in which the interpretation of one (called an anaphoric expression) is in some way determined by the interpretation of the other (called an antecedent (1)). In other words, in an anaphoric relation, an anaphoric expression takes its meaning or reference from its antecedent. E.g. in *John said that he would sell his small restaurant as a going concern*, the referent of the pronouns *he* and *his* is derived via their antecedent *John*. Many aspects of anaphora are pragmatic in nature. Also termed **anaphoric reference**. *See also* attributive anaphora; bound-variable anaphora; bridging cross-reference anaphora; coreferential anaphora; non-coreferential anaphora; deep anaphora; surface anaphora; E-type anaphora; identity of reference anaphora; identity of sense anaphora; metonymic anaphora; partonymic anaphora; toponymic anaphora; referential anaphora. **2.** An anaphoric relationship in which the antecedent comes earlier than the anaphoric expression, as in the above example. Originally, 'anaphora' was a term for a relation 'up' (Greek *aná*). Anaphora (2) is also called variously **forward anaphora**, **backward-looking anaphora**, or **retrospective**

anaphora. Contrasted with **cataphora**, **anticipatory anaphora**, and **prospective anaphora**. See Huang (2000a).

anaphoric ambiguity *See* referential ambiguity.

anaphoric expression *See* anaphor.

Andeutung A term borrowed from German and used by the American linguist Laurence Horn to refer to the British philosopher H. P. Grice's notion of *conventional implicature, based on the German philosopher, mathematician, and logician Gottlob Frege's discussion of it. According to Horn, Frege's discussion of the *Andeutung* relation is a direct precursor of Grice's concept of conventional implicature. More recently, Horn has translated *Andeutung* as **F-implicature**. See Huang (2011).

Anglo-American tradition (of pragmatics) One of the two main schools of thought in contemporary pragmatics. Within the Anglo-American conception of linguistics and the philosophy of language, pragmatics is defined as the systematic study of meaning by virtue of, or dependent on, the use of language. The central topics of inquiry include implicature, presupposition, speech acts, deixis, and reference, all of which originate in the 20th-century analytic(al) philosophy. This is known as the **component view** of pragmatics. On this view, a linguistic theory consists of a number of core components: phonetics, phonology, morphology, syntax, and semantics. Each of these core components has a relatively properly demarcated domain of inquiry. Pragmatics, then, is just another core component placed in the same contrast set within a linguistic theory. By contrast, other 'hyphenated' branches of linguistics such as anthropological linguistics, educational linguistics, and sociolinguistics lie outside this contrast set of core components. The component view of pragmatics is to some extent a reflection of the modular conception of the human mind, namely, the claim that the mental architecture of *homo sapiens* is divided roughly between a central processor and a number of distinctive, specialized mental systems known as modules. Also known as **Anglo-American pragmatics**. See Huang (2010c). Contrasted with **Continental tradition** (of pragmatics).

Anglo-Saxon approach (to pragmatics) A term that is often encountered in the history of pragmatics for the British mode of thought that grew out of *ordinary language philosophy within analytic(al) philosophy. The philosophers J. L. Austin, Gilbert Ryle, H. P. Grice, John R. Searle, and the later Wittgenstein are widely credited with the founding of this historical tradition. Topics of common interest to this school include meaning, intention, use, implicature, and speech acts. The Anglo-Saxon approach to pragmatics has its deep roots in antiquity, i.e. rhetoric, as one of the three elemental subjects of the *trivium* (Latin). It is built to some extent upon the German philosopher Immanuel Kant's philosophy of 'active (transcendental) subjects' and the English philosopher John Locke's philosophy of 'semiotic acts'. It was also affiliated in one way or another with *American pragmatism. It was developed simultaneously with but independently of the school of *British contextualism and functionalism. Contrasts with the **French approach** (to pragmatics), **German approach** (to pragmatics), **American pragmatism**, and **British contextualism and functionalism**. See Nerlich (2010).

answer condition A set of conditions for an interrogative sentence, modelled on *truth conditions for a declarative sentence. Answer conditions specify a range of possible answers to a question that can be asked by using an interrogative sentence. They are considered to be constitutive of satisfaction conditions. *See also* compliance condition.

antagonym Also called variously an **auto-antonym**, **contranym**, **self-antonym**, and **antilogy**. The term is used to refer to a single lexical item that has opposite meanings. E.g. the verb *shop* can mean either 'to search with the intent to buy things (in shops)', as in *John shopped for an iPod at several stores*, or 'to search with the intent to sell things to someone', as in *John shopped his manuscript to several publishers*. Since the two senses of the verb contradict each other, *shop* is an antagonym. Sometimes, antagonyms are also placed under the larger rubric of *enantiosemy.

antecedent **1.** A linguistic expression that determines in one way or another the interpretation of an anaphoric expression (*see* anaphor), whether it comes earlier or later than the anaphoric expression. E.g. *Mary* can function as the antecedent for *she* in *Mary said that she didn't ring the door bell*. **2.** A linguistic expression that determines in one way or another the interpretation of an anaphoric expression, and it comes earlier than the anaphoric expression. Contrasted with a **postcedent**.

anthropological pragmatics *See* cultural pragmatics.

anticipatory anaphora *See* cataphora.

anti-iconicity, anti-iconic *See* iconicity, iconic.

anti-inferential model (of communication) A model which goes against the assumption that communication is achieved by expressing and recognizing a speaker's intentions. This approach is represented by the American philosophers Tyler Burge and Ruth Millikan. Their alternative is a perceptual account of utterance interpretation, according to which an utterance produces a belief in more or less the same way as perception does. *See also* code model (of communication); inferential model (of communication).

antilogy *See* antagonym.

antipodal A variety of *directional oppositeness. The pairs are at the opposite ends along an axis within a certain entity. The domains to which antipodal pairs apply can be non-spatial as well as spatial. E.g. the sense relation between *top* and *bottom*, *front* and *back*, and *introduction* and *conclusion*. *See also* converseness; counterpart; opposite direction; reversive.

antitopic A sentence topic (3) that is placed at the end of the sentence. E.g. *John and Sophia* in *How far away do they live, John and Sophia?* Also known as **afterthought** or **right dislocation**.

antonymy, antonym **1.** = lexical oppositeness. **2.** A type of *lexical oppositeness in which the opposition is one of degree. E.g. the meaning relation between *big* and *small*. These antonyms are graded against different standards or norms, depending on e.g. context and real-world knowledge. E.g. compare *a big mouse* and *a big elephant*. Clearly even a very small elephant is still much bigger than a very big mouse, for *small* means 'small as elephants go' and *big* means 'big as mice go'. In such a sense relation, one term is often neutral. Thus if one wants to know the size of something, one will normally use the positive or 'supra' term, asking *How big is it?* without implying that it is big. Therefore, *big* is the unmarked term. On the other hand, the negative or the 'sub' term of the pair *small* cannot in general be used in such a way. The use of *How small is it?* does presume that the entity in question is small. Therefore, *small* is the marked term. Antonyms typically have a contrary relationship, because denying what is denoted by one term does not automatically assert what is denoted by the other. *The elephant is not big* does not entail that the elephant is small, for it is possible that it is neither big nor small. Therefore, antonyms are also called **gradable contraries**. Four main types of antonyms can be identified: (i) *gradable, (ii) *equipollent, (iii) *overlapping, and (iv) *privative. *See also* complementarity; directional oppositeness; incompatibility.

apodosis *See* conditional.

apology A *speech act performed by an apologizer to remedy the offence for which he or she is responsible, thus addressing the face-needs of the person who has been offended. In the last three decades, apology has attracted attention especially in *sociopragmatics, *cross-cultural pragmatics, and *interlanguage pragmatics.

***Appell* 'appeal' function** *See* functions (of language).

appellative function *See* functions (of language).

applied conversation analysis (applied CA) *See* pure conversation analysis (pure CA).

applied pragmatics Any application of the concepts and findings of theoretical pragmatics to practical tasks such as the diagnosis, assessment, and treatment of pragmatic disorders, human–computer interaction, and the teaching and learning of second and foreign languages. In the last connection, the field is often called **second and foreign language (L2) pragmatics**. *See also* applying pragmatics.

applied timeless meaning *See* timeless meaning.

applying pragmatics A term introduced by the Hong Kong-based linguist Leo Hoey within the Continental tradition of pragmatics for any dynamic, user-oriented, problem-solving activity employing pragmatic knowledge in the real-world context especially of the social struggle *See also* applied pragmatics.

approbation maxim One of a set of *maxims of politeness proposed by the British linguist Geoffrey Leech, which is addressee-oriented. What the principle basically states is: maximize praise but minimize dispraise of others. More recently Leech has preferred to use the term 'pragmatic constraint' over the term 'maxim'. See Leech (2007). *See also* agreement maxim; generosity maxim; modesty maxim; sympathy maxim; tact maxim.

appropriacy condition *See* felicity conditions.

approximation **1.** A variety of *lexical broadening, whereby a word with a relatively strict meaning is interpreted not literally but pragmatically as an approximation. E.g. the use of *bald* in *John is bald* in a situation in which John still has quite a few wispy strands of hair on his head. *See also* category extension. **2.** A type of sentence non-literality defined by the American philosopher Kent Bach, in which a sentence contains an approximation that is not expressed explicitly. E.g. when someone says *My home town is one hundred miles from London*, what he or she means is that his or her home town is approximately rather than exactly one hundred miles from London.

arbitrary reference *Reference expressed by the phonetically unrealized subject of a finite clause in a language like Spanish, represented by small *pro* in the American linguist Noam Chomsky's generative syntax, and of a non-finite clause in a language like English, represented by big *PRO*. E.g. *pro llaman a la puerta* ('people are knocking at the door') in Spanish and *PRO smoking/to smoke kills* in English. In sentences like these, the phonetically unrealized subject is understood as 'for anyone'. Reference in such a sentence is called arbitrary. See Huang (2000a).

areal (cultural) script A *cultural script that expresses broad cultural themes which are normally played out in detail by way of whole families of related speech practices shared by a number of speech cultures in a geographic area. E.g. a West African cultural script for name avoidance in adult address is like this: if I think about someone like 'This person is not a child' when I want to say something to this person, I can't say this person's name. See Goddard and Wierzbicka (2004). *See also* high-level (cultural) script; low-level (cultural) script.

argument A term taken from mathematical logic for any syntactic element seen as required by a relational predicate such as a verb. E.g. in

John hates Gordon, *John* and *Gordon* are the arguments of the two-place predicate *hate(s)*.

argument structure The number and type of arguments that a relational predicate such as a verb may or must be combined with. E.g. the argument structure of *give* requires an agent, a theme and a recipient, as in *John gave Mary a book*.

argumental underdetermination A term employed by the American philosopher Kent Bach to refer to a case of semantic *underdetermination whose source or locus is an argument. E.g. in *Gentlemen prefer blondes*, what is underdetermined is an argument like *to brunettes*.

Argumentation Theory (AT) A pragmatic theory of rational persuasion associated most closely with the work of the French linguist Oswald Ducrot. It promotes argumentation to the fundamental organizational force behind all linguistic communication. It studies persuasion through argumentation, investigating logical arguments and fallacies and the use of them. According to this theory, an utterance contains not only informational content but also **argumentative orientation**. The argumentative orientation is claimed to provide an account of a range of linguistic phenomena. See Anscombre and Ducrot (1989).

articulated constituent *See* unarticulated constituent.

articulatory inertia *See* speaker's economy.

artificial intelligence (AI) A branch of computer science, artificial intelligence is the science and engineering of designing and building intelligent machines, i.e. machines which can do the kind of things that human beings can. Main research topics within AI include knowledge and reasoning, problem solving, natural language processing, visual recognition, and game playing. AI is particularly relevant to *computational pragmatics.

assertability condition *See* assertion condition.

assertion A term deployed in the philosophy of language, pragmatics, and semantics to refer to (i) the *speech act of putting forward a statement or proposition as true, and/or (ii) the statement or proposition thus produced. E.g. the act of presenting a true statement that the dog is gnawing a bone, and the statement *The dog is gnawing a bone*.

assertion condition A term that is used usually for a set of three principles proposed by the American philosopher Robert Stalnaker, following the insights of the British philosopher H. P. Grice's theory of rational, co-operative communication. The first of these principles requires a speaker to be both consistent and informative. By the second condition, a speaker is expected to use only sentences whose presuppositions have already been placed in the common ground. The third principle dictates that a speaker should avoid ambiguity. Also called the **assertability condition**. See van Rooij (2004).

assertionalism The view that non-declarative sentences or utterances are derivative from and parasitic on the declarative use of language and as such they can be reduced to declarative sentences. It is this thesis that the British philosopher J. L. Austin challenged in the development of his *speech act theory. Also known as **descriptivism**.

assertive *See* representative.

assertive speech act *See* representative.

assertive verb A type of *illocutionary verb that names the assertive or representative speech act it performs. E.g. *allege*, *assert*, and *state*.

associate anaphora *See* bridging cross-reference anaphora.

association rights A term used by the British linguist Helen Spencer-Oatey for a type of sociality rights which refers to the belief that people are entitled to associate with others in accordance with the type of social relationship they have with them. Association rights are social. Contrasted with **equity rights**.

associative meaning Non-linguistic associations or *connotations (1) of a linguistic expression, especially a lexeme. E.g. the meaning of *war* is associated with destruction, death, etc. *See also* encyclopedic meaning.

asymmetric conjunction A *conjunction in which '*p* and *q*' and '*q* and *p*' are not understood as equivalent. E.g. the conjunction in *The police moved in and the suspects were arrested*. The reversal of the order of the two conjuncts here affects the meaning of the whole conjunction. Contrasts with **symmetric conjunction**.

asymmetry of politeness *See* pragmatic paradox (of politeness).

AT = Argumentation Theory.

attitudinal deixis *See* social deixis.

attitudinal meaning *See* expressive meaning.

attributive addressee A term invented by the American psycholinguists Herbert Clark and Thomas Carlson for an *addressee that is specified attributively. E.g. *the last one of you to leave* in John to David, Mary, and Sophia: 'The last one of you to leave, please close all the windows.'

attributive anaphora An anaphoric relation in which the anaphoric expression attributes a certain property to the entity referred to by its antecedent. E.g. the relationship between *the idiot* and the person denoted by its antecedent *John* in *John promised to come to Mary's wedding, but the idiot missed the train*. In this sentence, the anaphoric expression *the idiot* attributes the property of being an idiot to the person referred to by *John*.

attributive use A term employed in relevance theory to refer to the case in which a linguistic expression is used to express a concept that a speaker attributes to someone else, which the speaker may or may not endorse. A concept that is thus expressed is sometimes known as an **attributive concept**. Attributive use is considered to be a variety of *interpretive use.

attributive use (of referring expressions) *See* referential use.

audibility A dimension of *space deixis, which is in general concerned with whether or not an entity referred to is audible or inaudible with respect to the *deictic centre, typically a speaker. Yucatec Maya is a language with audibility markers. E.g. *hé?eb'*? meaning 'listen to the one audible to us'. *See also* visibility.

audience implicature A term used by the British philosopher Jennifer Saul to refer to a *conversational implicature or speaker meaning that is recognized by the addressee but not intended by the speaker. In contrast, by **utterer implicature** is meant a conversational implicature or speaker meaning that is intended by a speaker but not recognized by the addressee. Together, audience implicature and utterer implicature are called **near-implicature**. See Saul (2002).

auditor's economy A principle of economy proposed by the American linguist George Zipf. It posits a tendency toward a vocabulary of many different words with one distinct meaning for each of the words, thus minimizing a hearer's effort. Auditor's economy is related to the American linguist Laurence Horn's *Q-principle. Also called the **force of diversification**. See Horn (2004); Huang (2007). Contrasts with Zipf's speaker's economy.

augmentative and assisted communication *See* communication aid.

augmentative or alternative communication *See* communication aid.

augmented inclusive person *See* minimal inclusive person.

***Ausdruck* 'expression' function** *See* functions (of language).

Austin, John Langshaw (1911–1960) British philosopher. Educated primarily as a classicist at the University of Oxford, he started his academic career by teaching philosophy at Magdalen College, Oxford. After a distinguished period in the military intelligence service during the Second World War, he returned to Oxford to become White's Professor of Moral Philosophy in 1952. He was a major figure of the postwar movement in philosophy known as '*ordinary language philosophy'. His most substantial contribution is the development of a general theory of *speech acts, which has remained one of the cornerstones of contemporary thinking in linguistic pragmatics and the philosophy of language. His main work, collected in *Philosophical*

Papers (1961) , *Sense and Sensibilia* (1962), and *How to Do Things with Words* (1962), was published posthumously.

Austinian semantics *See* situation semantics.

auto-antonym *See* antagonym.

auto-hyponymy, auto-hyponym The phenomenon whereby a polysemic or polysemous lexical item functions in one of its senses as the superordinate to itself in another sense. E.g. the sense relation between *animal* in the meaning of 'mammal' and *animal* in the meaning of 'beast'.

auto-meronymy, auto-meronym The phenomenon whereby a polysemic or polysemous lexical item serves in one of its senses as the *holonym (the term referring to the whole) to itself as a *meronym (the term designating the part) in another sense. E.g. the meaning relation between *body* in the sense of 'the whole physical structure of a human being or an animal' and *body* in the sense of 'the main part of a body not including the head, or not including the head, arms, and legs'.

autonymy The use of a linguistic expression to refer to itself rather than its referent. E.g. '*Paris*' is used to refer to the five-letter word *Paris* rather than the capital city of France. *See also* mention.

availability A notion put forward by the French philosopher François Recanati which claims that normal conversational participants have conscious access to what is said and what is implicated of an utterance, and to the inferential mechanism that effectuate them. See Recanati (2004).

availability principle A principle proposed by the French philosopher François Recanati which states that in determining whether a pragmatically enriched aspect of utterance meaning is part of *what is said or a *conversational implicature, speakers' pre-theoretical intuitions are needed. See Recanati (1993).

avoid ambiguity A sub-*maxim of conversation introduced by the British philosopher H. P. Grice which goes under the *maxim of Manner. By this sub-maxim, a speaker is expected not to use any linguistic expressions or structures which may give rise to *ambiguity.

avoid ambiguity principle A pragmatic principle put forward by the American linguist David Dowty which predicts that if a language has two syntactic structures A and B, such that A is ambiguous between meanings X and Y, but B has only meaning X, speakers of that language would tend to reserve A for communicating meaning Y. This is because since B would have been available for communicating meaning X unambiguously, if meaning X was what is intended, speakers of that language would have used it. E.g. given that the syntactic structure *John hates himself* is unambiguous in that *himself* is obligatorily co-indexed with *John*, the syntactic structure *John hates him* is reserved to express non-coreference between *him* and *John*. See Huang (1994/2007).

avoid obscurity A sub-*maxim of conversation proposed by the British philosopher H. P. Grice which falls under the *maxim of Manner. Given this sub-maxim, a speaker is expected to express him- or herself in such a way that what he or she has said can be easily understood.

avoidance style Also called **avoidance language, respect language**, or **avoidance register.** A linguistic variety of speech that is used in talking in the presence of a certain 'taboo' kin of a speaker, prototypically a mother- or brother-in-law. One of the interesting characteristics of such a linguistic variety is that a part or nearly all of the language's vocabulary has to be replaced by special avoidance lexical items. The use of avoidance style is widespread in Australian aboriginal languages like Dyirbal, Guugu Yimidhirr, and Umpila. Avoidance style is a means to encode *bystander honorific. Other terms are **alternative style** and **respect style**. Sometimes avoidance style is also known as a **mother-in-law language**, **brother-in-law language**, or **taboo language**.

axioms of non-controversiality A set of dictums proposed by the American philosopher Jay Atlas and the British linguist Stephen Levinson, which states that (i) a proposition is not controversial if there is a topic NP in the statement that expresses the proposition, and (ii) the obtaining of stereotypical relations among individuals is not controversial. E.g. in *The teacher told the pupil that he had passed the examination*, the assumption that a pupil normally has to sit examinations is not controversial. *See also* maxim of relativity.

B

B-first analysis (of anaphora) A version of the *neo-Gricean pragmatic theory of anaphora developed by the British linguist Stephen Levinson and the British Chinese linguist Yan Huang. In this account, the pattern predicted by the American linguist Noam Chomsky's binding condition B is taken to be the basic pattern, from which the patterns regulated by binding conditions A and C are then derived for free by the systematic interaction of the *I- and *M-principles. See Levinson (2000); Huang (2004). *See also* A-first analysis (of anaphora); B-then-A analysis (of anaphora).

B-then-A analysis (of anaphora) A version of the *neo-Gricean pragmatic theory of anaphora developed by the British linguist Stephen Levinson. In this analysis, it is assumed that reflexives are historically derived from emphatic pronouns and that the *A-first system is developed out of the *B-first system. The interpretation of various anaphoric expressions is subject to the systematic interaction of the *I- and *Q-principles. Also referred to as **A-first plus B-first analysis** (of anaphora). See Levinson (2000); Huang (2004).

Bach–Peters sentence Named after the American linguists Emmon Bach and Stanley Peters, the term is used to refer to a sentence in which each of the two NPs contains a pronoun that is anaphoric to the other. E.g. *Every pilot who shot at it hit some MIG who chased him*. In this example, the first pronoun *it* is coreferential with the second NP *some MIG who chased him* and the second pronoun *him* is coreferential with the first NP *every pilot who shot at it*. Also called the **Bach–Peters paradox**. *See also* E-type anaphora; donkey sentence; pronoun of laziness.

back-channelling A term used in *conversation analysis and related areas to refer to the use by a listener of a short response, verbal or non-verbal, to react to what the speaker is saying without intending to interrupt him or her or take over his or her *turn. E.g. the use of *mm, uh huh*, and *yeah*. The short utterance is known as a **back-channel**, **back-channelling cue** or **continuer**. A back-channelling cue usually displays a rising contour and overall higher pitch than the other words in conversation. A listener who does the back-channelling is called a **back-channeller**. *See also aizuchi*.

background assumption General presumptions, information, or knowledge about the world that speakers and addressees can be assumed to share as a framework for communicating with one another, thus also known as **background information** or **background knowledge** *See also* mutual knowledge; world knowledge.

background knowledge context *See* general knowledge context.

backgrounded proposition *See* foregrounded proposition.

backgrounding, backgrounded *See* foregrounding.

backward anaphora *See* cataphora.

bald on-record *See* on-record without redress.

bald on-record impoliteness *See* on-record impoliteness.

banter principle A principle of *politeness proposed by the British linguist Geoffrey Leech, which dictates that in order to show solidarity with the addressee, a speaker should say something which is (i) obviously untrue and (ii) obviously impolite to him or her. E.g. the use of *Here comes trouble* when uttered to greet a good friend. The banter principle, together with the British philosopher H. P. Grice's theory of *conversational implicature, allows the speaker to be polite by being superficially rude and the addressee to draw an inference to that effect.

basic explicature *See* higher-level/order explicature.

basic-level concept A concept at the neutral level of inclusion like DOG in comparison with ANIMAL on the one hand and SPANIEL on the other. Concepts at this level are of particular communicative and psychological significance. From a communicative point of view, they are used most frequently and are highly informative; from a psychological perspective, they come to mind most readily and are typically the earliest learned. Lexical items that are related to basic-level concepts are called **basic-level terms**. Concepts at the next higher level such as ANIMAL are labeled **superordinate-level concepts**, and concepts at the next lower level such as SPANIEL are called **subordinate-level concepts**.

basic marker A type of *pragmatic marker (1), which conveys the force of the propositional content of the sentence that holds it. E.g. *I regret* in *I regret that the President hasn' t resigned*. The term 'basic marker' is due to the American linguist Bruce Fraser.

battle for politeness *See* pragmatic paradox (of politeness).

BDI = belief, desire, and intention.

Bedeutung German for *reference or *meaning. Appeared in the title of the German philosopher, mathematician, and logician Gottlob Frege's famous paper *Über Sinn und Bedeutung* (On sense and reference) published in 1892. Contrasted with **Sinn**.

'beforehand' pragmatics A term used by the American linguist Paul Portner for what one knows pragmatically before one hears a linguistic expression. Contrasts with **'afterwards' pragmatics**, which refers to what one knows (pragmatically) after one hears the linguistic expression. E.g. the knowledge of who *he* refers to in *He has a gun!* belongs to 'beforehand' pragmatics, and the knowledge that the uttering of that sentence performs, for instance, a *speech act of warning is part of 'afterwards' pragmatics. See Portner (2005).

behabitive A type of *speech act defined by the British philosopher J. L. Austin which gives reaction to or expresses attitudes or emotions toward the conduct, fortune, and attitudes of others. Paradigmatic cases include apologizing, thanking, congratulating, applauding, and welcoming. E.g. *I apologize for being late*. Behabitive speech acts are similar to *acknowledgement speech acts in the American philosophers Kent Bach and Robert Harnish's classification and *expressive speech acts in the American philosopher John Searle's typology. See Austin (1962). *See also* commissive; exercitive; verdictive; expositive.

behaviourist theory (of meaning) A theory which states that the meaning of a linguistic expression is either the stimulus that evokes it or the response that it evokes, or a combination of both, on a particular occasion of utterance. See Lyons (1995). *See also* meaning-is-use theory (of meaning); mentalistic theory (of meaning); referential theory (of meaning); truth-conditional theory (of meaning); verificationist theory (of meaning).

Beleuchtung German for *tone.

belief, desire, and intention model (of speech act interpretation) *See* plan-based (inference) model (of speech act interpretation).

biconditional A *proposition of the form 'if *p* then *q* and if *q* then *p*'. In other words, biconditional is equivalent to the conjunction of two conditionals, one going in each direction. It is standardly written as '*p* iff *q*'.

bidirectional optimality-theoretic pragmatics (Bi-OT pragmatics) A particular version of *optimality-theoretic pragmatics or optimality-theory pragmatics. What takes centre-stage in bidirectional optimality-theoretic pragmatics is the insight that in communication, not only does the addressee need to determine the optimal interpretation of a given form, but the speaker also needs to express the meaning by selecting the optimal form. Consequently one needs a two-dimensional search for both **interpretive optimality** and **expressive optimality** in terms of form–meaning pairs. This bidirectional approach was partially motivated by the American linguist Laurence Horn's reduction of the British philosopher Grice's *maxims of conversation to the addressee-oriented *Q- and speaker-oriented *R-principles (1); the British linguist Stephen Levinson's, to the Q- and *I-principles. In these principles, the perspective of the speaker and that of the addressee are conditioned on each other. Also known as **bidirectional optimality-theory pragmatics**. See Blutner and Zeevat (2004).

big-tent pragmatics A metaphor coined by the Israeli linguist Mira Ariel to refer to the heterogeneous nature of pragmatics. Within the big-tent pragmatics, there are two types of pragmatics: **problem-solver pragmatics** and **border-seeker pragmatics**. Problem solvers are pragmaticists who aim to provide an account of issues that cannot be tackled by formal grammar including semantics, and border seekers endeavour to draw a distinction between pragmatics and formal grammar. See Ariel (2010).

binary antonymy, binary antonym *See* complementarity.

Bi-OT pragmatics = bidirectional optimality-theoretic pragmatics; bidirectional optimality-theory pragmatics.

bivalence *See* law of bivalence.

blocking The phenomenon whereby the appropriate use of a lexical expression formed by a relatively productive process is apparently prevented by the prior existence of a synonymous or occasionally homophonous lexical item. The process applies to both derivation (e.g. *arrival* blocks **arrivement*); inflection (e.g.*went* pre-empts **goed*). Furthermore, blocking can take place between morphologically unrelated stems, as in *queen* overriding **kingess*. In one respect, blocking can be divided into *synonymy blocking and *homonymy blocking, and in another, a distinction can be made between *full blocking and *partial blocking. Blocking has recently become a topic in lexical pragmatics, especially in neo-Gricean lexical pragmatics. Also referred to as **lexical blocking** or **lexical pre-emption**. The opposite term is **deblocking**. See Huang (2009).

body language *See* non-verbal communication.

Boolean semantics *See* algebra semantics.

border-seeker pragmatics, border seeker *See* big-tent pragmatics.

both words-to-world and world-to-words (directions of fit of a speech act) A type of relationship between words and world, in which words and the world match each other. This is the case of the performance of the speech act of *declarations. E.g. *I declare the bridge open*. *See also* direction of fit (of a speech act); world-to-words (direction of fit of a speech act); words-to-world (direction of fit of a speech act); none (direction of fit of a speech act).

bottom-up pragmatic process A pragmatic process that is linguistically controlled, i.e. triggered by a linguistic expression in a sentence. E.g. *saturation from *Max was late* to 'Max was late for the meeting'. Contrasts with a **top-down pragmatic process**.

bound variable *See* variable.

bound-variable anaphora An anaphoric relation in which an anaphoric expression does not refer to any fixed entity in the external world, but is interpretable by virtue of its dependency on some quantificational expression in the same sentence or discourse, thus seeming to be the natural language counterpart of a bound variable in first-order logic. E.g. the relationship between *he* and *everybody* in *Everybody said that he likes Chinese cuisine.*

bridging A term introduced by the American psycholinguist Herbert Clark to refer to the phenomenon whereby the links between expressed contents of two or more sentences are assumed or inferred via the addition of background assumption, information, or knowledge. What is tacitly bridged is typically the information that is not structurally retrievable from either the sentence or discourse that triggers the inferential process. E.g. in *John walked into a concert hall. The chandeliers were magnificent*, what is bridged is the information that the chandeliers were the chandeliers of the concert hall John walked into. In the process of bridging, the accessibility of background assumptions plays an important role. If the gap is too large, bridging becomes inappropriate. If the extra information bridged is inferred, it is called **bridging inference**. If it is implicated, it is known as **bridging implicature**. For some scholars, bridging inference is considered to be a type of Gricean implicature.

bridging cross-reference anaphora An anaphoric relation in which a definite NP is used to establish a link of association with a preceding linguistic expression in the same sentence or discourse through the addition of background assumptions. E.g. the anaphoric relation between *went for a walk* and *The Italian garden* in *Mary went for a walk after lunch. The Italian garden was beautiful.* The interpretation of bridging cross-reference anaphora is subject to the *I-principle in neo-Gricean pragmatics. Also called **associate anaphora, indirect anaphora**, and **inferable anaphora**.

British contextualism and functionalism A term often found in the history of pragmatics for the approach associated with work by the British Egyptologist Sir Alan Henderson Gardiner, the Polish-born British social anthropologist Bronisław Malinowski, and the British linguist J. R. Firth. Gardiner investigated 'acts of speech'. Malinowski treated meaning as action. Firth emphasized that language should be analysed as part of a social process, and postulated a contextual theory of meaning, with its focus on *context of situation. Many of Firth's ideas were later developed by the British linguist M. A. K. Halliday and other systemic-functional linguists. Key themes in this historical tradition included context, function, and situation. Also known as **contextualist-functionalist pragmatics**. Contrasted with the **Anglo-Saxon approach** (to pragmatics), the **French approach** (to pragmatics), the **German approach** (to pragmatics), and **American pragmatism**. See Nerlich (2010).

broad context A notion put forward by the American philosopher Kent Bach. In opposition to **narrow context**, broad context is taken to be any contextual information that is relevant to the working out of what a speaker overtly intends to mean, and to the successful and felicitous performance of *speech acts. Defined thus, broad context is pragmatic in nature. Also called **wide context**.

broadening *See* lexical broadening.

brother-in-law language *See* avoidance style.

building block metaphor *See* principle of compositionality.

bystander A speech event participant who observes the speech event that is happening, but is not involved in it. *See also* addressee; addresser; eavesdropper; hearer; overhearer; speech event participant; ratified participant.

bystander honorific A variety of *relational social deixis that holds between speakers or addressees and bystanders including participants in the role of audience or non-participant overhearers. Bystander honorifics are linguistic forms that are used by a speaker to show respect towards a bystander. A classical example is the use of so-called 'avoidance' or 'mother-/brother-in-law' languages in Australian aboriginal languages. *See also* addressee honorific; referent honorific.

C

c-content (of what is said) *See* what is said.

CA = **1.** conversation analysis. **2.** componential analysis.

calculability, calculable A property of *conversational implicature. Basically, the claim that a conversational implicature can transparently be worked out via the British philosopher H. P. Grice's *co-operative principle and its component *maxims of conversation. See Huang (2007). *See also* defeasibility; indeterminacy; non-conventionality; non-detachability; reinforceability; universality.

calendrical usage (of a time unit) A usage in which a time measure period designates a fixed length of sequence of naturally given time units. E.g. 'July'. **Calendrical time units** can further be divided into **positional units** such as 'Monday', 'January', and 'morning' and **non-positional units** such as 'week', 'month', and 'year'. By contrast, **non-calendrical usage** is one in which a time measure period is used only as a unit of measure relative to certain fixed point of interest. E.g. 'fortnight'. It is with these calendrical and non-calendrical time units that *time deixis interacts.

call A type of *vocative. Calls are usually utterance-initial. E.g. *Daddy* in *Daddy, look, a spider in the corner!* Only some of them can be used as *addresses. Also referred to as a **summons**.

cancellability, cancellable *See* defeasibility, defeasible.

cancellation analysis (of presupposition) An analysis developed by the British linguist Gerald Gazdar. The crucial assumption underlying this account is that a presupposition is cancellable (*see* presupposition). Thus, what a presupposition trigger engenders is merely a potential presupposition. A potential presupposition will become an actual presupposition, unless it is defeated. With respect to the *presupposition projection problem, what the cancellation theory predicts is that each and every presupposition of an embedded clause will become an actual presupposition of the complex sentence unless it is cancelled by certain linguistic and non-linguistic factors. Furthermore, if a potential presupposition is defeated, then the cancellation must proceed in a fixed order of priority. See Huang (2007). *See also* filtering-satisfaction analysis (of presupposition), accommodation analysis (of presupposition), neo-Gricean analysis (of presupposition).

canonical request *See* request.

canonical speech act A term coined by the American psychologists Herbert Clark and Thomas Carlson to refer to a *speech act made by a single speaker to a single addressee. In other words, in a canonical speech act there is only one addressee. E.g. John to Mary: *Can you pass me that handbook?* Contrasts with a **collective speech act**.

CAPPA = Conversation Analysis Profile for People with Aphasia.

cataphor, cataphoric expression A linguistic expression that derives its interpretation from an antecedent (*see* antecedent 1) which comes later than it or from a *postcedent. E.g. *she* in *After she graduated, Jane worked in a supermarket*. Contrasted with **anaphor, anaphoric expression (2)**.

cataphora, cataphoric An anaphoric (*see* anaphora 1) relationship in which the antecedent of an anaphoric expression comes later than the anaphoric expression itself. Put the other way round, an expression 'looks forwards' for its antecedent. Cataphora is a term for a relation 'down'(Greek *katá*). E.g. if referring to the same person, *he* and *John* form a cataphoric relation in *After he entered the kitchen, John turned the heater on*. A sentence like *Near him, John saw a spider* constitutes a special type of cataphora that is termed **counter-unidirectional anaphora**. Also called variously **anticipatory anaphora, backward anaphora, forward-looking anaphora, prospective anaphora**, and **cataphoric reference**. Contrasts with **anaphora (2)**. *See also* endophora; exophora.

category extension A type of *lexical broadening, whereby a salient word (such as a brand name, a proper name, and even a common noun) is used to denote a broader category. E.g. in the utterance *Have you got any Kleenex?*, the brand name *Kleenex* can be understood as referring to any kind of disposable tissue. *See also* approximation (1).

causal theory (of reference) A theory of proper names (*see* proper noun) put forward by the American philosopher Saul Kripke. According to this theory, unlike *definite descriptions, proper names do not have any sense and therefore are non-descriptive in nature. Rather, they refer directly. The reference of a proper name used on a given occasion works via a causal or historical chain of communication. It is fixed through an initial act or event of naming. After that original act, the proper name is passed on from link to link in the community. In other words, on Kripke's view, it is the causal or historical connection of a proper name that is responsible for the reference of that name to be fixed. Thus William Shakespeare is called *William Shakespeare* because there is a continuous causal or historical chain of cultural transmission that leads from the original event of naming William Shakespeare to the present use of that name. Another way of putting it is that William Shakespeare is named *William Shakespeare* because he was so called initially by someone, somewhere, some time, and the proper name has since been passed on. Also referred to as the **causal chain theory, causal historical theory**, and **direct reference theory**. See Green (1996); Portner (2005).

cautious optimism A term used in relevance theory for the level of pragmatic development that is higher than *naïve optimism but lower than *sophisticated understanding. On this level, an addressee interprets an utterance in such a way as if he or she knows that a speaker is not always competent—e.g. sometimes the speaker may express him- or herself unclearly—but did not know that the speaker is not always benevolent—e.g. sometimes he or she may tell a lie. See Allott (2010).

CCC = Children's Communication Checklist.

CCSARP = Cross-Cultural Speech Act Realization Project.

CD = communicative dynamism.

central discourse topic *See* topic (1).

central speech act *See* ground-floor speech act.

ceremonial illocutionary act *See* conventional illocutionary act.

CF-reduplication = contrastive focus reduplication (*see* lexical cloning).

change of state predicate A predicate such as *begin, continue*, and *stop*, the use of which will trigger a *presupposition. E.g. the use of the change of state verb *stop* in *John has stopped beating his partner* gives rise to the presupposition that John had been beating his partner.

character/content distinction A distinction introduced by the American philosopher and logician David Kaplan between the level of linguistic meaning that does not vary with *context (character); the level of linguistic meaning that does (content).

Characters are functions from contexts of use to contents relative to such contexts. By contrast, **contents** or intensions are functions from world/time pairs to extensions. In other words, they are determined by characters and contexts. Thus, in the case of an indexical or demonstrative, its character is the rule that determines its referent as a function of context; its content is the entity the indexical or demonstrative refers to; and its reference is determined by content and what Kaplan calls 'circumstances of evaluation'. Consequently, an indexical or demonstrative has the same character in all contexts, but different contents in different contexts. See Kaplan (1989); Spencer (2010).

charity *See* pragmatic interpretation; principle of charity (1).

Children's Communication Checklist (CCC) One of the most prominent pragmatic assessment instruments used in clinical pragmatics to identify pragmatic language impairments in children. The checklist is intended to be used with children aged 4–16, and can be completed by a caretaker, a teacher, or a speech and language pathologist. It comprises ten scales covering areas such as coherence, inappropriate initiation, use of context, non-verbal communication, and social relations. Based on the scales, there are also two composites in the checklist: the **General Communication Composite** and the **Social Interaction Deviance Composite**. The former is employed to identify children with clinically significant communication problems, and the latter to identify children who may need further assessments for an autistic spectrum disorder. The checklist has been used extensively with a wide range of clinic groups of children. See Cummings (2009).

Chinese-style topic construction A *topic–comment construction whose comment clause is not syntactically but semantically and/or pragmatically related to the topic. E.g. schematically *That fire, fortunately the fire brigade came quickly*. Also known as a **pragmatic topic construction**. See Huang (2000). Contrasts with an **English-style topic construction**.

Chomskyan module *See* competence module.

circumlocution A *figure of speech which employs a prolix or convoluted form of words, or more words than are required, to avoid speaking or writing in a clear, direct way. E.g. the uttering of *The corners of John's lips turned slightly upward* to suggest or imply that John did not exactly smile. Circumlocution is subject to the *M-principle to engender an *M-implicature in neo-Gricean pragmatics. Also called **periphrasis**.

circumscription A concept developed in artificial intelligence and computational pragmatics for the restriction of entities in a domain to those that comply with predicates and/or those that are known to exist. Circumscription is deployed in certain *non-monotonic inference or reasoning systems. Also known as **domain circumscription**.

circumscriptive reference The process through which a collection of referents in a discourse is identified and a new referent which represents that collection of referents as a unit is established. E.g. the use of *that* in *The packers broke a vase and damaged a chandelier. That was all very careless.*

circumstance of evaluation *See* context of use (2).

clarity *See* principle of clarity.

class system *See* gender system.

classical pragmatics A term frequently used to refer to pragmatic theories of meaning and context developed by *ordinary language philosophers, especially the British philosopher J. L. Austin's *speech act theory and the British philosopher H. P. Grice's theory of *conversational implicature, before pragmatics emerged as a distinct field of linguistics in the 1980s. Both theories are classical in two senses. First, they are original. Secondly, they represent the establishment within the discipline. See Chapman (2011). Often contrasted with **modern pragmatics**.

classical pragmatism *See* pragmatism (1).

classificatory first-order politeness *See* first-order politeness.

cleft presupposition A *presupposition that is triggered by the use of a cleft sentence. There are two types of cleft sentence: cleft and pseudo-cleft. They give rise to two distinct presuppositions. Thus, the uttering of the cleft sentence *It wasn't John who studied the feathered dinosaurs in China* engenders the **cleft presupposition** that someone studied the feathered dinosaurs in China, while the uttering of the pseudo-cleft sentence *What John didn't study was feathered dinosaurs in China* generates the **pseudo-cleft presupposition** that John studied something.

clinical pragmatics A branch of pragmatics that involves the application of pragmatic concepts, theories, and findings to the assessment, diagnosis, and treatment of pragmatic aspects of language disorders. It studies such pragmatic concepts/phenomena as the British philosopher H. P. Grice's co-operative principle and its attendant maxims of conversation, conversational implicature, speech acts, inferences, context, non-literal meaning, deixis, and structure of conversation and discourse from a clinical perspective. The profiles of pragmatic deficits have been examined in a variety of clinical groups with different medical conditions or settings including developmental language disorder, autism, learning disability, left- or right-hemisphere damage of the brain, closed-head injury, Alzheimer's disease, and schizophrenia. Insofar as most of these clinical groups are defined by an underlying neurological condition, and a large amount of research involves children, clinical pragmatics overlaps to some degree with developmental pragmatics and neuropragmatics. See Cummings (2009). *See also* developmental pragmatics; neuropragmatics.

code model (of communication) In opposition to **inferential model**, this is the model which dictates that communication is accomplished by encoding and decoding messages, i.e. a communicator encodes his or her intended message into a signal, which is then decoded by the audience using an identical copy of the code. Much of animal communication utilizes this model. This, for instance, is the case for the bee dance employed to indicate the direction and distance of nectar. See Sperber and Wilson (1995); Huang (2007).

coding time (CT) The moment an utterance is produced. Contrasted with **receiving time (RT)**.

coercive impoliteness A term employed by the British linguist Jonathan Culpeper for the variety of impoliteness that attempts a rebalance of values between a speaker and his or her target so that the speaker can gain, maintain, and reinforce his or her benefits. It usually involves a conflict of interests and an imbalance of power. It is a typical means of pursuing power through language. E.g. *Shut up, or I'll cut your throat! See also* affective impoliteness; entertaining impoliteness.

cognitive anthropology The comparative study of the interrelations between language, thought, and culture. The principal concerns of cognitive anthropology are cultural models, everyday reasoning in its cultural context, the Sapir–Whorf hypothesis, situated language use, universal and cultural-specific principles of language use in context, spatial language and cognition, semantic categories in particular domains, and social interaction in all its multimodal complexity (such as speech, gesture, gaze, and kinesics). Construed thus, cognitive anthropology overlaps with cognitive, cultural, and sociopragmatics. Originally called **ethnosemantics** or **ethnographic semantics**.

cognitive context A type of *context concerned with *inference and other forms of reasoning. A cognitive context includes mental representations, propositions, contextual and factual assumptions, and meta-representations. Psychologically it is considered by some scholars to be conceptualized in terms of the *figure/ground distinction.

cognitive default A term employed in *default semantics for a default meaning or default interpretation that arises from human mental processes. E.g. the default interpretation of the sentence *The best British linguist supervised John's thesis*, namely, the best British linguist whose identity the speaker knows supervised John's thesis, is a cognitive default. Contrasts with **social, cultural**, and **world-knowledge default**.

cognitive effect *See* relevance.

cognitive environment *See* manifestness.

cognitive factive presupposition A *factive presupposition that is triggered by the use of a **cognitive factive verb** such as *realize*, which is concerned with knowledge of fact. E.g. the uttering of the sentence *John realized that her sister was unhappy with her new job* engenders the cognitive factive presupposition that John's sister was unhappy with her new job. Also called **epistemic factive presupposition**. *See also* emotional factive presupposition.

cognitive holism *See* holism.

cognitive linguistics Rooted in the emergence of modern cognitive science in the 1970s, cognitive linguistics has been a major school of thought in linguistics and cognitive science since the 1980s. It represents a systematic study of the relationship between language, the mind, and socio-physical experience. Opposed in particular to the view advocated by the American linguist Noam Chomsky and his followers that knowledge of language constitutes an independent mental system interfacing with others, cognitive linguistics assumes that our linguistic ability goes hand in hand with other cognitive abilities. The two most important branches of cognitive linguistics are cognitive grammar and *cognitive semantics. Leading thinkers in cognitive linguistics include the American linguists Charles Fillmore, George Lakoff, Ronald Langacker, and Leonard Talmy and the French linguist Gilles Fauconnier. *See also* construction grammar (1); cognitive pragmatics (1).

cognitive meaning *See* propositional meaning.

cognitive modularity *See* modularity.

cognitive pragmatics **1.** In its broad sense, the term refers to any pragmatic theory that investigates language in use primarily from a cognitive perspective. In other words, cognitive pragmatics studies the mental processes of language users in communicative interaction. A typical example of cognitive pragmatics in this broad sense is *relevance theory. **2.** In its narrow sense, the term makes reference to a particular cognitive pragmatic approach termed **cognitive pragmatics theory** developed by the Italian linguist Bruno Bara and his associates. Cast in the tradition of the Austrian-born British philosopher Ludwig Wittgenstein's concept of *language games, it provides an explanation of the cognitive processes involved in intentional verbal and non-verbal communication. The proponents of this approach contend that a 'partner' (addressee) in communication establishes the communicative intention of an 'actor' (speaker) by identifying the behaviour game that the actor intends him or her to play. Pragmatic phenomena are accounted for in terms of the complexity of the inferential steps (the 'inferential load') needed to refer an utterance to a particular behaviour game, and the complexity of the associate underlying mental representations. Cognitive pragmatics theory has been applied to studies of *developmental pragmatics in children, the comprehension of pragmatic phenomena in brain-injured patients, and pragmatic decay in subjects with Alzheimer's disease. In these cases, cognitive pragmatics theory overlaps with *clinical and *neuropragmatics. See Bara (2010).

cognitive principle of relevance One of the two main principles of *relevance in relevance theory, which states that human cognition tends to maximize relevance. The principle is claimed to apply to all areas of cognition including attention, inference, and memory, as well as utterance interpretation. Also termed the **first principle of relevance**. Contrasts with the **communicative principle of relevance**.

cognitive semantics A part of *cognitive linguistics. The term is best seen as representing an approach rather than a theory. Cognitive semantics studies the relationship between experience, the conceptual system, and the semantic structure of language. Four guiding principles of cognitive semantics can be identified: (i) the notion of embodied cognition, (ii) the idea that semantic structure reflects conceptual structure, (iii) the thesis that meaning representation is encyclopedic, and (iv) the idea that meaning construction is conceptualization. The family of cognitive semantics includes *frame semantics, *encyclopedic semantics, and *mental space(s) semantics. See Evans (2007).

cognitivism A term that is used to refer to the cognitive strand of pragmatic theorizing, represented by e.g. relevance theory.

Cohen–Recanati principle *See* scope principle.

coherence The logical well-connectedness between different parts of a piece of spoken or written language, which distinguishes it from a random assemblage of sentences or utterances. This type of well-connectedness relies on the working out of connected events rather than linguistic means. In other words, coherence is a matter of meaning compatibility. Two approaches to the study of coherence are of particular interest. In the first, **informational approach**, coherence is established on the basis of the necessary inference being drawn to satisfy the constraints imposed by a set of coherence relations. The informational model has been applied mainly to monologues. By contrast, the second, **intentional approach** maintains that a plan-based speaker's intention plays the most important role in establishing coherence in a discourse. The intentional approach has been applied predominantly to dialogues. It has also been argued that both approaches are interconnected and therefore are needed simultaneously. Also called **discourse coherence**. The concept is of particular relevance to *text pragmatics, *discourse deixis, and *conversation analysis. See Kehler (2004). Contrasted with **cohesion**.

coherence theory (of truth) A theory of truth which says that truth is a matter of internal consistency within the whole system of propositions. In other words, coherence theory is dependent on the fact that all the propositions within the whole system cohere with each other. Put in slogan form, a belief is true if and only if it coheres with other ideas. E.g. the practice of cross-examination is based on this theory. Also known as the **idealist theory** of truth. *See also* correspondence theory (of truth); deflationist theory (of truth); performative theory (of truth); pragmatist theory (of truth).

cohesion A term in *discourse analysis, *conversation analysis, *text pragmatics, and other related areas to make reference to the use of various phonological, grammatical, and/or lexical means to link sentences or utterances into a well-connected, larger linguistic unit such as a paragraph or chapter. In other words, cohesion achieves well-connectedness by means of linguistic forms. The use of an anaphoric expression is one of the most common ways of connecting different parts of a text, as in *Mary is a secretary. She works in a law firm.* Also referred to as **discourse cohesion**. Contrasts with **coherence**.

co-hyponymy, co-hyponym *See* hyponymy.

collaborative performative Also called **collaborative speech act**. The term refers to a *performative or *speech act whose success depends essentially on particular *uptakes by the addressee. Examples include bequeathing, betting, and challenging. *See also* group performative; joint speech act.

collective face *See* social identity face.

collective request *See* request.

collective speech act A term introduced by the American psycholinguists Herbert Clark and Thomas Carlson for a *speech act made by a single speaker to more than one addressee. E.g. Mary to John and Bill: *Can you please bring a cake?* A collective speech act can have a distributive and a collective reading. In the above example, Mary may intend that John and Bill are to bring a cake together (collective reading) or that each of them is to bring a cake separately (distributive reading). In addition, for a collective speech act, it is in general not necessary to inform all the addressees jointly. E.g. Mary can promise something to John and Bill collectively without telling them jointly that she is doing so. An exception is the performance of the speech act of pronouncing a couple married by uttering *I now pronounce you man and wife*, in which the groom and bride have to be informed jointly. Contrasts with a **canonical speech act**.

collectivistic face *See* social identity face.

co-meronymy, co-meronym *See* meronymy.

command An utterance that constitutes an order. E.g. *Go back to your room immediately! See also* mand.

comment The part of a sentence which says something about the *topic in a topic–comment construction. E.g. *you shouldn't smoke* in *Cheap cigarettes, you shouldn't smoke*. Contrasts with a **topic**.

commentary marker A type of *pragmatic marker (1), which comments on aspects of the propositional content of the sentence that contains it. E.g. *reportedly* in *Reportedly, the Berlin Wall has fallen*.

commissive A variety of *speech act proposed by the British philosopher J. L. Austin and the American philosopher John Searle, by which a speaker commits him- or herself to some future course of action. It expresses the speaker's intention to do something in the future. Paradigmatic cases include offers, pledges, promises, refusals, and threats. E.g. *I'll be back in ten minutes*. Also known as a **commissive speech act**. See Austin (1962); Searle (1975). *See also* representative; directive; expressive; declaration.

commissive verb A type of *illocutionary verb that names the commissive speech act it performs. E.g. *offer*, *promise*, and *volunteer*.

common background belief *See* mutual contextual belief.

common ground A term introduced by the American philosopher Robert Stalnaker on the basis of the notion of *common knowledge proposed by the American philosopher David Lewis. By common ground is meant aspects of background knowledge that are taken for granted and shared by a speaker and an addressee in communication. The knowledge involved includes contextual knowledge, linguistic knowledge, and real-world knowledge. According to the American psycholinguist Herbert Clark, the notion can be further divided into **communal command ground** and **personal common ground**. Communal common ground is the background knowledge shared by members of a speech community. In other words, it is based on community membership. By contrast, personal common ground refers to the body of background knowledge two members of a speech community share from their past experience, i.e. it is based on the joint perceptual and linguistic experience of two community members. The term 'common ground' is sometimes used loosely as synonymous with the term '*context', but it is better considered to be a particular variety of context. Often contrasts with **privileged ground**. *See also* context; background assumption; encyclopedic knowledge.

common knowledge A term coined by the American philosopher David Lewis for whatever knowledge people share to coordinate themselves. Common knowledge is an essential property of a speech community. It plays an important role in pragmatics. *See also* common ground; mutual knowledge.

common knowledge context *See* general knowledge context.

common-sense knowledge context *See* general knowledge context.

communal common ground *See* common ground.

communication The transmission and reception of information between a sender and a receiver using a signalling system. A distinction is frequently made between **verbal** (linguistic); **non-verbal** (non-linguistic) **communication.** As a branch of linguistics, pragmatics falls within the province of **communication science**—the systematic study of all aspects of communication.

communication aid A low- or high-tech system or device that presents **augmentative and assisted communication** or **augmentative or alternative communication (AAC)** possibilities for communicators who have difficulties using speech and/or writing for communication or who are disabled by environmental circumstances. In other words, a communication aid provides a means of supplementing or substituting for normal speech or writing. It includes a **voice output communication aid (VOCA)**. Since mid-1980s, there has been a shift in augmentative and assisted/augmentative or alternative communication research away from the linguistic structure to the pragmatics of communication.

communication disorder Any deficit involving communication, which includes but is not restricted to *pragmatic disorder. Cases of communication disorder have been investigated in *clinical and *neuropragmatics. Also known as **communication deficit** and **communication impairment**.

communication failure Lack of success in the transmission and reception of information between a sender and a receiver using a signalling system. In human communication, communication failure consists often of an unsuccessful attempt on the part of a speaker to have his or her intentions recognized by the addressee. Defined thus, **pragmatic failure** is a type of communication failure. Contrasts with **communication success**.

communication science *See* communication.

communication success The completion of transmission and reception of information between a sender and a receiver using a signalling system. In human communication, communication success can be defined in terms of an addressee's recognition of the speaker's intentions. Contrasted with **communication failure**.

communicative act Any act of communication, by speech or by other actions. Defined thus, both *linguistic acts and *speech acts fall under the category of communicative act.

communicative competence A concept introduced by the American anthropological and sociolinguist Dell Hymes in the late 1960s by analogy with the American linguist Noam Chomsky's notion of linguistic or grammatical competence. Communicative competence is concerned with an individual speaker's knowledge of the total set of rules, principles, and conventions governing the appropriate use of language in a society and his or her capacity to develop linguistically and become a skilful native speaker to communicate effectively and efficiently. In short, it constitutes a native speaker's ability to communicate in a language. It consists of at least linguistic, pragmatic, sociolinguistic, sociocultural, and sociopragmatic competence. E.g. a speaker's knowledge of when to speak and when not to speak, how to speak, and how much information to provide.

communicative dynamism (CD) A notion in the *Functional Sentence Perspective. It refers to the degree to which an element of a sentence or utterance contributes to the achievement of a communicative goal in terms of its *information structure. The concept of communicative dynamism presupposes a continuum of *givenness. Sentence elements are assumed to carry varying degrees of communicative dynamism: a high degree is linked with newness or *rheme and a lower degree is associated with givenness or *theme. Elements of a sentence or utterance that have an intermediate degree are taken to form a transition between theme and rheme.

communicative illocutionary act An *illocutionary act that is neither conventional nor ceremonial. Intention and inference rather than convention are assumed to play a central role in the performance of a communicative illocutionary act. E.g. *I promise to show you how to use an iPad.* Contrasts with a **conventional illocutionary act**.

communicative intention **1.** A concept developed by the British philosopher H. P. Grice in the context of his theory of *meaning$_{nn}$ or speaker meaning (*see* utterance meaning). A communicative intention is characterized by three properties. First, it always takes place in the context of an interaction with an audience. Secondly, it is overt in the sense that it is intended to be recognized. Thirdly, the success of a communicative intention depends on the intention being recognized by the audience. The notion of communicative intention plays a fundamental role in pragmatics and related disciplines: it distinguishes between communicative and non-communicative forms of interaction, and draws an outer boundary on the communicative effects that a theory of communication is responsible for. See Grice (1989). *See also* meaning$_{nn}$. **2.** A term used in relevance theory for a higher-order speaker intention to make it mutually manifest to an audience and a communicator that the communicator has a particular *informative intention. Contrasted with an **informative intention**.

communicative presumption (CP) A term used by the American philosophers Kent Bach and Robert Harnish for the general mutual belief in a speech community that whenever a member of the speech community says something to another member of the same speech community, he or she is doing so with some recognizable illocutionary intent, i.e. he or she intends to carry out some identifiable illocutionary act. See Sadock (2004). Contrasts with **linguistic presumption**.

communicative principle A general pragmatic principle proposed by the Danish linguist Jacob Mey which states that people talk with the intention to communicate something to someone, which forms the foundation of all linguistic behaviour.

communicative principle of relevance One of the two main principles of *relevance in relevance theory, which states that every utterance (or other ostensive stimulus) conveys a presumption of its own optimal relevance. Give this postulate, a speaker is expected to make his or her utterance as relevant as possible. Also called the **second principle of relevance**. Contrasted with the **cognitive principle of relevance**.

communicative rationality *See* formal pragmatics (2).

competence Related to the Swiss linguist Ferdinand de Saussure's notion of **langue*, and introduced by the American linguist Noam Chomsky in the 1960s, the concept refers to an abstract system of unconscious knowledge possessed by an idealized native speaker-hearer of his or her own language, as represented by a generative grammar. One of the major differences between competence and *langue* is that the former is conceived as a mental ability and the latter as a social reality.

When applied to pragmatics, the concept becomes highly controversial. Also referred to as **linguistic competence** or **grammatical competence**. More recently, Chomsky has replaced competence with the term *'I[nternalized]-language'. Contrasted with **performance**. *See also* communicative competence.

competence module A module that constitutes a system of mental representation. Competence modules are said to contain linguistic knowledge, biological knowledge, psychological knowledge, physical knowledge, and mathematical knowledge. Also referred to as a **Chomskyan module** or **information module**. Contrasts with a **performance module**. See Carston (2010).

complaint A *face-threatening speech act in which a disappointment, dissatisfaction, or grievance is expressed. Complaints are divided into two types: **direct** or **instrumental complaints** and **indirect complaints**, frequently called 'whinges'. The former is involved with an explicit or implicit accusation and at least an explicit or implicit directive. By comparison, the latter contains a long or repeated expression of dissatisfaction or discontent without intending to improve the dissatisfactory situation. In recent years, complaints have been carefully studied especially in cultural, cross-cultural, and interlanguage pragmatics.

complementarism A term used by the British linguist Geoffrey Leech with regard to the relationship and interface between pragmatics and semantics. On a complementarist view, the division between pragmatics and semantics can in principle be retained. Within complementarism, a further distinction can be made between **radical pragmatics** and **radical semantics**. See Huang (2007). Contrasted with **reductionism**.

complementarity, complementary A type of *lexical oppositeness. It refers to the *sense relation between two lexical items that are mutually exclusive or incompatible. In other words, the choice of one lexical item excludes the use of the other lexical item in a pair. E.g. the meaning relation between *true* and *false*: if something is true it cannot be false, and vice versa. In neo-Gricean lexical pragmatics, the use of complementary lexical items or complementaries is analysed as generating a weak, unordered *Q-implicature. See Huang (2009). Also called **binary antonymy, binary antonym**. *See also* incompatibility; antonymy (2); directional oppositeness.

complete blocking *See* full blocking.

complete definite description A *definite description, the descriptive content of which applies uniquely to the intended referent. E.g. *the author* in *Her uncle met the author of* Lady Chatterley's Lover *in 1922*. Contrasts with **incomplete definite description**.

complete synonymy, complete synonym A term used by the British linguist Sir John Lyons for synonyms that are synonymous in all relevant dimensions of meaning. According to this view, two or more lexical items are complete synonyms if and only if they are identical on every relevant dimension of meaning. Complete synonyms are very rare. *See also* total synonymy; full synonymy.

completion A pragmatic process postulated by the American philosopher Kent Bach which provides extra contextual content or information to a *propositional radical. E.g. the proposition expressed by the sentence *Mary is not slim enough* is conceptually incomplete. Consequently, it needs to be completed or filled in contextually to become minimally but fully propositional, as, for example, in *Mary is not slim enough to be a fashion model*. The completed, full proposition can then be assigned a truth value. See Bach (2004). *See also* expansion; saturation; free enrichment.

complex indirect = non-conventional indirect speech act.

complex proposition A *proposition that contains two or more simple propositions joined by one or more (logical) connectives. E.g. *Jane is beautiful and Jenny is intelligent*. Also called a **compound proposition**. Contrasts with a **simple proposition**.

compliance condition A set of conditions for an imperative sentence, modelled on *truth conditions for a declarative sentence. Compliance conditions specify a range of possible actions to a *speech act that can be made by using an imperative sentence. They are taken to be part of *satisfaction conditions. *See also* answer condition.

compliment A *speech act in which praise or admiration is expressed to the addressee or a third party. One of the main functions of compliments is to make known the speaker's positive psychological attitude towards what has been done by the recipient. Compliments are thus intrinsically polite in nature. They serve to assist in 'greasing the social wheels'. They are highly sensitive to sociological assumptions and values such as *face. Two types of compliment are sometimes identified: **internal** and **external compliments**. Internal compliments refer to aspects that are inherent part of the complimentee such as his or her personal traits. In contrast, by 'external compliment' is meant aspects that are not intrinsically part of the complimentee such as his or her possession. There are cross-cultural similarities and differences in both compliment expressions and responses. Compliments have recently become one of the central topics of inquiry especially in socio-, cultural, cross-cultural, applied, and interlanguage pragmatics.

component view (of pragmatics) *See* Anglo-American tradition (of pragmatics).

componential analysis (CA) A formal approach to *lexical meaning, in which the total sense of a lexeme is analysed and described in terms of a set of simpler, indivisible atoms, elements or components of meaning known variously as **semantic components**, **sense components**, **semantic features**, and **semantic primes**. E.g. in componential analysis, *man* is analysed as [+HUMAN, +MALE, +ADULT]. Componential analysis represents an atomistic approach to lexical meaning. Also called **lexical decomposition, componential semantics** and **semantic feature theory**. *See also* meaning postulate.

compositional expression *See* principle of compositionality.

compositional meaning *See* principle of compositionality.

compositional pragmatics *See* pragmatic compositionality (view).

compositional semantics Any semantic theory in which the notion of (semantic) compositionality plays a central part.

compositionality *See* principle of compositionality; pragmatic compositionality (view).

compound hedge A *hedge that is made up of two or more single hedges. Compound hedges include double hedges (e.g. *it probably indicates that*), triple hedges (e.g. *it seems likely to assume that*), quadruple hedges (e.g. *it may appear somewhat reasonable that*), etc.

compound proposition *See* complex proposition.

computational module *See* performance module.

computational pragmatics The systematic study of the relation between utterances and contexts from an explicitly computational point of view. This includes the relation between utterances and action, the relation between utterances and discourse, and the relation between utterances and their uttering time, place, and environment. Two sides to the question of how to compute the relation between linguistic aspects and contextual aspects can be identified. On the one hand, given a linguistic expression, one needs to work out how to compute the relevant properties of the context. On the other hand, in the case of language generation, the task is to construct a linguistic expression that encodes the contextual information a speaker intends to convey. Given the relevant properties of the context, one needs to work out how to compute the relevant properties of the linguistic expression. This study of the relation between linguistic aspects and contextual aspects requires the building up of explicit computational representations at either side of the relation. A particularly important topic of inquiry in computational pragmatics is *inference. *Abduction, the resolution of *reference, the generation and interpretation of *speech acts, and the generation and interpretation of discourse structure and *coherence relations have figured prominently in computational pragmatics. See Bunt and Black (2000); Jurafsky (2004).

computer corpus (*pl.* corpora) *See* corpus pragmatics.

conative function *See* functions (of language).

concept A mental construct or representation that stores knowledge about **conceptual categories**, i.e. classes of entities in the external world such as DOG, GREEN, and WORK. Simply put, a concept is an idea of a certain class of objects in the external world. It mediates between a word and whatever it denotes or is used to refer to. Thus, the concept DOG can be seen as mediating between *gou* in Chinese, *dog* in English, and *chien* in French and the set of animals denoted by them. Concepts can be grouped according to different levels of inclusiveness: **basic**, **superordinate**, and **subordinate concept**s. No adequate theory of meaning can ignore concept, but concept plays a particularly important role in cognitive pragmatic theories. *See also* conceptualist theory (of meaning).

concept signified *See* sign (2).

conceptual blend *See* mental space(s) semantics.

conceptual blending theory *See* mental space(s) semantics.

conceptual grinding The phenomenon whereby count nouns obtain a mass noun interpretation that denotes the stuff the individual objects are made of. E.g. *Cat is all over the house.* Recently conceptual grinding has been discussed with respect to *blocking and *deblocking in lexical pragmatics. See Blutner (2004).

conceptual meaning (1) = propositional meaning.

conceptual meaning (2) In opposition to **procedural meaning**, the term is used in relevance theory for any meaning that contributes concepts to the logical form of a sentence or utterance. Put slightly differently, in conceptual encoding, linguistic forms or words encode conceptual information. E.g. *lamb, sleep*, and *happy* are lexical items that encode conceptual information. Also referred to as **representational meaning**.

conceptual pragmatic marker A *pragmatic marker (2) that encodes conceptual information. E.g. *fortunately* encodes the concept FORTUNATE. Two types of conceptual pragmatic marker are usually identified: **epistemic** and **evaluative conceptual pragmatic markers**. Contrasts with a **non-conceptual pragmatic marker**.

conceptual semantics (1) A term employed in relevance theory for the category of linguistic semantics whose domain contains linguistic forms whose encoded meaning contributes concepts to the logical form of a sentence or utterance. The opposite term is **procedural semantics**.

conceptual semantics (2) A type of *componential semantics associated with the work of the American linguist Ray Jackendoff. Underlying this approach is the belief that meaning is essential conceptual in nature. The meaning of a sentence constitutes a conceptual complex made up of a set of more basic conceptual components. A set of universal basic ontological categories is deployed to provide a semantic analysis of the sentence, yielding its conceptual structure. The conceptual structure is then mapped to the syntactic structure of the sentence.

conceptualist theory (of meaning) *See* mentalistic theory (of meaning).

concretion A term used in *computational pragmatics for an operation that gives rise to an *inference to a more specific interpretation than can be maintained on a strictly logical basis. E.g. an inference from 'use an umbrella' to 'use an umbrella to protect oneself from the rain or hot sun', though one could use an umbrella for many other purposes.

conditional Any proposition or sentence of the form 'if *p* then *q*'. The condition hypothesized, *p*, is termed the **antecedent** of the conditional, and *q*, the **consequent**. For a conditional sentence, the conditional clause is traditionally called the **protasis** (Greek 'premise'), and the main clause, the **apodosis** (Greek 'response'). E.g. *If you don't go to her seminar, Dr Smith would be unhappy*. Conditionals are considered to be at least partially pragmatic.

conditional perfection A term introduced by the American linguists Michael Geis and Arnold Zwicky for the pragmatic inferential process to change or 'perfect' a conditional into a corresponding biconditional. E.g. the uttering of a sentence such as *If you give me a free Haydn, I'll buy five Mozarts* gives rise to the conversational implicature that if and only if the addressee gives the speaker a free Haydn will the speaker buy five Mozarts. Conditional perfection is taken to be an instance of *I-implicature in neo-Gricean pragmatics.

conditional relevance (of adjacency pairs) The requirement that given a first pair part of an *adjacency pair, the second pair part is immediately relevant and expectable.

confirmation holism *See* holism.

Confucian pragmatics A term used to refer to the thinking of the ancient Chinese philosopher Confucius (551–479 BC) on language use and users, especially his famous doctrine of *zheng ming* 'correction of names'. In this theory, Confucius stressed the performative dimensions of language use and communication. The acts of naming and correcting names are not a matter of describing a world that already exists; on the contrary, it is through these acts that rulers or language users constitute that very world, i.e. the very social realities they are describing. Next, he emphasized the role of authority and symbolic power that are involved in successful naming and other speech acts. Thirdly, on Confucius' view, education, ritual, and language shape the *de* or habitus of an individual as much as they are shaped by him or her. Finally, Confucius treated linguistic normativity in terms of rites rather than universal laws or rules. See Leezenberg (2010).

conjunction A term of logic which refers to the joining together of two propositions or sentences *p* and *q* to obtain a proposition or sentence in the form of *p* & *q*. The propositions or sentences *p* and *q* are in this context described as **conjuncts**. Logical conjunction is truth-functional; it is true if and only if each of the conjuncts is true. Conjunctions can be divided into **symmetric** and **asymmetric conjunctions**. Contrasts with **disjunction**.

conjunction buttressing A term used to refer to the pragmatic enrichment from the use of '*p* and *q*' to '*p* and then/therefore/in order to cause *q*' in an *asymmetric conjunction. E.g. from *John turned the key and the safe opened*, we obtain 'John turned the key and then/thereby caused/ in order to make the safe open'. The pragmatic enrichment involved is treated as an *I-implicature in neo-Gricean pragmatics. Also known as **conjunction reduction**.

connectionism, connectionist A model of mental processes inspired by the physical connections within the human brain. There are billions of nerve cells, called neurons, in the brain. During any brain activity many brain cells are active, transmitting signals to other neurons. While some of these signals are 'excitatory' (causing excitement/excitation), others are inhibitory (causing inhibition). The outcome is a network of simple, neuron-like processing units. These units are densely interconnected. The main thesis of the connectionist model is that human cognition operates through the interaction of these large networks of units in the brain. The units are linked in such a way that each can either arouse or suppress others. There are no specialized modules in the Fodorian sense. Also referred to as the **neural network** or **parallel distributed processing model**, because information is considered to be processed in a highly 'distributed' way (i.e. in different places); 'in parallel' (i.e. at the same time). The simultaneous, distributed processing is thought to operate in the entire system. This is in contrast to **serial** or **sequential processing**, in which operations of different sorts are carried out in sequence, each having access only to the outputs of its previous ones. Recently, the connectionist model of the mind has become very influential in computational linguistics and certain theories of pragmatics. See Aitchison (2003). *See also* modularity.

connotation (1) Aspects of communicative value of a linguistic expression that cannot be reduced to its core, descriptive meaning. One such aspect is concerned with the expressive, affective or emotive component of meaning, especially the use of expressions which have 'favourable' or 'unfavourable' overtones. E.g. in the classical example provided by the British philosopher Bertrand Russell, *I am firm, you are obstinate, he is pig-headed*, where *firm* rates high on the good/bad scale, while *obstinate* and *pig-headed* rate lower on that scale. Another aspect involves the social and situational circumstances of use. Finally, connotation can reflect the cultural associations of a linguistic expression. E.g. *dragon* in English and its broad equivalent *long* in Chinese have quite different cultural connotations.

connotation (2) In *philosophical semantics, the term, due to the British philosopher J. S. Mill, is usually contrasted with or opposed to **denotation**. Thus, while *cat* denotes the set of all cats in the external world, it connotes the property of being a cat. In this usage, the term is deployed in a way equivalent to **intension** and **sense (3)**. *See also* denotation; intension; sense (3).

constancy under negation A property of *presupposition, which dictates that a presupposition generated by the use of a *presupposition trigger remains in force when the sentence containing that trigger is negated. E.g. the uttering of both *The boy cried wolf again* and *The boy didn't cry wolf again* presupposes that the boy had cried wolf before. See Huang (2007).

constant reference *Reference in which a referring expression normally refers to the same entity in the external world, i.e. the referring expression has the same referent. E.g. the referring expressions *the sun, London*, and *the Forbidden City in Beijing* have constant reference. Contrasted with **variable reference**.

constative **1.** A concept developed by the British philosopher J. L. Austin for an utterance that is employed to make an *assertion or a statement. E.g. *When John backpacked around China, he met his future wife.* Occasionally, the term **explicit constative** is used to refer to a statement-making utterance containing an assertive verb such as *assert, state*, and *hypothesize*. E.g. *I state that John is running a hedge fund*. See Austin (1962). The opposite term is **performative**. **2.** A type of communicative *illocutionary act proposed by the American philosophers Kent Bach and Robert Harnish, which is equivalent to the American philosopher John Searle's speech act type of *representative. Paradigmatic cases include affirming, claiming, denying, informing, and stating. E.g. *I deny that I know him. See also* effective; acknowledgement.

constative pragmatics Usually discussed in opposition to **performative pragmatics**, constative pragmatics represents a cognitive or relational approach to language in use. It is oriented to the study of abstract patterns of language use that are taken to be more or less context-invariable. These include *context types, speaker/addressee types, and *speech act types. See e.g. Robinson (2005). *See also* performative pragmatics.

constative speech act One of the three types of *speech act proposed by the German philosopher Jürgen Habermas. 'Constative speech act' is his term for *assertion. E.g. (*I assert that*) *John's moods oscillated wildly between depression and elation. See also* expressive speech act; regulative speech act.

constituent non-literality *See* sentence non-literality.

constitutive rule (of a speech act) A precondition or prerequisite that makes a *speech act what it is. In other words, constitutive rules create or constitute a speech act itself, without which the speech act will not be carried out. E.g. the rule connecting an *illocutionary force linking device (IFLD) and its corresponding illocutionary act: if I warn you not to binge-drink, it counts as an undertaking that it is not in your best interests to binge-drink. The violation of a constitutive rule will normally terminate the purported speech act. Often contrasts with the **regulative rule** (of a speech act). See Searle (1969).

construction grammar **1.** In its broad sense, the term refers to any of a range of grammars set within the framework of cognitive linguistics, pioneered by the American linguists Charles Fillmore, Paul Kay, and George Lakoff in the late 1980s. Construction grammar takes its name from the view held in cognitive linguistics that the basic unit of a language is a pair between form and meaning, called a 'construction'. One of the central theses in construction grammar is the belief that a 'cognitively realistic' or 'psychologically real' grammar can be modelled in terms of constructions. Four versions of construction grammar can be identified: (i) **'classical' construction grammar** championed by Fillmore and Kay, (ii) **'new' construction grammar** developed by the American linguist Adele Goldberg, (iii) **embodied construction grammar (ECG)**, and (iv) **radical construction grammar**. Given that constructions interact with *context or *common ground, and are influenced by pragmatic information, construction grammar and pragmatics share certain common interests. **2.** In its narrow sense, construction grammar designates the 'classical' version put forward by Fillmore and Kay, based in part on an analysis of *idioms. In this variety of construction grammar, the lexicon and syntax are on a continuum rather than being treated as separate, independent components. The representations comprise not only syntactic but also semantic and pragmatic information. **3.** In its narrow sense, the term is also used with reference to the 'new' version of construction grammar developed by Goldberg. Goldberg extended Fillmore and Kay's classical analysis from 'special, irregular' idioms to 'regular, ordinary' constructions, focusing on verb argument constructions. She called the lexicon–grammar continuum she had proposed the 'construction'. Incorporating insights also from *cognitive semantics, she produced a new version of construction grammar to explain argument structure patterns. See Evans (2007).

constructional presupposition trigger Any linguistic structure whose use triggers a *presupposition. E.g. the use of the temporal clause in *After she entered the room, Jane took her gloves off* presupposes that Jane entered the room. Also called a **structural presupposition trigger**. *See also* lexical presupposition trigger.

content 1. A term used in the philosophy of language to refer to the representational aspect of mental states. The content of certain mental states is considered to be propositional. Therefore, the content of a sentence constitutes the proposition expressed by the sentence. **2.** *See* character/content distinction.

content-descriptive (speech act) verb A term employed by the British linguist Geoffrey Leech for the type of *speech act verb that describes the content or matter of a speech act. E.g. *describe, request* and *persuade*. This type of speech act verb consists of three subtypes: **locutionary, illocutionary**, and **perlocutionary speech act verbs**. *See also* phonically descriptive (speech act) verb; neutral (speech act) verb.

context Generally, any relevant features of the dynamic setting or environment in which a linguistic unit is systematically used. Context can be seen as composed of a number of different sources: **physical, linguistic, social, and general knowledge context**—a view known as the 'geographic' division of context. It is relevant to both semantics and pragmatics but plays a more central role in pragmatics. Some of the semantic phenomena and most of the pragmatic phenomena are context-dependent or context-sensitive. In the philosophy of language and formal pragmatics, context is often taken as *common ground. See Huang (2007). *See also* broad context; narrow context; cognitive context; cultural context; default context; global context; macro context; opaque context; situational context; context of situation; context of use.

context-bound presupposition *See* pragmatic presupposition.

context change potential In *file change semantics and other dynamic semantic theories, the term is used with reference to the potential ability of a sentence, when uttered, to alter dynamically the environment or context in which it is used. It includes patterns of change produced by a sentence on the information status of the participants in a discourse or conversation.

context change semantics *See* file change semantics.

context dependence *See* context sensitivity.

context dependency *See* context sensitivity.

context-dependent expression *See* context-sensitive expression.

context-dependent scale *See* pragmatic scale.

context-independent scale *See* semantic scale.

context of culture *See* cultural context.

context of situation A term originated with the Polish-born British social anthropologist Bronisław Malinowski and associated also with the British linguist J. R. Firth. It refers to the whole set of relevant circumstances in which a specific act of speech takes place. *See also* situational context.

context of use **1.** = context. **2.** A term used by the American philosopher David Kaplan to refer to one of the two distinct roles played by context he has identified. A **context of use** plays the role of supplying content for a *context-sensitive or context- dependent expression such as an *indexical. In other words, it helps to determine what a speaker says. By contrast, a **circumstance of evaluation** plays the role of evaluating the content of a sentence uttered. Put slightly differently, it represents an actual or merely possible situation or context in which the truth or falsity of what is said is determined.

context of utterance *See* linguistic context.

context principle A principle in the philosophy of language and formal pragmatics and semantics which states that a word has meaning only in the context of a sentence. In other words, the principle claims that only a sentence has meaning in isolation. Proponents of the principle include such eminent philosophers as Gottlob Frege, Ludwig Wittgenstein, and W. V. O. Quine.

context-sensitive expression A linguistic expression the interpretation of which is sensitive to or dependent on context of use. In other words, a context-sensitive or -dependent expression is one that relies on the context of use to select an interpretation. A typical example is a *deictic or *indexical expression like *I*, *here*, and *now*. Such an expression is context-sensitive or -dependent in two senses. First, context helps to decide what a sentence containing a context-sensitive or -dependent expression says. Secondly, context also determines whether what a speaker says is true or false. But for some scholars, a phrase such as *the high standards* also falls under the category of context-sensitive or -dependent expression. Currently, the scope and nature of context-sensitive or -dependent expressions is a hotly debated topic between *contextualists and *semantic minimalists in the philosophy of language and formal pragmatics and semantics. Also called a **context-dependent expression**.

context sensitivity The property that the interpretation of certain linguistic expressions is sensitive to or dependent on context. Also known as **context dependence** or **context dependency**.

context set A term used by the American philosopher Robert Stalnaker for the set of *possible worlds in which every proposition in the common ground is true.

context-shift A term used by the French philosopher François Recanati to refer to the change from (aspects of) one context to (those of) another context. We usually interpret an utterance with respect to the context in which it is used. But occasionally we have to interpret it with respect to a different context. This is called context shift. Context shift is considered a *primary pragmatic process in Recanati's theory. *See also* language-shift.

contextual anaphora *See* exophora.

contextual determinacy The thesis that through contextual constraints, linguistic meaning or interpretation can acquire certain degrees of determinacy, i.e. it can become contextually determinate enough for the interaction to be successful.

contextual effect *See* relevance.

contextual implication One of the three main types of cognitive effects (*see* relevance) in *relevance theory, which refers to a conclusion inferred from a set of premises containing both old and new information together, but not containing either old or new information alone. The other two types of cognitive effects are (i) supporting and strengthening an existing assumption and (ii) contradicting and cancelling an existing assumption.

context(ual) increment(ation) *See* Gazdar's basket.

contextual inference theory (of scalar implicature) The view that the derivation of *scalar implicatures depends heavily on contextual factors. In other words, scalar implicatures can only be derived if the context warrants it. This position is associated with the work of relevance theorists. *See also* default inference theory (of scalar implicature); structural inference theory (of scalar implicature).

contextual modulation A term introduced by the British linguist D. A. Cruse for the phenomenon whereby a meaning of a word can be modified by different contexts. E.g. the interpretation 'male cousin' in *My cousin had a vasectomy last week* and the interpretation 'female cousin' in *My cousin is pregnant* are the effects of the influence of the respective linguistic contexts in which the word *cousin* is used. Also referred to as **sense modulation**. *See also* contextual selection; lexical adjustment.

contextual parameter An aspect or component of a context. According to the American philosopher David Lewis, a context consists of three parameters: a language, a situation, and a circumstance of evaluation or a possible world. Furthermore, the contextual parameter of situation of utterance contains a number of **contextual sub-parameters** such as speaker, addressee, time, and place.

contextual selection (of senses) A term used by the British linguist D. A. Cruse to refer to the phenomenon whereby context plays a role in selecting a single sense from among those senses associated with an ambiguous word form. E.g. given an appropriate context, the 'contest' sense of the word *match* is selected.

contextualism, contextualist A broad school of thought in the contemporary *philosophy of language and pragmatics and semantics, which endeavours to provide an account of contextual variations in semantic content in terms of a criterion of contextual best fit. According to this view, pragmatically enriched entities such as *speech acts are the primary bearers of truth-conditional content. Only in the context of an utterance does a sentence express a determinate semantic content. In other words, semantics covers only part of the computation of utterance meaning, and it is pragmatic enrichment that completes the process as a whole. Two versions of contextualism can be identified: **moderate** and **radical contextualism**. Also called **contextualist semantics** in opposition to **minimal(ist) semantics** and occasionally **maximalism** in contrast to **minimalism**. See Recanati (2005). For some scholars, this contextualist position can be distinguished from a '**pragmatist**' position or **pragmatism**. One main though subtle difference between the two positions is that while the former appeals primarily to facts about linguistic meaning, the latter involves pragmatic principles or maxims. See Carston (2010b). Often contrasted with **literalism** or **semantic minimalism**.

contextualization cue A term introduced by the American sociolinguist John Gumperz for linguistic devices that are used to signal the situated understanding of the sociocultural aspects of meaning. These include *back-channelling cues, code switching, and prosodic markers. The study of contextualization cues is important for socio- and cultural pragmatics.

contextualize, contextualization To put a linguistic unit such as a word, phrase, or sentence into a context, in order e.g. to work out its intended meaning. Contrasts with **decontextualize, decontextualization**.

Continental philosophy A term that is used to refer to a type of philosophy put forward in Continental Europe in the 20th century, in which language has played a central part. This philosophical school is associated particularly with the work of the French philosophers Michel Foucault and Jacques Derrida. Its method is based on rhetoric and argument. This philosophical tradition rejects the idea that meaning is fixed and therefore the possibility of attaining understanding by rigorous analyses of the language in which philosophical problems are expressed. Also known as **European Continental philosophy**. Often contrasted with **analytic(al) philosophy**. See Chapman (2000).

Continental tradition (of pragmatics) One of the two main schools of thought in contemporary pragmatics. Within the Continental conception of linguistics, the view that pragmatics should be treated as a core component of a linguistic theory, in conjunction with phonetics, phonology, morphology, syntax, and semantics, is rejected. Instead, pragmatics is taken to present a functional perspective on all core components and 'hyphenated' areas of linguistics and beyond. According to e.g. the Belgian linguist Jef Verschueren, pragmatics constitutes 'a general functional (i.e. cognitive, social and cultural) perspective on linguistic phenomena in relation to their usage in forms of behaviour'. Consequently, within the wider Continental tradition, the empirical orbit of pragmatics has been considerably widened, encompassing not only much that goes under the rubric of those non-core branches of linguistics such as sociolinguistics, psycholinguistics, and discourse analysis, but also some that falls in the province of certain neighbouring social sciences. This represents the '**perspective view**' of pragmatics. Also called the **European Continental tradition** (of pragmatics) and **Continental pragmatics**. See Verschueren (1999); Huang (2007). Contrasted with the **Anglo-American tradition** (of pragmatics).

contingent sentence A sentence that is neither necessarily true nor necessarily false, but is dependent on the nature of external reality to be assigned a truth value. E.g. *Oil floats on water* is a logically contingent sentence, i.e. it is true but need not be. In other words, this contingently true sentence could be false in a different world. Thus, the notion is linked to that of *possible worlds in possible-worlds semantics.

continuer *See* back-channelling.

contraction approach (to incomplete definite description) *See* incomplete definite description.

contradictory (Propositions, sentences, terms, etc.) of which only one can be true and only one can be false. Thus, for example, two propositions stand in a contradictory relation to each other if the truth of one entails the falsity of the other, and the falsity of one entails the truth of the other. E.g. the relation between *No one likes dark tourism* and *At least someone likes dark tourism*. This logical relationship underlies the notion of *complementarity in lexical semantics. *See also* contrary.

contranym *See* antagonym.

contrary (Propositions, sentences, terms, etc.) of which only one can be true though both can be false. Thus, for example, two propositions are contrary if the truth of one entails the falsity of the other, but the falsity of one does not entail the truth of the other. E.g. the relation between *The skirt is blue* and *The skirt is red*. This logical relationship underlies the notion of *incompatibility in lexical semantics. *See also* contradictory.

contrast *See* principle of contrast.

contrastive focus *See* focus (3).

contrastive focus reduplication *See* lexical cloning.

contrastive pragmatic marker A *non-conceptual pragmatic marker that indicates a speaker's belief that there is a contrast between the two propositions of the sentence uttered. E.g. *but* in *John is poor but he is honest*.

contrastive pragmatics A branch of pragmatics in which aspects of language in use in different languages are systematically investigated from a contrastive view.

convention, conventionality, conventional The relationship between linguistic forms and meanings that is set up by virtue of an agreement among speakers. Four types of conventional item are identified: (i) vocabulary items, (ii) syntactic constructions, (iii) pronunciation items, and (iv) patterns of usage. See Clark (2007). While the first three are similar to the American linguist Jerry Morgan's concept of *convention of language, the last is akin to his notion of *convention of usage. In Gricean pragmatics, the notion of conventionality is used to define both *what is said and what is conventionally implicated (*see* conventional implicature).

convention of form *See* convention of means.

convention of language A term used by the American linguist Jerry Morgan to refer to the convention that yields the *literal meaning of a sentence. By contrast, a **convention of usage** is one that governs the use of a sentence. It comprises three ingredients: occasion, purpose, and means. E.g. the convention concerning what one should say on an occasion of departure. An example of both a convention of language and a convention of usage is the use of *Can you turn on the heater?* to perform a speech act of requesting indirectly. On the one hand, by the convention of language, the sentence has the literal meaning of a question about the addressee's abilities. On the other, the sentence constitutes a standard way of making a request indirectly, which is due to the convention of usage.

convention of means The American psycholinguist Herbert Clark's term for the convention that regulates the linguistic devices by which an *indirect speech act can be performed. E.g. the use of *Can you tell me how your father was persecuted in Mao's Cultural Revolution in China?* to make a request indirectly is determined by the convention of means. In addition, the **convention of form** specifies the exact wording of the linguistic device used in making an indirect speech act. Both conventions belong to the *convention of usage.

convention of usage *See* convention of language.

conventional expression *See* formula.

conventional gender *See* natural gender.

conventional illocutionary act An *illocutionary act of a certain sort by virtue of satisfying certain socially or institutionally recognized conditions for being an illocutionary act of that sort. In the performance of this type of speech act, convention is the primary illocutionary mechanism. E.g. the *effective act of sentencing a convicted criminal performed by a judge in uttering the sentence *I* *hereby sentence you to six months in prison*. Also referred to as **ceremonial illocutionary act**. Contrasted with a **communicative illocutionary act**.

conventional implicature One of the two types of *implicature (1) proposed by the British philosopher H. P. Grice. A conventional implicature is an aspect of non-truth-conditional meaning, which is not derivable from any general considerations of cooperation and rationality, but arises solely from the conventional features attached to particular lexical items and/or linguistic constructions. E.g. the use of *but* in *We want peace but they want war* gives rise to the conventional implicature that there is a contrast between the information contained in the first conjunct and that contained in the second conjunct of the sentence. Conventional implicatures are distinguished by a number of properties: (i) *conventionality (*see* convention and principle of conventionality), (ii) non-truth conditionality, (iii) commitment, (iv) independence, (v) *subjectivity, (vi) *speaker orientation, (vii) infallibility, (viii) occurency, (viii) dependency, and (x) *context-sensitivity. Also termed **what is conventionally implicated**. See Grice (1989); Feng (2010). Contrasts with **conversational implicature**. *See also Andeutung.*

conventional implicature trigger Any linguistic expression whose use engenders a *conventional implicature. E.g. the use of *managed to* in *Jennifer managed to type accurately* gives rise to the conventional implicature that it was difficult for Jennifer to type accurately.

conventional indirectness An indirect strategy that is constrained by convention. In other words, conventional indirectness is dependent on the conventions of both the propositional content or sentence meaning and the linguistic form of a sentence to yield the pragmatic force of the sentence uttered. It is subject to both the *convention of language and the *convention of usage. It also displays *pragmatic duality. E.g. the use of *Could you please pass me the iPod?* to perform the indirect speech act of requesting the addressee to pass the iPod to the speaker. Contrasted with **non-conventional indirectness**.

conventional pragmatics A term used by the American linguist Adele Goldberg for the conventional association of certain formal properties of language with some *pragmatic constraints on contexts of use. With regard to sentence structure, for instance, conventional pragmatics conforms largely with the ways in which a language packages *information structure. Contrasts with **non-conventional pragmatics**. See Goldberg (2004).

conventionalism A term deployed by the French philosopher François Recanati for the view that the truth-conditional content of a sentence (even in a given context) is fully determined by the rules of language, i.e. the conventional meaning of the sentence disregarding any pragmatic considerations such as the speaker's intentions.

Conventionalism is considered to be a stage in the development of *literalism. See Recanati (2005).

conventionality *See* convention; principle of conventionality.

conventionalized implicature A conversational implicature that has largely been semanticized and/or grammaticalized. In other words, a certain interpretation for the conversational implicature has been strongly preferred or sanctioned. E.g. the conversational implicature that the speaker does not drink alcohol engendered by the uttering of the sentence *I don't drink* is a conventionalized implicature. The mechanism of the conventionalization of conversational implicature is called **fossilization**—a term coined by the American linguists Michael Geiz and Arnold Zwicky in 1980s. By contrast, a conversational implicature that has not been fossilized into a conventional meaning is called a **'live' implicature**.

conversation analysis (CA) Also known as **conversational analysis**. A branch of *macropragmatics. Grown out of a break-away group of sociologists known as *ethnomethodologists within micro-sociology, conversation analysis represents an empirical, procedural and inductive approach to the analysis of (the audio and/or video recordings of) naturally occurring, spontaneous conversations or 'talks in (face-to-face) interaction'. It is concerned with the discovery and description of the methods and procedures that conversational participants employ systematically to display their understanding of the infrastructure of conversation. In conversation, there are rules governing its sequential organization such as the *turn-taking system, the formulation of *adjacency pairs, and the mechanism for opening and/or closing a conversation. There are also norms regulating participating in a conversation such as how to hold the *floor, how to interrupt, and how to remain silent. Other interesting structural devices of conversation include the *preference organization, the *pre-sequence system, and the *repair mechanism. Given that conversation is the primary spoken manifestation of language, conversation analysis is closely linked to prosodic pragmatics. Furthermore, since rules, norms, and regulations for conversational interaction may vary from culture to culture, society to society, and language to language, conversation analysis overlaps with the *ethnography of speaking and *cross-cultural pragmatics. For some scholars, it is opposed to **discourse analysis**. Conversation analysis can also be divided into **pure conversation analysis (pure CA)** and **applied conversation analysis (applied CA)**. Occasionally also called **conversation pragmatics** or **conversational pragmatics**. See Sacks (1992); Hutchby and Wooffitt (2008); Sidnell (2011).

Conversation Analysis Profile for People with Aphasia (CAPPA) A test used in *clinical pragmatics to assess the conversational skills of aphasic adults and their conversational partners. Based on the insights from *conversation analysis, the assessment tool consists of a structured interview, an analysis of a ten-minute sample of conversation made between a patient and his or her conversational partner, and a profile summarizing the information gleaned from both the interview and the conversation analysis. In the conversation analysis part of the test, three central areas of conversation management are examined: (i) initiation and turn-taking, (ii) repair, and (iii) topic management.

conversation pragmatics *See* conversation analysis.

conversational analysis *See* conversation analysis.

Conversational Coaching A pragmatic therapy programme deployed in *clinical pragmatics. Developed out of the Functional Communication Treatment, the therapy teaches patients how to control the quality of monologue in various situations.

conversational contract model (of politeness) An approach to *politeness developed by the American linguist Bruce Fraser, in which politeness is explained within the terms of a conversational contract. This involves the understanding conversational interlocutors have of their rights and obligations in an interaction and the norms of the interaction in which they participate. *See also* conversational maxim model (of politeness); face-saving model (of politeness); pragmatic scale model (of politeness); social norm model (of politeness).

conversational disability A term used in *clinical pragmatics for any deficit or disorder in the production and/or comprehension of conversation. Conversational disability is a type of *pragmatic disorder.

conversational implicature One of the two types of *implicature (1) proposed by the British philosopher H. P. Grice. A conversational implicature is any meaning implied by a speaker and inferred by the addressee which goes beyond *what is said in the strict sense. It is derived from a speaker's saying of what is said via the *co-operative principle and its attendant *maxims of conversation. Thus, the uttering of the sentence *There is a Chinese supermarket just around the corner* may implicate, in an appropriate context, that the addressee can buy soy sauce there. In one approach, conversational implicatures can be divided into ***conversational implicature$_O$** and ***conversational implicature$_F$**. In another approach, conversational implicatures can be grouped into ***generalized conversational implicature (GCI)** and ***particularized conversational implicature (PCI)**. Conversational implicatures are characterized by a number of distinctive properties: (i) cancellability or *defeasibility, (ii) *non-detachability, (iii) *calculability, (iv) *non-conventionality, (v) *reinforceability, (vi) *universality, and (vii) *indeterminacy. See Grice (1989); Huang (2007). Also termed **what is conversationally implicated**. Contrasts with **conventional implicature**. *See also* what is said; impliciture; explicature.

conversational implicature trigger Any linguistic expression whose use gives rise to a *conversational implicature. E.g. *pale red* in *Mary has a pale red skirt*, the use of which generates the conversational implicature that Mary has a dress whose colour cannot be described exactly as pink.

conversational implicature$_F$ A term coined by the British Chinese linguist Yan Huang which refers to a *conversational implicature that is generated by way of a speaker's deliberately *flouting or exploitation of one or more of the *maxims of conversation. E.g. in the following conversation: John: *Susan can be such a cow sometimes!* Mary: *Oh, what a lovely day today!*, Mary's utterance may give rise to the conversational implicature that one shouldn't speak ill of people behind their back. This conversational implicature is derived from the speaker's *flouting or exploitation of the British philosopher H. P. Grice's *maxim of Relation. See Huang (2007). Contrasted with **conversational implicature$_O$**.

conversational implicature$_O$ A term introduced by the British Chinese linguist Yan Huang which is used with reference to a *conversational implicature that is engendered by way of a speaker's directly observing the *maxims of conversation. E.g. the uttering of the sentence *The tea is warm* gives rise to the conversational implicature that the tea is not hot. This conversational implicature is derived from the speaker's observation of the British philosopher H. P. Grice's first sub-*maxim of Quantity. Also called **standard conversational implicature**. Contrasts with **conversational implicature$_F$**.

conversational impliciture *See* impliciture.

conversational inference The predicting of what will come next in a conversation in the light of previous interactive experience.

conversational knowledge *Pragmatic knowledge about rules, norms, and regulations that govern conversational interaction, how to use language appropriately and effectively in a particular conversational context, and the intentional states of the participants in a conversation.

conversational maxim model (of politeness) An approach to *politeness developed by the British linguist Geoffrey Leech in which politeness is accounted for in terms of a *politeness principle and a set of *maxims of politeness. *See also* conversational contract model (of politeness); face-saving model (of politeness); pragmatic scale model (of politeness); social norm model (of politeness).

conversational maxims *See* maxims of conversation.

conversational paradox A term used by the Greek linguist Savas Tsohatzidis for the contradiction arising from the apparent incompatibility of the British philosopher H. P. Grice's *co-operative principle with the kind of reasoning required for the calculation of *conversational implicatures. In order to understand an addressee's uncooperativeness in conversational interaction, he or she has to be co-operative, hence the paradox.

conversational postulate A rule or principle of *inference that is modelled on a *meaning postulate but takes contextual factors into account. From the literal meaning and force of a sentence and the context, the rule derives the relevant indirect force of the sentence. Thus, if a speaker utters *Can you pass me the English–Chinese dictionary?* in a context in which the question reading is ruled out, by the conversational postulate, the utterance will then be inferred as conveying the indirect force of making a request. Conversational postulates are considered by some scholars as a conventionalized strategy of *conversational implicature.

conversational pragmatics **1.** = conversation analysis. **2.** A term used by the American linguist Laurence Horn to refer to work by the British philosophers J. L. Austin and H. P. Grice, and the American philosopher John Searle in pragmatics and especially *philosophical pragmatics. *See also* functionalist pragmatics.

conversational repair *See* repair.

conversational turn *See* turn.

converseness, converse A variety of *directional oppositeness. Converse refers to the *sense relation in which pairs of lexical items exhibit the reversal of a semantic relationship between them. E.g. the meaning relation between *parent* and *child*. Thus, if John is Bill's parent, then Bill must be John's child. Also called **relational opposite**. *See also* antipodal; counterpart; opposite direction.

co-operative principle An overarching pragmatic principle put forward by the British philosopher H. P. Grice in his theory of *conversational implicature, which determines the way in which language is used most efficiently and effectively to achieve co-operative, rational interaction in communication. By this guideline, participants are normally expected to co-operate with each other in the process of communication. The principle is instantiated by a set of nine *maxims of conversation. See e.g. Grice (1989); Huang (2007).

coreference, coreferential The relation between two linguistic expressions that share the same reference. E.g. in *As soon as Susan$_1$ left school, she$_1$ worked in a supermarket*, *Susan* and *she* are said to be coreferential. If two linguistic expressions do not have the same reference, they are **non-coreferential** or **disjoint in reference**. E.g. in *As soon as Susan$_1$ left school, she$_2$ worked in a supermarket*, *Susan* and *she* are disjoint in reference.

coreferential anaphora An anaphoric relation in which an anaphoric expression and its antecedent have the same reference. E.g.

he and *John* form such a relationship in *John*$_1$ *said that he*$_1$ *can play the harp*. Often contrasted with **non-coreferential anaphora**.

corpus pragmatics Corpus (*pl* corpora) is a systematic collection of naturally occurring spoken or written language or a variety of such language, which can be searchable online. When it is accessible on a computer, it is called computer corpus or corpora. By corpus pragmatics is meant the investigation of language use on the basis of the analysis of corpora. It is part of *empirical pragmatics. Corpus pragmatics can be divided into two types: (i) **corpus-based pragmatics** and (ii) **corpus-driven pragmatics**. In the former, researchers approach the corpora with a set of assumptions and expected findings. By contrast, the latter investigates linguistic forms and pragmatic functions that emerge from the corpora in order to discover things that have not been recognized. Much of the current research in corpus pragmatics is corpus-based rather than corpus-driven. From a methodological point of view, corpus pragmatics can be either **form-based** (i.e. it takes a linguistic structure as its starting point and examines the range of pragmatic functions the form serves in a corpus) or **function-based** (i.e. it takes a particular pragmatic function as a point of departure and studies how such a function is actually realized). Finally, corpus-based or driven research in pragmatics can be either **qualitative** (treating corpora primarily as a source of natural data) or **quantitative** (studying patterns of frequency, distribution and collocation using statistical techniques). See Andersen (2011); Rühlemann (2011).

correspondence theory (of meaning) A theory which states that there is a direct relationship between a linguistic expression and the entity it denotes, as in the case of onomatopoeic words such as *cuckoo*, *murmur*, and *splash*. Given that the relationship between most linguistic expressions and their entities is arbitrary, the theory is frequently termed the **correspondence fallacy**.

correspondence theory (of truth) A theory which says that a statement or proposition is true if and only if it corresponds to the reality or the way the world actually is. Also called variously the **corresponding, realist, realistic**, or **simple theory** of truth. Put in slogan form, a belief is true if and only if it corresponds to reality. *See also* coherence theory (of truth); deflationist theory (of truth); performative theory (of truth); pragmatist theory (of truth).

co-text *See* linguistic context.

counterfactive A predicate such as a verb that can take a complement clause, the use of which presupposes the falsity of the proposition expressed in the complement clause. E.g. the verb *pretend* in *John pretends that he is a professional footballer*, which gives rise to the *presupposition that John is not a professional footballer.

counterfactual conditional A conditional that expresses a condition which is in fact not met, the use of which normally yields a *presupposition. E.g. the use of *If an ant was as big as a human being, it could run five times faster than an Olympic sprinter* gives rise to the presupposition that an ant is not as big as a human being. Alternative terms are a **hypothetical, remote**, and **unreal conditional**.

counterpart A type of *directional oppositeness in which the defining directions of an entity and its counterpart are reversed. E.g. the sense relation between *hill* and *valley*, *bump* and *dent*, and *convex* and *concave*. *See also* antipodal; converseness; opposite direction.

counter-unidirectional anaphora *See* cataphora.

courteous belief A term coined by the British linguist Geoffrey Leech for an attribution of some positive value to an addressee and others and/or of some negative value to the speaker him- or herself. In contrast, by **discourteous belief** is meant an attribution that has some positive value to a speaker and/or some negative value to the addressee and others. Compare e.g. *You're coming to have dinner with us this weekend, I insist* and *I'm coming to have dinner with you this weekend, I insist*. The distinction represents a case of asymmetry of politeness (*see* pragmatic paradox of politeness). See Leech (2007).

covert indexical *See* indexicalism; incomplete definite description.

CP = **(1)** co-operative principle. **(2)** communicative presumption.

critical pragmatics (1) A term used by the Danish linguist Jacob Mey for the work done in *sociopragmatics that follows the tradition of critical linguistics, particularly **critical discourse analysis**. Critical discourse analysis deals with the relationship between language and power in society, especially the way in which discourse is ideologically influenced by, and can itself have an impact on, social power. Like in critical discourse analysis, in critical pragmatics (1), great emphasis is also put on the relationship between language and social power and between language and ideology.

critical pragmatics (2) A term employed by the American philosopher John Perry and the Basque philosopher Kepa Korta for the position in formal pragmatics that takes the contents of an utterance as central and critical to both pragmatics and semantics. According to critical pragmatics (2), language is a way of doing things with words, meanings of linguistic expressions and contents of utterances come ultimately from intentions, and language combines with other factors to allow people to attain communicative goals. See Korta and Perry (2011).

cross-cultural communication Communication between speakers from different cultures or societies. It is an important topic in *cross-cultural pragmatics. Also called **intercultural communication**.

cross-cultural pragmatics **1.** In its narrow sense, cross-cultural pragmatics is the systematic study of language in use, especially pragmatic differences across different cultures and languages. Since the 1980s, a principal concern of cross-cultural pragmatics has been the issue of how particular kinds of *speech acts, especially such *face-threatening acts (FTAs) as requests, apologies, and complaints, are realized across different cultures and languages. Also called **intercultural pragmatics**. See Cheng (2010). **2.** In its wide sense, cross-cultural pragmatics covers four distinct research areas: (i) *contrastive pragmatics, (ii) cross-cultural pragmatics (1) or intercultural pragmatics, (iii) a combination of contrastive pragmatics and *interlanguage pragmatics, and (iv) a combination of cross-cultural pragmatics (1)/intercultural pragmatics and interlanguage pragmatics. See Kraft and Geluykens (2007).

Cross-Cultural Speech Act Realization Project (CCSARP) A large-scale and influential research project conducted by a group of American, German, and Israeli scholars in the 1980s. In this project, the realization patterns of the *speech acts of requesting and apologizing in a number of cultures/languages were compared and contrasted. These cultures/languages include German, Hebrew, Danish, Canadian French, Argentinean Spanish, and British, American, and Australian English. The research project has since generated an exceptionally large amount of research in this area. See Blum-Kulka, House, and Kasper (1989)

CT = coding time.

cue A term borrowed from psychology for a specific surface feature that is considered to be an aid to the perception of some other feature, structure or force. Cues can be grouped into **lexical**, **syntactic**, **prosodic**, and **discourse**. They are, for example, probabilistically associated with certain *speech acts or *dialogue acts in *computational pragmatics.

cue-based model (of speech act interpretation) A *computational pragmatic model of *speech act interpretation. It treats the surface form of an input utterance as a set of lexical, syntactic, discourse, and prosodic cues to a speaker's intention. It concentrates on the statistical examination of these cues, utilizing probabilistic reasoning to generate the most probable dialogue act of the utterance as the output, and hence is also called the **probabilistic model**. See Jurafsky (2004). *See also* plan-based (inference) model (of speech act interpretation).

cue phrase *See* discourse marker.

cultural context A large and complex body of knowledge shared among members of a particular *culture including knowledge about the attitudes, beliefs, customs, behaviours, myths, arts, sciences, languages, ideologies, modes of perception, habits of thought, and social organizations and institutions of that culture. *See also* general knowledge context; linguistic context; physical context; social context.

cultural pragmatics A branch of pragmatics, sometimes known also as **anthropological pragmatics** and **ethnographic pragmatics (1)**. It is the systematic study of language in use and its place in the functioning of human communities and institutions from a cultural or anthropological view, especially but not exclusively focusing on a non-Western culture or cultures. It overlaps with the *ethnography of communication and the *ethnography of speaking. *Ethnopragmatics is thus a variety of cultural pragmatics, and so are *emancipatory pragmatics and *ethnographic pragmatics (2). *See also* cross-cultural pragmatics.

cultural script A term used in *natural semantic metalanguage and *ethnopragmatics for a cultural norm, a formula that articulates such a form, or the technique for articulating cultural norms, values, and practices using semantic primes (*see* natural semantic metalanguage) as a medium of semantic and pragmatic description. E.g. an Anglo cultural script against 'telling people what to do' is like this: when I want someone to do something I can't say something like *I want you to do it, because of this you have to do it*. Cultural scripts come in different levels of generality: some are **high-level** or **master scripts**, others are **areal scripts**, still others are **low-level scripts**. Also called **ethnopragmatic script**. See Goddard and Wierzbicka (2004).

culture The way of life of a particular people, community, or country. It includes the attitudes, beliefs, customs, behaviours, myths, arts, sciences, languages, modes of perception, habits of thought, and social organizations of that people, community or country. E.g. the Chinese culture. Given that language and use of language are not only a part of a culture but also an important means of conveying and acting out that culture, this anthropological notion of culture plays a crucial role in cultural pragmatics, cross-cultural pragmatics, ethnopragmatics, ethnography of communication, ethnography of speaking, and related areas. *See also* high-context culture.

cyberpragmatics A term that is used to refer to a newly emerged research area in which internet-mediated interactions are analysed mainly from a cognitive pragmatic point of view. A wide variety of interactions on the internet are dealt with. These include emails, web pages, chat rooms, social networking sites, blogs, 3D virtual worlds, instant messaging, and videoconferencing. See Yus (2011).

D

DA = discourse analysis.

DAMSL = Dialogue Act Makeup in Several Layers

***Darstellung* '(re-)presentation' function** *See* functions (of language).

Darwinian module *See* modularity.

Davidsonian semantics A formal approach to meaning inspired by the work of the British philosopher Donald Davidson. The central tenet of Davidsonian semantics is the belief that the meaning of a sentence lies in its truth-conditions. However, the theory rejects the idea that the meaning of a sentence consists of a set of *possible worlds. Davidsonian semantics is to some extent *holistic in nature.

DCT = Discourse Completion Test, Discourse Completion Task.

de dicto Latin for 'about what is said' as opposed to ***de re***, which is Latin for 'about a/the thing'. With a long tradition in philosophy, *de dicto* is concerned with the belief in the truth of a proposition, whereas *de re* is concerned with the belief about an individual in the actual world. E.g. the definite description *the woman who has cheated on him* in *John believes that the woman who has cheated on him is a feminist* can be taken to refer either to the woman about whom John thinks that she has cheated on him (*de dicto*) or the woman who has actually cheated on him (*de re*). This kind of ambiguity is often called a ***de dicto/de re* ambiguity**. In the case of the *de dicto* interpretation, while the *intension is committed, the *extension is left open. *See also de se.*

***de facto* accommodation** = global accommodation.

***de jure* accommodation** = local accommodation.

de re *See de dicto.*

de se Latin for 'of oneself'. The term is used to refer to the general phenomenon of self-locating beliefs, i.e. beliefs about the self. Sometimes it is also deployed for the property theory of content advocated by the American philosopher David Lewis. According to this theory, a speaker ascribes to him- or herself the property rather than the proposition denoted by the predicate that contains a *de se* expression. The study of *de se* beliefs constitutes an important topic in the philosophy of language, pragmatics, semantics, and the philosophy of mind. *See also de dicto; de re.*

deblocking The cancellation of *blocking under certain conditions, some of which are pragmatic in nature. E.g. while the food-denoting term *beef* usually blocks the *conceptual grinding mechanism with regard to the use of its animal-denoting counterpart *cow*, as in *John doesn't like eating beef/*cow*, deblocking occurs in *Hindus are forbidden to eat cow/?beef*. See Blutner (2004); Huang (2009). Contrasts with **blocking**.

declaration A type of *speech act proposed by the American philosopher John Searle which effects immediate changes in some state of affairs in the external world. In other words, in performing this type of speech act, a speaker brings about changes in the outside world. Declaration tends to rely on elaborate extralinguistic institutions for its successful performance. Paradigmatic cases include bidding in bridge, declaring war, excommunicating, firing from employment, and sentencing a convicted criminal. E.g. *I name this ship the Princess Elizabeth*. Occasionally also called **declarative**. See Searle (1975); Huang (2007). *See also* commisssive; representative; directive; expressive; institutionalized speech act.

declaration verb A type of *illocutionary verb that names the institutionalized *speech act it performs. E.g. *declare* (war), *name* (a ship), and *sentence* (a convicted criminal).

decoding In opposition to **encoding**, this is a term borrowed from communication theory to refer to a message being deciphered. In linguistics including pragmatics, it means roughly understanding speech.

decontextualize, decontextualization To abstract a linguistic expression such as a word, phrase, and sentence away from any context in which it might be used in order e.g. to judge a sentence to be grammatical or ungrammatical. Contrasted with **contextulize, contextualization**.

decontexulized pragmatics The label given to a pragmatic paradox by the Polish linguist Roman Kopytko, according to whom, there is an inconsistency that arises from methodological reductionism in rationalistic pragmatics (*see* empirical pragmatics). Methodological reductionism leads to abstraction away from context, i.e. decontexualization. However, in order to understand the abstract theoretical constructs, they must be contextually situated.

de-deictification A process in which deictic distinctions of a linguistic expression is neutralized. E.g. the development of Latin demonstratives into definite articles in modern Romance languages.

deduction, deductive A process of *reasoning or *inference from the general to the particular. In other words, a **deductive reasoning** or **deductive inference** can be characterized as one in which if a set of premises are true, the conclusion must also be logically true. Often contrasts with **induction, inductive**. *See also* abduction.

deep anaphora A term initiated by the American linguists Jorge Hankamer and Ivan Sag for *anaphora that does not need a linguistic antecedent and therefore is pragmatically licensable. E.g. in the context in which John attempts to open a safe, one can ask him 'Are you able to do it?' *Do it* is a deep anaphora. Contrasts with **surface anaphora**. *See also* pragmatic ellipsis.

deep structure structural ambiguity *See* syntactic ambiguity.

default In general, what obtains unless there is some reason to suggest otherwise. Thus, the **default meaning** of a word is the meaning it is intuitively given, unless in a particular context in which the word is used, some other meaning is indicated. E.g. the default meaning of the verb *hear* is 'to be aware of sounds with one's ears'. The default meaning or **default interpretation** of an utterance is the salient, unmarked, and presumptive meaning or interpretation the utterance has in the absence of any specific context. In other words, it is the meaning or interpretation of an utterance that the addressee will arrive at without a conscious inferential process. E.g. the default meaning or interpretation of the sentence *You should meet the love of your life and get married* uttered is that the addressee should meet the love of his or her life first and then get married. A **default inference** is an inference that is automatic and subconscious. A **default context** is an unmarked context. A **default rule** or **principle** is a rule or principle that is assumed to operate if no other is specified. Since default constitutes one of the characteristics of pragmatics, it plays an important role in a number of contemporary pragmatic theories including *Gricean and *neo-Gricean pragmatics, *optimality-theoretic pragmatics, and *truth-conditional pragmatics.

default inference theory (of scalar implicature) The view that *scalar implicatures convey default meaning, i.e. the meaning of a scalar implicature is automatically worked out by an addressee on encountering a *scalar implicature trigger. In other words, according to this analysis, scalar implicatures are inferences that do not need a conscious inferential process and are independent of a particular context. This position is represented by the British linguist Stephen Levinson. Also called **defaultism**. See Levinson (2000). *See also* contextual inference theory (of scalar implicature); structural inference theory (of scalar implicature); default model.

default model (DM) A term used especially in *experimental pragmatics to refer to the pragmatic processing model that is equivalent to what is labelled the **default inference theory** or the **local theory**. Contrasted with the **underspecification model**.

default semantics (DS) A radical *contextualist approach to the modelling of utterance meaning, combining features of both post-Gricean *truth-conditional pragmatics and formal *Discourse Representation Theory. In this account, pragmatic information is allowed to contribute to the truth-conditional representation of an utterance in the form of conscious inference or default interpretation (both cognitive and sociocultural). In other words, where context and inference are not needed, they have no role to play in the construction of meaning. But unlike other contextualist analyses, default semantics rejects the level of meaning at which the *logical form can be pragmatically enriched. Instead, as in discourse representation theory, it treats *dynamic semantics as context change implemented in semantic representation, and argues that utterance and discourse meaning is essentially compositional. See Jaszczolt (2010).

defaultism = default inference theory (of scalar implicature). Two versions are identified: **strong** and **weak defaultism**. The former is represented by the work of the British linguist Stephen Levinson and the latter by the work of the American linguist Laurence Horn.

defeasibility, defeasible A term borrowed from the law which refers to the property of a meaning, proposition, or inference that can be cancelled or suspended. E.g. the uttering of the sentence *John's wife is often complaining* generates the *conversational implicature that John's wife is not always complaining. This conversational implicature, however, is overridden if a phrase such as *in fact always* is added to the original sentence, as in *John's wife is often, in fact always, complaining*. Such defeasibility is **explicit defeasibility**, because the conversational implicature in question is explicitly cancelled by the addition of a semantic entailment. By contrast, defeasibilty can also be implicitly accomplished. E.g. in the case of *The Americans and the Russians tested an atom bomb in 1962*, the cancellation of the 'togetherness' conversational implicature is due to real-world knowledge, and is thus an instance of **implicit defeasibility**. Defeasibility is an essential property of a meaning, proposition, or inference that is pragmatic in nature. While both conversational implicatures and (pragmatic) presuppositions are defeasible, (semantic) entailments are not. Also called **cancellability, cancellable**. See Huang (2007).

deference (1) In opposition to **familiarity**, deference refers to the distance and respect one shows to others by virtue of their higher social status, greater age, etc. Defined thus, deference constitutes a subcategory of *politeness.

deference (2) *See* deferred interpretation.

deferential form A type of *honorific or polite form. This refers to any linguistic form including one of a pair of lexical items that a speaker uses to show respect to the addressee. E.g. the use of *guifu* '(your) honourable residence' as opposed to *hanshe* '(my) humble hut' in Chinese. Contrasts with a **humiliative form**.

deferred interpretation A term used for the phenomenon whereby an expression can be used to refer to an entity that is not explicitly included in the conventional denotation of that expression. E.g. the use of *Picasso* in *John has recently bought an expensive Picasso* to refer to his painting. See Nunberg (2004). Also known as **deference (2)**.

deferred reference = reference transfer.

definite description A term used in the *philosophy of language which refers to a subtype of definite NP which contains two parts: a descriptive part and a referential part. E.g. *the city*, *the author of* Pragmatics, and *the girl over there*. A definite description denotes and identifies a definite entity or set of entities in part by means of its descriptive content. Definite descriptions are divided into **complete** and **incomplete definite descriptions**. Since the publication of the British philosopher Bertrand Russell's classic essay in 1905, the debate over the proper analysis of definite descriptions has been a central concern in the philosophy of language.

definite reference *Reference to a specific entity or set of entities. E.g. in the sentence *Inside the safe he found the original manuscripts*, both the definite NP *the safe* and the definite pronoun *he* refer to a specific entity, and the definite NP *the original manuscripts* makes reference to a set of specific entities that can be identified by the addressee. Contrasted with **indefinite reference**.

deflationist theory (of truth) Also called **deflationism** or the **deflationary**, **disquotational**, or **redundancy theory**. A theory of truth put forward by the British philosopher Frank Ramsey, based on the idea originally entertained by the German philosopher, mathematician, and logician Gottlob Frege. According to this theory, to say of a sentence that it is true is not to say anything else about it. In other words, if someone says '*p*', he or she is already saying that '*p* is true'. What the statement '*p* is true' does is nothing but make explicit what the statement '*p*' states implicity. The deflationist theory is further developed by the British philosopher A. J. Ayer, who reached the conclusion that *true* is an empty predicate. This version is known as the **disappearance** or **no truth theory** of truth. *See also* coherence theory (of truth); correspondence theory (of truth); pragmaticist theory (of truth); performative theory of (truth).

deictic *See* deictic expression.

deictic adverb of space An adverb of space that encodes *space deixis such as *here* and *there*.

deictic adverb of time An adverb of time that encodes *time deixis such as *now* and *then*.

deictic category *See* deixis.

deictic centre The central anchorage point around which *deixis is organized. The default *deictic centre or the **deictic *origo*** (the ground zero or zero point) of the three major categories of deixis, namely, person, time, and space deixis, is (i) the person who is speaking, (ii) the time at which the speaker produces the utterance, and (iii) the place where the speaker produces the utterance. This property is called the

egocentricity of deixis. The notion of *origo* was first defined in the 1930s by the German psychologist Karl Bühler as the centre for deixis.

deictic context A term used by the British linguist Sir John Lyons for the spatio-temporal environment in which an utterance occurs. *See also* physical context.

deictic directional A linguistic form that is connected with the direction in which an entity is moving. E.g. *come* and *go*. Deictic directionals can be grouped into two categories: **deictic motion affixes, morphemes and particles**, and **deictic motion verbs**.

deictic expression A linguistic expression that has the deictic usage as basic or central. Demonstratives, first- and second-person pronouns, tense markers, adverbs of time and space, and motion verbs are typical deictic expressions. Deictic expressions can be further divided into **pure** and **impure deictic expressions**. By contrast, a **non-deictic expression** is a linguistic expression that does not have a deictic usage as basic or central. For example, third-person pronouns in English are not taken to be deictic expressions. Also called a **deictic form** or **deictic**. *See also* indexical.

deictic field (German *Zeigfeld*) A term that was introduced by the Austrian-born German psychologist Karl Bühler for the context in which a sign is uttered, in contrast with his notion of a **symbolic field** (German *Symbolfeld*), i.e. a context that is formed by (other) signs that make up an utterance. Bühler's notion of deictic field originated the modern conception of *deixis. In contemporary usage, the term refers to the psychosocial construct that consists (i) the relationship between a speech event participants such as a speaker, addressee, and others, (ii) the positions occupied by objects of reference, and (iii) the multiple dimensions whereby the speech event participants have cognitive access to objects such as relative proximity. See Hanks (2011).

deictic motion affix, morpheme, and particle An affix, morpheme, or particle that marks the direction in which an entity is moving. E.g. in Somali, *soo* and *sii* are used with a verb to indicate that the motion proceeds towards or away from the speaker, respectively. *See also* deictic motion verb.

deictic motion verb Any verb that marks the direction in which an entity is moving. E.g. *come* and *go*. *See also* deictic motion affix, morpheme, and particle.

deictic *origo* *See* deictic centre.

deictic parameter A range of values of some characteristic property that is used to specify a limited set of alternatives or dimensions of contrast in the description of *deixis. E.g. *visibility used to indicate whether an entity referred to is within sight of the deictic centre, typically the speaker or not, in space deixis. See Huang (2007).

deictic pre-emption The phenomenon whereby the use of an appropriate deictic expression has priority over the use of another expression. Thus, speakers of English will normally avoid saying *Saturday* if either today or tomorrow is Saturday, because on a Saturday they would say *today* and on a Friday they would say *tomorrow*. In other words, *today* on a Saturday or *tomorrow* on a Friday pre-empts *Saturday*.

deictic presentative A presentative that can be used deictically. E.g. *voici* and *voilà* in French, *ecce* in Latin, and *vot* and *von* in Russian.

deictic projection The phenomenon whereby the default deictic centre, typically the speaker, is shifted or projected onto some other participants in the speech event, most commonly the addressee. Compare *I'll go to your office* and *I'll come to your office*. In the former, the use of *go* encodes movement away from the default deictic centre, i.e. the speaker, and therefore we do not have a deictic projection. By contrast, in the latter the use of *come* denotes motion towards the addressee, and therefore we have a deictic projection. In some languages, deictic projection is formally marked. This is the case in Inuktitut.

deictic reference *Reference that is determined deictically. E.g. the reference of *I* in *I hope coffee is soon*. *See also* demonstrative reference.

deictic simultaneity An assumption which says that in the canonical situation of utterance, the coding time (CT) and receiving time (RT) of an utterance are identical. In other words, the temporal zero point is the same for both the speaker and addressee.

deictically marked third-person pronoun A pronoun that is marked to specify the location of the intended referent with respect to the speaker. E.g. in Punjabi, *eh* is used to mark *proximal, and *oh* is employed to encode *distal. See Huang (2007).

deixis The phenomenon whereby features of context of utterance or speech event are encoded by lexical and/or grammatical means in a language. This includes the identification of a specific speaker, addressee, time, and place of an utterance. There are three major categories of deixis: **person**, **space**, and **time deixis** and two minor categories: **social** and **discourse deixis**. *See also* delivery deixis; empathetic deixis; emphatic deixis; gestural deixis; symbolic deixis; perceptual deixis; primary deixis; secondary deixis; referential deixis; socio-person deixis; indexicality.

delivery deixis A term employed by the American linguist George Lakoff for the type of deixis used in examples like *Here's your pizza*.

delocutivity A term used in the French approach to pragmatics for the phenomenon whereby the reflexivity of certain **verba dicendi* appears from their being derived from locutions. E.g. the delocutive verb *ok* comes from the locution *OK*. See Verschueren (1999).

demonstrative A lexical item that is used to find a referent in relation especially to a speech event participant such as a speaker or an addressee. Demonstratives can be divided into (i) **demonstrative pronouns** (e.g. *That* in *That is a ravenous dog.*), **demonstrative adjectives** or **determiners** (e.g. *This* in *This candidate expected to impress the review panel.*), **demonstrative adverbs** (e.g. *here* in *Come here.*), **demonstrative verbs**, and **demonstrative identifiers**. Demonstrative verbs are reported to exist in Boumaa Fijian and Dyirbal. Demonstrative identifiers are demonstratives used in copular and non-verbal clauses, as in languages such as Ambulas. An alternative typology is to group demonstratives into three types: (i) **nominal demonstratives**, which include both demonstrative pronouns and adjectives, (ii) **adverbial demonstratives**, and (iii) **verbal demonstratives**. Demonstratives are commonly used to express especially *space deixis.

demonstrative reference A category of *deictic reference in which reference is made by the use of a demonstrative. E.g. the reference of *This* in *This is splendid!*

denotation The relation that holds primarily between a linguistic expression and the objects including individuals, properties, and events it is used to refer to in the external world. Thus, *dog* can be said to denote the class of all dogs in the external world. The class of entities etc. referred to by a linguistic expression is called a **denotatum**. There are two aspects of denotation: **intension** and **extension**. *See also* connotation (2); sense (3); reference.

denotational theory (of meaning) *See* referential theory (of meaning).

Description of Speech Acts A University of Minnesota website that contains descriptions of six well-studied speech acts— apologies, complaints, compliments and their responses, requests, refusals, and thanks—with examples drawn from a number of languages including Chinese, English, German, Hebrew, Japanese, and Spanish. The resource is of particular interest to teachers of second and foreign languages. URL:

SEE WEB LINKS

- http://www.carla.umn.edu/speechacts/descriptions.html

descriptive content *See* expressive content.

descriptive fallacy A term introduced by the British philosopher J. L. Austin for the view that the only philosophically interesting function of language is that of making true or false statements. In other words, the primary use of language is to producing statements of facts or descriptions of reality. The view is particularly linked with *logical positivism.

descriptive function *See* functions (of language).

descriptive indexical An anaphoric expression that is indexically used to stand for a *definite description, which is made sufficiently salient by the context of utterance. E.g. *He* in [With a gesture at a portrait of President Obama] John said: *'He is usually white'*. In this example, *He* is normally interpreted as a definite description, namely *the President of the United States of America*.

descriptive meaning *See* propositional meaning.

descriptive negation As opposed to **metalingustic negation**, descriptive negation is taken to be **ordinary**, **regular**, or **standard negation**. It represents the truth-functional use of negation and is concerned with the truth-conditional semantic content of a sentence. E.g. *He was not born in Beijing, he was born in Tokyo*.

descriptive pragmatics The study of the patterns of and conditions on language use in a particular language. In this sense, one can talk of Chinese pragmatics, English pragmatics, etc. In contrast, by **general pragmatics** is meant the study of conditions on language use in general.

descriptive synonymy, descriptive synonym *See* synonymy, synonym.

descriptive representation *See* representation.

descriptively used representation *See* representation.

descriptivism *See* assertionalism.

developmental interlanguage pragmatics *See* interlanguage pragmatics.

developmental pragmatic disorder A variety of *pragmatic disorder which has its onset in the developmental period, i.e. before pragmatic skills have been fully acquired. E.g. a child with an autistic spectrum disorder fails to acquire certain pragmatic skills such as the ability to identify the *illocutionary force of speech acts. Contrasts with an **acquired pragmatic disorder**.

developmental pragmatics A heterogeneous research field within *psychopragmatics. It studies the empirical development of *pragmatic competence in young children to use language appropriately and effectively, utilizing both observations and experiments. Topics that have been discussed in developmental pragmatics include communicative intentions, conversational skills, discourse rules, politeness principles, the acquisition of scalar implicature, metaphor, and irony. Sometimes also known as **acquisitional pragmatics**.

diachronic historical sociopragmatics *See* historical sociopragmatics.

diachronic modularity A term used by the British philosopher Gabriel Segal for a cognitive module that follows a genetically and developmentally determined pattern of growth. By contrast, **synchronic modularity** refers to a module that is static.

diachronic pragmaphilology A research trend in *historical pragmatics, which is placed between *pragmaphilology on the one hand and *diachronic pragmatics on the other.

diachronic pragmatics **1.** In its broad sense, = historical pragmatics. 'Diachronic' means literally 'through time', hence 'historical'. Contrasts with **synchronic pragmatics**. **2.** In its narrow sense, the term refers to a particular research trend in historical pragmatics. Diachronic pragmatics represents a 'micro-approach' to change in pragmatic phenomena over time, focusing on the interface between a linguistic structure and its communicative use across different historical stages of the same language. Furthermore, a methodological distinction is made between the 'form-to-function' and 'function-to-form' modes. The former, called **pragmalinguistic diachronic pragmatics**, is semasiological and the emphasis is on how a particular linguistic form has undergone functional changes; the latter, called ***sociopragmatic diachronic pragmatics**, is onomasiological and the focus is on how a particular pragmatic function has changed the form it uses. Diachronic pragmatics in this sense is closely related to *diachronically oriented discourse analysis in historical discourse analysis. See Traugott (2004); Culpeper (2010). *See also* pragmaphilology; pragma-historical linguistics.

diachronic textlinguistics *See* historical pragmatics.

diachronically oriented discourse analysis A type of historical discourse analysis, which takes a micro approach and investigates the evolution of forms or systems that have a discourse function. Diachronically oriented discourse analysis is closely linked to *diachronic pragmatics (2) in historical pragmatics. See Traugott (2004). *See also* discourse-oriented historical linguistics; historical discourse analysis proper.

dialogue act Also called a **dialogue move**. The term used in *computational pragmatics for **1.** a speech act in the context of a dialogue. In other words, dialogue acts represent actions carried out by a speaker in a dialogue. **2.** An act that has internal structures, which are related specifically to its dialogue function. **3.** A combination of a speech act and the semantic force of an utterance. See Jurafsky (2004).

Dialogue Act Makeup in Several Layers (DAMSL) A dialogue act tagging scheme in *computational pragmatics, which can codify a variety of dialogue information about utterances.

dialogue analysis A term used for *discourse analysis of spoken language in the German-speaking world, which is strongly based on speech acts and speech act theory. Also called **dialogue grammar**.

dialogue move *See* dialogue act.

dictionary meaning Meaning of a word or lexeme as found in a dictionary definition. E.g. one of the dictionary meanings of *head* is 'the part of the body on top of the neck'. *See also* encyclopedic meaning.

dictiveness, dictive A term used by the British philosopher H. P. Grice to refer to part of what is said. It is used in contrast to the term **formality (2)**, by which is meant part of the conventional meaning of a linguistic expression. The dictiveness/formality distinction can be illustrated by a Gricean example: if someone says *He's just an evangelist*, he or she may mean that the person referred to by *he* is a sanctimonious, hypocritical, racist, reactionary money-grubber. What the speaker means here is the dictive content of meaning but not the formal content or meaning.

direct access view (of context effects) The pragmatic processing view that context affects language comprehension entirely. At an early stage, *top-down or contextual and *bottom-up or lexical processes interact with each other. If context is rich, it can infiltrate lexical processes and pick up the appropriate meaning. Contrasted with the **modular view** (of context effects). See Peleg, Giora, and Fein (2004).

direct complaint *See* complaint.

direct illocution An illocution that is most directly indicated by a literal reading of the grammatical form and vocabulary of a sentence uttered. By contrast, an **indirect illocution** is any further illocution that the utterance may have. E.g. the direct illocution of the utterance *Can you pass the cream, please?* is an enquiry about the addressee's ability to pass the cream. The indirect illocution is a request that the addressee pass the cream. *See also* illocutionary act; direct illocutionary act.

direct illocutionary act An *illocutionary act that is performed directly. By contrast, an **indirect illocutionary act** is one that is performed indirectly, i.e. by performing another illocutionary act. See Bach (2004). *See also* direct illocution.

direct implicature The American philosopher Robert Harnish's term for a *conversational implicature$_O$.

direct reference theory (of reference) *See* causal theory (of reference).

direct refusal *See* refusal.

direct request *See* request.

direct speech The direct quotation of an actual utterance, etc. E.g. John said: 'I have a large family to feed.' In more technical writings, direct speech is also known by its Latin name ***oratio recta***. Contrasts with **indirect speech**. *See also* free direct speech; free indirect speech.

direct speech act A *speech act whose *illocutionary force and sentence type are directly matched. Thus, when an imperative is used to make a request, as in *Move out of the way*, we have a direct speech act. In addition, an *explicit performative, which happens to be in the declarative form, is also taken to perform a direct speech act, because it has its illocutionary force explicitly named by the *performative verb in the main part or matrix clause of the sentence. E.g. *I order you to shut up.* Contrasted with an **indirect speech act**. See Huang (2007).

direction of fit (of a speech act) A term found in the American philosopher John Searle's speech act theory to refer to the relationship or 'fit' between words and world in the performance of a speech act. E.g. in the performance of the speech act type of a *commissive such as *I'll show you around the cathedral*, the direction of fit is **world-to-words**, because the world is adapted to fit the words via the speaker. The other three types of direction of fit are: **words-to-world**, **both words-to-world and world-to-words**, and **none**, i.e. there is no or empty direction of fit.

directional oppositeness A variety of *lexical oppositeness that involves a basic directional opposition or represents a conceptual or metaphorical extension of it. E.g. the sense relation between *in* and *out*, *head* and *toe*, and *ascend* and *descend*. Five types can be identified: (i) **antipodal**, (ii) **counterpart**, (iii) **opposite direction**, (iv) **reversive**, and (v) **converseness** or **relational oppositeness**. *See also* antonymy (2); complementarity; incompatability.

directive A type of *speech act proposed by the American philosopher John Searle by which a speaker attempts to get the addressee to do something. It expresses the speaker's desire or wish for the addressee to do something. Paradigmatic cases include advice, commands, orders, questions, and requests. E.g. *Turn the TV down, please.* See Searle (1975). Directives are sometimes divided into **embedded** and **explicit directives**. Also called a **directive speech act**. *See also* commissive; representative; expressive; declaration.

directive verb A type of *illocutionary verb that names the directive speech act it performs. E.g. *ask*, *forbid*, and *request*.

directness *See* indirectness.

directedness *See* intentionality.

disambiguate, disambiguation The process of resolving an *ambiguity, which frequently involves context, world knowledge, and pragmatic inference such as conversational implicature in classical and neo-Gricean pragmatics or explicature in relevance theory. E.g. *The bill is large* is lexically ambiguous, but if we add *but need not be paid*, then the ambiguity disappears.

disappearance theory (of truth) *See* deflationist theory (of truth).

discourse analysis (DA) **1.** In its broad sense, the term refers to any study of **discourse**, namely a continuous stretch of spoken or written language larger than a sentence, which includes conversation analysis (CA). **2.** In its narrow sense, the term is defined in opposition to

conversation analysis (CA), especially in terms of the theoretical orientation and methodology it adopts.

discourse coherence *See* coherence.

discourse cohesion *See* cohesion.

Discourse Completion Test (DCT) A written questionnaire with an incomplete discourse sequence for a particular *speech act. It also contains brief descriptions of particular speech situations. Subjects are requested to complete a dialogue that is appropriate for a particular context in which the speech act is performed. This test has been widely used in the cross-cultural and cross-linguistic study of speech act realization patterns. Also called a **Discourse Completion Task**.

discourse connective *See* discourse marker.

discourse deixis The use of a linguistic expression within some utterance to point to the current, preceding, or following utterances in the same spoken or written discourse. E.g. the use of the distal demonstrative *that* in *That is tonight's evening news* to refer back to a preceding segment of the discourse. Also known as **text deixis** or **textual deixis**.

discourse logophoric domain *See* logophoric domain.

discourse marker (DM) **1.** In its broad sense, the term is largely interchangeable with **pragmatic marker (1)**. **2.** In its narrow sense, the term refers to any lexical expression that marks boundaries between, and/or connect different units of discourse. Discourse markers are usually syntactically optional, and arguably do no contribute to the semantic meaning of the second discourse segment of which they occur as a part. Instead they signal a specific semantic relationship between the relevant discourse segments. E.g. *and*, *but*, and *so*. Discourse markers in the narrow sense constitute a subset of pragmatic markers (1). Also variously called a **discourse connective**, a **discourse operator**, and a **cue phrase**. See Fraser (2010). *See also* discourse particle.

discourse-old Information that has been explicitly given in the previous discourse. E.g. in *The poet will come tomorrow. She's a woman of great charm and style*, *she* represents information that is discourse-old. Contrasts with **discourse-new**, i.e. information that has not been evoked explicitly in the previous discourse. E.g. *the poet* in the above example represents information that is discourse-new.

discourse operator *See* discourse marker; pragmatic marker (1).

discourse-oriented historical linguistics A type of *historical discourse analysis, which takes a 'macro' approach and studies the origins of or motivations for change in discourse. Closely related to *pragma-historical linguistics in *historical pragmatics. See Brinton (2001). *See also* diachronically oriented discourse; historical discourse analysis proper.

discourse particle Any linguistic unit that is used to express an attitude of a speaker toward what is being said in discourse. Unlike *discourse markers, discourse particles do not indicate the demarcation of the boundaries between discourse segments. They do not have any truth-conditional, semantic content. E.g. *well, uh, gosh, I mean*, and *you know*. See Green (2010). *See also* pragmatic marker (2).

discourse pragmatics *See* text pragmatics.

discourse reference, discourse referent A technical term introduced by the Finnish linguist Lauri Karttunen in the 1960s to refer to the referential relationship that exists between *it* and *John* in a two-sentence discourse such as *John has a yacht. It is white*. Contrast the above with the ungrammatical *John doesn't have a yacht. *It is white.* Discourse reference is distinguished from reference to real-world entities. See Abbott (2010).

Discourse Representation Structure (DRS) A level of semantic representation in the *Discourse Representation Theory (DRT), which contains sets of discourse referents that allow anaphoric expressions etc. to be formally identified. A Discourse Representation Structure is derived cumulatively, sentence by sentence, by rules operating on the syntactic structure of these sentences, and is therefore dynamic in nature.

Discourse Representation Theory (DRT) A type of *dynamic semantics developed by the Dutch-born German philosopher Hans Kamp and his associates. It extends *model-theoretic semantics to discourse to account for sequences of sentences, concerning itself particularly with anaphoric dependencies across sentence boundaries. It formalizes an intermediate level of semantic representation called a **Discourse Representation Structure (DRS)**. On this level of representation, the meaning of a sentence can be dynamically modified by its *context change potential. One central part of the theory which is relevant to pragmatics is the postulation of a discourse level of representation. This is further developed in the **Segmented Discourse Representation Theory (SDRT)** advanced by the American linguists Nicholas Asher and Alex Lascarides. In this descendant of the Discourse Representation Theory, formal coherence relations between sentences in discourse are established. More recently, attempts have been made to set up the **Layered Discourse Representation Theory (LDRT)** to represent different types of linguistic content such as assertions, presuppositions, and implicatures on different layers. Since their inception, various versions of the Discourse Representation Theory have been an influence especially in *formal pragmatics. *See also* file change semantics.

discourse topic *See* topic (1).

discourteous belief *See* courteous belief.

disjoint reference presumption (DRP) A pragmatic principle put forward by the American linguist Ann Farmer and the American philosopher Robert Harnish which states that the arguments of a predicate are intended to be disjoint in reference, unless marked otherwise. This pragmatic principle predicts that *him* and *John* in *John admires him* tend to be disjoint in reference and *himself* and *John* in *John admires himself* tend to be coreferential.

disjunction A term of logic which links two *propositions *p* and *q*, called in this context **disjuncts**, in the form of $p \vee q$. **Inclusive disjunction** allows that both disjuncts may be true, e.g. *The successful candidate will be a university graduate or someone with teaching experience*; **exclusive disjunction** allows that only one disjunct is true, e.g. *Were you in the study or the dining room?* Contrasts with **conjunction**.

displaying face *See* normative face.

dispreferred second turn A second pair part of an *adjacency pair that is not the most likely one to occur in response to its first pair part from a structural point of view. The dispreferred status is often signalled by e.g. delays, prefaces, and explanations. E.g. refusal is the dispreferred second turn with respect to an invitation, as illustrated in B's turn. A: *Uh if you'd care to come and visit a little while this morning I'll give you a cup of coffee.* B: *Hehh well that's awfully sweet of you, I don't think I can make it this morning. Hh uhm I'm running an ad in the paper and and uh I have to stay near the phone.* Also called a **marked second turn**.

dispreferred turn *See* dispreferred second turn; preference organization.

disquotational theory (of truth) A term generally attributed to the American philosopher W. V. O. Quine which is largely equivalent to the **deflationist theory** (of truth). Also known as **disquotationism**.

distal A term used in the description of *distance in *space deixis. It indicates that the entity referred to is remote from the speaker, and/or close to the addressee. E.g. *nali* in Chinese, *there* in English, and *ott* in Hungarian. Contrasts with **proximal**. *See also* medial.

distal context *See* macro context.

distance A *deictic parameter used in the description of *space deixis which indicates the distance between the speaker or addressee and the entity identified. E.g. *this* used in *this side of the road*. In a language which has a bipartite system of demonstratives and deictic adverbs of space, a fundamental distinction is made between *proximal and *distal. In a language which has a basic tripartite system, *medial is added to proximate and distal. See Huang (2007). *See also* visibility; elevation; side; stance.

distance-oriented three-term system (of space deixis) A system in which the middle or medial term points to a location relative to the *deictic centre, typically the speaker. E.g. Classical Arabic, Scottish

English, and Yimas have this system. See Huang (2007). Contrasted with the **person-oriented three-term system**.

distributed spatial semantics An approach to the semantics of spatial language within the framework of cognitive linguistics. The central tenet of distributed spatial semantics is that spatial meaning is distributed over several grammatical classes of lexical items and characterized by many-to-many meaning–form mappings. Some mappings are many-to-one (conflation), others are one-to-one (compositional), and still others are one-to-many (distribution). There is also a typological difference between languages. Some languages (like Japanese) have an overt distributed spatial semantics. Others (such as English) display a covert distributed spatial semantics. See Evans (2007).

division of pragmatic labour A *neo-Gricean communicative equilibrium between the *Q- and *R-principles proposed by the American linguist Laurence Horn. What it basically says is that the R-principle generally takes precedence until the use of a marked, contrastive linguistic form induces a *Q-implicature to the non-applicability of the pertinent *R-implicature. E.g. in the following pair of sentences *John went to university* and *John went to the university*, while the use of the unmarked former engenders an R-implicated unmarked, stereotypical meaning, use, or situation, the use of the marked latter gives rise to a Q-implicated marked meaning, use, or situation outside the stereotype. Also called the **pragmatic division of labour**. See Horn (2009). *See also* resolution schema (for the interaction of the Q-, I-, and M-principles).

DM 1. = discourse marker. **2.** = default model

domain circumscription *See* circumscription.

domain of discourse *See* universe of discourse.

domain restriction A term used in formal semantics and formal pragmatics for domain constraints on the interpretation of tripartite quantificational structures and referring expressions. Tripartite quantificational structures are constructions that consist of a quantifier, domain, and nuclear scope. E.g. *Every book in the Library of Congress has been catalogued*. Research shows that context plays an important role in the determination of the domain of quantification and therefore the interpretation of the quantificational domain is associated in part with pragmatics, and especially formal pragmatics.

donkey sentence A sentence of the type *If a man owns a donkey, he beats it* or *Everyman who owns a donkey beats it*. The anaphoric relation between *it* and *a donkey* in this type of sentence is called **donkey anaphora**. There is no consensus on exactly what the pronoun *it* means here. Donkey sentences were brought to the attention of modern linguistics by the

British philosopher Peter Geach. *See also* E-type anaphora; Bach–Peters sentence; pronoun of laziness.

double construction *See* lexical cloning.

double hedge *See* compound hedge.

downgrader A modality marker, which is used to mitigate or play down the impact an utterance is likely to have on the addressee. E.g. *a trifle* in *Sue seems a trifle worried*. Many linguistic devices can be employed as a downgrader. These include politeness markers, hedges, understaters, downtoners, 'minus' committers, and syntactic, 'play down' devices. The notion is frequently used in the analysis of the *illocutionary force of a speech act. Contrasted with an **upgrader**.

downtoner A type of downgrader, which is used to play down the impact an utterance is likely to have on the addressee. E.g. *just* in *Can't you just get up a bit earlier?*

downward entailment An *entailment from a set to a subset. In other words, the direction of downward entailment is from less specific to more specific. E.g. the sentence or the proposition expressed by the sentence *No woman is cooking* entails the sentence or the proposition expressed by the sentence *No woman is roasting beef*. Also called **downward entailing** or **monotone decreasing**. The opposite term is **upward entailment**.

DRP = disjoint reference presumption.

DRS = Discourse Representation Structure.

DRT = Discourse Representation Theory.

DS = default semantics.

dthat An expression introduced by the American philosopher David Kaplan as a formal substitute for the English demonstrative *that*.

dual pragmatics In the *philosophy of language, a term introduced by the British philosopher Emma Borg for any theory, approach, or position which posits two distinct roles played by pragmatics in utterance comprehension: (i) pre-semantically to determine the *truth-conditional content of a sentence as uttered in a given context, and (ii) post-semantically to derive any *conversational implicature of an utterance. Neo-Gricean pragmatics, relevance theory, contextualism, Discourse Representation Theory, and file change semantics are said to belong to this camp. See Borg (2004). *See also* contextualism; pragmatic intrusion.

dynamic semantics A form of semantics that models the influence of discourse context on meaning in a formal way. One of the central questions dynamic semantics explores is how sentences affect, and are affected by, the flow of information in discourse. Dynamic semantics allows the integration of meaning below the sentence level with meaning above the sentence level. It endeavours to provide a systematic explanation for the interaction between language and context, thus having a pragmatic flavour. Discourse Representation Theory, file change semantics, and Dynamic Montague Grammar, for instance, are typical examples of dynamic semantics. Contrasted with **static semantics**.

dysphemism *See* euphemism.

E

E-language. Also known as **Externalize-language** A term introduced by the American linguist Noam Chomsky in the mid-1980s to describe a language conceived as a collection or system of observable spoken and written utterances or other linguistic units that are external to, or externalized by, a native speaker. In other words, the understanding of such linguistic units is independent of the properties of the human brain/mind. Contrasts with **I-language**. *See also* performance.

E-principle A pragmatic principle in *bidirectional optimality-theoretic/theory pragmatics put forward by the Dutch linguist Robert van Rooij. E stands for 'effort minimization'. This principle requires a speaker to keep effort to a minimum. Contrasts with the **R-principle (2)**. *See also* principle of least effort.

E-type anaphora Named after the British philosopher Gareth Evans. It refers to a type of anaphora which for technical reasons is neither pure *referential anaphora nor pure *bound-variable anaphora, but which nevertheless seems to constitute a unified semantic type of its own. E.g. the anaphoric relation between *it* and *donkey* in *Most people who bought a donkey have treated it well. See also* Bach–Peters sentence; donkey sentence; pronoun of laziness.

eavesdropper A person who is listening secretly to what participants of a speech event are talking. *See also* bystander; hearer; overhearer; addresser; addressee; speech event participant; ratified participant.

ECG = embodied construction grammar.

echoic use A term deployed in relevance theory to refer to the use of a representation (utterance or thought) to attribute another representation to someone else or to oneself at a different time and to convey an attitude to it. E.g. Mary's utterance in John: *I'm going to teach in Tibet.* Mary: *You're going to teach in Tibet! Fantastic!* Defined thus, echoic use is a type of attributive use and interpretively used *representation. The notion of echoic use was developed in relevance theory as part of the use/*mention distinction to provide an analysis of irony.

ecological pragmatics An account of language especially the activity of conversing within the theoretical framework of a general, ecological, values-realizing approach to psychology sometimes known as **values-pragmatics theory**. It argues that linguistic activities are better interpreted in terms of ecological, values-realizing dynamics than in terms of rule-governed processes, and treats conversing as a perceptual mechanism, an action, and a caring system. See Hodges (2009).

economic versatility *See* principle of economic versatility.

economy *See* auditor's economy; speaker's economy; expression minimization; semantic minimalism; principle of least effort.

EEG = electroencephalogram, electroencephalography.

effective A type of *conventional illocutionary act proposed by the American philosophers Kent Bach and Robert Harnish which is largely equivalent to the American philosopher John Searle's speech act type of *declaration. Paradigmatic cases include abdicating, banning, indicting, sentencing, and vetoing. E.g. *I hereby veto the bill. See also* constative (2); acknowledgement; verdictive.

effective means *See* principle of effective means.

egocentricity (of deixis) *See* deictic centre.

egocentrism A property of language being centred on the 'here' and 'now' of the person who is speaking, i.e. 'I' (Latin *ego*). Egocentrism is of fundamental importance to *deixis. *See also* deictic centre.

elaborative pragmatic marker A *non-conceptual pragmatic marker which indicates a speaker's conception that the proposition to which the elaborative pragmatic marker is attached is an elaboration or conclusion of, or more important than, the previous proposition. E.g. *Moreover* in *Rosemary can read Chinese. Moreover, she can write poems in the language*.

electroencephalogram, electroencephalography, electroencephalograph (EEG) A non-invasive, direct measure of the physiological activity within the brain, made by placing electrodes on a subject's scalp. These electrodes record the electrical activity of the cortex and transmit the electrical signals to bio-amplifiers. The bio-amplifiers will then covert the information to digital signals that can be stored in a computer. Electroencephalograms have been used in *neuro- and *experimental pragmatics. However, given that they engender high temporal resolution but low spatial resolution, sometimes they are used simultaneously with **functional magnetic resonance imaging (fMRI)** to measure and record brain activity. See Coulson (2004).

elevation A term used in the description of *space deixis. It refers to the physical dimension of height relative to the deictic centre, typically the speaker. In a language that utilizes this **geometric parameter** of space deixis, the deictic centre, typically the speaker, will set a horizontal line as the zero point. When the entity referred to is above the line, 'up' or 'upwards' is used; when it is below the line, 'down' or 'downwards' is employed. One variant of elevation is where height is marked in terms of 'uphill' vs. 'downhill' and/or 'upriver' vs. 'downriver' depending partially on the geographic environment in which a particular language is spoken. This is called the **geographic parameter** of space deixis. See Huang (2007). *See also* distance; stance; side; visibility.

EM = ethnomethodology.

emancipatory pragmatics A recently emerged research framework in pragmatics that attempts to free the study of language in use from the confines of the theoretical and methodological orthodoxies grounded in the dominant thought and practice derived from Anglo-American and European languages and ways of speaking, with the attendant premises of individualism, rationality, and market economy, thus the term 'emancipatory'. The focus of emancipatory pragmatics is placed on non-Western languages and ways of speaking and on describing a language and/or culture strictly in its own terms. See Hanks, Ide, and Katagiri (2009). *See also* enthnopragmatics; ethnographic pragmatics (2).

embedded directive A *directive speech act that is performed by means of a *conventionally indirect strategy. E.g. the use of *Can you pass me the glue?* to make an indirect request. It is contrasted with an **explicit directive**, which is carried out directly. E.g. *Take off your helmet.*

embedded implicature A term that is used to refer to an (apparent) *conversational implicature that is engendered locally, typically triggered in a clause embedded under a propositional attitude verb. E.g. the implicature that John believes that not all of his colleagues are rude arising from the uttering of the sentence *John believes that some of his colleagues are rude*. For some scholars, embedded implicatuers are calculated locally, at the level of the embedded sentence. Recently, embedded implicature has generated a heated debate between the philosophy of language, pragmatics, and semantics.

embedded utterance *See* utterance[E].

embedded utterance cluster *See* utterance cluster[E].

embodied construction grammar (ECG) A recent variety of *construction grammar (1) developed by the American linguist Benjamin Bergen and his associates. In this model, constructions are considered to form the basis of linguistic knowledge, and the focus is placed on how they are processed in online or dynamic language processing, in particular language comprehension with regard to embodied cognition. See Evans (2007).

emotional factive presupposition A *factive presupposition that is triggered by the use of an **emotional factive verb**, which is concerned with emotional attitude towards fact. E.g. the uttering of the sentence *The prime minster regretted that the government hadn't responded quickly* engenders the emotional factive presupposition that the government hadn't responded quickly. *See also* cognitive factive presupposition.

emotional function *See* functions (of language).

emotive function *See* functions (of language).

emotive meaning *See* expressive meaning.

empathetic deixis A term that refers to a speaker's identification and reflection of the point of view of another person in a speech event or situation. *See also* emphatic deixis.

empathy A speaker's identification with another person who participates in the event or state that he or she describes. Empathy may vary in degree, ranging from the speaker's total identification to a lack of identification with another person. See Kuno (2004). *See also* point of view; logophoricity; humanness empathy hierarchy; topic empathy hierarchy; speech act empathy hierarchy; surface structure empathy hierarchy.

emphatic Marking of emphasis. E.g. *himself* in *Mary met the president himself.* In this sentence, *himself* is used as an emphatic pronoun, which is a type of an **emphatic marker**. Emphasis is frequently accommodated in terms of the *M-principle in neo-Gricean pragmatics.

emphatic deixis A term used by the British linguist Sir John Lyons for *deixis that is employed to encode emotional proximity or distance between the speaker and aspects of a speech event. This includes a shift from the use of a *distal to a *proximal deictic expression to show empathy, as in from *What's that?* to *What's this?*; and from the use of a proximal to a distal deictic expression to show emotional distance, as in from *this woman* to *that woman*. *See also* empathetic deixis.

empirical pragmatics A controversial view of pragmatics advocated by the Polish linguist Roman Kopytko. On Kopytko's view, pragmatic theorizing should be based on empirical findings rather than rationalistic assumptions. In other words, empirical pragmatics is data- rather than theory-driven. It should be (i) non-essentialist, (ii) non-modular, (iii) non-reductionist (i.e. not simplify and generalize for complex data), (iv) non-deterministic, (v) non-categorical, and (vi) contextual. By contrast, Kopytko called the rationalist assumption-based and theory-driven approach to pragmatics **rationalistic pragmatics**, which is characterized in terms of (i) philosophical essentialism, (ii) modular pragmatics, (iii) reductionism, (iv) postulation of rationality of human behaviour analysed in terms of idealized rational agents, etc., (v) categorical pragmatics, and (vi) the deductive-nomological, i.e. deterministic and predictive approach. According to Kopytko, most of the current influential pragmatic theories such as Gricean pragmatics, relevance theory, and the face-saving model of politeness belong to rationalistic pragmatics. See Kopytko (1995).

empty (direction of fit of a speech act) *See* none (direction of fit of a speech act).

empty pragmatic category *See* pragmatic zero anaphor.

enantiosemy A variety of *polysemy in which one sense of a lexical item is the opposite of another sense of that lexical item. E.g. the sense of *dust* in *Mary dusted the desk* vs. that of *dust* in *Mary dusted the cake with sugar*. In the first sentence, *dust* means 'to remove (dust)'; in the second sentence, it means 'to apply or add (fine particles)'. *See also* antagonym.

encoding A term borrowed from communication theory for a message being put into a code to be sent. In linguistics including pragmatics, it means roughly producing speech. Contrasts with **decoding**.

encyclopedic knowledge = world knowledge.

encyclopedic knowledge context *See* general knowledge context.

encyclopedic meaning Meaning of a word or lexeme that is related to everything known about the referent of that word or lexeme. E.g. the encyclopedic meaning of the word *cat* may include such matters as typical appearance and behaviour of cats, cats are born blind, the usefulness of cats, how cats should be looked after. *See also* dictionary meaning.

encyclopedic semantics A perspective on the study of meaning within *cognitive semantics, which is characterized by a number of assumptions. First, encyclopedic semantics does not distinguish between semantics and pragmatics. Secondly, it assumes that encyclopedic knowledge represents a structured body of knowledge or information. Thirdly, it maintains that encyclopedic meaning emerges in context of use. Fourthly, it regards lexical items as points of access to encyclopedic knowledge. Finally, it holds that the encyclopedic knowledge that a lexical item has access to is dynamic. *See also* frame semantics; mental space(s) semantics.

endophora, endophoric Also called **endophoric reference.** A term that is sometimes used to subsume *anaphora (2); *cataphora, viewed as a relation in which an anaphoric expression and its antecedent are within ('*endo-*') the same sentence or discourse. Contrasted with **exophora**, **exophoric**.

English-style topic construction A*topic–comment construction whose comment clause is syntactically related to the topic. E.g. *Labour, my street voted in the last election*. Also termed a **syntactic topic construction** and **left-dislocation**. Contrasts with a **Chinese-style topic construction**.

entailment Derived from formal logic, the term refers to a semantic relation that can be defined in terms of *truth, i.e. a proposition (or sentence expressing a proposition) *p* entails a proposition (or sentence expressing a proposition) *q* if and only if the truth of *p* guarantees the truth of *q*. In other words, if *p* entails *q*, then *q* can be taken as following logically and inescapably from *p*. If *p* is true, then *q* is also true. E.g. *All of the university's professors are hard-working* entails *Some of the university's professors are hard-working* provided that the university in question has professors. By contrast, if *p* is false, nothing is said about the *truth value of *q*. Defined thus, entailment represents a *truth-functional relationship in the sense that its function is to predict the truth value of a proposition from what is known of the truth value of another. It is not *defeasible. See Huang (2011). Also called **entailingness** and **semantic entailment**. *See also* pragmatic entailment; downward entailment, upward entailment.

entertaining impoliteness A term introduced by the British linguist Jonathan Culpeper for the type of impoliteness that involves a speaker's exploitative entertainment at the expensive of a target. E.g. in reply to Miss Havisham's invitation to play cards with Pip, Estella said: *With this boy! Why, he is a common labouring-boy* (Dickens, *Great Expectations*). *See also* affective impoliteness; coercive impoliteness.

enthymeme A term encountered in rhetoric to refer to an argument that has the form of a syllogism but contains unexpressed premises or conclusions. In other words, an enthymeme is logically incomplete, because it is often based on what is commonly accepted or likely rather than what is valid. E.g. the dialogue Sue: *'Let's walk along Waterloo Lane.'* Mary: *'It's too dark'* expresses an enthymeme. Construed thus, enthymemes have a clear pragmatic base. *See also* abduction.

epistemic factive presupposition *See* cognitive factive presupposition.

epistemic meaning *Meaning that encodes a speaker's degree of commitment to the truth of the propositional content of the sentence he or she utters.

epistemic pragmatic marker A *conceptual pragmatic marker which indicates the degree of commitment of a speaker to the truth of what he or she says. E.g. *Clearly* in *Clearly, John has sprained his ankle*. From a structural point of view, a distinction can be made between **epistemic adverbial pragmatic makers**, as in the above example, and **epistemic clausal pragmatic markers**, as in e.g. *I believe* in *The Berlin Wall was destroyed in 1989, I believe*.

epistemic subjectivity *See* metaphysical subjectivity.

epithet Typically a noun used derogatively. E.g. *idiot* in *John promised to come to Mary's wedding, but the idiot missed the train*. As this example shows, an epithet phrase can sometimes function as an *anaphoric expression.

eponymy, eponym A relation between an individual name and a common noun that is (believed to be) named after it. E.g. the relation between the name *Lord Wellington* and *wellington (boot)*.

equipollent antonymy, equipollent antonym A variety of *antonym (2). E.g. the sense relation between *hot* and *cold*. One characteristic of equipollent antonyms is that, like overlapping antonyms, each term has its own scale, but unlike overlapping antonyms, both scales point outwards from a common zero value. For *hot* and *cold*, we have a scale of hotness and a scale of coldness, which point in the opposite direction. Both scales share a common zero value, which is the absence of a temperature sensation. Most of equipollent antonyms denote sensations, e.g. *sweet* vs. *bitter*, or emotions, e.g. *happy* vs. *sad*. *See also* gradable antonymy; overlapping antonym; privative antonym.

equity rights A term used by the British linguist Helen Spencer-Oatey for a type of social rights which refers to the belief that people are entitled to personal consideration from others, to be treated fairly, and not to be unduly imposed upon. Equity rights are personal and are similar to the notion of *negative face postulated by the American linguist Penelope Brown and the British linguist Stephen Levinson. Contrasted with **association rights**.

ERP = event-related potential; evoked response potential.

essential condition A kind of *felicity condition which defines the essential nature of the *speech act being performed, namely, (i) a speaker has the intention that his or her utterance will count as the identifiable act, and (ii) this intention is recognized by the addressee. Thus in the case of a promise, a speaker must intend his or her utterance to count as putting him or her under an obligation to carry out what is promised. For a request, a speaker must intend his or her utterance to count as an attempt to get the addressee to do what is requested. Failure to satisfy the essential condition has the consequence that the act has not been performed successfully.

essential indexical *See* pure indexical.

eternalism A term used by the French philosopher François Recanati for the view that from a theoretical perspective, given the **eternalization principle**, the phenomenon of *indexicality is a practical convenience, but not an essential feature, of natural language. Eternalism is taken to be a stage in the development of *literalism. See Recanati (2005).

eternalization principle A principle which states that for every statement that can be made in a natural language utilizing a *context-sensitive sentence in a given context, there is an eternal sentence in that language which can be employed to make the same statement in any context. To achieve this, one has only to replace the context-sensitive constituent of the context-sensitive sentence by a non-context-sensitive constituent with the same semantic content. See Recanati (2005).

ethnographic pragmatics **1.** Roughly = cultural or anthropological pragmatics. **2.** A term used in its narrow sense to refer to the ethnographically oriented approach to context-sensitive language use associated particularly with the work of the American linguist Michael Silverstein and his students. Influenced by his teacher, the Russian-born American linguist Roman Jakobson, research conducted in Silverstein's ethnographic pragmatics has focused largely on non-Western cultures, societies, and languages. *See also* cultural pragmatics; ethnopragmatics; emancipatory pragmatics.

ethnographic semantics *See* ethnosemantics.

ethnography of communication A term largely identical in reference to **ethnography of speaking**. The main difference is that non-verbal communication is included in ethnography of communication.

ethnography of speaking A term introduced by the American anthropological linguist Dell Hymes in the early 1960s, 'ethno-' being from the Greek word for a people or nation. Ethnography of speaking represents an approach within anthropological linguistics to the investigation of speech as a series of cultural or social events to be analysed utilizing ethnographic techniques, especially by a speech event participant-observer who records naturally occurring discourses in their cultural context. The emphasis is on language used by a particular group, community, or society rather than on the abstract linguistic system. The notion of *communicative competence is a central concept in ethnography of speaking. Ethnography of speaking is clearly relevant to *conversation analysis and *cultural and *cross-cultural pragmatics. *See also* ethnography of communication.

ethnomethodology (EM) A breakaway movement in micro-sociology that argues for the study of social interaction in terms of categories, methods, and techniques utilized by the members of a society themselves, hence the term 'ethnomethodology', with 'ethnic' meaning 'participants' own'. Scholars belonging to this movement are called **ethnomethodologists**. The main relevance of ethnomethodology to pragmatics is the methodology it has offered to *conversation analysis.

ethnopragmatic script *See* cultural script.

ethnopragmatics An approach to pragmatics that is semantically grounded in *natural semantic metalanguage developed by the Polish-born Australian linguist Anna Wierzbicka and her colleagues. Utilizing *cultural scripts and semantic or reductive paraphrase explications (*see* natural semantic metalanguage) as analytical tools, practitioners of ethnopragmatics aim to find out more about speech practices and language use of particular, local cultures, contextualized and understood in terms of the beliefs, norms, and values of speakers themselves. In other words, the emphasis is on culturally anchored analyses and explanations. Ethnopragmatics rejects universal(ist) pragmatics. Overlaps with *cultural and *cross-cultural pragmatics. *See also* universal(ist) pragmatics; ethnosemantics. See Goddard (2006).

ethnosemantics As part of the cognitive revolution in the late 1950s, ethnosemantics represented an anthropological approach to the study of meaning in relation to cognitive science. It investigated ways in which meaning is structured in a particular culture or cultures. Topics of common interest to the subject area involved included the structure of kinship systems, universal in colour terminology, ethnobiological terms, discourse structure of speech events, and conditions governing culturally constrained semantic variation. When the study is conducted from a diachronic perspective, it is called **historical ethnosemantics**. Historical ethnosemantics is particularly concerned with the investigation of a reconstructed proto-vocabulary and the cultural and historical paths by which it evolved into the vocabularies found in individual languages. Also referred to as **ethnographic semantics**. Its modern incarnation is known as **cognitive anthropology**. *See also* ethnopragmatics.

etiolation (of language) A term used by the British philosopher J. L. Austin to refer to the non-performance or void of a *performative that is uttered or a *speech act that is performed in the playful use of language such as on stage, in a poem or in a soliloquy. E.g. an onstage promise. It may bind the character in the play but does not bind the actor who plays the character. However, there seem to be cross-cultural and/or linguistic variations. In some Muslim cultures, an unintentional, onstage performance of the speech act of divorcing can effect a divorce between the actual actors if they happen to be husband and wife in real life. See Huang (2007).

euphemism An indirect word or phrase that is often used by a speaker to refer to something embarrassing or unpleasant, sometimes to make it seem less offensive, indecent, or alarming than it really is. E.g. *working girl* used in place of *prostitute*. Many euphemisms have their origin in the pragmatic use of language governed by the *maxims of conversation proposed by the British philosopher H. P. Grice. Contrasts with **dysphemism**—language deployed to emphasize the unpleasant aspects of something. E.g. the used of *rag* for 'newspaper'.

European Continental philosophy = Continental philosophy.

European Continental tradition (of pragmatics) = Continental tradition (of pragmatics).

European functionalism *See* functionalism.

evaluative meaning A type of non-propositional meaning by virtue of which a speaker expresses his or her attitude to or evaluation of what is being said. E.g. the meaning of *amazingly* in *Amazingly, John survived. See also* expressive meaning.

evaluative pragmatic marker A *conceptual pragmatic marker which indicates a speaker's attitude toward, emotion, and evaluation of the propositional content of a sentence uttered. E.g. *Unfortunately* in *Unfortunately, Mary lost her job.*

Evans-type anaphora = E-type anaphora.

event(-based) semantics A variety of neo-Davidsonian semantics devoted especially to the analysis of thematic roles. Under this approach, a verb is taken to be a one-place predicate of events, and a thematic role is treated as two-place relations between individuals and events.

event-related potential (ERP) Electrical brain activity which can be measured and related to an external stimulus event. This can be done by presenting a particular stimulus to a subject, recording his or her electroencephalograph (derived from **electroencephalogram**), and averaging his or her brain response to the stimulus. The method or technique has been used in the cognitive neuroscience of language, and in recent years has been increasingly applied to pragmatic language comprehension in *neuro- and *experimental pragmatics. Also called **evoked response potential**. See Coulson (2004).

event-related potential component (ERP component) A series of deflections contained in a brain waveform, which appear to the eye as positive or negative peaks. Evoked response potential components are distinguished in terms of (i) **polarity**—whether they are positive- or negative-going, (ii) **latency**—the time point at which they reach their largest amplitude or size, and (iii) **scalp distribution**—the pattern of relative amplitudes a component has across all the recording sites. See Coulson (2004).

evidential A linguistic element used to express a speaker's degree of certainty or strength of commitment to a proposition or a statement in term of the reliability of the evidence available. The use of an evidential can distinguish propositions based on personal experience, direct (e.g. sensory) evidence, indirect (e.g. inferable) evidence, reported evidence or hearsay, and guesswork. Cross-linguistically, **evidentiality** can be encoded morphologically, as in certain American Indian languages; syntactically, as in Japanese, Tibetan, and Turkish; and/or lexically, as in English. Evidentiality and evidentials have been extensively studied in pragmatics.

evincive The American linguist Lawrence Schourup's term for *discourse particles such as *like*, *uh*, and *well*, which are used to express how a speaker feels about the semantic content that follows the particles.

evoked response potential *See* event-related potential.

exaggeration *See* hyperbole.

exclusive disjunction *See* disjunction.

exclusive person A type of plural first-person marking in opposition to ***inclusive person**, meaning 'we-exclusive-of-addressee'. In other words, 'exclusive person' refers to the speaker but not any of the addressees. E.g. *ame* in Gujarati, *kami* in Malay, and *nii* in Zayse.

Occasionally, the term applies also to second-person plural, which means 'you-exclusive-of-speaker'.

exercitive A type of *speech act defined by the British philosopher J. L. *Austin, which gives a decision for or against a course of action. It is a legislative or executive act. Paradigmatic cases include appointing, bequeathing, ordering, sentencing, and voting. E.g. *I hereby sentence you to ten years in prison*. See Austin (1962). *See also* commissive; verdictive; behabitive; expositive.

exhaustivity *See* law of exhaustivity.

exhibitive utterance A term used by the British philosopher H. P. Grice to refer to an *utterance by the use of which a speaker intends to show an addressee that he or she (the speaker) has a certain *propositional attitude. In contrast, by **protrepic utterance** is meant an utterance by the use of which a speaker intends to get the addressee to share his or her (speaker's) propositional attitude. E.g. the uttering of *Gordon got himself into trouble* is an exhibitive one if the speaker of that utterance intends his or her addressee to take it as evidence that the speaker believes that Gordon got himself into trouble. On the other hand, the utterance is a protrepic one if the speaker intends to get the addressee to believe that the speaker believes that Gordon got himself into trouble. The **exhibitive/protrepic utterance distinction** can be applied to other types of sentences such as the imperative.

existential presupposition A *presupposition that is triggered by the use of a *definite description. E.g. the uttering of the sentence *The king of France is bald* induces the existential presupposition that there is or exists a king of France.

existential quantifier *See* quantifier.

exophora, exophoric In opposition to **endophora, endophoric**, the term refers to a relation in which the *referent of an *anaphoric expression lies outside ('*exo-*') what is said or written. E.g. *He's not the suspect; he is*, where the different referents of the two instances of *he* are in the physical context in which the sentences are uttered. Also called **contextual**, **exophoric** or **situational anaphora**, and **exophoric reference**. *See also* deixis.

expansion A pragmatic process postulated by the American philosopher Kent Bach to flesh out or elaborate on a minimal though full proposition, generating a pragmatically enriched proposition that is identified with what a speaker has intentionally meant. E.g. the proposition expressed by the sentence *Mary has nothing to wear* needs to be expanded to something like 'Mary has nothing suitable to wear for John's party', thus allowing the assignment of an appropriate *truth value to the proposition. See Bach (2004). *See also* saturation; completion.

expansion approach (to incomplete definite description) *See* incomplete definite description.

experimental paradox A well-known dilemma in experimental psycholinguistics, and also relevant to *experimental, *neuro-, and *clinical pragmatics. The dilemma is that the more perfect an experiment, the less like the real speech situation it is, and the more likely that subjects of the experiment will produce unnatural responses. On the other hand, the more the experiment resembles the real speech situation, the less easy for the experimenters to control the external factors that may interfere with the experiment. The consequence of this paradox is that it is almost impossible to design a perfect experiment. See Aitchison (2003).

experimental pragmatics **1.** In its broad sense, experimental pragmatics refers to any investigation through experiments of any phenomenon or issue that is considered to be pragmatic, using both psycholinguistic and neurolinguistic methods. Topics include the Gricean theory of conversational implicature, indirect speech acts, presupposition, the given/new information distinction, pragmatic competence, theory of mind, and the processing of metaphorical, metonymical and ironical uses of language. **2.** In its narrow sense, experimental pragmatics refers to a recent development in psycholinguistics, pragmatics, and the psychology of reasoning that investigates, through carefully controlled psycholinguistic experiments, a particular set of issues at the interface between pragmatics and semantics. These issues, phenomena, and theories include scalar implicatures, default vs. contextual inference, the felicity conditions on speech acts, reference, the neo-Gricean pragmatic theory, relevance theory, and children's pragmatic competence. Methodologies typically adopted in psychology and neuroscience such as reaction times, eye movements, and *event-related potentials are used in experimental pragmatics. See Noveck and Sperber (2004); Bezuidenhout (2010).

explicated inference Inference that forms part of an *explicature.

explicature A controversial term used in relevance theory to refer to a pragmatically inferred, explicitly communicated component of what is said (i.e. the **explicit content**) rather than of what is conversationally implicated (*see* conversational implicature) (i.e. the **implicit content**). In other words, an explicature consists of the explicit assumptions communicated by an utterance. It functions to inferentially flesh out or explicate the linguistically given incomplete conceptual representations or logical form of the sentence uttered, yielding fully propositional content. E.g. Depending on the context, the explicature of *Everyone enjoys classical music* may be 'Everyone in John's class enjoys classical music'. An explicature corresponds roughly to the American philosopher Kent Bach's notion of *impliciture and the French philosopher François Recanati's notion of *pragmatically enriched said. Explicatures can be divided into **basic** and **higher-level/order explicatures**. Contrasts with an **implicature** or **r-implicature**.

explicit constative *See* constative (1).

explicit defeasibility *See* defeasibility.

explicit directive *See* embedded directive.

explicit illocutionary act An *illocutionary act that is performed explicitly, i.e. the performer of the illocutionary act fully spells out what he or she means. By contrast, an **inexplicit illocutionary act** is one that is not performed explicitly, i.e. the performer of the illocutionary act does not fully spell out what he or she means. E.g. someone may say *I haven't had my breakfast* to perform an indirect illocutionary act of requesting the addressee to provide him or her with some food, but what he or she is likely to mean is that he or she has not had his or her breakfast this morning. Therefore *I haven't had my breakfast* has to be expanded to 'The speaker hasn't had his or her breakfast this morning'. See Bach (2004).

explicit performative A *performative which contains a performative verb that makes explicit what kind of act is being performed. E.g. *I promise to come to your seminar tomorrow*. Contrasts with an **implicit performative**.

explicit suspension (of presupposition) The cancellation of a *presupposition by suspending it explicitly in an *if* clause that follows. E.g. in *I'm sure John's wife is a binge drinker, if he has a wife*, the potential presupposition engendered in the first clause that John has a wife is cancelled by the speaker's explicit suspension of it in the *if* clause. *See also* overt denial (of presupposition).

explicitness maxim *See* maxim of explicitness.

exploit, exploitation *See* flout.

expositive A type of *speech act defined by the British philosopher J. L. Austin which is used to express views, conduct arguments, and clarify usages and reference in a context of argument or conversation. Paradigmatic cases include denying, informing, accepting, postulating, and analysing. E.g. *I turn next to the issue of inheritance tax*. See Austin (1962). *See also* commissive; exercitive; behabitive; verdictive.

expression meaning The cover term for word meaning and sentence meaning.

expression minimization Opposed to **semantic minimization**, the term is used by the British linguist Stephen Levinson to refer to the view that 'shorter' linguistic expressions are preferred to 'longer' ones. E.g. the use of *modem* instead of *modulator demodulator*. Also known as **expression economy** or **expression brevity**. See Levinson (2000).

expressive A type of *speech act proposed by the American philosopher John Searle which expresses a psychological attitude or state in a speaker such as joy, sorrow, and likes/dislikes. Paradigmatic cases include apologizing, blaming, congratulating, praising, and thanking. E.g. *Well done, Elizabeth!* Also called an **expressive speech act**. See Searle (1975). *See also* commissive; representative; directive; declaration.

expressive content A term used in the *philosophy of language to refer to the case where a linguistic expression is used to express rather than describe something, and hence has expressive rather than descriptive content. E.g. while the use of *John has been to the Tate in London* expresses a proposition, the uttering of *wow* does not express a proposition but expresses the speaker's amazement.

expressive first-order politeness *See* first-order politeness.

expressive function *See* functions (of language).

expressive meaning A type of non-propositional meaning by virtue of which a speaker expresses rather than describes his or her beliefs, attitudes and emotions. E.g. *clever* and *cunning* have different expressive meanings. Expressive meaning falls at least in part within pragmatics. Other terms which overlap with 'expressive meaning' include **affective**, **attitudinal**, **emotive**, and **evaluative meaning**.

expressive politeness A term used by the British linguist Gino Eelen for an occasion where interlocutors explicitly endeavour to produce politeness language. E.g. the use of polite formulae like *please*.

expressive speech act **1.** = expressive. **2.** One of the three types of speech act proposed by the German philosopher Jürgen Habermas. An expressive speech act is one that conveys the speaker's communicative intentions and expresses his or her *subjectivity and attitudes. E.g. *I honestly believe that the military is taking de facto control of the country. See also* constative speech act; regulative speech act.

expressive verb A type of *illocutionary verb that names the expressive speech act it performs. E.g. *apologize*, *commiserate*, and *pardon*.

extended performative hypothesis *See* performative hypothesis.

extension, extensional The set of entities that a word may properly apply to in the external world. E.g. the extension of the word *dog* is the set of all dogs in the external world. In one analysis, the **intension/extension distinction** allows one to distinguish between words like *dog* and words like *unicorn*. While *dog* has both intension (the property of being a dog) and extension (the set of all dogs), *unicorn* has intension but not extension in the real world. Contrasted with **intension**.

external compliment *See* compliment.

externalized-language *See* E-language.

F

F-implicature *See Andeutung.*

face Developed into a technical term first by the Canadian-born sociologist Erving Goffman and then by the American linguist Penelope Brown and the British linguist Stephen Levinson to refer to a basic 'want' of every individual member of a society to have self-respect. In other words, face is the public self-image that an individual claims for him- or herself. If such a public self-image is not conveyed or accepted by others, loss of face will result. Face is the fundamental concept underlying the now classical Brown and Levinson *face-saving model of politeness. In one respect, face is divided into **positive face** and **negative face**. In another, it is further analysed into **first-order face (face 1)** and **second-order face (face 2)**. Face as defined by Goffman and Brown and Levinson represents second-order face. The technical notion of face is believed to be introduced to the West by the Chinese anthropologist Hsien Chin Hu in the 1940s. See Brown and Levinson (1987). *See also* group face; quality face; social identity face; normative face.

face 1 *See* first-order face.

face 2 *See* second-order face.

face-enhancing act Any *speech act which by its nature boosts the face of an addressee. A typical example is complimenting. Also called a **face-flattering act**. Contrasts with **face-threatening acts**.

face-saving model (of politeness) The most influential approach to politeness developed by the American linguist Penelope Brown and the British linguist Stephen Levinson, in which politeness is accounted for in terms of the concept of face. According to this model, the basic strategy of politeness is to minimize the threat to an addressee's negative face and maximize his or her positive face as much as possible. The model endeavours to develop a theory of **universal politeness**. Brown and Levinson's now classic face-saving theory has generated a huge industry of cross-cultural and cross-linguistic analyses of politeness. Also called the **face-oriented model** (of politeness); the **face-management model** (of politeness). See Brown and Levinson (1987). *See also* conversational contract model (of politeness); conversational maxim model (of politeness); pragmatic scale model (of politeness); social norm model (of politeness).

face-threatening act (FTA) Any *speech act which by its nature threatens the face of an addressee. Examples include complaints, disagreements, and requests. Contrasted with a **face-enhancing act**. *See also* incidental face damage; intentional face damage.

face-to-face interaction Any interactive communication between two or more physically present participants. A typical example is conversation. Studies of face-to-face interaction are important for pragmatics, especially *conversational pragmatics.

face work **1.** Any work involved in the construction, maintenance, enhancement and/or damage of *face as defined by the Canadian-born sociologist Erving Goffman and by the American linguist Penelope Brown and the British linguist Stephen Levinson. **2.** A dispreferred, alternative term for **relational work**, given that the notion of face occupies a central part in the process of defining relationships in interaction in this framework. But the concept of face in relational work is defined largely in the sense of Goffman rather than of Brown and Levinson.

factive A predicate such as a verb, adjective, or even NP that can take a complement clause, and which presupposes the truth of the proposition expressed in the clause. E.g. *realize*, *sorry*, and *a shame* in *John realized that /John was sorry that/It was a shame that the new apartment blocks are ugly*. Factives can further be divided into two types: (i) **cognitive** or **epistemic factives** and (ii) **emotional factives**. *See also* counterfactive.

factive presupposition A *presupposition that is triggered by the use of a factive verb such as *know*, a factive adjective such as *happy*, or a factive NP such as *the fact/knowledge*. E.g. the uttering of the sentence *John knows that the team has flown to Beijing* gives rise to the factive presupposition that the team has flown to Beijing. Factive presuppositions can be divided into two subtypes: (i) **cognitive** or **epistemic factive presuppositions** and (ii) **emotional factive presuppositions**.

falsity, false *See* truth.

familiar form Any *form of address that is used to mark familiarity with an addressee. A typical example is the use of T pronouns (see *tu/vous* distinction) such as *ni* in Chinese, *tu* in French, and *ty* in Russian. *See also* polite form.

far-side pragmatics A term used by the American philosopher John Perry and the Basque philosopher Kepa Korta for pragmatics on the far side of what is said, i.e. pragmatics that generates *conversational implicatures. Often contrasted with **near-side pragmatics**. *See also* post-semantic pragmatics.

'fast and frugal' heuristic *See* heuristic.

felicitous utterance Any utterance which satisfies the *felicity conditions on speech acts. In contrast, by **infelicitous utterance** is meant any utterance which fails to satisfy the felicity conditions on speech acts. Consequently, an infelicitous utterance cannot perform the relevant speech act appropriately or successfully.

felicity conditions A set of conditions introduced by the British philosopher J. L. Austin and systemized by the American philosopher John Searle. Felicity conditions are the conditions that the world must meet for a performative or speech act to be appropriately or successfully performed. They comprise four categories: (i) the **propositional content condition**, (ii) the **preparatory condition**, (iii) the **sincerity condition**, and (iv) the **essential condition**. Also known as the **happiness conditions** or the **appropriacy condition**. See Austin (1962); Searle (1969); Huang (2007).

felicity judgement task A technique devised by the Italian linguist Gennaro Chierchia and his associates in *experimental pragmatics. In the task, a pair of sentences to describe the same speech situation is presented to children. The two sentences have the same *truth value but differ in appropriateness. The objective of the test is to determine if children can distinguish between the two descriptions. See Chierchia et al. (2004).

feminist pragmatics An approach to the study of gender and language use incorporating insights from both feminism and pragmatics. Within this approach, it is assumed that on the one hand, if pragmatics is to provide a theoretical framework for the investigation of gender and language use, it has to be informed by the findings of feminist scholarship. On the other hand, pragmatics can inform feminist research on gender and language in a wide range of contexts. See Christie (2000).

figurative (sense, meaning, use, etc.) From the traditional notion of *figures of speech, the term is used to refer to an extension of a basic or linguistically encoded literal meaning of a linguistic expression. Some words have a **figurative sense**. The **figurative use** of language refers to the ways of using language non-literally to convey or suggest a meaning that goes beyond its literal meaning. A **figurative language** is a non-literal language or a style of language employing 'figures'. The study of the figurative use of language constitutes an important research area in pragmatics.

figure The concept was developed in Gestalt psychology in its analysis of perception. The basic idea is that human perception tends to segregate a given spatial scene into two parts: a figure and a ground. A figure is the most salient entity, i.e. some portion of the perceptual field that is highlighted. A **ground** is the rest of the scene that is relegated to background. Attention is normally focused on a figure, which stands out against the ground. The **figure/ground distinction** has been applied especially in cognitive linguistics, including the cognitive pragmatic analyses of spatial reference.

figure of speech A traditional term for a linguistic expression used in a different way from its usual, literal meaning in order to create a particular rhetorical effect. The concept is used extensively in rhetoric.

Stock examples of figures of speech include metaphor, hyperbole, and irony.

file change semantics A type of *dynamic semantics developed by the American linguist Irene Heim. It uses the metaphor of 'files' for the update of a speaker's information state in discourse. Meaning is viewed as the potential to change context. There are many similarities between it and the Discourse Representation Theory. *See also* Discourse Representation Theory.

filled pause *See* pause.

filter A term used by the Finnish linguist Lauri Karttunen which refers to a *presupposition operator which prevents some but not all of the presuppositions of an embedded or lower clause from being projected to the matrix clause. E.g. logical connectives like *and*. *See also* plug; hole.

filtering condition (on presupposition for a conditional) A condition proposed by the Finnish linguist Lauri Karttunen, which states that in the case of a conditional 'if *p* then *q*', if the presupposition that would have been engendered by the second clause is entailed by the first clause, it will be filtered out, as in *If the bishop promotes the politically incorrect, then he will regret doing so*. Otherwise the presupposition will survive to be projected to the whole sentence, as in *If Susan returned to England, then she would be arrested*. See Huang (2007).

filtering condition (on presupposition for a conjunction) A condition put forward by the Finnish linguist Lauri Karttunen which states that in the case of a conjunction '*p* and *q*', if the presupposition that would have been generated by the second conjunct is entailed by the first conjunct, it will be ruled out, as in *John has three children, and all his children are intelligent*. Otherwise the presupposition will survive to be projected to the whole sentence, as in *John has three children, and he regrets that he didn't study developmental psychology in university*. See Huang (2007).

filtering condition (on presupposition for a disjunction) A condition proposed by the Finnish linguist Lauri Karttunen, which states that in the case of a disjunction '*p* or *q*', the presupposition of the second disjunct will be eliminated if it is entailed by the negation of the first disjunct, as in *Either the bishop will not promote the politically incorrect, or he will regret doing so*. Otherwise the presupposition will survive to be projected to the whole sentence, as in *Either Susan will return to England, or she will flee to Spain*. See Huang (2007).

filtering-satisfaction analysis (of presupposition) An analysis developed by the Finnish linguist Lauri Karttunen and the American philosopher Robert Stalnaker which represents the first systematic study of presupposition within the context of modern linguistics. The central idea is that a presupposition is not cancellable. Rather, it has to be entailed or satisfied by its local context, which is conceived mainly as a set of propositions. The local context is constructed in a dynamic way, thus making it possible for an unwanted presupposition to be filtered out during the derivation of a sentence in a bottom-up manner. In order to handle the **presupposition projection problem**, presupposition operators are classified into three types: (i) **plugs**, (ii) **holes**, and (iii) **filters**. See Huang (2007). *See also* cancellation analysis (of presupposition); accommodation analysis (of presupposition); neo-Gricean analysis (of presupposition).

first-order concept A term used by the proponents of the 'post-modern' or 'discursive' approach to *politeness to refer to a commonsense concept, i.e. a concept as perceived and talked about by lay members of a sociocultural and/or speech community. By contrast, a **second-order concept** is a scientific one. In other words, it is an abstract, theoretical construct defined within a theory of politeness. Second-order concepts are informed by first-order concepts. They are used in a number of theoretical models to provide an account of politeness universals. The distinction between first- and second-order is applied to concepts such as *face, *politeness, and *impoliteness. See Watts, Ide, and Ehlich (2005).

first-order face In contrast to **second-order face**, this is the commonsense notion of face, i.e. a lay person's understanding of face, as in the everyday notion of 'losing face'. Also known as **face 1**.

first-order impoliteness The commonsense notion of impoliteness, i.e. judgement about whether a particular behaviour is impolite or not in accordance with the norms of a society, made by lay members of a sociocultural and/or speech community. Also called **impoliteness 1**. Contrasts with **second-order impoliteness**.

first-order politeness The commonsense notion of politeness, i.e. judgement about whether a particular behaviour is polite or not in keeping with the norms of a society, made by lay members of a sociocultural and/or speech community. First-order politeness consists of three components. Firstly, **expressive first-order politeness** refers to the politeness intention a speaker displays through speech. Secondly, **classificatory first-order politeness** is concerned with the classification of a particular behaviour as being polite or not on the basis of the addressee's evaluation. Thirdly, there is **metapragmatic first-order politeness**. It refers to the various ways in which politeness is conceptualized. Also described as **politeness 1**. Contrasts with **second-order politeness**. See Felix-Brasdefer (2008).

first pair part (FPP) *See* adjacency pair.

first person *See* person.

first-person logophoric marking A first-person verbal affix is used in a subordinate clause embedded under a logocentric predicate to encode logophoricity.

first principle of relevance *See* cognitive principle of relevance.

fixed expression *See* formula.

floor A term used metaphorically in *conversation analysis to refer to an arena in which interaction among conversational participants takes place. Thus, *taking/getting the floor, holding the floor*, and *yielding the floor* mean that a speaker starts speaking, continues to speak, and is replaced by another speaker, respectively.

flout, flouting A technical term used by the British philosopher H. P. Grice to refer to a speaker's deliberate and conscious non-observance of a maxim of conversation, which results in a *conversational implicature$_F$. Thus, if someone says *Stalin was a great democrat*, he or she is flouting the maxim of Quality, by which a speaker is expected to tell the truth. Consequently, the utterance of the sentence generates the conversational implicature$_F$ that Stalin was no democrat at all. Also called **exploit, exploitation**.

fMRI = functional magnetic resonance imaging.

focus **1.** The centre of attention. **Psychological focus** may involve differences in importance of a referent, in attention in a referent, or in activation of a referent in memory. E.g. *He* in *John has changed. He looks more like his elder brother now* is the psychological focus, because its referent is in the addressee's focal attention. **2.** The new material or information in a sentence that provides an answer to the relevant *wh*-question. **Information** or **semantic focus** is given prominence typically by means of prosodic highlighting of some kind, e.g. with prominent stress and/or intonation. Other linguistic means that mark information or semantic focus include word order, focus particles, and special syntactic structures. E.g. *JOHN* in A: *Do you know who gave up smoking?* B: *JOHN gave up smoking* expresses the information or semantic focus that identifies the one who gave up smoking as John. **3.** The material that a speaker calls to the attention of an addressee, thus often evoking an explicit contrast with a limited set of entities that may occupy the same position. E.g. the topic *that BOOK* in *We have to withdraw some of these books from the library. That BOOK you are holding in your right hand I think we can give to a charity* can receive a **contrastive focus**. One of the primary functions of focus is pragmatic, marking presuppositions. **4.** = comment. See Huang (2000); Gundel (2010). *See also* intonational focus.

focusing device *See* foregrounding.

Fodorian (cognitive) modularity *See* modularity, modular.

folk pragmatics A term used to refer to pre-theoretical, often popular assumptions, beliefs, expectations, and knowledge about aspects of language in use such as face, inference and politeness.

force **1.** = illocutionary force (*see* illocutionary act). **2.** = pragmatic force.

force of diversification *See* auditor's economy.

force of unification *See* speaker's economy.

foregrounded proposition For some scholars, a foregrounded proposition is one that is explicitly stated or logically entailed. By contrast, a **backgrounded proposition** is one that is taken for granted or presupposed. Thus, when one says *The king of France is bald*, the proposition that the king of France is bald is what is explicitly said or logically entailed, and therefore it is a foregrounded proposition. By contrast, the proposition that he exists is what is assumed or presupposed, and consequently it is a backgrounded proposition.

foregrounding, foregrounded A term used to refer to relative prominence in a sentence or discourse. Foregrounding can be achieved by various linguistic means such as the use of emphatic stresses and cleft constructions. The linguistic forms deployed to increase the salience of the element of the sentence or discourse are called **focusing devices** and the foregrounded part is termed **focus (2)**. E.g. *ROSEMARY* in *Martin is married to ROSEMARY*. The rest of the sentence or discourse that is not highlighted is **backgrounding** or is **backgrounded**. Foregrounding is closely linked to **focus (2)** and **presupposition**. Also called **highlighting, highlighted**.

form-based corpus pragmatics *See* corpus pragmatics.

formal form *See* polite form.

formal level (of pragmatic analysis) *See* pragmatic analysis level.

formal linguistic semantics The British linguist Sir John Lyons' term for **formal semantics**.

formal pragmatics **1.** An approach to pragmatics characterized by adopting the basic tools, notations, and techniques from logic and mathematics. It is to some extent an extension of *formal semantics to the domain of pragmatics. Examples of the formal approach to pragmatics include *optimality-theoretic/theory pragmatics and *game- and decision-theoretic pragmatics. **2.** A philosophically inspired pragmatic theory developed by the German philosopher Jürgen Habermas. Combining elements of both Continental and analytic(al) philosophy, especially the speech act theory, formal pragmatics lies at the very heart of Habermas' theory of communicative action. This research programme endeavours to identify and reconstruct the universal conditions underlying a speaker's communicative competence and his or her successful communication with other individuals, thus also the term **'universal pragmatics'**. Later on, Habermas preferred to use the term 'formal pragmatics' to distinguish it from his Frankfurt colleague Karl-Otto Apel's alternative theory of **transcendental pragmatics** and to emphasize its close links with formal semantics. The core assumption of formal pragmatics (2) is that not only language but also speech/utterance is amenable to a formal philosophical analysis. Its central hypothesis is that communication is governed by what Habermas called **communicative rationality**—a formal rationality based on the procedure in which mutual understanding is reached. Habermas utilized rational reconstruction as the method of investigation. This methodology is concerned with the reconstruction of a normal, competent speaker's *a priori* knowledge of how to produce appropriate utterances in communication.

formal semantics An approach to natural language meaning, especially sentence meaning, using a logical and mathematical system. Over the last 30–40 years formal semantics has been systematically applied to the study of meaning in natural language, especially in the work of the American logician Richard Montague. The term covers a family of semantic theories such as *model-theoretic semantics, *truth-conditional semantics, *possible-worlds semantics, and *situation semantics. One interesting characteristic of formal semantics is that it normally presupposes and operates in conjunction with a particular syntactic model. Formal semantics and indeed other formal approaches to semantics are labelled **objectivist semantics** by cognitive linguists, because on their view, formal approaches to semantics make the assumption that language refers to a cognitively independent 'objective' reality. Also known as **formal linguistic semantics**.

formalism The term refers to a variety of schools of thought in linguistics that have three characteristics in common. In the first place, the formalist approach focuses on the form of language and attempts to provide a description of the form of language independently of some other aspects of language such as its function. Secondly, it aims to express generalizations about language in terms of formalism, i.e. a mathematical system. Thirdly, on the formalist view, the form of language is assumed to be an autonomous system. One position is that the autonomous system is realized by a knowledge system in a speaker's mind/brain, known as the **language faculty**. Both children's acquisition of language and linguistic universals can be explained in terms of this genetically determined mental device. This mentalist approach is the one adopted by the American linguist Noam Chomsky. Another, narrower formalist position treats language as an abstract object, as is frequently encountered in the logical tradition of formal semantics. Also called **formalist linguistics**. See ten Hacken (2010). Usually discussed in opposition to **functionalism**.

formalist literary pragmatics A term used by the Finland-based linguist Roger Sell to refer to one of the two sub-branches of *literary pragmatics. Formalist literary pragmatics seeks to characterize literariness in terms of the pragmatic properties of literary texts, concentrating on formal analyses which are based on formal systems or pragmatic processes. Key research themes include speech acts in literary communication and free indirect discourse. See Pilkington (2010). Contrasts with **historical literary pragmatics**.

formality (1) A variety of *relational social deixis that holds between speaker (and perhaps other participants); speech setting. Formality refers to degrees or levels of compliance with the kind of language behaviour expected in different social situations, ranging from the most to the least strictly regulated. In some of the world's languages such as Balinese, Japanese, and Thai, levels of formality are firmly grammaticalized and/or lexicalized.

formality (2) *See* dictiveness, dictive.

forms of address Any of the forms or terms that is used by a speaker to address other people. Examples include the choice between T or familiar and V or polite pronouns (*see tu/vous* distinction), personal names, titles (e.g. *doctor*), rank terms (e.g. *colonel*), *kinship terms (e.g. *uncle*), and terms of endearment (e.g. *honey*). Forms of address are used to perform a variety of socially deictic functions, expressing such social relationships as power, status, and solidarity. In all cultures, societies, and speech communities, there are norms concerning who should use which form to address whom, what the social implications are of selecting one form over another, and on which occasions particular forms must and may be used. It is not unreasonable to say that in natural languages there is no such thing as a socially neutral form of address. Also called **terms of address**. See Huang (2007).

formula Also called a **conventional** or **formulaic expression**. A specific form of linguistic expressions used in a specific, especially a ritualized, context. Those expressions that have a very clear pragmatic function, such as a greeting (*How do you do?*), a responding to thanks (*You're welcome*) and a warning (*Watch out!*) are referred to as **pragmatic formulas**. Other possible alternative terms may include an **idiom** and a **fixed**, **set**, and **frozen expression**. These terms are difficult to distinguish. *See also* idiom.

forward anaphora = anaphora (2).

fossilization *See* conventionalized implicature.

fourth person *See* obviation.

FPP = first pair part (*see* adjacency pair).

frame-based inference A pragmatic inference that is generated within a semantic frame. It is taken to be an *I-implicature within *neo-Gricean pragmatics. E.g. the uttering of *Mary pushed the cart to the checkout* yields the I-implicature that Mary pushed the cart full of groceries to the supermarket checkout in order to pay for them, and so on.

frame of (spatial) reference A term deployed in Gestalt psychology for a coordinate system used to compute and specify the location of objects with respect to other objects. Cross-linguistically, there are three main linguistic frames of reference to express spatial relation between an entity to be located or a *figure and a ground: (i) **intrinsic**, (ii) **relative**, and (iii) **absolute**. Also called **reference frame**. Frames of (spatial) reference are relevant for the study of *space deixis. See Levinson (2003).

frame semantics An account of meaning developed by the American linguist Charles Fillmore since the 1970s. The central idea of frame semantics is that the meaning of a word can be properly understood only against a **semantic frame**—a particular body of assumptions and knowledge—in which the word is used. E.g. *serve* has different meanings in a restaurant frame and a tennis frame. *See also* encyclopedic semantics; mental space(s) semantics.

frame topic A Chinese-style or pragmatic topic that provides a spatial, temporal, or individual framework within which the main predication holds true. In other words, a frame topic limits the applicability of the main predication to a certain restricted domain of reference. E.g. 'elephant' in the Lahu topic–comment construction, schematically, 'Elephant, nose (is) long'. In this example, the topic establishes a universe of discourse with respect to which the comment clause provides some relevant information. *See also* instance topic; range topic. See Huang (2000).

free direct speech A category that lies in between *direct and *indirect speech. Free direct speech is basically a form of direct speech, but it differs from direct speech in the lack of an accompanying reporting, inquisitive or framing clause. E.g. *Mao caused tens of thousands of intellectuals to die during China's Cultural Revolution*. Also referred to as **free direct style**. *See also* free indirect speech.

free enrichment A type of *primary pragmatic process, postulated by the French philosopher François Recanati, whereby the linguistically decoded logical form of a sentence uttered is conceptually enriched by the addressee. Free enrichment is typically an optional and contextually driven *top-down pragmatic process. It is 'free' because it is entirely pragmatic but not linguistic in nature. E.g. the proposition expressed by the sentence *I haven't brushed my teeth* needs to be freely enriched to a proposition such as 'The speaker hasn't brushed his teeth this morning'. There are two types of free enrichment: **strengthening** and **expansion**. See Recanati (2004). *See also* saturation; completion.

free indirect speech A category that lies between *direct and *indirect speech. Free indirect speech is basically a form of indirect speech, but it differs from indirect speech in two major respects. First, the accompanying reporting, inquisitive or framing clause is often dropped. Second, the syntactic structure of direct speech is normally retained. E.g. *So that was his plan, was it? She well knew his tricks, and would show him a thing or two before she left the company* (with *she thought* etc. understood). The stylistic device is commonly found in narrative writing, especially in fiction, representing a protagonist's stream of thought. Also known as **free indirect style**. *See also* free direct speech.

free variable *See* variable.

Frege, (Friedrich Ludwig) Gottlob (1848–1925) German mathematician, logician, and philosopher. Educated at the universities of Jena and Göttingen, he started his academic career by becoming a *Privatdozent* in mathematics at the University of Jena in 1874. He was later promoted to professor of mathematics. He retired from the University of Jena in 1918. Frege was one of the greatest intellectual figures of his time, and is the father of the modern discipline of mathematical logic. As a mathematician and logician, he invented the notion of a formal system, established the distinction between axioms and rules of inference, and worked out the device to render modern logic superior to its predecessors. As a philosopher of language, he was one of the founders of analytic(al) philosophy. His thinking had an enormous impact on the development of philosophical logic, the philosophy of language, and linguistic semantics and pragmatics. In semantics, he is best known for the distinction he drew between an expression's sense and reference and for his principle of compositionality of meaning. In pragmatics, he introduced the concept of opacity, and a context principle. He was generally recognized as the first scholar in modern times who (re)introduced the philosophical study of *presupposition. His concept of **Andeutungen* is a precursor of the British philosopher H. P. Grice's notion of *conventional implicature.

Frege–Church argument *See* slingshot.

Fregean principle (of compositionality of meaning) *See* principle of compositionality.

French approach (to pragmatics) A term often encountered in the history of pragmatics for the French school that is associated with work by the French linguists Émile Benveniste and Oswald Ducrot. Benveniste's important contributions to pragmatics included his work on the nature of communication, the act of utterance, subjectivity, indexicality, and his theory of enunciation. Ducrot's distinction between producer, locutor, and enunciator as distinct aspects of a speaker and his reformulation of the speech act theory as a general theory of argumentation has been influential. This European tradition of pragmatic thinking has its deep roots in antiquity, i.e. rhetoric, as one of the three elemental subjects constituting the *trivium* (Latin). It is built, to some extent, upon the German philosopher Immanuel Kant's philosophy of 'active (transcendental) subjects' and the English philosopher John Locke's philosophy of 'semiotic acts'. It was also affiliated in one way or another with American pragmatism and was influenced by analytic(al) philosophy. Contrasts with the **Anglo-Saxon approach** (to pragmatics), **German approach** (to pragmatics), **American pragmatism**, and **British contextualism and functionalism**. See Nerlich (2010).

'from-old-to-new' principle *See* 'given precedes new' principle.

frozen expression *See* formula.

frozen pragmatics The view that pragmatics often engenders conventional properties of language through a process of grammaticalization. On this view, many syntactic and semantic facts are seen as frozen pragmatics. Thus, if a particular structure in a language is used very frequently due to some general human preferences, the language may conventionalize that structure. As pointed out by the American linguist Laurence Horn, 'what starts life as a *conversational implicature becomes conventionalized'; according to another American linguist, John Du Bois, 'grammars code best what speakers do most'.

FSP = Functional Sentence Perspective.

FTA = face-threatening act.

full blocking Complete *blocking of the occurrence of an innovative lexical expression, thus also called **complete blocking**. E.g. *bad* pre-empts **ungood*. In contrast, by **partial blocking** is meant blocking that is not complete. E.g. while *glory* blocks **gloriosity*, it does not prevent *gloriousness*.

full-fledged contexualism, full-fledged contextualist A term used by the French philosopher François Recanati for *contextualism or *radical contextualism.

full-fledged speech act *See* primitive speech act.

full logophoric language Any language which has special morphological and/or syntactic forms that are employed only in *logophoric domains, be the form a *logophoric pronoun, a *logophoric addressee pronoun, and/or a *logophoric verbal affix. Babungo, Pero, and Ekpeye, for instance, are such languages. Also called **pure logophoric language**. By contrast, any language which has no such special morphological and/or syntactic forms is a **non-logophoric language**. English is such a language. See Huang (2000).

full synonymy, full synonym A term used by the British linguist Sir John Lyons for *synonyms that are synonymous in all their sub-meanings. In other words, according to this view, two or more lexical items are full synonyms if and only if all their sub-meanings are identical. Full synonyms are very rare. *See also* total synonym; complete synonym.

function-based corpus pragmatics *See* corpus pragmatics.

Functional Communication Treatment A formal pragmatic therapy programme developed in *clinical pragmatics for aphasics. In this therapy, aphasic patients, confronted with simulated everyday life situations, are trained in the use of non-verbal communicative strategies.

functional independence principle A principle proposed by the New Zealand-born linguist Robyn Carston, which states that if the role played by a pragmatically derived aspect of utterance meaning subsumes the role of *what is said, then the pragmatically determined element of utterance meaning is part of what is said. On Carston's view, pragmatic aspects of what is said and conversational implicatures should play independent roles in an addressee's mental life.

functional magnetic resonance imaging (fMRI) A specialized brain-imaging scan, which measures changes in blood flow related to neural activity in the brain. In general, the more complex the task a patient or subject is requested to perform, the greater the blood flow. In recent years, the technique has been used in *neuro- and *clinical pragmatics. However, given that functional magnetic resonance imaging gives rise to good spatial but poor temporal resolution, it is sometimes used with **electroencephalograms** to measure brain activity. *See also* electroencephalogram.

functional pragmatics **1.** = functionalist pragmatics (2). **2.** The label given to the approach advocated by the Austrian-born German linguist Konrad Ehlich which combines the insights of the British philosopher J. L. Austin and the American philosopher John Searle's speech act theory and the German linguist Karl Bühler's theory of linguistic fields. According to this approach, language provides a main means of transferring knowledge and obtaining mutual understanding.

Functional Sentence Perspective (FSP) A theory of the *information structure of a sentence or an utterance developed within the framework of **Prague School functionalism**. It provides an account of an utterance or a text in terms of the information a sentence or an utterance conveys, and evaluates it in terms of its semantic contribution to the text as a whole, utilizing the notion of *communicative dynamism.

functionalism The name given to a variety of schools of thought in linguistics that attach great importance to the functions of language. Functionalism considers communication to be the primary function of language, which shapes the forms a language takes. It attempts as far as possible to explain linguistic phenomena in terms of their external, functional (e.g. cognitive, cultural, and social) motivations. It accounts for children's acquisition of language in term of the development of communicative needs and abilities in society. Currently, a distinction can be drawn between **European** and **North American functionalism**. The former includes **Functional Grammar** developed by the Dutch linguist Simon Dik, **Functional Discourse Grammar** advanced by the Dutch linguists Kees Hengeveld and Lachlan Mackenzie, and **systemic-functional grammar** initiated by the British linguist M. A. K. Halliday. The latter encompasses **Role and Reference Grammar** advanced by the Australian linguist William

Foley and the American linguist Robert Van Valin, work by the American linguist Talmy Givón within so-called **West Coast Functionalism** and a number of **usage-based functionalist-cognitive models** including the American linguist Paul Hopper's **emergent grammar** and work by the American linguists Joan Bybee and Sandra Thompson. Functionalism overlaps with cognitive grammar and variants of cognitively oriented construction grammar, as well as with pragmatics. Also called **functional linguistics**. Contrasts with **formalism**. See Butler (2010).

functionalist pragmatics **1.** In its narrow sense, the term refers to the study of the *information structure of a sentence or discourse from a pragmatic point of view. **2.** In its broad sense, the term is sometimes used for the pragmatic study of language functions in general. Also called **functional pragmatics**.

functions (of language) The various purposes or roles played by language. E.g. language may be used to communicate an idea, to express an attitude, or to get an addressee to do something. Two typologies of language functions are particularly influential. In the Austrian-born German linguist Karl Bühler's 'organon-model' proposed in the 1930s, there are three functional dimensions of language: (i) the ***Darstellung*** **'(re-)presentation' function** (representing the states of affairs in the world), (ii) the ***Ausdruck*** **'expression' function** (expressing a speaker's states of mind), and the ***Appell*** **'appeal' function'** (appealing to an addressee). This classification had a great influence on the Russian-born American structural linguist Roman Jakobson's typology of six language functions in the 1960s. These are **referential** or **descriptive** (= representation), **expressive**, **emotive**, or **emotional** (= expression), **conative** or **appellative** (= appeal function), **phatic** (developing and maintaining contact between interlocutors), **metalingual** or **metalinguistic** (using a language to talk about itself or any other language), and **poetic** (paying attention to the form of the utterance) functions.

future tense *See* tense.

G

game- and decision-theoretic pragmatics (GDT pragmatics) Although its roots can be traced back to the late 1960s, game- and decision-theoretic pragmatics is a newly emerged formal pragmatic approach to language use. It endeavours to combine some of the central ideas of both **game** and **decision theory** and *Gricean (*see* maxims of conversation) and *neo-Gricean pragmatics and to apply them to the pragmatic use of language. At the heart of game- and decision-theoretic pragmatics lie two basic assumptions. First, utterance interpretation is treated as a game. Secondly, there is a decision problem in an utterance game. The success of utterance interpretation relies on how the utterance game is played by its speaker and addressee and the overall preference of the players over the ultimate outcomes of the game. In addition, insights from **evolutionary game theory**—a branch of game and decision theory—are borrowed to explain the emergence of regularities or conventions of language use. Game- and decision-theoretic pragmatics is to some extent linked with *optimality-theoretic/theory pragmatics. See Benz, Jäger, and van Rooij (2006).

game-theoretical semantics (GTS) A semantic theory developed by the Finnish philosopher Jaakko Hintikka and his associates. It owes its philosophical roots to the Austrian-born British philosopher Ludwig Wittgenstein's concept of language games. A synthesis of the *verificationist and *truth-conditional accounts of meaning, game-theoretical semantics makes extensive use of semantic games to elucidate the meaning of natural languages. A game is introduced by a set of rules which specify how moves are to be made in it. Such a game is associated with each sentence in a language to provide meaning to connectives, quantifiers, and other types of lexical items.

GAPP = Golden Age of Pure Pragmatics.

GAPS = Golden Age of Pure Semantics.

Gazdar's basket Named after the British linguist Gerald Gazdar to refer metaphorically to the mechanism proposed by him whereby the informational content of an utterance is incremented in accordance with an order of priority: background assumptions, contextual factors, semantic entailments, conversational implicatures, and presuppositions. Each augmentation must be consistent with the communicative content that has already been put in the common ground metaphorically referred to as the 'basket'. See Levinson (2000); Huang (2007).

GCI = generalized conversational implicature.

GDT pragmatics = game- and decision-theoretic pragmatics.

gender A category that divides nouns etc. into classes largely on the basis of biological sex. A variety of gender systems are found in the world's languages, but two are most common: that with the division between **masculine** and **feminine**, and that with the division between masculine, feminine, and **neuter**. Gender is commonly grouped into **grammatical** or **semantic gender** and **natural** or **conventional gender**. Gender marking on personal pronouns is an important aspect of *person deixis. See Huang (2007). *See also* person; number.

gender system One of the four main types of *reference-tracking systems. In this system, an NP is morphologically classified for *gender or class according to its inherent features, and is tracked through a discourse via its association with the gender or class assigned. Thus, NPs of the same gender or class can be interpreted as *coreferential, while those of different genders or classes cannot. The term 'gender' is used in a broad sense here, and is intended to cover what are traditionally treated as agreement features such as *person and *number. Also called the **class system**. *See also* inference system; switch-reference system; switch-function system.

general knowledge context One of the main types of *context. General knowledge context refers to the knowledge shared between a speaker and an addressee. E.g. the information derived from this type of context explains why whereas *I went to Beijing last month. The Forbidden City is magnificent* is pragmatically well-formed, *I went to Paris last month. The Forbidden City is magnificent* is pragmatically anomalous. This is because given real-world knowledge, while we know that there is a Forbidden City in Beijing, there is no such tourist attraction in Paris. In relevance theory, this type of context is conceived as a cognitive phenomenon. In other words, it is seen as a psychological construct. Alternative terms include a **background knowledge context**, **common knowledge context**, **common-sense knowledge context**, **encyclopedic knowledge context**, **mutual knowledge context**, and **real-world knowledge context**. *See also* physical context; linguistic context; social context.

general pattern (of anaphora) A pattern of *anaphora (1) which states that reduced, semantically general anaphoric expressions tend to favour locally coreferential interpretations, but full, semantically specific anaphoric expressions tend to favour locally non-coreferential interpretations. E.g. *The rose*$_1$ *on the windowsill has come into blossom. The flower*$_1$ *was beautiful.* vs. *The flower*$_1$ *on the windowsill has come into blossom. The rose*$_2$ *is beautiful.*

general pragmatics *See* descriptive pragmatics.

General Semantics A philosophical movement in the 1930s developed by the American thinker Alfred Korzybski. The approach devoted special attention to the conventional relationships between words and things.

general term *See* singular term.

general world knowledge = world knowledge.

generalized conversational implicature (GCI) A term introduced by the British philosopher H. P. Grice for a *conversational implicature which arises without requiring any particular contexts. E.g. the utterance of the sentence *Some of John's students like Wikipedia* engenders the generalized conversational implicature that not all of John's students like Wikipedia. This conversational implicature has a very general currency and goes through without needing any particular contexts. See Grice (1989); Levinson (2000); Huang (2007). Contrasts with a **particularized conversational implicature (PCI)**.

generalized conversational implicature scale (GCI scale) A semantic scale from which a generalized conversational implicature (GCI) arises. A representative example is a *Horn scale. E.g. <always, often>. Contrasted with a **particularized conversational implicature scale (PCI scale)**.

generalized invited inference *See* invited inference (2).

generative semantics A school of thought within generative grammar that was prominent from the late 1960s to the mid-1970s. Its leading figures are the American linguists George Lakoff, James McCawley, Paul Postal, and John R. Ross. According to the proponents of this approach, called **generative semanticists**, the semantic component of a grammar is taken to be the generative base from which syntactic structures can be derived, and no distinction is drawn between a sentence's deep structure and its semantic interpretation. The term 'generative' used in generative semantics thus has a narrower sense than that used in generative grammar or generative linguistics. The relevance of generative semantics for pragmatics is that generative semanticists challenged the American linguist Noam Chomsky's treatment of language as an abstract, mental device divorced from the use and functions of language. In their search for the means to undermine Chomsky's position, they were attracted to the work of the British philosophers J. L. Austin, H. P. Grice, and Peter Strawson and the American philosopher John Searle. In this way, they helped empty what the Israeli philosopher Yehoshua Bar-Hillel had called the '*pragmatic wastebasket', and thereby encouraged a great deal of important research on pragmatics in the 1970s. In addition, generative semantics served as one of the precursors of what came to be known as cognitive linguistics in the 1980s.

generic proposition A *proposition that makes a statement about a species, i.e. an entire class of individuals etc. rather than specific members in the class. E.g. LIONS ARE DANGEROUS ANIMALS.

generic reference *Reference to an entire class of entities rather than to a specific or non-specific member of that class. E.g. *Giant pandas live on bamboo shoots*, *The giant panda lives on bamboo shoots*, and *A giant panda lives on bamboo shoots* are all sentences that can be used to make generic reference in English. In contrast, by **specific reference** is meant reference to a specific member of a class of entities. E.g. in *A giant panda is sleeping in the cage*, the reference is specific because the speaker is talking about a specific member or a specimen of the class 'giant pandas'. *See also* definite reference; indefinite reference.

generosity maxim One of a set of *maxims of politeness proposed by the British linguist Geoffrey Leech which is speaker-oriented. What the maxim basically states is: minimize benefit but maximize cost to self. This maxim is particularly applicable to *speech acts like *directives and *commissives. More recently Leech has preferred to use the term **pragmatic constraint**. See Leech (2007). Contrasts with the **tact maxim**.

genre Traditionally, a particular type or style of literature that one can recognize by virtue of its form or function. E.g. epic poetry, the romantic novel, and the detective story. In its extended sense, the term is used with reference to any formally distinguishable variety of text, whether in speech or writing, that has achieved a general level of recognition. E.g. lecture. The study of genre is relevant to pragmatics. Sometimes also called **speech genre**.

'geographic' division (of context) *See* context.

geographic parameter (of space deixis) *See* elevation.

geometric parameter (of space deixis) *See* elevation.

German approach (to pragmatics) A term often encountered in the history of pragmatics to refer to the mode of thought that is associated with the critical theory movement championed by the German philosophers Jürgen Habermas and Karl Otto Apel. The German approach regarded pragmatics as part of a general theory of communicative action. It can be traced back to antiquity as rhetoric, one of the three elemental subjects of the *trivium*. It is based to some extent on the German philosopher Immanuel Kant's philosophy of 'active (transcendental) subjects' and the British philosopher John Locke's philosophy of 'semiotic acts'. It also has links with American pragmatism. Central topics of enquiry included agenthood of (transcendental) subject, dialogue, and speech acts. Contrasted with the **Anglo-Saxon approach** (to pragmatics), **French approach** (to pragmatics), **American pragmatism**, and **British contextualism and functionalism**. See Nerlich (2010).

gestural deixis A term used to refer to *deixis that is accomplished by the gestural use of a deictic expression. In contrast, by **symbolic deixis**

is meant deixis that is established by the symbolic use of a deictic expression.

gestural reference *Reference in which the identity of the *referent of a *referring expression is achieved by way of a physical demonstration (such as a selecting gesture or eye contact) of some sort on the part of the speaker. See Lyons (1995). *See also* demonstrative reference; deixis; indexical.

gestural use (of a deictic expression) The basic use of a deictic expression. Gestural use can be properly interpreted only by direct, moment by moment monitoring of some physical aspects of the speech event by the addressee. E.g. in *You and you, but not you, stand up* the three uses of the deictic expression *you* can only be interpreted if they are accompanied by physical demonstrations (such as three selecting gestures or eye contacts) of some sort on the part of the speaker. Contrasts with the **symbolic use** (of a deictic expression).

gesture Any voluntary movement of the body or limbs as a means of communicating meaning, e.g. a shrug. Such a movement may sometimes accompany speech, as in the case of the use of a deictic expression. The study of gesture is sometimes called **kinesics**.

GIIN = generalized *invited inference.

given Also called **givenness, given information** and **old information**. One of the two main constituents of the *information structure of a sentence or an utterance. **1.** Defined in terms of predictability or recoverability, **given-p[redictability]** is the information that is predictable or recoverable either linguistically or situationally. **2.** Stated in terms of psychological saliency, **given-s[aliency]** is the information that a speaker assumes to be in the consciousness of the addressee at the time of utterance. **3.** Defined in terms of shared knowledge (*see* mutual knowledge), **given-k[nowledge]** is the information that a speaker believes that the addressee already knows and can identify uniquely. Contrasts with **new, newness**, and **new information**, i.e. information that is not recoverable, not salient, and/or not shared. For some scholars, the **given/new information distinction** can further be grouped into two types: **referential** and **relational givenness/newness**. See Huang (1994/2007).

'given precedes new' principle A principle of *information structure which states that given information tends to be placed before new information in a sentence. This may apply only to SV languages. VS languages seem to display the reverse order: new information tends to be placed before given information. See Ward and Birner (2004).

global accommodation *Accommodation that arises from the amendment of a global context. Also known as ***de facto* accommodation**. In contrast, by **local accommodation** is meant accommodation that stems from the amendment of a local context (*see* global context). Also referred to as ***de jure* accommodation**.

global context A term used by the American linguist Irene Heim for the linguistic context against which a sequence of sentences or clauses are evaluated. Global contexts yield global accommodation. By contrast, **local context** refers to the linguistic context against which parts of a sentence are evaluated. Local contexts give rise to local accommodation. **Intermediate context** is the term used by the Dutch linguist Rob van der Sandt for the linguistic context between a local and a global context.

global theory (of a conversational implicature) A term used by the French linguist Anne Reboul to refer to the view that a *conversational implicature is a *nonce inference, and as such can be accessed only at the end of the sentence uttered, i.e. at a global (sentential) level. A proponent of such a view is called a **globalist**. Relevance theory is considered to represent a global theory. Contrasts with the **local theory**. See Reboul (2004). *See also* contextual inference theory (of scalar implicature); underspecification model.

Goffman, Erving (1922–1982) Canadian-born sociologist. Educated at the universities of Manitoba, Toronto, and Chicago, he worked at a number of American universities and institutes. He was Professor of Sociology and Benjamin Franklin Professor of Anthropology and Sociology at the University of California at Berkeley and the University of Pennsylvania, respectively. He died of cancer in 1982. As a sociologist, Erving Goffman is best known for his pioneering study of *face-to-face interaction and for having developed a 'dramaturgical' approach to human interaction. His work has also had a profound influence on anthropology, linguistics, and psychiatry. His primary contribution to pragmatics is in *sociopragmatics. Being the first to develop *face into a technical notion, he has been regarded as one of the key founders of modern *politeness theory.

Golden Age of Pure Pragmatics (GAPP) A term invented by the American linguist Laurence Horn for the traditional, 'received' view of pragmatics and the interaction between pragmatics and semantics. According to this view, the output of semantics provides input to pragmatics, which then maps literal meaning to speaker meaning. In other words, during GAPP, *pragmatic intrusion, i.e. pre-semantic pragmatics helping to determine the truth-conditional content of a sentence uttered was not allowed. The term is modelled after the ***Golden Age of Pure Semantics**.

Golden Age of Pure Semantics (GAPS) A term coined by the American philosopher David Kaplan to refer to the status of semantic theory before the problems caused by demonstratives and proper names were widely noted. *See also* Golden Age of Pure Pragmatics.

gradable antonymy, gradable antonym The prototype of *antonymy (2). E.g. the meaning relation between *fast* and *slow*. Also called '**polar antonymy, polar antonyms**'. *See also* equipollent antonymy; overlapping antonymy; privative antonym.

gradable contrary *See* antonymy, antonym (2).

graded salience hypothesis A hypothesis of pragmatic processing put forward by the Israeli linguist Rachel Giora and her associates. The hypothesis can best be seen as a version of the *modular view of context effects. Like the modular model, it makes the assumption that there are independent systems involved in comprehension: one bottom-up, sensitive only to domain-specific, linguistic information, and the other top-down, sensitive to all kinds of (linguistic and extralinguistic) information. But unlike the modular view, the hypothesis maintains that the modular lexical access mechanism is itself ordered, i.e. more salient responses or meanings are accessed faster than, and arrive at a level of sufficient activation before, less salient ones. See Peleg, Giora, and Fein (2004).

grammatical ambiguity *See* syntactic ambiguity.

grammatical competence *See* competence.

grammatical gender A grammatical category in which gender is defined solely by grammatical behaviour. E.g. masculine for *Löffel* (spoon), feminine for *Gabel* (fork), and neuter for *Messer* (knife) in German. Also called **semantic gender**. Contrasted with **natural gender**.

grammatical meaning In opposition to **lexical meaning**, the term is usually used to refer to any aspect of meaning considered as part of the syntax and morphology of a language. Grammatical meaning may include (i) meaning of grammatical elements such as affixes, articles, and prepositions, (ii) meaning of grammatical constructions, (iii) meaning a lexical item has by virtue of belonging to a particular grammatical category, especially noun, verb, and adjective, and (iv) meaning expressed by syntactic functions such as subject of a verb and case of a noun. See Cruse (2006). Also called **structural meaning**.

grammatical performativity The indication of *illocutionary force of an utterance by grammatical means. E.g. the use of a grammatical imperative to signal the *illocutionary act of ordering *Stop whining!*

grammatical pragmatics A term employed by the Israeli linguist Mira Ariel to refer to pragmatics that deals with aspects of meaning that are encoded but non-truth conditional such as *conventional implicature proposed by the British philosopher H. P. Grice.

grammaticality, grammatical *See* acceptability.

grand strategy of politeness (GSP) A super-pragmatic constraint on *politeness proposed by the British linguist Geoffrey Leech. What the strategy basically says is that in order to be polite, a speaker should express or imply meanings that associate a high value with others, especially the addressee, or associate a low value with him- or herself. See Leech (2007).

Grice, Herbert Paul (1913–1988) British philosopher. Educated at Oxford, he was elected to a Fellowship at St John's College, Oxford in 1939. In 1967 he emigrated to a Chair at the University of California at Berkeley, retiring in 1980. His wide-ranging body of philosophical work addressed topics of inquiry as diverse as reference, metaphysics, philosophical biology, philosophical psychology, and Kantian ethics, but his most influential contribution was to develop a theory of meaning in terms of speakers' *communicative intentions and to put forward a concept of *implicature. The notion of implicature was introduced by him in the William James Lectures delivered at Harvard in 1967. In these lectures, he presented a panorama of his thinking on meaning and communication for a systematic, philosophically inspired pragmatic theory of language use, which has since come to be known as Gricean pragmatics. Since its inception, the Gricean paradigm has revolutionized pragmatic theorizing and remains one of the cornerstones of contemporary thinking in linguistic pragmatics and the philosophy of language. His main work, collected in *Studies in the Way of Words* (1989) and *The Concept of Value* (1991), was published posthumously.

Gricean maxims *See* maxims of conversation.

Gricean pragmatics School of thought in pragmatics associated particularly with the insights of the British philosopher H. P. Grice. These include Grice's theory of meaning in terms of intentions, co-operation and rationality, and his theory of conversational implicature. Occasionally also called **Gricean semantics** by semanticists and **Griceanism** in the philosophy of language. See Grice (1989); Huang (2007). *See also* neo-Gricean pragmatics; post-Gricean pragmatics.

Gricean pragmatics 1 *See* pre-semantic pragmatics.

Gricean pragmatics 2 *See* post-semantic pragmatics.

Griceanism *See* Gricean pragmatics.

Grice's circle Named after the British philosopher H. P. Grice to refer to the issue of explaining how what is conversationally implicated can be defined in contrast to, and calculated on the basis of, what is said, given that what is said both determines and is determined by what is conversationally implicated. See Levinson (2000).

ground *See* figure.

ground-floor speech act Usually discussed in opposition to the notion of **higher-order speech act**, the term was used by the British philosopher H. P. Grice to refer to a *speech act performed by an utterance without a lexical item that triggers a *conventional implicature. By contrast, a higher-order speech act is one performed by a *conventional implicature trigger. The primary function of the higher-order speech act is to comment on the interpretation of the ground-floor speech act. E.g. in uttering *John is poor but he is honest* the speaker is performing a ground-floor speech act of asserting that John is poor and that he is honest. In addition, by using *but* he or she is also performing a higher-order speech act of making a contrast between the information contained in the first conjunct and that contained in the second one. Ground-floor speech acts are also called **central speech acts** and higher-order speech acts, **non-central speech acts**.

group face The public self-image or self-worthiness of the social group to which an interlocutor belongs. The notion was put forward in the analysis of certain African cultures and/or languages, in which any behaviour capable of lowering or 'darkening' the group face of, say, a speech community is avoided. *See also* social identity face.

group performative A term used by the British linguist Jenny Thomas for a *performative that is commonly or necessarily carried out by more than one person. E.g. the uttering of the sentence by the chairman of a disciplinary committee *We do not judge you to be guilty of professional misconduct*. *See also* collaborative performative; joint speech act.

GSP = grand strategy of politeness.

GTS = game-theoretical semantics.

H

happiness conditions *See* felicity conditions.

hard pragmatics A trend in pragmatics that studies language use from a philosophical, logical, and (formal) linguistic perspective. In contrast, by **soft pragmatics** is meant a trend in pragmatics that investigates language use from a social, cultural and sociocultural point of view.

hardcore pragmatics = (roughly) theoretical, pure, or micropragmatics.

head act Usually the nucleus or the core part of a *speech act. In other words, it is the part of the sentence that serves to realize a speech act independently of other parts. E.g. *how about going to the museum tomorrow afternoon* in *John, how about going to the museum tomorrow afternoon, since we'll have no lectures?* constitutes the head act of the speech act of suggesting.

hearer A person who hears an utterance, whether as an *addressee or not. *See also* addresser; bystander; overhearer; eavesdropper; speech event participant; ratified participant.

hearer-old Information that is assumed to be already known to a hearer or addressee. E.g. in *The president will come tomorrow to give a speech*, *The president* represents information that is hearer-old. Contrasts with **hearer-new**, i.e. information that is not known to the hearer or addressee. E.g. *a speech* in the above example represents information that is hearer-new.

'hearer preference' felicity condition A term that is used to refer to one of the two preparatory conditions for the performance of the speech act of promising: the speaker believes that the addressee would prefer the promised action to be accomplished. This explains why a speaker normally will not promise to beat the addressee up. *See also* 'non-evident' felicity condition; 'obligation' felicity condition.

hearer('s) maxim *See* speaker('s) maxim.

hedge Any linguistic expression used to express imprecision or qualification. E.g. instead of saying *A cultural exchange has been arranged between Japan and New Zealand*, one may employ a hedge *As far as I know* and say *As far as I know, a cultural exchange has been arranged between Japan and New Zealand*. Other examples of hedge include *sort of*, *perhaps*, and *in my view*. One of the earliest studies of hedge was conducted by the American linguist George Lakoff. Also termed **verbal hedge**. *See also* compound hedge; maxims of conversation hedge; kinesic hedge; prosodic hedge.

hedged performative A *performative accompanied by a hedge to modify its *illocutionary force. E.g. *We regret to have to inform you that you have not been appointed to the committee.*

***hereby* test** A test to determine whether an utterance in English is a *performative or *constative one. If a sentence can be accompanied by the adverb *hereby* immediately before the verb, then the uttering of that sentence constitutes a performative utterance. E.g. *Applicants are hereby reminded that your applications must be submitted to the Dean's Office by July 3rd.* The test was proposed and then rejected by the British philosopher J. L. Austin because *hereby* can also be used with a constative utterance, as in *I hereby state that the earth is round.* This was one of the reasons why Austin abandoned the **performative/constative dichotomy** in favour of a general theory of *speech acts.

hermeneutics The art, theory, science, or methodology of interpretation as well as a philosophical movement in 20th-century German philosophy. The hermeneutic approach starts with the insight that interpretation is both *holistic and circular. It is holistic because the interpretation of any part of a text depends on the understanding of the other parts of the text and/or the whole text; it is circular because any interpretation rests on a prior interpretation. This problem is known as the **hermeneutic circle**. Two competing positions can be identified within hermeneutics. One views interpretation as a method for the social, historical, and human sciences; the other sees it as an interaction between an interpreter and a text. The ideas of hermeneutics have been introduced to linguistics since the 1970s, in opposition especially to the doctrines advocated by the American linguist Noam Chomsky. For some philosophers and linguistic pragmaticists, a pragmatic interpretation is hermeneutic in nature.

heteronymy **1.** A sense relation in which two or more lexical items have the same meaning, though used by different speakers or in different dialects, as distinct from **homonymy**. E.g. the meaning relation between *bucket* and *pail*. **2.** = **homography** or **homophony**, where homonymy is in writing only or in pronunciation only, but not in both.

heuristic A term used in computing and cybernetics for a 'rule of thumb' process or procedure of discovery or problem-solving that is based on the exploration of the most plausible possibilities including using the trial-and-error method as opposed to an algorithm, which examines every possibility in a mechanical way. Some heuristics are **'fast and frugal'** ones, because they arrive at decisions fast and expend as little cognitive effort as possible. This specific mode of investigation has been adopted in pragmatic theories. E.g. in *neo-Gricean pragmatics, pragmatic principles are recast as heuristics and three heuristics are proposed.

hic et nunc Latin for 'here and now', and hence of a place and time of speaking, e.g. as a *deictic centre.

hidden indexical *See* indexicalism; incomplete definite description.

hidden indexicalism, hidden indexicalist *See* indexicalism.

high-context culture A *culture in which context plays a relatively more important role in communication and interaction. In such a culture, relatively little language is needed. Language is used typically to reinforce externally perceived social structures. A high context culture is claimed to be shame-driven in the sense that an individual's behaviour is constrained by the opinions of others. It is characterized by *deference and the maintenance of relative social positions. By contrast, a **low-context culture** is one where context plays a relatively less important part in communication and interaction. In such a culture, relatively more language is thus needed. Language typically has the function of creating new social structures. A low-context culture is guilt-driven in that an individual is accountable to him- or herself for his or her behaviour. It is characterized by courtesy and the possibility of social mobility. See Grundy (2000).

higher-level/order explicature An *explicature which involves the embedding of a propositional form of an utterance or one of its constituent propositional forms under a high-level description such as a *propositional attitude description, a *speech act description, and an *evidential marker. E.g. 'The speaker is angry that her husband is an alcoholic' is a higher-level/order explicature for the utterance *My husband is an alcoholic*. By contrast, a **non-higher-level/order explicature** is called **basic explicature** in relevance theory. E.g. 'The speaker's husband is an alcoholic' is the basic explicature of the above utterance.

higher-order speech act *See* ground-floor speech act.

high-level script (cultural) A *cultural script that expresses broad cultural themes which are normally played out in detail by way of whole families of related speech practices in a particular speech culture. E.g. a Russian cultural script for 'expressiveness': people think like this: it is good if someone wants other people to know what this someone thinks, it is good if someone wants other people to know what this someone feels. Also called a **master cultural script**. See Goddard and Wierzbicka (2004).

highlighting, highlighted *See* foregrounding.

hint Something one says or does in an indirect way to suggest what one is thinking or wants to happen. Many instances of *indirect speech acts are accomplished via hints. E.g. the uttering of *You have left the bathroom in a mess* to perform the indirect speech act of requesting the addressee to clean up the bathroom. In a similar way, many cases of *conversational implicature are induced via hints, triggered by the exploitation of the maxims of conversation proposed by the British philosopher H. P. Grice. E.g. the uttering of *I am Italian* to implicate that the speaker knows how to cook pasta.

Hirschberg scale Named after the American linguist Julia Hirschberg. A Hirschberg scale is a contextually given *ad hoc* scale (*see* scalar expression). The relation between the ordered elements in such a scale is not that of semantic entailment. The scale can be based on any partially ordered contrast sets in a contextually salient way. E.g. <divorce, separate>, <Barack Obama's autograph, Hillary Clinton's autograph> and <president, prime minister>. Also known as a **context-dependent scale**. See Huang (2010). *See also* Horn scale; rank order.

historical discourse analysis Any analysis of historical discourse. This overlaps considerably with *historical pragmatics, given that textual data is used heavily in both fields. A threefold typology primarily based on the methodological perspective has been established: (i) **historical discourse analysis proper**, (ii) **diachronically-oriented discourse analysis**, and (iii) **discourse-oriented historical linguistics**. The first represents a 'macro' approach; the second and third, a 'micro' one. See Brinton (2001).

historical discourse analysis proper A type of historical discourse analysis which takes a 'macro' approach and is essentially synchronic. It examines pragmatic factors such as orality, text type, and narrative markers at a particular language stage. Closely related to *pragmaphilology in *historical pragmatics. See Brinton (2001); Traugott (2004). *See also* discourse-oriented historical linguistics; diachronically oriented discourse analysis.

historical ethnosemamatics *See* ethnosemantics.

historical literary pragmatics A term used by the Finland-based linguist Roger Sell to refer to one of the two sub-branches of *literary pragmatics. Interdisciplinary in nature, historical literary pragmatics places an emphasis on the interconnections between literary studies, history studies, sociocultural studies, and pragmatic studies. For example, it uses the insights of the American linguist Penelope Brown and the British linguist Stephen Levinson's face-saving model of politeness to characterize the relationship between language users, i.e. writers and readers, in a literary context. See Pilkington (2010). Contrasted with **formalist literary pragmatics**.

historical pragmatics A branch of pragmatics that emerged in the 1990s. It is concerned with the investigation of language change between two given points in time in individual languages and in language generally from a pragmatic perspective. There are two main research trends that correspond roughly to the distinction between 'external' and 'internal' language change. The first, 'external' research strand is called '**pragmaphilology**', The second, 'internal' one, '**diachronic pragmatics**'. Since the boundary between pragmaphilology and diachronic pragmatics is sometimes not clear-cut, an intermediate category dubbed '**diachronic pragmaphilology**' has also been proposed. In addition to the two main approaches, there is another research trend, which is termed '**pragma-historical linguistic**'. Given that textual data is heavily used in both historical pragmatics and historical discourse analysis, there is considerable overlap between the two fields. At the early stage of its development, historical pragmatics was also called '**new philology**' or '**diachronic textlinguistics**'. See Jacobs and Jucker (1995); Traugott (2004); Culpeper (2010). Contrasts with **synchronic pragmatics**.

historical sociopragmatics A recently emerged research domain that involves the interaction between *historical pragmatics and *sociopragmatics. According to some scholars, historical sociopragmatics is more closely related to the pragmaphilology research trend in historical pragmatics. It constitutes a systematic study of interaction between aspects of social context and particular historical language uses that give rise to pragmatic meanings. Historical sociopragmatics can be either synchronic or diachronic. **Synchronic historical sociopragmatics** studies how language use shapes and is shaped by social context at a certain moment of time in the past. By contrast, **diachronic historical sociopragmatics** traces how changes in language use shape social context, changes in social context shape language use, and/or changes take place in the relationship between language use and social context. See Culpeper (2009).

hole A term coined by the Finnish linguist Lauri Karttunen, which refers to a presupposition operator which lets all the presuppositions of an embedded or lower clause to ascend to become presuppositions of the matrix clause. E.g. factive verbs like *know* and modal operators like *likely*. *See also* plug; filter.

holism, holistic The thesis that a complex whole consists of more than the sum of its parts, and therefore no single part can be adequately characterized without reference to the whole to which it belongs. Various types of holism can be identified. First, there is holism about meaning, according to which the meaning of a linguistic expression in a language is dependent on the meanings of all the other linguistic expressions in that language. This type of holism is called **semantic holism**. Semantic holism of some sort is considered to be an essential feature of a pragmatic system by certain pragmaticists. Secondly, **translation holism** holds that how one word is translated relies on how other words in the same language are translated. Thirdly, we have holism about evidence known as **confirmation holism**, the view that whether some empirical discovery confirms a given proposition is dependent on the confirmation status of a great number of other propositions, and ultimately of all the other propositions. Finally, there is holism about psychological explanation. Given **cognitive holism**, it is assumed that human mental content is holistic. See Barber (2009).

holonym *See* meronymy.

holophrase A single word used to represent a whole phrase or sentence in early child language. A holophrase is often employed in conjunction with extralinguistic means such as a gesture. It represents a highly effective way of utilizing the resources available. E.g. the use of *nana* to mean 'I want a banana'. The importance for pragmatics is that the phenomenon shows that young children intend to communicate more than what they can express linguistically.

homography, homograph A variant of *homonymy. Homographs are lexical items that are the same in written form, i.e. spelt in the same way, but are different in sound. They generate lexical ambiguity in written language. E.g. the relation between *lead* 'metal' and *lead* 'a long piece of leather etc. for holding a dog' is homography. *See also* homophony.

homonymy, homonym The phenomenon of different lexical items having the same linguistic form. In such a case, the meanings of the lexical items must be different and unrelated. E.g. the relation between $bank_1$ 'financial institution' and $bank_2$ 'sloping side of a river'. The two *banks* are called **homonyms**. There are two varieties of homonymy: **homograph** and **homophony**. From a different perspective, another two types of homonymy can be identified: **absolute** and **partial homonymy**. Absolute homonyms must satisfy three conditions. First, their forms must be unrelated in meaning. Secondly, all their forms must be identical. Thirdly, identical forms must be syntactically equivalent. $Sole_1$ 'bottom of a shoe' and $sole_2$ 'kind of fish' are an instance of absolute homonymy. Partial homonymy is homonymous, but not absolutely so, as in the relation between the adjective *last* and the verb *last*. See Lyons (1995). Often contrasts with **polysemy**. *See also* homophony; homography.

homonymy blocking *Blocking of a lexical expression by another homonymous/homophonous but distinct lexical expression. E.g. *liver* 'inner organ' blocks **liver* 'someone who lives'. Contrasts with **synonymy blocking**.

homophony, homophone A variant of *homonymy. Homophones are lexical items that are the same in sound, i.e. pronounced in the same way, but are spelt differently. They give rise to lexical ambiguity in spoken language. E.g. the relation between *site* and *sight* is an instance of homophony. *See also* homonymy; homography.

honesty *See* principle of honesty.

honorific A grammatical or lexical form that is used as a sign of *deference, especially in relation to someone who is of higher social status. E.g. the avoidance of the use of a second-person pronoun, and the use instead of a professional title, kinship term, or a combination of a kinship term and an honorific ending to address a superior in languages such as Dzongkha, Korean, and Japanese. A common distinction is made between **referent**, **addressee**, and **bystander honorific**. The system of honorifics constitutes an integrated component of the politeness aspect of language use. Also called an **honorific form**.

honorific register A model of sociopragmatic conduct that treats certain behaviours, including the use of honorific forms, as stereotypically indicative of *deference (1). See Agha (2010).

Horn scale Named after the American linguist Laurence Horn. A Horn scale contains a set of linguistic alternates such that a semantically strong linguistic expression unilaterally entails the semantically weaker ones. All the linguistic alternates in the set should be of the same word class, from the same register, and about the same semantic relation. E.g. <boiling, hot, warm>. There are two types of Horn scale: **positive Horn scale** and **negative Horn scale**. The use of a semantically weak linguistic expression in a Horn scale gives rise to a $Q_{\text{-scalar}}$ implicature. Also called a **scalar scale**, **Q-scale**, or **$Q_{\text{-scalar}}$ scale**. See Huang (2010). *See also* Hirschberg scale; rank.

humanness empathy hierarchy A scale which states that it is easiest for a speaker to empathize with a human; next easiest, with a non-human animate entity; and next easiest, with an inanimate entity. In other words, E (human) > E (non-human animate) > E (inanimate). See Kuno (2004). *See also* topic empathy hierarchy; speech act empathy hierarchy; surface structure empathy hierarchy.

humiliative form A type of *honorific or *polite form. It refers to any linguistic form including lexical items that a speaker uses to humble him- or herself, his or her relatives, etc. in order to show *deference (1) to the addressee. E.g. the use of *hanshe* '(my) humble hut' as opposed to *guifu* '(your) honourable residence' in Chinese. Also called a **humbling form**. Contrasts with a **deferential form**.

humour A non-literal use of language which involves (stylistic) incongruity derived from linguistic constructions or the events described. In other words, humour can be seen as arising from the perception of two opposite concepts that co-occur in the same discourse. If it is based on linguistic constructions, the incongruity can operate at any level of language or discourse. Humour is considered to be universal. Its use may violate or exploit pragmatic principles such as the British philosopher H. P. Grice's *co-operative principle.

hypallage A *figure of speech in which a linguistic expression is syntactically linked with one linguistic expression but is semantically or pragmatically more naturally related to some other linguistic expression. E.g. *the opposition leader's angry speech*, where *angry* syntactically goes with *speech* but semantically and/or pragmatically it is the leader who was angry.

hyperbole A *figure of speech in which something is deliberately exaggerated by being made to sound e.g. better, more exciting, and more dangerous, to increase impact or to attract attention. The exaggeration may be positive or negative. E.g. *That woman never stops nagging!* As an instance of *figurative (non-literal) use of language, hyperbole has been a subject of study in pragmatics. In *Gricean pragmatics, it is considered to be a violation or exploitation of the British philosopher H. P. Grice's first sub-maxim of Quality. For some scholars, hyperbole can be divided into two types: **lexical** and **propositional hyperbole**. In lexical hyperbole, the exaggeration can be attributed to a particular lexical expression. E.g. *That woman*... By contrast, in a propositional hyperbole, the exaggeration cannot be ascribed to a particular lexical expression. Rather, the whole proposition expresses an overstatement. E.g. *If this had happened earlier in his career, Gordon would definitely have resigned.* Also known as an **overstatement** or **exaggeration**. *See also* meiosis.

hyponymy, hyponym An asymmetrical sense relation between two or more lexical items such as *stallion* and *horse*. The relation is usually defined as one of inclusion, but it can be examined from two distinct perspectives. Looked at from the intensional point of view, the meaning of *stallion* includes that of *horse*. By contrast, in extensional terms, the category of horses includes that of stallions. The term for the inclusive category, e.g. *horse*, is called the **hyper(o)nym** or **superordinate**, and the term for the included, e.g. *stallion*, is known as the **hyponym**. Hyponyms of the same hyperonym or superordinate, e.g. *stallion*, *mare*, and *colt*, are called the **co-hyponyms**. *See also* meronymy.

hypothesis *See* inference to the best explanation.

hypothetical conditional = counterfactual conditional.

I

i-content (of what is said) *See* what is said.

I-heuristic *See* I-principle.

I-implicature Also known as **informativeness-implicature** or **informative implicature**. A neo-Gricean *conversational implicature that is derived via the operation of the *I-principle. E.g. the uttering of the sentence *If you let me see the manuscript, I'll make a donation to the library* generates the I-implicature that if and only if the addressee lets the speaker see the manuscript will the speaker make a donation to the library. Also called **I-inference**. See Levinson (2000); Huang (2010a). *See also* Q-implicature; M-implicature.

I-language Also known as **Internalized language** A term introduced by the American linguist Noam Chomsky in the mid-1980s to refer to the system of knowledge of language ('*competence') seen as internalized in the brain/mind of a native speaker. Contrasts with **E-language**.

I-principle Also known as the **informativeness-principle** or **informative-principle**. One of the three *neo-Gricean pragmatic principles proposed by the American philosopher Jay Atlas and the British linguist Stephen Levinson. 'I' stands for 'informativeness'. The I-principle has two sides: a speaker's maxim, by which a speaker is expected not to say more than is required, and a recipient's corollary, which allows an addressee to I-implicate that what is generally said is stereotypically exemplified. In other words, given the I-principle, the use of a semantically general linguistic expression I-implicates a semantically more specific interpretation. E.g. the uttering of the sentence *John and Mary bought an apartment in Paris* gives rise to the I-implicature that John and Mary bought an apartment in Paris together. The I-principle is sometimes recast as the **I-heuristic** in the form of 'Speaker: Do not say more than is required. Addressee: What is generally said is stereotypically and specifically exemplified.' See Levinson (2000); Huang (2007; 2010a). *See also* R-principle (1); Q-principle; M-principle.

IAP = illocutionary act potential.

iconicity, iconic A relationship between semantic and/or conceptual notions that is represented or reflected in the formal patterns of a language. Some *pragmatic principles can be recast in terms of iconicity. E.g. the British philosopher H. P. Grice's fourth sub-maxim of manner (Be orderly). By this sub-maxim, a speaker is expected to arrange events in the order in which they take place and the addressee is expected to draw an inference in such a way. In other words, the ordering of the linguistic elements is expected to reflect iconically that of the events. In contrast, by **anti-iconicity** is meant such semantic and/ or conceptual relations that are not reflected in the formal patterns of a language by which they are realised. E.g. an unmarked linguistic form is used to express a marked meaning, and a marked linguistic form is associated with an unmarked interpretation. The term 'iconicity' originated with the American philosopher Charles Peirce's theory of signs, but is now used largely independently in linguistics and pragmatics.

ideal language philosophy A term used by the French philosopher François Recanati by analogy with **ordinary language philosophy**. Ideal language philosophy is a loosely structured school of thought or movement within *analytic(al) philosophy, whose central ideas were originated with the philosophers Gottlob Frege, Alfred Tarski, Bertrand Russell, and the early Ludwig Wittgenstein. The philosophers involved were primarily interested in the study of the logical system of artificial language. However, the partially successful application of its theory and methodology to natural language in the 1950s and 1960s by followers of the movement such as the American logician Richard Montague, the British philosopher David Donaldson, and the American philosopher David Lewis led to the development of today's *formal semantics. Often contrasted with **ordinary language philosophy**. *See also* system perspective.

idealist theory (of truth) *See* coherence theory (of truth).

ideational theory (of meaning) *See* mentalistic theory (of meaning).

identical constituent compounding *See* lexical cloning.

identity of reference anaphora An anaphoric relation in which the anaphoric expression and its antecedent have identical *reference. E.g. the relation between *he* and *John* in *John*$_1$ *said that he*$_1$ *was a music lover*. Contrasts with **identity of sense anaphora**. *See also* coreferential anaphora.

identity of sense anaphora In opposition to **identity of reference anaphora**, the term refers to an anaphoric relation in which the anaphoric expression and its antecedent are related in terms of *sense. E.g. the anaphoric relation between the zero anaphor Ø and *favourite composer of the Baroque era* in *John's favourite composer of the Baroque era is Bach, but Bill's Ø is Handel*. *See also* non-coreferential anaphora.

idiom Also called an **idiomatic expression**. A formulaic or set expression in which two or more words are syntactically related, but where the overall meaning of the expression is not given as a function of the meanings of its individual constituents. In other words, a prototypical idiom has two characteristics: it is syntactically fixed or frozen, and it is non-compositional. E.g. *let the cat out of the bag*. In cognitive linguistics, four pairs of contrast have been identified: (i) **decoding** vs. **encoding idioms**, (ii) **grammatical** vs.

extragrammatical idioms, (iii) **substantive** vs. **formal idioms**, and (iv) ***idioms with pragmatic point** vs. **idioms without pragmatic point**. Idioms have been extensively studied especially in *cognitive, *experimental, and *clinical pragmatics. *See also* formula.

Idiom Comprehension Test A test deployed in *clinical pragmatics to examine patients' ability to understand idioms. It has been used with aphasic, schizophrenic, and depressive patients, patients with learning disabilities and communication disorders, and patients with probable early Alzheimer's disease.

idiom model (of indirect speech act interpretation) A model which assumes that an *indirect speech act is interpreted as an idiom that does not involve any *inference. Thus, for a sentence like *Can you pass the salt?* the request interpretation is seen as constituting a speech act idiom, and the uttering of the sentence is simply recognized as performing a speech act of requesting with no speech act of questioning being perceived. Contrasts with the **inferential model** (of indirect speech act interpretation).

idiom with pragmatic point An idiomatic expression that serves a clear pragmatic function. E.g. *How are you?* used in a greeting. By contrast, an **idiom without pragmatic point** is one that is pragmatically neutral and can be used in any context of utterance. E.g. *on the whole.* See Evans (2007).

idiomatic expression *See* idiom.

idiomaticity *See* maxim of idiomaticity.

iff Used in logic for 'if and only if'.

IFID = illocutionary force indicating device

IIN = invited inference.

IITSC = Invited Inference Theory of Semantic Change.

illocutionary act A concept developed by the British philosopher J. L. Austin for one of the three types of *speech act simultaneously performed by a speaker when he or she says something. An illocutionary act is an act or action intended to be performed by a speaker in uttering a linguistic expression, by virtue of the conventional force associated with it, either explicitly or implicitly. In other words, an illocutionary act refers to the type of function a speaker intends to fulfil or the type of action he or she intends to accomplish in the course of producing an utterance. It is an act accomplished in speaking and defined within a system of social conventions. Thus, if John says to Mary *Pass me the glasses, please,* he performs the illocutionary act of requesting or ordering Mary to hand the glasses over to him. The functions or actions just mentioned are also referred to as the **illocutionary force** or **illocutionary point** of the speech act. The illocutionary force of a speech act is the effect a speech act is intended to have by a speaker. Indeed, the term 'speech act' in its narrow sense is often taken to refer specifically to illocutionary act. Also known as **illocution**. See Austin (1962); Huang (2007). *See also* locutionary act; perlocutionary act; explicit illocutionary act; direct illocutionary act; literal illocutionary act; direct illocution.

illocutionary act potential (IAP) A view put forward by the American philosopher William Alston. According to this view, given the conventions of the language, a declarative sentence, when uttered, has the potential of performing a range of *illocutionary acts but not others. What particular illocutionary act is produced depends on particular circumstances and *contexts. Thus, in uttering the sentence *The baby spilled the milk over the table*, a speaker can be said to be performing a range of illocutionary acts such as asserting, admitting, and requesting. But in a specific situation, the illocutionary act the speaker intends to perform may be that of requesting. In other words, according to Alston, the meaning of a sentence consists in its having a single illocutionary act potential that is closely and conventionally associated with its form. On this view, to know what a sentence means is to know what range of illocutionary acts it can conventionally be used to perform. See Alston (1994); Sadock (2004). *See also* indirect speech act.

illocutionary denegation An act to deny a certain *illocutionary force. E.g. the uttering of the sentence *I don't promise to come* indicates that the speaker is not undertaking the illocutionary act of promising. Illocutionary denegation can be achieved by the negation of a *performative verb, as in the above example, or by the use of a *performative verb of denegation. See Searle and Vanderveken (1985).

illocutionary force *See* illocutionary act.

illocutionary force hedge *See* performative hedge.

illocutionary force indicating device (IFID) A linguistic device used to convey an illocutionary force, the most direct and conventional type of which is an explicit performative, as in *I hereby pronounce you man and wife*.

illocutionary metonymy *See* metonymy.

illocutionary point *See* illocutionary act.

illocutionary verb A type of *content-descriptive speech act verb that names the illocutionary act it performs. E.g. *announce, suggest*, and *promise*. *See also* performative verb; locutionary verb; perlocutionary verb.

illocutionary verb fallacy The thesis that performativity is associated with the *performative verb overtly represented in an utterance.

illocutionary type *See* speech act type.

immediate inference A term in traditional logic for an *inference in which a conclusion is drawn from a single premise. E.g. the move from 'Every Nobel laureate is a genius' to 'No Nobel laureate is not a genius'. Contrasts with **mediate inference**.

implicate *See* implicature.

im-plicate *See* im-plicature.

implicated conclusion *See* r-implicature.

implicated premise *See* r-implicature.

implication A logical relation such that, if *p* is true, the *q* is also true. Commonly written as $p \rightarrow q$.

implicational universal (for logocentric predicates) *See* logocentric predicate.

implicative predicate A predicate such as *forget*, *manage*, and *happen*, the use of which will engender a *presupposition. E.g. the use of the implicative verb *manage* in *Gordon didn't manage to give up gambling* triggers the presupposition that Gordon tried to give up gambling.

***implicatum* (pl. *implicata*)** Latin for 'what is implicated' or '*implicature'. The term is due to the British philosopher H. P. Grice. Nowadays the term 'implicature' is used more commonly than '*implicatum*'.

implicature **1.** A concept originally developed by the British philosopher H. P. Grice, though some proto-Gricean ideas can be traced back at least to the rhetorical tradition in ancient Greek thought. Some of these ideas were later reiterated by the 19th-century British philosophers John Stuart Mill and Augustus De Morgan and the German philosopher, mathematician, and logician Gottlob Frege. An implicature is what a speaker intends to mean beyond what he or she strictly says. Thus, in the following conversation: John: *How about going out to play football?* Bill: *It's snowing heavily*, Bill's utterance may **implicate** that he and John can't play football outside. A distinction is made between **conversational implicature** and **conventional implicature**. Also termed **what is implicated** in contrast to **what is said**. **2.** = conversational implicature. See Grice (1989); Huang (2010d). *See also* explicature; impliciture; additive implicature; subtractive implicature; audience implicature; politeness implicature; impoliteness implicature; sentence implicature; embedded implicature; nonce implicature; short-circuited implicature; alienable possession implicature; inalienable possession implicature; direct implicature; indirect implicature; scalar implicature; non-conventional implicature; Q-implicature; I-implicature; M-implicature; R-implicature; r-implicature; im-plicature; conventionalized implicature.

im-plicature The British linguist Gerald Gazdar's technical term for a potential *conversational implicature or **potential implicature**, i.e. a conversational implicature the uttering of a sentence could possibly give rise to prior to cancellation. E.g. if someone utters the sentence The *Americans and the Russians tested an atom bomb in 1962*, he or she would **im-plicate**, i.e. generate the potential conversational implicature that the Americans and the Russians tested an atom bomb in 1962 together. However, this potential conversational implicature will then be defeated by real-world knowledge. If a potential conversational implicature is not cancelled, it will become an actual conversational implicature or an **actual implicature**.

implicature theory (IT) A term used to refer to the classic Gricean position that apart from the role played by pragmatics to identify reference, fix deixis, and resolve ambiguity, all other pragmatic contributions to speaker meaning belong to what is conversationally implicated. This is in contrast to the version of **truth-conditional pragmatics (TCP)** advocated by the French philosopher François Recanati, in which much of what is implicated in the Gricean sense is placed on the side of what is said, i.e. the proposition expressed.

implicature trigger Any linguistic expression the use of which engenders an implicature. E.g. given stereotypical assumptions, the use of *secretary* in *The principal's secretary likes to take a summer break* triggers the conversational implicature that the principal's female secretary likes to take a summer break. There are two types of implicature trigger: **conversational implicature trigger** and **conventional implicature trigger**.

implicit content *See* explicature; r-implicature.

implicit defeasibility *See* defeasibility.

implicit performative A *performative which does not contain any *performative verb that makes explicit what kind of speech act is being performed. E.g. *I'll come to your seminar tomorrow*. Also called a **primary performative** by the British philosopher J. L. Austin. Contrasted with an **explicit performative**.

implicit qualification A type of sentence non-literality pointed out by the American philosopher Kent Bach, in which a sentence contains a qualification that is not explicitly expressed. E.g. the implicit qualification of *All birds can fly* is something like [except ostriches, penguins, etc.].

implicit quantifier domain A type of sentence non-literality observed by the American philosopher Kent Bach in which *expansion is needed to make explicit what the quantifier domain is. Thus, for a sentence like *Everyone was touched by* Captain Corelli's Mandolin, a quantifier domain such as [who went to see the film] may need to be added to represent the contextual meaning of the sentence.

impliciture A term coined by the American philosopher Kent Bach by analogy with the British philosopher H. P. Grice's notion of implicature. An impliciture is a pragmatically enriched proposition of *what is said. It accounts for aspects of what has to be understood in a context that is neither what is said nor what is implicated (*see* implicature). In other words, it is a third category of speaker meaning that is implicit in what is said and that is intermediate between what is said and what is implicated. It thus contributes to the implicit *completion and/or *expansion of the proposition expressed by a sentence. E.g. one of the implicitures for *John is too young* may, in an appropriate context, be 'to vote', so the proposition expressed by the sentence can be completed to become 'John is too young to vote'. Also called a **conversational impliciture** in opposition to Grice's term '**conversational implicature**'. See Bach (1994); Huang (2010e). *See also* explicature.

impoliteness Any *face-aggravating behaviour relevant to a particular context. For some scholars, impoliteness has to be intentional (on the part of the speaker), and has to be perceived or constructed as intentional (on the part of the addressee). For others, intentions play no part in impoliteness. If intentions and recognition of intentions are involved, then **rudeness** rather than impoliteness occurs. More recently impoliteness has been classified into three types: (i) **affective**, (ii) **coercive,** and (iii) **entertaining impoliteness**. Defined in such a way, the notion of impoliteness here is that of a ***second-order impoliteness**. See Culpeper (2011). Contrasts with **politeness**. *See also* instrumental impoliteness; mock impoliteness; off-record impoliteness; on-record impoliteness; negative impoliteness; positive impoliteness.

impoliteness 1 *See* first-order impoliteness.

impoliteness 2 *See* second-order impoliteness.

impoliteness implicature A term employed by the Australian linguist Michael Haugh for a *conversational implicature that engenders *impoliteness. In other words, by virtue of implying something, a speaker expresses impoliteness. Contrasted with **polite implicature**. See Haugh (2011).

impoliteness theory The term is employed to refer to a number of recent investigations that focus on impolite behaviours in linguistic interactions that are argumentative, conflictual, and/or hostile. In linguistic exchanges of this type, interlocutors may deliberately perform a *face-threatening act to damage each other's *face. Key research themes that have figured prominently in impoliteness studies include (i) when and how impoliteness is prompted, (ii) how impolite acts are sequenced in a particular interaction, (iii) how arguments and other kinds of conflict progress, and (iv) how impoliteness can be solved. See Bousfield and Locher (2008); Chapman (2011). Contrasted with **politeness theory**.

improper definite description *See* incomplete definite description.

impure deixis A term used by the British linguist Sir John Lyons for a linguistic expression whose meaning is partly deictic and partly non-deictic. E.g. *that person* in *Who's that person?* Contrasts with **pure deixis**. *See also* deictic expression.

impure textual deixis A term employed by the British linguist Sir John Lyons to refer to the use of an anaphoric and/or deictic expression whose function seems to fall somewhere between anaphora and textual deixis. E.g. the use of *that* in A: *Sue has a police cadet boyfriend.* B: *That's not true* is strictly speaking neither anaphoric nor textual-deictic but falls somewhat in between. By contrast, if a deictic expression is used within some utterance to point purely to the current, preceding, or following utterances in the same text, it is called **pure textual deixis**.

inalienable possession implicature A *conversational implicature that stems from the use of an indefinite expression which denotes inalienable possession. E.g. the uttering of *John cut a finger* invites the conversational implicature that the finger in question was John's own finger. This is because fingers are inalienable possessions of a person. Contrasted with an **alienable possession implicature**.

incidental face damage Any harm to *face that is not intended by the speaker and is perceived by the addressee as unintentional on the part of the speaker. Incidental face damage is thus an unplanned by-product of the interaction. Contrasts with **accidental face damage (1)** and **intentional face damage**.

inclusive disjunction *See* disjunction.

inclusive person A type of plural first-person marking, which means 'we-inclusive-of-addressee'. In other words, inclusive person refers to the speaker plus at least one addressee. E.g. *aapNe* in Gujarati, *kita* in Malay, and *nuy* in Zayse. Occasionally, inclusive person applies also to second-person plural, which means 'you-inclusive-of-speaker'. Two subtypes of inclusive person can be identified: **minimal** and **augmented inclusive person**. Contrasted with **exclusive person**.

incompatibility, incompatible A type of *lexical oppositeness. It refers to the sense relation between lexical items in a set that are mutually exclusive. In other words, the choice of one lexical item excludes the use of all the other lexical items in that set. E.g. the meaning relation between *table* and *chair* in the furniture set: if something is a table it cannot be a chair, and vice versa. In neo-Gricean lexical pragmatics, the use of incompatibles is analysed as generating a weak, unordered *Q-implicature. Also known as **multiple incompatibility**. *See also* antonymy (2); complementarity; directional oppositeness.

incomplete definite description A *definite description the descriptive part of which does not apply uniquely to the intended referent or anything else. E.g. *the window* in *The window is open*. Also called an **indefinite definite description**, **improper definite description**, or **pragmatic definite**. Generally speaking, there are two main approaches to incomplete definite description: the **expansion approach** and the **contraction approach**. In the former, an incomplete definite description is expanded in some way so as to become complete. E.g. *the window* is expanded to *the window of this bedroom*. By contrast, in the contraction approach, an incomplete definite description is required to apply uniquely only within the relevant *universe of discourse rather than the whole universe utilizing covert or hidden indexicals (*see* indexicalism). Alternative terms for the two approaches include the **explicit** vs. **implicit approach** and the **semantic** vs. **pragmatic approach**. Contrasts with a **complete definite description**. See Reimer and Bezuidenhout (2004); Abbot (2010).

incomplete predicate A term used in the philosophy of language and formal pragmatics and semantics to refer to a predicate that when combined with an NP in a certain way, forms a sentence that is not truth-conditionally evaluable, even relative to its context of use. E.g. *rain* in *It is raining*, *be ready* in *John is ready*, and *be nine o'clock* in *It's nine o'clock*. *See also* unarticulated constituent; under-articulation.

indefinite addressee A term coined by the American psycholinguists Herbert Clark and Thomas Carlson for an addressee who is not named but is encoded in terms of an indefinite pronoun like *anyone* and *someone*. E.g. *Anyone wanting to see the new photo* in John to David, Mary, and Sophia: *Anyone wanting to see the new photo, please come with me*, and *Someone* in *Someone move the chair, please*.

indefinite definite description *See* incomplete definite description.

indefinite description A subtype of indefinite NP such as *a musician*, *an American*, and *a certain town*. Sometimes an indefinite description can be ambiguous. E.g. *John wants to marry a Chinese* has two interpretations, one specific and the other non-specific. Contrasted with a **definite description**.

indefinite reference *Reference to an entity or set of entities, the identification of which is not known to the addressee. E.g. the indefinite NP *A young lady* in *A young lady was here looking for you a few minutes ago* refers to a person who may not be known to the address. Indefinite reference can further be divided into **specific indefinite reference** and **nonspecific indefinite reference**. In the former, the speaker has a specific entity in mind, as in the above example; in the latter, the speaker may not have a specific entity in mind, as in *My boyfriend will buy me something expensive for Christmas*. Contrasts with **definite reference**.

indeterminacy (1) A property of *conversational implicature. What it basically says is that in certain cases, the range of associated conversational implicatures engendered by the uttering of a sentence may be indeterminate. E.g. the uttering of *Bill's a machine* may give rise to a set of different conversational implicatures such as 'Bill is cold', 'Bill is efficient', and 'Bill has never stopped working'. Also called **pragmatic indeterminacy**. See Huang (2007). *See also* calculability; defeasibility; non-conventionality; non-detachability; reinforceability; universality.

indeterminacy (2) *See* underdetermination.

indexical A term used in the *philosophy of language for a *deictic expression such as *I*, *here*, and *now*. Indexicals are token reflexive, because they can be defined in terms of the locution 'this token', where the latter (reflexively) self-refers to the very token used. E.g. *I* can be defined in terms of 'the person who utters this token'. Also referred to as an **indexical expression** or **indexical form** and rather uncommonly as an **indicator word** or **indicator term**.

indexical *origo* *See* indexicality.

indexical pragmatics Pragmatics used to interpret a *context-sensitive expression such as an indexical.

indexical reference A term used in the *philosophy of language for *deictic reference.

indexical semantics The British linguist Sir John Lyons' term for *model-theoretic semantics.

indexicalism, indexicalist A term used by the French philosopher François Recanati for the position in the contemporary *philosophy of language and pragmatics and semantics according to which there is a role for the speaker's meaning to play in the determination of the *truth-conditional content of a sentence, but only when a slot is set up by the sentence itself to be pragmatically filled in its logical form. To this end, a range of '**covert**' or '**hidden indexicals**' is posited to provide syntactic triggers for the additional context sensitivity demanded by **indexicalists,** thus also called **hidden indexicalism, hidden indexicalist**. No top-down pragmatic influence is allowed to affect the truth-conditional content of the sentence. The position is represented by the work of the American philosopher Jason Stanley and his colleagues. See Recanati (2004). Indexicalism is considered to be a version of *moderate contextualism by *semantic minimalists, and a variety of *literalism by *contextualists.

indexicality A term used in the *philosophy of language for *deixis. But indexicality is both narrower and broader than deixis. It is narrower in the sense that it is sometimes restricted to such context sensitivity as affects the truth-condition of a sentence; it is broader in the sense that it sometimes also covers cases of *anaphora. The central anchorage point around which indexicality is organized is called '**indexical *origo***'.

indicative act A communicative act of indicating. A speaker's displaying his or her signals to others affords a good example of an indicative act.

indicator term The label given to **deixis** by the American sociologist Harvey Sacks, and an uncommon name for **indexical** in the philosophy of language.

indirect anaphora *See* bridging cross-reference anaphora.

indirect complaint *See* complaint.

indirect illocution *See* direct illocution.

indirect illocutionary act *See* direct illocutionary act.

indirect implicature The American philosopher Robert Harnish's term for a *conversational implicature$_F$.

indirect quotation test (IQ test) A test proposed by the American philosopher Kent Bach to decide on whether an element of a sentence is part of *what is said. According to this test, a constituent of a sentence is constitutive of what is said if and only if it can be straightforwardly embedded in an indirect quotation.

indirect refusal *See* refusal.

indirect request *See* request.

indirect speech The reporting of an actual utterance etc. with grammatical modification such as the adaption of deictic expressions to the point of view of the reporter. E.g. *John said that his examination results were neither good nor bad*. An alternative term is **reported speech**. In more technical writings, indirect speech is also known by its Latin name ***oratio obliqua***. Contrasted with **direct speech**.

indirect speech act (ISA) A *speech act whose *illocutionary force and sentence type are not directly matched. Thus, when an interrogative is used to make a request, as in *Can you turn down the TV a bit?*, we have an indirect speech act. Contrasts with a **direct speech act**. See Searle (1975).

indirectness The opposite of **directness**, especially avoiding saying what one means in a clear and obvious way. The concept is applied to the non-literal use of language, *speech act theory, and *conversation analysis. It has now been established, for example, that there is extensive cross-cultural and linguistic variation in directness/indirectness in the realization of speech acts, especially in face-threatening acts such as requests, complaints, and apologies.

induction, inductive A process of *reasoning or *inference from the particular to the general. In other words, an **inductive reasoning** or **inductive inference** can be characterized as one that moves from premises to conclusions supported in some way by the premises or rendered plausible in the light of them, but not deductively entailed by them. Contrasts with **deduction, deductive**. *See also* abduction.

inexplicit illocutionary act *See* explicit illocutionary act.

infelicitous utterance *See* felicitous utterance.

inferable anaphora *See* bridging cross reference anaphora.

inference As one of the basic forms of *reasoning, inference is a process of accepting a statement or proposition (called the **conclusion**) on the basis of the (possibly provisional) acceptance of one or more other statements or propositions (called the **premises**). It includes deduction, induction, and abduction. It also includes entailment, presupposition, and conversational implicature. Some inferences are logical in nature; others are non-logical. Inference plays an important role in pragmatics. See Huang (2011). See also ampliative inference; nonce inference; scalar inference.

inference system (of reference tracking) One of the four main types of *reference-tracking systems. In this pragmatic system, reference tracking is characterized by (i) the heavy use of *zero anaphora, (ii) the appeal to sociopragmatic devices such as the use of *honorifics, and (iii) the resorting to *pragmatic inference, hence the name. The inference system is particularly common in some East and Southeast Asian languages such as Chinese, Korean, and Thai. *See also* gender system (of reference tracking); switch-reference system (of reference tracking); switch-function system (of reference tracking). See Huang (2000a).

inference to stereotype A pragmatic enrichment to a stereotypical interpretation, be it social, cultural, political, racial, gender, etc. The *inference is taken as an *I-implicature within neo-Gricean pragmatics. E.g. the enrichment from *John's new friend is a nurse* to *John's new friend is a female nurse.*

inference to the best explanation A concept put forward by the American philosopher Gilbert Harman, though the idea can arguably be traced back to the American philosopher Charles Peirce. It refers to a process of drawing a conclusion on the grounds that it best explains one's premises. Also called **hypothesis**. *See also* abduction.

inferential A linguistic element that is used to indicate that what a speaker says is based on *inference rather than direct observation. E.g. schematically, *There INFERENTIAL was a full-scale public inquiry.*

inferential model (of communication) A model which dictates that communication is achieved by the expression and recognition of *intentions. That is to say, a communicator provides evidence of his or her intention to convey a certain meaning, which is then inferred by the audience on the basis of the evidence presented. The theoretical foundation of the inferential model is largely laid by the British philosopher H. P. Grice's original theory of *meaning$_{\text{-nn}}$. Many pragmatic theories of communication, including both the classical and neo-Gricean pragmatic theory and relevance theory, fall under this model. See Sperber and Wilson (1995); Huang (2007). Contrasts with the **code model** (of communication).

inferential model (of indirect speech act interpretation) A model which assumes that an *indirect speech act is interpreted via some kind of *inference either in terms of the British philosopher H. P. Grice's *conversational implicature including the American linguist Jerry Morgan's *short-circuited implicature or in terms of the American linguists David Gordon and George Lakoff's inference rule called *conversational postulates. Contrasted with the **idiom model** (of indirect speech act interpretation).

inferential pragmatic marker A *non-conceptual pragmatic marker that indicates a speaker's belief that there is an inferential relation between the two propositions of the sentence uttered. E.g. *so* in *Mary is taking Chinese cookery lessons. So her boyfriend has bought a wok for her.*

inferential pragmatics Pragmatics used to infer the conveyed meaning of a sentence or discourse. A typical example of inferential pragmatics is relevance theory.

inferentialism A variety of *pragmatism (1) and of the *use theory of meaning associated with the work of the American philosopher Robert Brandom. Inferentialism endeavours to explain meaning in terms of inferential rules rather than regularities of usage.

information flow Change in the status of information during language production and comprehension through time such as variations in the *givenness and newness of information throughout a discourse.

information focus *See* focus.

information module *See* competence module.

information structure The structure of a sentence or discourse viewed as a means of conveying information to an addressee. Described variously in terms of given vs. new information, given vs. old information, topic vs. comment, topic vs. focus, and theme vs. rheme, with regard to the intonational pattern by which these information units are marked. No theory of information structure can ignore pragmatics.

informational account (of discourse) A model of discourse interpretation in *computational pragmatics that pays special attention to the information conveyed explicitly or implicitly by the discourse. By contrast, the **intentional account** is one that concentrates on describing how a discourse realizes a speaker's *intentions or, more generally, his or her plans to achieve certain goals. Both models are needed for discourse interpretation. But for some scholars, the informational account should be embedded in the intentional one.

informational approach (to coherence) *See* coherence.

informative implicature *See* I-implicature.

informative intention A term used in relevance theory for an *intention to make a set of assumptions manifest or more manifest to an audience. Contrasts with **communicative intention (2)**.

Informativeness-heuristic *See* I-principle.

Informativeness-implicature *See* I-implicature.

Informativeness-principle *See* I-principle.

insensitive semantics A variety of *semantic minimalism in the contemporary philosophy of language and linguistic semantics and pragmatics, represented by work of the Norwegian philosopher Herman Cappelen and the American philosopher Ernest Lepore. Insensitive semantics takes the view that, apart from a very specific and limited set of linguistic expressions such as *I*, *foreigner*, and *local*, which are context-sensitive, all other linguistic expressions have constant meanings. The semantic meaning of a sentence expresses a complete truth-conditional proposition independently of contexts of use. In other words, semantics is 'insensitive' in that it operates independently of, or is not sensitive to, any features of contexts of utterance. Insensitive semantics is supplemented by Cappelen and Lepore's *speech act pluralism. See Cappelen and Lepore (2005). *See also* speech act pluralism; minimal semantics (2); radical semantic minimalism.

insertion sequence A term used in *conversation analysis to refer to a sequence that is inserted into another sequence, e.g. when one *adjacency pair is embedded within another, as in: Customer: *Can I have a bottle of red wine?* Shop assistant: *May I ask how old you are?* Customer: *Twenty-two*. Shop assistant: *Yes*.

instance topic A Chinese-style or pragmatic topic that represents an instance of the object about which a predication is made. E.g. 'this matter' in the Chinese topic–comment construction, schematically 'This matter, he is too serious'. *See also* frame topic; range topic.

instantiated pragmatic act (ipra) A term used by the Danish linguist Jacob Mey within the *Continental tradition of pragmatics for an individual *pragmatic act. It refers to a particular *pragmeme as its realization. E.g. the uttering of the sentence by an interviewer to a candidate at an job interview, *Could you please tell us why you've decided to apply for this post?* constitutes an instantiation of the pragmatic act of fishing for compliments. Also called **prac**. See Mey (2001). *See also* allopract.

institutional pragmatics An area of research in pragmatics which investigates the use of language in institutions and in an institutionalized context, such as courtroom interaction, job interviews, and police interrogations. See Roberts (2010). *See also* institutionalized speech act.

institutionalized speech act A *speech act that is heavily associated with rituals and is crucially dependent on elaborate extralinguistic institutions for its successful performance. Paradigmatic examples include declaring war, naming a building, and baptizing a child into the Christian faith. Institutionalized speech acts tend to be culturally specific. Also referred to as an **institutionalized**, **ritual**, or **ritualized performative**. *See also* declaration.

instructional pragmatics Pragmatics that is concerned with how to teach and learn pragmatics in language, especially second and/or foreign language, instruction. It constitutes part of and has close links with *applied, *cross-cultural, *interlanguage, and *second and/or foreign language pragmatics (*see* applied pragmatics). See Ishihara and Cohen (2010).

instrumental complaint *See* complaint.

instrumental impoliteness Impoliteness the main goal of which is to affect the target of it so that he or she acts in a certain setting-specific, linguistic or extralinguistic way. When it is successfully conveyed, it intends to impinge *negative face.

instrumental rationality *See* rationality.

intensifier A variety of *upgrader, by means of which one strengthens the proposition of a sentence uttered. E.g. *really* in *I'm really surprised that he has left his wife*.

intension, intensional In opposition to **extension**, intension refers to the property that defines a word or concept. E.g. the intension of the word *dog* is the property something must have in order to count as a dog.

intensional context = opaque context.

intensional verb *See* opaque context.

intention (1) The phenomenon of being in a mental state that is favourably directed towards doing something now or in the future. Defined thus, intention is both a feature of one's mind (as when one has an intention to act in a certain way) and a characteristic of one's action (as when one acts with a certain intention). On one dimension, intention can be divided into **prior**, **immediate**, **future intention**, and **action**, **aim**, and **motor intention**. On another, a distinction can be made between **collective** or ***we*-intention** and **individual** or ***I*-intention**. The concept of **communicative intention (1)** developed by the British philosopher H. P. Grice is of fundamental importance to pragmatics. *See also* intentionality. **(2)** = *communicative intention (1).

intention-based pragmatic semantics *See* pragmatic semantics.

intention-based pragmatics *See* Gricean pragmatics.

intention-based semantics *See* Gricean pragmatics.

intentional account (of discourse) *See* informational account (of discourse).

intentional approach (to coherence) *See* coherence.

intentional face damage Any *face attack that is intended by a speaker and is so perceived by the addressee. In other words, the face damage is planned and purposefully performed by the speaker and the speaker's intention to harm the addressee's face is recognized by the addressee. Contrasted with **incidental face damage**.

intentional theory (of reference) A theory that maintains that *reference is irreducibly intentional. In other words, the gap between reference and meaning can be bridged by the fact that when a speaker uses a referring expression, he or she has the intention of communicating about a particular entity or referent in his or her mind. The American philosopher Keith Donnellan is considered to be one of the leading proponents of this theory. Sometimes contrasts with the **causal theory** (of reference).

intentionalist pragmatics *See* Gricean pragmatics.

intentionalist semantics *See* Gricean pragmatics.

intentionality A term used in *the philosophy of mind and the *philosophy of language for the **directedness** or **aboutness** of mental acts or states, i.e. the semantic or meaningful relation between the mind and the world. Many if not all conscious mental acts or states such as beliefs, desires, dreams, expectations, wishes, wants, and thoughts are directed at objects. In other words, they are about things. Furthermore, the linguistic expressions we use to express these mental acts or states are also about things. The concept of intentionality is of paramount importance to pragmatics simply because intentional acts provides the meaning of linguistic expressions. Also known as **aboutness, directness**, and **representationality**. *See also* intention.

interactional level (of pragmatic analysis) *See* pragmatic analysis level.

interactional sociolinguistics A branch of macro-sociolinguistics particularly associated with the work of the American sociolinguist John Gumperz. It studies interactions among speakers in face-to-face communication, focusing on how interlocutors use language to define, reflect, maintain, refine, and develop social relationships. It overlaps with *conversation analysis and *sociopragmatics in areas such as turn-taking, forms of address, and politeness.

intercultural communication *See* cross-cultural communication.

intercultural pragmatics *See* cross-cultural pragmatics (1).

interest principle A pragmatic principle proposed by the British linguist Geoffrey Leech which dictates that in a conversation, participants should say what is unpredictable and new rather than what is predictable and old, thus making the conversation an interesting one.

interlanguage pragmatics An **interlanguage** is a stage on a continuum within a ruled-governed language system that is developed by second or foreign language (L2) learners on their path to acquiring the target language. This language system is intermediate between the learner's native language and his or her target language. It gives rise to the phenomenon of what the American psycholinguist Dan Slobin called 'first language thinking in second language speaking'. The notion of interlanguage was introduced by the American linguist Laurence Selinker. Interlanguage pragmatics is at the interface between pragmatics and second language acquisition. It studies how non-native speakers of a language acquire and develop their ability to understand and produce pragmatic features in a second language, i.e. an interlanguage. Central research topics include pragmatic awareness, pragmatic transfer, the development of pragmatic competence, speech act comprehension and production, and the relationship between second language grammar and pragmatics. The sub-branch of interlanguage pragmatics that investigates the empirical acquisition and development of pragmatic competence in children is called **developmental interlanguage pragmatics**. The best-studied interlanguage is that developed by speakers of English as a second language. Other interlanguages that have been investigated include Chinese, German, Hebrew, Japanese, and Spanish. See Kasper (2010).

intermediate context *See* global context.

internal compliment *See* compliment.

internalist theory (of meaning) *See* mentalistic theory (of meaning).

Internalized-language *See* I-language.

International Pragmatics Association (IPrA) Established in 1986, an international organization devoted to the study of pragmatics in the broad, European Continental sense. It has published the journal *Pragmatics* since 1991.

interpersonal meaning Meaning that pertains to the shaping of social relations such as the expression of one's personality, social role, etc. Interpersonal meaning constitutes a topic of inquiry especially in interpersonal and sociopragmatics.

interpersonal pragmatics A research area in pragmatics that concentrates on the interpersonal and relational aspects of language in use, especially how interlocutors utilize language to establish and maintain social relations, and how interactions between interlocutors both affect and are affected by their own and others' understanding of culture, society, etc. Central topics of inquiry include *face, *politeness/ *impoliteness, respect/deference, identity, gender, and mitigation. Interpersonal pragmatics overlaps with *socio- and *cultural pragmatics. See Locher and Graham (2010).

interpretive use *See* representation.

interpretively used representation *See* representation.

intersubjectivity, intersubjective *See* subjectivity, subjective.

intonational focus Any *focus that is marked by prominent pitch accent, commonly put in capitals when written. E.g. *JOHN* in A: *Who recommended Mary for the post?* B: *JOHN recommended her for the post.*

intrinsic frame (of spatial reference) A linguistic *frame of reference to express a spatial relation between a *figure and a ground. An intrinsic frame is an object-centred coordinate system, where the coordinates are determined by inherent features such as the sideness or facets of the object to be used as a ground. E.g. in *The dog is behind the car*, the sideness of the car is used to specify the spatial relation between the figure (the dog) and the ground (the car). See Levinson (2003). *See also* absolute frame (of spatial reference); relative frame (of spatial reference).

intrusive construction A term used by the British linguist Stephen Levinson to refer to a construction in which the *truth conditions of the whole depend partially on the *conversational implicatures of the parts. E.g. the truth-conditional content of the conditional construction *If the old king has died of a heart attack and a republic has been declared, John will be quite content* is dependent crucially on the generalized conversational implicature (GCI) stemming from the use of *and* to mean 'and then'. Other intrusive constructions include logical connective constructions such as comparatives, disjunctions, and *because*-clauses. See Levinson (2000). *See also* pragmatic intrusion.

intuition Introspective judgements (native) speakers have or may have about aspects including pragmatic aspects of their own language.

invisibility *See* visibility.

invisibility marker In contrast to a **visibility marker**, the term refers to any linguistic expression that is used to mark invisibility in the description of *space deixis. E.g. the suffix *-pa/pe* in Daga.

invisible-occlusion A type of invisibility in the description of *space deixis. It denotes the marking of entities that are behind an obstacle or inside a container. *See also* invisible-remote; invisible-periphery.

invisible-periphery A variety of invisibility in the description of *space deixis. It refers to the marking of entities that are out of sight but audible and/or olfactory, i.e. things that the deictic centre, typically the speaker, can hear and/or smell but cannot see. *See also* invisible-occlusion; invisible-remote.

invisible-remote A type of invisibility in the description of *space deixis. It refers to the marking of entities that are out of sight and far away from the deictic centre, typically the speaker. *See also* invisible-occlusion; invisible-periphery.

invited inference **1.** A term introduced by the American linguists Michael Geis and Arnold Zwicky for a class of *conversational implicature that arises from cases such as *conditional perfection, inclusive *or*, and inferred causation. This type of implicature is treated as an *I-implicature in neo-Gricean pragmatics. E.g. the uttering of the sentence *After a warm bath, Jane slept soundly* gives rise to the inference or implicature that taking a warm bath is a cause of or reason for Jane's sound sleep. **2.** A term used by the American linguist Elizabeth Traugott in *historical pragmatics for conversational implicature in general. On Traugott's view, the term is preferable to 'conversational implicature' because it reflects the dual role played by the speaker and the addressee in a dyadic speech event where the speaker strategically generates conversational implicatures and invites the addressee to infer a meaning. Accordingly, in Traugott's model, generalized conversational implicatures (GCIs) are restyled **generalized invited inferences (GIINs)**, and particularized conversational implicatures (PCIs) are renamed **invited inferences (IINs)**. Inferences of this type are invited because they are engendered by the context. See Traugott (2004).

Invited Inference Theory of Semantic Change (IITSC) An analysis developed by the American linguist Elizabeth Traugott in *historical pragmatics to account for the pragmatic factors involved in the regularities in semantic change leading to grammaticalization. The main claim of the theory is that form–meaning reanalysis is the outcome of situated language use. In other words, semantic change is largely usage-based in nature. The IITSC provides a step-by-step analysis of how pragmatic meanings develop, utilizing neo-Gricean pragmatic principles. Also called the **Invited Inferencing Theory of Semantic Change**. See Traugott (2004).

ipra *See* instantiated pragmatic act.

IPrA = International Pragmatics Association.

IQ test = indirect quotation test.

irony A figure of speech in which one thing is said but the opposite is meant by the speaker. E.g. *Stalin was a democratic leader!* The literal meaning of a linguistic expression that is used ironically typically echoes the words, thoughts, or views the speaker tacitly attributes to someone other than him- or herself at the time of speaking. Irony is used mainly to mock or ridicule. As a variety of *figurative (non-literal) use of language, irony has been the subject of extensive study in pragmatics. Also called **verbal irony**. In American English, the term **sarcasm** is sometimes used as a synonym for irony. In British English, sarcasm is often taken to be mocking or contemptuous irony.

irony principle A principle proposed by the British linguist Geoffrey Leech which states that if one has to cause offence, one should at least do it in a way that does not clash with what is required by the politeness principle, but allows the addressee to work out one's offensive point indirectly, by way of a *conversational implicature.

irreducibility thesis (of pure indexical) A term used in the philosophy of language for the view that in a direct speech, a *pure indexical such as *I* cannot be explained away by a coreferential expression without ruining the cognitive impact its use conveys. On the other hand, in indirect speech, the cognitive impact conveyed by the use of a pure indexical such as *I* can only be retained by a *quasi-indicator such as *he himself.*

irregular negation *See* metalinguistic negation.

ISA = indirect speech act.

IT = implicature theory.

iterative Any linguistic expression or device indicating repetition, the use of which usually gives rise to a *presupposition. E.g. the use of the iterative adverb *again* in *The boy cried wolf again* triggers the presupposition that the boy has cried wolf before.

J

joint speech act **1.** A term coined by the American psycholinguists Herbert Clark and Thomas Carlson to refer to a speech act that is performed by two or more people including addressees, who must intentionally coordinate their separate acts in order to achieve success. **2.** = collaborative performative. *See also* collaborative performative; group performative.

judicial act *See* verdictive.

jussive Verb forms or sentence types that are used to express a command. The term is encountered especially in the speech act theory. E.g. an imperative such as *Hands up! See also* command; mand.

K

kinesic hedge In contrast to a **verbal hedge**, the term refers to a *hedge that is encoded by kinesic means. E.g. the use of the raised eyebrow, the earnest frown, etc. to indicate the presence of a *face-threatening act, whose *illocutional force the speaker wants to soften. See Brown and Levinson (1987). *See also* prosodic hedge.

kinesics *See* gesture.

kinship-based request An 'exotic' *speech act of requesting that is found in the Australian aboriginal language Walmajarri. Based on kinship rights and obligations, this speech act conveys the message meaning roughly 'I request you to do X for me, and I expect you to do it simply because of how you are related to me'. Thus, for the speakers of Walmajarri, it is very difficult to refuse such a request. See Huang (2007).

kinship term Any term that is used to label personal relationships within a family. E.g. *grandfather*, *aunt*, and *daughter*. All human societies have the same family relationships, but different ones group and identify them in linguistically different ways. A system of oppositions among kinship terms in a given language and/or culture to express family relationships is known as the **kinship system**. Kinship terms are a topic of enquiry in *social deixis, and therefore are of interest to *sociopragmatics.

L

L-tense = linguistic tense.

L2 pragmatics = second and foreign language pragmatics (*see* applied pragmatics).

langage *See langue.*

language game A concept originating with the Austrian-born British philosopher Ludwig Wittgenstein, which gradually replaced his earlier **picture theory** of language. On Wittgenstein's view, 'the speaking of language is part of an activity, or a form of life'. Consequently, knowing the meaning of a word is to specify the language game or language games that constitute its 'logical home'. Language games are a complex of activities in which language is used. It is via language games that language is linked to reality. Wittgenstein's theory of language games has a profound impact on the development of the speech act theory in pragmatics.

language of thought *See* mentalese.

language shift A special case of **context shift**. Language shift involves the change of linguistic meaning under certain circumstances. Suppose both John and his addressee know that Mary is wrong about the use of the linguistic expression *plenary speaker* in that she misunderstands it as meaning *keynote speaker*. John then says, *Mary says Professor Lyons is the 'plenary speaker'*. In this case, the speaker does not use *plenary speaker* in its normal sense, but in the sense Mary uses the expression, where it means 'keynote speaker'. We thus have a language shift. *See also* context shift.

language sign *See* sign (2).

language user Any member of a speech community who, in using a language, endeavours to attain an interactional goal or goals.

langue A term borrowed from French and originally introduced by the Swiss linguist Ferdinand de Saussure. *Langue* is an abstract system of a language shared by a community of native speakers of that language. It is also conceived as a social fact or reality ('*fait social*'), held together tightly in a system that no individual speaker can change. The term stands in contrast to both ***langage*** (the phenomenon of language in general) and ***parole*** (the concrete, individual use of the abstract language system). *See also parole*; competence.

latched turn *See* adjacency pair.

latency, latent A latent expression is one which has to be recovered from the context if that expression is to be interpreted properly. E.g. the direct object of the verb *watch* in *The children are watching*.

law of abbreviation A principle proposed by the American linguist George Zipf, which postulates an inverse relation between a lexical item's frequency of use and its length: the more use, the shorter. E.g. from *pianoforte* to *piano*. Contrasts with Zipf's **principle of economic versatility**.

law of bivalence A principle in classical logic which states that every *proposition is either true or false. In other words, there are just two truth values a proposition may have. Also known as the **principle of bivalence**.

law of exhaustivity A pragmatic principle proposed by the French linguist Oswald Ducrot, which requires a speaker to provide his or her addressee with the strongest information. This principle is similar to the British philosopher H. P. Grice's first sub-maxim of *Quantity.

law of least effort *See* principle of least effort.

law of parsimony *See* Occam's razor.

Layered Discourse Representation Theory (LDRT) *See* Discourse Representation Theory.

'lazy' pronoun *See* pronoun of laziness.

LDRT = Layered Discourse Representation Theory.

least effort *See* principle of least effort.

left-dislocation *See* English-style topic construction.

legal pragmatics A research area in pragmatics. Originating in part from the work of the British philosopher J. L. Austin, legal pragmatics is concerned mainly with the study of legal documents and spoken legal discourse in the courtroom from a pragmatic point of view. Pragmatic features in written legal texts and spoken legal discourses that have been analysed include speech acts such as legal performatives, presuppositions, turn-taking, question–answer adjacency pairs, and silence. The sociopragmatic concepts of power and politeness have also been used in these studies. See Kurzon (2010).

Leibniz's Law *See* opaque context.

lexeme A grammatical entity in abstraction from the set of specific word forms it takes in specific syntactic environments. E.g. the verb 'work' in abstraction from the various word forms *work*, *works*, *worked*, and *working*. It is to lexemes rather than word forms that meaning is assigned, hence the term **lexical meaning**. Consequently, a lexeme is the basic unit of lexical semantics and lexical pragmatics.

lexical adjustment The pragmatic adjustment of *lexical meaning. E.g. when the sentence *How do you like our new secretary?* is used, the meaning of the word *secretary* in the sentence is pragmatically adjusted to 'female secretary'. There are two main types of lexical adjustment: **lexical narrowing** and **lexical broadening**. In its broad sense, the term may also cover adjustment of meaning in cases such as hyperbole, metaphor, and metonymy. Also called **lexical modulation**. See Huang (2009); Wilson and Carston (2007). *See also* lexical narrowing; lexical broadening.

lexical ambiguity *Ambiguity through the ascription of two or more (unrelated) meanings to a single word (in the sense of word form). E.g. *John went to the bank.* Here the word *bank* can be assigned two quite different interpretations: 'a financial institution' and 'a sloping side or margin of a river'. *See also* syntactic ambiguity; semantic scope ambiguity; pragmatic ambiguity; lexico-syntactic ambiguity.

lexical blocking *See* blocking.

lexical broadening One of the two main types of the pragmatic process of *lexical adjustment. The term refers to the phenomenon whereby the use of a word pragmatically conveys a more general meaning than the word's lexically encoded meaning. E.g. the use of *rectangle* in the sentence *There is a rectangle of lawn at the back of his house.* Here the rectangle is likely to be approximately rectangular, hence what is expressed is not the encoded concept RECTANGLE, but a broadened or loosened concept RECTANGLE*. Also referred to as **lexical loosening** or **lexical weakening**. See Huang (2009). Contrasts with **lexical narrowing**.

lexical cloning The phenomenon whereby there is a modifier reduplication of a lexical item. The reduplicated modifier is used to single out some privileged sense, in contrast to other senses, of an ambiguous, polysemous, or vague lexical expression. E.g. *late late* in *Honey, I'm sorry. Am I late late or just late?* The **lexical clone** *late late* means 'really late' here. Lexical cloning has been studied in neo-Gricean lexical pragmatics. Also called variously a **contrastive focus reduplication (CF-reduplication),** a **double construction**, and **identical constituent compounding**. See Huang (2009).

lexical decomposition *See* componential analysis.

lexical field theory (of word meaning) *See* structural semantics.

lexical hyperbole *See* hyperbole.

lexical meaning The meaning of a full lexical item or *lexeme such as a noun, a verb, or an adjective. E.g. the lexical meaning of the adjective *hectic* is 'very busy'. Often contrasted with **grammatical meaning**.

lexical modulation *See* lexical adjustment.

lexical narrowing One of the two main types of the pragmatic process of *lexical adjustment. It refers to the phenomenon whereby the use of a word pragmatically conveys a more specific meaning than the word's lexically encoded meaning. E.g. *drink* is used to mean 'alcoholic drink' in *I don't drink; milk* is used to mean 'cow's milk' in *John had a glass of milk for breakfast this morning*; and *smell* is used to mean 'stink' in *Something smells here!* Also known as **lexical strengthening**. See Huang (2009). Contrasted with **lexical broadening**.

lexical oppositeness, lexical opposite A sense relation in which lexical items have opposite meanings. E.g. the meaning relation between *hot* and *cold*. In other words, *hot* is a **lexical opposite** of *cold* and vice versa. Lexical oppositeness has four main types: (i) **incompatibility**, (ii) **complementarity**, (iii) **antonymy (2)**, and (iv) **directional oppositeness**. Also known traditionally as **antonymy, antonym (1)**. Contrasts with **synonymy, synonym**.

lexical pragmatics A newly emerged branch of pragmatics that makes a systematic study of aspects of meaning-related properties of lexical items that are dependent on or modified in language use, i.e. that part of *lexical meaning which is parasitic on, but is not part of, what is coded. E.g. the meaning of 'romantic' or 'sexual' arising from the use of *relationship* in *I don't know if John's already in a relationship*. Central topics of inquiry include *lexical adjustments including both lexical broadening and narrowing, *lexical cloning, and lexicalization asymmetry of logical operators. Lexical pragmatics is a hot pursuit of neo-Gricean pragmatics, bidirectional optimality-theoretic/theory pragmatics and relevance theory. See Huang (2009).

lexical pre-emption *See* blocking.

lexical presupposition trigger Any lexical item the use of which triggers a *presupposition. E.g. *know*, *stop*, and *again*.

lexical relation *See* sense relation.

lexical scale *See* semantic scale.

lexical semantics A subfield of semantics that is concerned with characterizing lexical or word meaning and lexical relations. Central topics include paradigmatic relations of meaning such as synonymy, antonymy (1), and hyponymy; syntagmatic relations of meaning; hierarchical relations of meaning such as hyponymy and meronymy; meaning change over time; and meaning extension such as metaphor and metonymy. *See also* lexical pragmatics.

lexical strengthening *See* lexical narrowing.

lexical underdetermination 1. *See* lexical underspecification. **2.** A term used by the American philosopher Kent Bach to refer to a case of semantic underdetermination whose source or locus is a lexical item. E.g. the underdetermination of *red as in red dress* and *red paint*.

lexical underspecification The view that every lexical item determines an unspecified representation. According to this view, a lexical item contains a single univocal, semantically broad sense with a set of defeasible pragmatic inferences. E.g. adjectives like *brown* used in *a brown cow/book/newspaper/crystal/paper bag/house/eye* are not treated as systematically ambiguous. Also referred to as **lexical underdetermination (1)**. See Blutner (2004).

lexical weakening *See* lexical broadening.

lexico-syntactic ambiguity *Ambiguity through both the ascription of multiple meanings to a single word (in the sense of word form); the assignment of different syntactic structures to a single string of words in a sentence. E.g. *The children saw her duck* is ambiguous. It can be understood either in the sense that the children saw her bird or as the manner that the children saw her lower her head. The ambiguity is lexical, because the two readings are associated with two different lexical meanings of the noun *duck* and the verb *duck*, and it is syntactic in the sense that the two interpretations are associated with two different grammatical structures.

linguistic act Any act performed by the utterance of a linguistic expression. E.g. the uttering of the sentence *Can't you cook the dinner?* constitutes a linguistic act. *See also* speech act.

linguistic action verb = speech act verb (1).

linguistic competence *See* competence.

linguistic context One of the main types of *context. Linguistic context refers to the preceding and following utterances and/or other linguistic units in a discourse or text. Also called a **context of utterance** or **co-text**. E.g. in the following conversation: John: *Who gave the waiter a large tip?* Mary: *Helen*, what has been mentioned in the previous discourse by John plays a crucial role in the understanding of the elliptical construction used by Mary. *See also* physical context; social context; general knowledge context.

linguistic direction principle A term used by the New Zealand-born linguist Robyn Carston for the principle which states that a pragmatically determined aspect of utterance meaning is part of *what is said if and only if it represents a case of *saturation, i.e. there is a slot or variable in the semantic representation of the sentence that has to be filled contextually.

linguistic impoliteness *See* impoliteness.

linguistic meaning *Meaning ascribed to a linguistic expression and/or construction such as a word, a phrase, or a sentence, abstracted away from any context of use. Also called **linguistically encoded meaning**.

linguistic performance *See* performance.

linguistic philosophy **1.** = the philosophy of language, but the emphasis is on the attempt to solve particular philosophical problems by studying the ordinary use of particular linguistic elements in a particular language. **2.** = analytic(al) philosophy. *See also* philosophy of language.

linguistic politeness *See* politeness.

linguistic pragmatics *See* pragmatics.

linguistic presumption (LP) A term used by the American philosophers Kent Bach and Robert Harnish for the general belief in a speech community that members in that speech community share the same language, and that whenever a member of that speech community says something to another member of the same speech community, he or she expects that the addressee will understand the language. Contrasts with the **communicative presumption (CP)**.

linguistic semantics *See* semantics.

linguistic sign *See* sign (2).

linguistic subjectivity *See* subjectivity.

linguistic tense *See* tense.

linguistic underdeterminacy thesis The view that the linguistically encoded meaning of a sentence radically underdetermines the proposition a speaker expresses when he or she utters that sentence. E.g. when one says: *I've got nothing to wear*, one would normally mean that one has nothing suitable to wear for a special occasion. See Huang (2007). *See also* underdetermination.

linguistically encoded meaning *See* linguistic meaning.

literal (meaning, sense, use) *See* figurative (sense, meaning, use, etc.).

literal force hypothesis The view that there is a direct structure–function correlation in *speech acts, and that sentence forms are by default direct reflexes of their underlying *illocutionary forces. The validity of the distinction between direct and indirect speech acts is dependent on that of the hypothesis. Also known as the **literal meaning hypothesis**. See Huang (2007).

literal illocutionary act An *illocutionary act that is performed literally, i.e. the performer of the illocutionary act means what the words he or she is using in performing that act means. By contrast, a **non-literal illocutionary act** is one that is not performed literally, i.e. the performer of the illocutionary act does not mean what the words he or she is using in performing that act means. E.g. one may say *I really admire your table manners* ironically to perform an indirect illocutionary act of, say, requesting the addressee to improve his or her table manners. See Bach (2004).

literal meaning Basic, usual meaning, i.e. meaning of a linguistic expression as determined solely by that of its component words or as (part of) what is said. Contrasts variously with **figurative meaning, metaphorical meaning**, or **what is implicated**. In the French philosopher François Recanati's theory, literal meaning is technically divided into **type-** or **T-literal, minimally** or **M-literal**, and **primary** or **P-literal meaning**. Type-literal meaning is meaning determined exclusively by linguistic conventions irrespective of context. By minimally literal meaning is meant meaning specified by type-literal meaning together with the aspects of context that are set by conventions, as in the fixing of an indexical. Primary literal meaning is meaning decided on by adjusting a minimally literal meaning to the utterance situation. The adjustment can be achieved in two ways: sense elaboration (enrichment) and sense extension (loosening). See Recanati (2004); Iglesias (2007). *See also* utterance meaning.

literal meaning hypothesis *See* literal force hypothesis.

literalism, literalist A term deployed by the French philosopher François Recanati for the broad approach in the contemporary philosophy of language and pragmatics and semantics, according to which, *truth-conditional content can legitimately be ascribed to a natural language sentence, independently of the *speech act the sentence is used to perform or what a speaker actually means in uttering the sentence. Contrasts with **contextualism, contextualist**. See Recanati (2005). *See also* semantic minimalism.

literary pragmatics The term can be best described as covering an area of research rather than a well-defined unified theory. Literary pragmatics represents a domain at the intersection of pragmatics, literary theory, and the philosophy of literature. It is the study of the use of linguistic forms in a literary text and the relationship between author, text, and reader in a sociocultural context from a pragmatic perspective, focusing on the question of what and how a literary text communicates. Two complementary aspects of literary pragmatics can be identified. On the one hand, how can the insights of pragmatic theories be employed for the study of literature? On the other, how can the insights of literary pragmatics contribute to general pragmatic theories? Literary pragmatics can further be divided into two sub-branches: **formalist** and **historical literary pragmatics**. See Pilkington (2010). *See also* pragmatic stylistics.

litotes = meiosis, especially by the 'ironic' use of a negative sentence. E.g. the uttering of *That wasn't a bad lecture* to mean it was a very good one.

'live' implicature *See* conventionalized implicature.

local accommodation *See* global accommodation.

local context *See* global context.

local deixis *See* space deixis.

local pragmatics A field primarily in *computational pragmatics that tackles problems which are posed within the scope of an individual sentence, though their solutions generally require greater context and real-world knowledge. Typical examples include resolving syntactic and lexical ambiguity, interpreting metonymy and metaphor, and determining reference. See Hobbs (2004).

local theory (of conversational implicature) A term used by the French linguist Anne Reboul to refer to the view that a *conversational implicature is a default inference engendered by a lexical trigger. It is accessed as soon as its trigger is met in the sentence uttered, i.e. at a local (subsentential) level. An advocate of such a view is called a **localist (1)**. The British linguist Stephen Levinson's theory of *generalized conversational implicature (GCI) is considered to be a stock example of a local theory. Contrasts with the **global theory**. See Reboul (2004). *See also* default inference theory (of scalar implicature).

localism The view that spatial expressions are grammatically and semantically more fundamental than non-spatial ones, and as such tend to extend into other linguistic domains. In the area of *deixis, localism amounts to saying that *spatial deictic expressions tend to be extended to other categories of deixis such as time, discourse and social deixis. A scholar who maintains the view is called a **localist (2)**. Also known as the **localist hypothesis**.

localist **1.** *See* local theory (of conversational implicature). **2.** *See* localism.

locational deixis *See* space deixis.

locution *See* locutionary act.

locutionary act A concept developed by the British philosopher J. L. Austin for one of the three types of *speech act simultaneously performed by a speaker when he or she says something. A locutionary act has to do with the simple act of a speaker saying something, i.e. the act of producing a meaningful linguistic expression. It consists of three sub-acts. They are (i) a **phonic act** of producing an utterance-inscription, (ii) a **phatic act** of composing a particular linguistic expression in a particular language, and (iii) a **rhetic act** of contextualizing the utterance-inscription. The first of these three sub-acts is concerned with the physical act of producing a certain sequence of vocal sounds (in the case of spoken language), which is also called a **phonetic act** or a set of written symbols (in the case of written language). The second refers to the act of constructing a well-formed string of sounds and/or symbols, be it a word, phrase, sentence, or discourse, in a particular language. These two sub-acts are grouped by the American philosopher John Searle as performing an **utterance act**. The third sub-act is responsible for tasks such as assigning reference, resolving deixis, and disambiguating the utterance-inscription. This is referred to as a **propositional act** by Searle. Thus, if John says to Mary, *Pass me the glasses, please*, meaning 'Hand the glasses over to me' with *me* referring to himself and *glasses* to spectacles, he performs the locutionary act of uttering the sentence *Pass me the glasses, please*. Also called **locution**. *See also* illocutionary act; perlocutionary act.

locutionary subjectivity *See* subjectivity.

locutionary verb A type of *content-descriptive speech act verb that describes the locutionary act. E.g. *define*, *describe*, and *refer*. *See also* illocutionary verb; perlocutionary verb.

logic The general science of *inference. Logic endeavours to make explicit the rules by which inference can be drawn rather than to study the actual human reasoning processes, which may or may not comply with these rules. Given that inference plays an important role in pragmatics, logic is relevant especially to *formal pragmatics. The two main systems of logic that are used in pragmatics and semantics are **propositional** and **predicate calculus**.

logic of conversation A term normally used to refer to the British philosopher H. P. Grice's theory of *conversational implicature.

logical atomism The view in the philosophy of language that there is a process of logical and philosophical analysis of language that ultimately terminates in 'atoms' of meaning, i.e. meaning elements which can specify the meaning of a linguistic expression independently of its relationship with other linguistic expressions in the language. The idea is advocated by the British philosopher Bertrand Russell and the Austrian-born British philosopher Ludwig Wittgenstein. *See also* holism.

logical constant A term used in *logic and sometimes in *formal semantics and pragmatics for the expressions that are considered to indicate the logical form of a sentence. While the exact membership of the set of logical constants is a matter of debate, it normally includes expressions for the truth functions: conjunctions (&), disjunctions (∨), implications (→), equivalence (↔); negation (~), the existential quantifier (∃); the universal quantifier (∀), and the identity relation (=). The parenthesis (( )), which indicates the scope of functions, may also be taken as logical constant. These expressions are also known as **logical** or **truth-functional operators** or **operators** for short.

logical empiricism = logical positivism

logical enrichment *See* strengthening.

logical form An informal representation of the structure of a sentence or proposition, shareable with other sentences or propositions, in terms related to those of formal logic. *See also* semantic representation.

logical inference An *inference that is logical in nature in the sense that it is monotonic, i.e. it is not *defeasible. A stock example is semantic entailments. Contrasts with **pragmatic inference**.

logical operator *See* logical constant; truth function, truth-functional.

logical positivism A movement in philosophy inspired by empiricism and verificationism, and developed by a group of philosophers, mathematicians, and physicists principally in Vienna between the 1920s and 1940s. The term is frequently applied in a vaguely opprobrious sense to *analytic(al) philosophy in general. One of the central doctrines of logical positivism is the *verification principle. According to this principle, the meaning of any statement is its method of verification by means of empirical observation, rejecting as meaningless many statements of religion, aesthetics, morality, literature, and metaphysics. It was against this philosophical background that the British philosopher J. L. Austin set about developing his theory of speech acts. Also known as **logical empiricism** and **scientific empiricism**.

logical semantics The study of natural language meaning by means of various systems of mathematical logic such as propositional calculus. Sometimes the term is also used to refer to **model-theoretic semantics**.

logocentric antecedent Any linguistic expression that can act as an antecedent for a *logophoric expression. Logocentric antecedents are usually constrained to be a core argument of the *logocentric predicate of the matrix clause. They are typically subjects. Also called a **logocentric trigger**.

logocentric complementizer A complementizer that can create a *logophoric domain. Logocentric complementizers are often homophonous with the verb 'say' and are frequently developed historically out of it. E.g. *be* in Ewe, *se* in Mundang, and *ga* in Tuburi.

logocentric licenser A linguistic expression that can create a *logophoric domain. Logocentric licensers are of two main types: **logocentric predicates** and **logocentric complementizers**.

logocentric predicate A predicate or verb that can establish a *logophoric domain. Logocentric predicates or **logocentric verbs** can largely be distinguished on a semantic basis. The most common types are predicates of speech 'say' and thought 'think'. But other types of predicate such as those of mental state 'be happy', knowledge 'know', and direct perception 'hear' can also trigger a logophoric domain. Cross-linguistically there is an **implicational universal** for logocentric predicates: speech predicates > epistemic predicates > psychological predicates > knowledge predicates > perceptive predicates. In other words, if a language allows, say, knowledge predicates to create a logophoric domain, then it will necessarily allow psychological, epistemic, and speech predicates to do the same. Also called a **logophoric verb**. See Huang (2000).

logocentric trigger *See* logocentric antecedent.

logophor, logophoric expression A linguistic expression that is used to encode *logophoricity. It includes (i) **logophoric pronouns**,

(ii) **logophoric addressee pronouns**, (iii) **logophoric cross-referencing**, (iv) **logophoric verbal affixes**, (v) **first-person logophoric marking**, and (vi) **long-distance reflexives**. E.g. *-ee* in Gokana is a logophor.

logophora = logophoricity.

logophoric addressee pronoun A special type of second-person pronoun that is used to mark *logophoricity. E.g. *gwar* in Mapun. The existence of logophoric addressee pronouns raises the issue of whether the logophoric complement should be seen as direct or indirect speech. *See also* logophoric pronoun; logophoric cross-referencing; first-person logophoric marking; logophoric verbal affix; long-distance reflexivization.

logophoric construction A construction in which *logophoricity is encoded morphologically and/or syntactically. Thus, schematically, *John said that LOG was happy*. Also called a **logophoric structure** or **logophoric sentence**.

logophoric cross-referencing A verbal form or affix that is used in a subordinate clause embedded under a logocentric predicate to mark logophoricity by indicating coreference with normally a subject in the matrix clause. Examples can be found in languages like Akɔɔse, Kaliko, and Moru. *See also* logophoric addressee pronoun; logophoric pronoun; first-person logophoric marking; logophoric verbal affix; long-distance reflexivization.

logophoric domain A sentence or stretch of discourse in which an internal protagonist's perspective is represented. The former constitutes a **sentential logophoric domain**. E.g. schematically, *John said that LOG is a taxi driver*. By contrast, the latter is called a **discourse logophoric domain**.

logophoric marking Marking of *logophoricity. Cross-linguistically, logophoricity can be morphologically and/or syntactically expressed or marked by one or more of the following mechanisms: (i) **logophoric pronouns**, (ii) **logophoric addressee pronouns**, (iii) **logophoric cross-referencing**, (iv) **logophoric verbal affixes**, (v) **first-person logophoric marking**, and (vi) **long-distance reflexives**.

logophoric pronoun A special type of pronoun that is used to encode *logophoricity. Logophoric pronouns may take free forms, as in Efik, or be cliticized to the verb, as in Ewe. They are particularly common in West African languages. E.g. *ye* in Mundani. *See also* logophoric addressee pronoun; logophoric cross-referencing; first-person logophoric marking; logophoric verbal affix; long-distance reflexives.

logophoric reference *See* logophoricity.

logophoric verb *See* logocentric predicate.

logophoric verbal affix A verb affix that is used to encode *logophoricity. E.g. *-ee* in Gokana. *See also* logophoric pronoun; logophoric addressee pronoun; logophoric cross-referencing, first-person logophoric marking; long-distance reflexives.

logophoricity The phenomenon whereby the perspective or *point of view of an internal protagonist of a sentence or discourse, as opposed to that of the current, external speaker, is being reported by utilizing some morphological and/or syntactic means. The technical term 'perspective' is intended to include words, thoughts, knowledge, emotion, perception, and space location. Logophoricity is commonly encoded by a logophor or logophoric expression. It is largely a pragmatic phenomenon. See Huang (2000). Also called **logophora** and **logophoric reference**.

long-distance reflexivization The phenomenon whereby a reflexive can have its antecedent outside its local syntactic domain. E.g. in Chinese, *ziji* 'self' can have its antecedent outside its embedded clause, as in schematically, *Xiaoming*$_1$ *think Xiaohua*$_2$ *love self*$_{1/2}$. A reflexive that can be used in such a way is called a **long-distance reflexive, long-range reflexive** or **long-distance anaphora**. Examples other than *ziji* in Chinese include *sig* 'self' in Icelandic, *zibun* 'self' in Japanese, and *aapan* 'self' in Marathi. Long-distance reflexives are commonly used to encode *emphasis/contrastiveness, *logophoricity, and **de se* ascription. They are given a pragmatic analysis in the *neo-Gricean pragmatic theory of anaphora. See Huang (2000). *See also* logophoric pronoun; logophoric addressee pronoun; logophoric verbal affix.

long-distance reflexivization language Any language that systematically allows a reflexive to have its antecedent outside its local syntactic domain. Chinese, Malay, and Russian are such languages. By contrast, any language that does not systematically license the use of a long-distance reflexive is a **non-long-distance reflexivization language**. One such language is English. See Huang (2000).

loose constative A statement-making utterance that may not be assessed strictly by means of *truth conditions. E.g. the Austinian example *France is hexagonal*.

loose use A term deployed in relevance theory for the use of one representation to represent another on the basis of a relation of non-literal resemblance. E.g. the use of the sentence *Holland is flat*. While this statement is not entirely false, it is not strictly speaking true, either, thus lying between literal and figurative use of language.

low-context culture *See* high-context culture.

LP = linguistic presumption.

lying A *speech act of saying something that the speaker knows is not true. This deliberate use of language as a tool demands an ability to deceive, and successful lying requires a person to have a *theory of mind. In recent years, lying has increasingly become a topic in pragmatics including the speech act theory, conversation analysis, neo-Gricean pragmatics, relevance theory, and developmental pragmatics.

M

M-heuristic *See* M-principle.

M-implicature Also called **Manner-implicature**. A neo-Gricean *conversational implicature that is derived via the operation of the *M-principle. E.g. in the following pair of sentences *John stopped the alarm* and *John caused the alarm to stop*, the uttering of the marked causative construction *John caused the alarm to stop* engenders the M-implicature that John didn't stop the alarm in the normal way. Also known as an **M-inference**. *See also* Q-implicature; I-implicature.

m-intention, m-intend The British philosopher H. P. Grice's term for a speaker's intention that the addressee recognizes his or her intention. 'M' stands for 'meaning'.

M-literal meaning = minimally *literal meaning.

M-principle Also known as the **Manner-principle**. One of the three *neo-Gricean pragmatic principles put forward by the British linguist Stephen Levinson. The M-principle operates primarily in terms of a set of alternates that contrast in form. It has two sides: a speaker's maxim, by which a speaker is expected not to use a marked linguistic expression without reason, and a recipient's corollary, which allows an addressee to infer that what is said in a marked way conveys a marked message. Thus, given the pair of the sentences *The tram comes frequently* and *The tram does not come infrequently*, the use of the marked double negative construction *The tram does not come infrequently* M-implicates that the tram comes less frequently than what the uttering of the unmarked *The tram comes frequently* would suggest. The M-principle is sometimes recast as the **M-heuristic** in the form of 'Speaker: Do not use a marked linguistic expression without reason. Addressee: What is said in a marked way is not unmarked'. See Levinson (2000); Huang (2007). *See also* R-principle (1); Q-principle (1); I-principle.

M-tense = metalinguistic *tense.

macro context A term used in *conversation analysis to refer to a context that lies outside the talk exchange in conversation, such as a conversational participant's age, sex, and social class. An alternative term for macro context is **distal context**. In contrast, by **micro context** is meant a context that is set up by the 'micro' domain of the talk exchange in conversation. More recently, it has been argued that context and talk shape each other in conversation. The distinction between macro and micro context is a controversial one. See Grundy (2000).

macropragmatics The systematic study of the use of language in all aspects. Macropragmatics includes e.g. computational, cross-cultural, and sociopragmatics. Often in contrast to **micropragmatics**.

mand An utterance by which a speaker attempts to get the addressee to do something. Paradigmatic cases include a command, demand, order and request. E.g. *Give your car a wash!*

Manichaeanism (in pragmatics) A term coined by the American linguist Laurence Horn for a dualistic model of pragmatic principles such as his own, in which there is a *Q-principle, and an *R-principle. Manichaeus or Manes was an ancient Persian teacher who advocated the doctrine, known as Manichaeanism, that the world is governed by a balance of the forces of good and evil.

manifestness, manifest A term used in relevance theory for the degree to which a person is capable of representing an assumption mentally and accepting that representation as true or probably true at a given time. However, the assumption in question does not in fact need to be true; a false assumption can also be treated as true. A set of assumptions manifest to a person at a given moment is called that person's **cognitive environment**, and a set of manifest assumptions shared by two or more persons is termed **mutual cognitive environment**. Every manifest assumption in a mutually cognitive environment is a **mutually manifest**. Construed thus, **mutual manifestness** plays a similar but perhaps weaker role than *mutual knowledge.

Manner hedge A type of *maxims of conversation hedge. It is oriented to the British philosopher H. P. Grice's *maxim of Manner. It is used to indicate that a speaker is opting out of the maxim, i.e. what he or she says, for example, may not be perspicuous. E.g. *I don't know if this is clear, but*... See also Quality hedge; Quantity hedge; Relation hedge.

Manner-heuristic *See* M-principle.

Manner-implicature *See* M-implicature.

Manner-inference *See* M-implicature.

Manner maxim *See* maxim of Manner.

Manner-principle *See* M-principle.

marked, markedness Any linguistic expression, unit, or construction that contains a feature or a value of a feature that is unpredicted or unexpected, i.e. derived, more complex, more special, unusual, less frequent, etc. In other words, a marked expression is one that is out of the ordinary. It can be formal, semantic, or distributional or a combination of any of these. By contrast, **unmarked** is not marked, i.e. not out of the ordinary. Within neo-Gricean pragmatics, the interpretation of an unmarked linguistic expression, unit, or construction is subject to the *I-principle, while that of a marked linguistic expression, unit, or construction falls under the *M-principle.

marked second part *See* dispreferred second turn.

massive modularity of mind thesis A version of the *modularity of mind thesis which takes the view that the human mind is largely, if not entirely, composed of *modules. The term 'massive modularity' was introduced by the French linguist Dan Sperber. Two forms of the massive modularity of mind thesis can then be identified. According to the **strong massive modularity of mind thesis**, the human mind does not contain any overarching general-purpose mechanism. In other words, every central process is modular. By contrast, the **weak massive modularity of mind thesis** maintains that while central processes are largely modular, there are also non-modular, general-purpose processes. The massive modularity of mind thesis is not, however, espoused by the American linguist Jerry Fodor. See Meini (2010).

master (cultural) script *See* *cultural script.

material implication A logical relation in which *p* materially implies *q* if it is not possible for *p* to be true and *q* false.

matrix wins hypothesis A hypothesis proposed by the British Chinese linguist Yan Huang which states that *conversational implicatures due to higher constructions may take precedence over those due to lower constructions, especially with regard to anaphora.

maxim of belief *See* maxim of Quality.

maxim of clarity *See* maxim of Manner.

maxim of evidence See maxim of Quality.

maxim of explicitness A sub-maxim of *Manner proposed by the Israeli linguist Tanya Reinhart, which requires a speaker to be as explicit as conditions permit.

maxim of idiomaticity A term introduced by the British Chinese linguist Yan Huang to refer to an additional *maxim of conversation put forward by the American philosopher John Searle. By this maxim, a speaker is expected to speak idiomatically unless there is some reason not to.

maxim of informativeness *See* maxim of Quantity.

maxim of Manner A super-*maxim of conversation propagated by the British philosopher H. P. Grice. According to this maxim, a speaker is expected to be perspicuous. Also called the **maxim of clarity**. There are four sub-maxims. The first sub-maxim dictates that a speaker should avoid obscurity. By the second sub-maxim, a speaker is expected to avoid ambiguity. The third enjoins a speaker to be brief. Finally, the fourth requires a speaker to be orderly. *See also* maxim of Quantity; maxim of Relation; maxim of Quality.

maxim of politeness **1.** Any general principle that directs a speaker to be polite. **2.** A principle of politeness proposed by the Greek linguist Alexandra Kallia, which requests a speaker to be appropriately polite in both form and content. It contains two attendant **sub-maxims of politeness**: (i) Do not be more polite than expected, and (ii) do not be less polite than expected. See Kallia (2004).

maxim of Quality A super-*maxim of conversation proposed by the British philosopher H. P. Grice, by which a speaker is expected to be truthful, hence also called the **maxim of truth** or **maxim of truthfulness**. The maxim consists of two sub-maxims. First, do not say what one believes to be false. This sub-maxim is also known as the **maxim of belief**. The second sub-maxim dictates that one should not say that for which one lacks adequate evidence. It is also referred to as the **maxim of evidence**. *See also* maxim of Quantity; maxim of Relation; maxim of Manner.

maxim of Quantity A super-*maxim of conversation put forward by the British philosopher H. P. Grice. Given this maxim, a speaker is expected not to say more or less than is required. Also called the **maxim of informativeness**. This maxim has two sub-maxims. First, do not say less than is required; secondly, do not say more than is required. *See also* maxim of Quality; maxim of Relation; maxim of Manner.

maxim of Quantity and Quality A maxim introduced by the American philosopher Robert Harnish, which collapses the British philosopher H. P. *Grice's *maxims of Quantity and Quality. What the principle dictates is that a speaker should make the strongest relevant claim justifiable by his or her evidence.

maxim of Relation A maxim of conversation postulated by the British philosopher H. P. Grice by which a speaker is expected not to be irrelevant. *See also* maxim of Quantity; maxim of Quality; maxim of Manner.

maxim of relativity A neo-Gricean principle proposed by the American philosopher Jay Atlas and the British linguist Stephen Levinson, which is a reformulation of the British philosopher H. P. Grice's *maxim of Quantity. It requires a speaker not to say what he or she believes to be highly non-controversial, and the addressee to take what he or she hears to be non-controversial to a low degree. *See also* interest principle.

maxim of strengthened belief A term used to refer to a strengthened version of the first sub-maxim of the British philosopher H. P. Grice's *maxim of Quality, namely not to say what one does not believe to be true.

maxim of strengthened evidence A term that is employed to refer to a strengthened version of the second sub-maxim of the British philosopher H. P. Grice's *maxim of Quality: not to say that for which one does not believe there is adequate evidence.

maxim of truth *See* maxim of Quality

maxim of truthfulness *See* maxim of Quality

maxims of conversation A term coined by the British philosopher H. P. Grice for the set of nine sub-principles of his *co-operative principle classified into four categories: the maxims of **Quality**, **Quantity**, **Relation**, and **Manner**. Together with the co-operative principle, the set of maxims of conversation ensures that in the process of communication, the right amount of information is provided, and that the interaction is conducted in a truthful, relevant, and perspicuous manner. Also called **conversational maxims**. See Grice (1989); Huang (2007).

maxims of conversation hedge A *hedge that is addressed to one or more of the British philosopher H. P. Grice's maxims of conversation. E.g. *I probably don't need to say this, but*... Four types of such hedge can be identified: **Quality**, **Quantity**, **Relation**, and **Manner hedge**. See Brown and Levinson (1987).

maxims of politeness A set of principles of *politeness proposed by the British linguist Geoffrey Leech. Some of the members of the set form a pair. This is the case for the *tact and *generosity maxims and the *approbation and *modesty maxims. Others, such as *agreement and *sympathy maxims, do not. More recently, Leech has preferred to use the term 'pragmatic constraint' over the term 'maxim'. See Leech (2007).

MCB = mutual contextual belief.

meaning What is conveyed or intended to be conveyed by a linguistic unit such as a word, sentence, and utterance. E.g. the sentence *I hate the Berlin Wall* is said to express the thought, judgement, or proposition 'I hate the Berlin Wall'. A distinction can be made between **word meaning** or **lexical meaning**, **sentence meaning**, and **utterance meaning**. Another distinction can be drawn between **propositional** and **non-propositional meaning**. See Lyons (1995). *See also* associative meaning; dictionary meaning; encyclopedic meaning; epistemic meaning; evaluative meaning; expressive meaning; interpersonal meaning; linguistic meaning; sentence meaning; utterance meaning.

meaning eliminativism (ME) A form, and perhaps the most radical form, of *contextualism. According to meaning eliminativism, the process of constructing or computing the contextual meaning of a linguistic expression on a particular occasion of use can proceed directly from the contextual meaning the linguistic expression has obtained on the previous occasions of use. In other words, the intermediate stage of abstraction from past uses and formulation of a core, context-independent (i.e. linguistic) meaning of the linguistic expression can be eliminated or is not needed. The views of the British philosopher J. L. Austin and the Austrian-born British philosopher later Ludwig Wittgenstein are considered to be close to this position. See Recanati (2005).

meaning-is-use theory (of meaning) A theory which states that the meaning of a linguistic expression is determined by its use in a language. This approach was inaugurated by the Austrian-born British philosopher Ludwig Wittgenstein and systematically developed by ordinary language philosophers. Also known as the **use theory** (of meaning). See Lyons (1995). *See also* behaviourist theory (of meaning); mentalistic theory (of meaning); referential theory (of meaning); truth-conditional theory (of meaning); verificationist theory (of meaning).

meaning$_{-n}$ = natural meaning.

meaning$_{-nn}$ Occasionally also known as **what is meant$_{-nn}$**. A concept put forward by the British philosopher H. P. Grice. Here 'nn' stands for 'non-natural'. **Non-natural meaning** consists of both *what is said and what is implicated (*see* implicature). It involves the expression and recognition of a speaker's *communicative intention, i.e. meaning which is intended to be recognized as having been intended. In the case of non-natural meaning, *x means that p* does not entail *p*. *Conversational implicature is a standard example of non-natural meaning. By contrast, **natural meaning**—sometimes abbreviated as **meaning$_{-n}$** or called **what is meant$_{-n}$**—does not involve any communicative intention on anyone's part. In the case of natural meaning, *x means that p* entails *p*. E.g. in the Gricean example *Those spots meant measles* there is a natural, fixed link between a certain type of spot and measles, which cannot be cancelled. Thus, while natural meaning or what is meant$_{-n}$ can only be a fact, non-natural meaning or what is meant$_{-nn}$ need not be. *See also* utterance meaning. See Grice (1989); Huang (2007).

meaning postulate A rule of *inference developed by the German-born American philosopher Rudolf Carnap. It formalizes the sense relation, in particular the paradigmatic sense relation between two or more lexical items of a language. It takes the form of an implication between *propositions that contain the lexical items. E.g. the relation of *hyponymy between *oak* and *tree* is represented: oak (*x*) → tree (*x*): 'if *x* is an oak, *x* is also a tree'. Meaning postulate presents an alternative to *componential analysis.

meaning transfer A pragmatic process whereby the concept literally expressed by an input proposition is transferred into a different concept, provided that there is a salient functional relation between the old and new concepts. E.g. in the sentence *Shakespeare is on the top shelf*, the proper name *Shakespeare*, which literally denotes a certain individual, is used to refer, through meaning or semantic transfer, to one or more books written by him, thus also called **semantic transfer**. See Recanatic (2004).

medial A term used in the description of *distance in *space deixis. It indicates that the entity referred to is in between proximal and distal. E.g. *that* in Scottish English, which is the middle point between the proximal *this* and the distal *yon*. *See also* proximal; distal.

mediate inference A term in traditional logic for an *inference in which a conclusion is drawn from two or more premises. E.g. the move from 'If it's snowing, it's cold' and 'It's snowing' to 'It's cold'. For some scholars, mediate inferences are particularly relevant to pragmatics. *See also* immediate inference.

meiosis A *figure of speech in which something is presented deliberately as less significant than it is. In other words, in meiosis the importance (e.g. quantity, intensity or seriousness) of something is understated or underemphasized. E.g. *I've made a small contribution to theoretical physics*, said by a Nobel laureate in physics. The use of meiosis can have a variety of pragmatic effects. As an instance of *figurative (non-literal) use of language, meiosis is a subject of study in pragmatics. Also known as **litotes** and **understatement**. *See also* hyperbole.

membership categorization A type of *I-implicature in *neo-Gricean pragmatics. E.g. the uttering of the sentence *The toddler cried. The dad gave him a cuddle* engenders the **member categorization implicature** that the dad was the father of the crying toddler. The term 'membership categorization' is taken from the **membership categorization analysis**, an offshoot of *ethnomethodology. In membership categorization analysis, the focus is on how 'member categories' referring to, for example, age, gender, and ethnicity are used in communication.

mental inertia *See* speaker's economy.

mental lexicon The permanent word-store as assumed by many psycho- and cognitive linguists to be represented in the human mind. The study of mental lexicon is particularly relevant to *cognitive pragmatics (1).

mental representation A technical term used in cognitive science to refer to a structured set of elements in the human mind. In some cognitive pragmatic theories, utterance interpretation is treated in terms of the generation and transformation of its mental representations.

mental space(s) semantics A semantic theory of dynamic meaning construction associated particularly with the work of the French linguist Gilles Fauconnier within *cognitive linguistics, A **mental space** is a region of a cognitive environment that contains specific kinds of information. It is constructed online, i.e. at the moment of thinking or speaking. Once a mental space is constructed, it is linked to the other mental spaces established as thought proceeds and discourse unfolds. This gives rise to a **mental spaces lattice**, namely a series of connected mental spaces. Mental space(s) semantics endeavours to show how certain long-standing issues in the philosophy of language and linguistic pragmatics such as indexicality, implicature, presupposition, and reference are constructed in a conceptual or mental space. Also known as **mental space(s) theory**. More recently, Fauconnier and the American linguist Mark Turner have extended mental space(s) semantics, engendering a new approach known as **conceptual blending theory**, which investigates how to amalgamate meanings or concepts in the interpretation of a complex linguistic expression. E.g. in the interpretation of the metaphor *That surgeon is a butcher*, we take out the relevant features from both the concept SURGEON and the concept BUTCHER and then utilize our knowledge about the world to form a new '**conceptual blend**', inferring that the surgeon in question is incompetent. See Evans (2007); Cruse (2006).

mentalese A term particularly associated with the American psychologist and linguist Jerry Fodor which refers to the innate language of thought.

mentalistic theory (of meaning) A theory which says that the meaning of a linguistic expression is the concept or the idea associated with it in the mind of anyone who knows the linguistic expression. Also referred to as the **ideational**, **internalist**, or **conceptualist theory** (of meaning). See Lyons (1995). *See also* behaviourist theory (of meaning); meaning-is-use theory (of meaning); referential theory (of meaning); truth-conditional theory (of meaning); verificationist theory (of meaning).

mention The use of a linguistic expression to represent itself. Thus, in *'Intrepid' has eight letters*, *Intrepid* is 'mentioned'. By contrast, when a linguistic expression is employed to stand for something, it is **used**. E.g. in *My friend is an intrepid exploiter*, *intrepid* is 'used'. The **use/mention distinction** is drawn originally from the philosophy of language. *See also* autonymy.

meronymy, meronym From the Greek word *meros* 'part', the term refers to a sense relation of inclusion, in which two or more lexical items form a 'part–whole' relationship. E.g. The meaning relation between *finger* and *hand*. The term for the part is called the **meronym**, and the term referring to the whole is known as the **holonym**. Meronyms of the same holonym are **co-meronyms**. Meronymy is a main type of lexical hierarchy. Also called **partonymy**. *See also* synecdoche; homonymy.

message A term deployed in information theory and the code model of communication for a signal encoded by a transmitter, to be transmitted to the receiver. In pragmatics, the term is often used loosely to refer to what a speaker intends to convey. *See also* signal; sign.

meta-implicature A term used by the British linguist Geoffrey Leech which refers to any *conversational implicature that contains a reference to another conversational implicature. According to this analysis, the uttering of *Let me take the box for you* may indirectly give rise to the meta-implicature that it is only because the speaker is being polite that he or she implicates that he or she wants to take the addressee's box.

metalinguistic Sometimes also called **metalingual**. The function or use of a language to make a statement about itself or any other language. A language that is used to comment on either itself or any other language is called **metalanguage**, and the language that is talked about is labelled **object language**. E.g. in the case of a grammar of English written in Chinese, Chinese is the metalanguage and English is the object language. In the case of a grammar of French written in French, French is both the meta- and object language. Note that a metalanguage does not need to be a natural language. The **meta-/object language distinction** seems to originate from formal logic.

metalinguistic negation Introduced by the French linguist Oswald Ducrot, the term refers to a device for rejecting a previous utterance on any grounds whatever, including its morphosyntactic form, its phonetic realization, or its style or register. In other words, metalinguistic negation represents the non-truth-functional use of negation and is concerned largely with the form rather than the meaning of an utterance. It is characterized by a number of distinctive properties. First, it consists of a negative sentence followed by a rectifying clause. Second, it is a rejoinder to a previous utterance, aspects of which it objects to. Third, taken descriptively, it constitutes a truth-conditional contradiction. Fourth, when spoken, it tends to occur with a special, so-called contradiction intonation contour. Fifth, it does not allow the use of negative polarity items like *any*. Sixth, it does not permit negative incorporation. Seventh, its interpretation is frequently the outcome of a reanalysis. Finally, it is essentially an instantiation of quotation, *mention, or representational use. E.g. *He was not born in Peking, he was born in Beijing*. Occasionally also referred to as **paradoxical negation**, **irregular negation**, or **pragmatic negation**. See Horn (1989); Huang (2007). Contrasts with **descriptive negation**.

metalinguistic performative A term used by the British linguist Jenny Thomas for a *performative that is always felicitous or successful as well as self-referential, self-verifying, and non-falsifiable. The success of a metalinguistic performative is not dependent on any rituals or extralinguistic institutions. Cross-linguistically, metalinguistic performatives are the most straightforward type of performative and tend to be universal. E.g. the uttering of the sentence *I promise to vote for abolishing the inheritance tax*.

metalinguistic tense *See* tense.

metaphor A *figure of speech in which a linguistic expression normally belonging to one field of reference is extended analogously to another. E.g. *All the world's a stage/And all the men and women merely players* (William Shakespeare, *As You Like It*). As an instance of *figurative (non-literal) use of language, metaphor has been extensively studied in pragmatics including both Gricean and neo-Gricean pragmatics, relevance theory, and experimental pragmatics.

metaphor from metonymy *See* metaphtonymy.

metaphoric reference *Reference to an entity that is evoked by whatever is pointed at and deictically referred to. Suppose one says, pointing to a particular copy of *The Times*, *The billionaire has just bought that for ten million pounds*. The use of *that* does not refer to the single copy of the newspaper but to its publisher, which is evoked.

metaphtonymy A blended term used to refer to the *figure of speech in which *metaphor and *metonymy interconnect with each other. Two types of metaphtonymy are found to be particularly commonly used: **metaphor from metonymy** and **metonymy within metaphor**. The first subtype can be illustrated by considering *The prisoner is often close-lipped*. In this example, the metaphoric interpretation that the prisoner often speaks but gives little away is based on the metonymic interpretation that the prisoner is often silent. A good example of the second subtype is *Mary has finally caught her boss's ear*, in which the metonymic reading 'ear for attention' is placed within the metaphoric reading 'attention is a moving physical entity'.

metaphysical subjectivity When one says *I have a toothache*, the judgement is **metaphysically subjective**, because the pain has to be experienced. By contrast, when one says *Paul Grice was a great philosopher*, the judgement is **epistemically subjective** because the truth or falsity of the sentence cannot be determined in an objective way. This is called **epistemic subjectivity**. The distinction originates in philosophy.

metapragmatic Function or use of language in commenting on pragmatic theories, glossing pragmatic functions of an utterance, and/or referring to the effects of language in use. E.g. the use of a *hedge like *I'm not sure this is true, but*... by a speaker to indicate his or her awareness of, and desire not to violate the Gricean *maxim of Quality.

metapragmatic ability *See* pragmatic ability.

metapragmatic device *See* metapragmatics.

metapragmatic first-order politeness *See* first-order politeness.

metapragmatics The study of the use of language by a speaker to discuss pragmatics, in particular, to indicate his or her awareness of pragmatic features and interpretations of an utterance. The pragmatic aspects being discussed are sometimes called **object pragmatics**. Metapragmatics is of a higher order than object pragmatics. It is viewed as a discussion of the descriptive, analytic, and theoretical aspects of pragmatics, of the conditions and possibilities that enable language users to do pragmatics by acting in a pragmatic way, and of language users' capacity to reflect upon language use in a reflexive (self-referring) way. **Metapragmatic devices** include linguistic action verbs, deictic expressions, contextualization cues, hedges, discourse markers, and formulaic constructions. The metapragmatic use of language is often captured under what is called **reflexivity**, **reflexiveness**, or **reflectiveness**—a design feature of language by virtue of which language can be used to talk about itself. See Overstreet (2010).

metarepresentation, metapresentational A representation of itself or any other representation. E.g. a painting of another painting of the Great Wall in China is a representation of the original painting, and a meta-representation of the Great Wall. For some scholars, both thoughts and utterances can be metarepresentational. In pragmatics, the concept is utilized especially in relevance theory.

metonymic anaphora An anaphoric relation between an anaphoric expression and its antecedent that is defined in terms of such continuity relations as part–whole, container–content, and location–object. E.g. in *The phone rang. John picked it up*, *it* refers to the receiver of the phone rather than the phone as a whole. There are two varieties of metonymic anaphora: **partonymic anaphora** and **toponymic anaphora**. Also called **metonymic reference**.

metonymy A *figure of speech in which a linguistic expression denoting one entity is used to refer to another entity that is associated with it in one way or another. Therefore, metonymy is a variety of *figurative (non-literal) use of language. E.g. the use of *the ham sandwich* in *The ham sandwich is at table nine* to refer to the customer who has ordered the ham sandwich. In one aspect, three types of metonymy have been identified: (i) **referential**, as in the example above, (ii) **predicational**, and (iii) **illocutionary metonymy**. Predicational metonymy is illustrated by examples like *John's new girlfriend is just a pretty face*, in which *a pretty face* is not used referentially but predicatively. Illocutionary metonym is exemplified by utterances such as *Can you lend me your mobile?* In another aspect, metonymy can be divided into two types: **source-in-target** and **target-in-source metonymy**. In the former, the source of the metonymic operation is in the target. E.g. in *The ham sandwich wants another glass of wine*, HAM SANDWICH is conceptualized as being in the domain RESTAURANT CUSTOMER. By contrast, in the latter, the target of the metonymic operation is in the source. E.g. in *John broke the window*, it is typically the windowpane rather than the window as a whole that is broken. Given that metonymic links are used for inferencing and that what is metonymically inferred can be defeated, metonymy is largely a pragmatic phenomenon. Often taken to include **synecdoche**. See Panther and Radden (2005). *See also* metaphor.

metonymy within metaphor *See* metaphtonymy.

micro context *See* macro context.

micro-sense *See* sub-sense.

micropragmatics The systematic study of language in use which is largely limited to central topics of enquiry such as implicature, speech acts, presupposition, deixis, and reference. Often contrasted with **macropragmatics**.

mindblindness *See* theory of mind.

mind-reading *See* theory of mind.

minimal inclusive person A type of *inclusive person, this term refers to a speaker plus at least one addressee. E.g. *kata* 'you and I' in Tagalog. It contrasts with **augmented inclusive person**, which makes reference to a speaker and addressee plus at least one other. E.g. *tayo* 'you and I and at least one other' in Tagalog.

minimal proposition A proposition that is a minimal projection from the semantic values of the semantically valued constituents of a sentence. It is derived from the combination of the lexical meanings of the basic parts of the sentence and the contextually determined values of any semantically or linguistically context-sensitive constituents of the sentence. Every part of a minimal proposition is semantically 'called for' by some constituent of the sentence. In other words, a minimal proposition is what is strictly and literally said. It corresponds most closely with the linguistic expressions used in the sentence and can be assigned a truth value. E.g. the minimal proposition expressed by the sentence *John weighs 65kg* may be that John weighs 65kg naked and without taking any breakfast. While semantic minimalists believe in minimal proposition, contextualists, especially radical contextualists reject the concept. See Taylor (2010). Also called a **skeletal proposition**. Often contrasts with a **pragmatically enriched proposition**.

minimal semantics **1.** = *semantic minimalism. **2.** A position within semantic minimalism whose main advocate is the British philosopher Emma Borg. On Borg's view, semantics should operate independently of, and prior to, the actual use of a linguistic expression by a speaker to communicate. The role of semantics is simply to explain formal linguistic meaning, but not to give a full account of the nature of meaning or indeed to explain communication. Consequently, Borg distinguishes between 'literal' truth conditions and verification conditions. While the former belongs to semantics, the latter falls outside it. *See also* insensitive semantics; radical semantic minimalism.

minimal(ist) semantics *See* contextualism; semantic minimalism.

minimal truth-evaluability principle A term used by the New Zealand-born linguist Robyn Carston for the principle which states that a pragmatically determined aspect of utterance meaning is part of what is said if and only if it is required to express a complete proposition that can be evaluated truth-conditionally.

minimalism, minimalist *See* semantic minimalism.

minimalist principle The French philosopher François Recanati's term for the *linguistic direction principle and the *minimal truth-evaluability principle. It is minimalist in the sense that both principles attempt to keep pragmatic contributions to what is said to a minimum. Also called the **mixed minimalist principle**.

minimally literal meaning *See* literal meaning.

minimax principle A principle proposed by the American linguists John Carroll and Michael Tanenhaus which states a minimax of effort and information or cost and benefit: 'The speaker always tries to optimally minimize the surface complexity of his utterances while maximizing the amount of information he effectively communicates to the listener.' *See also* principle of effective means.

'minus' committer A variety of *downgrader which is employed to lower a speaker's degree of commitment to the state of affairs referred to in the proposition of a sentence uttered. E.g. *I guess* in *I guess you haven't read the book*. Contrasts with a **'plus' committer**.

mirror maxim A term that is used to refer to a pragmatic principle proposed by the American philosopher Robert Harnish, which states that one should make one's sayings mirror the world. An instance is the pragmatic enrichment from 'A and B do C' to 'A and B do C together'. The pragmatic inference is taken to be an *I-implicature within the neo-Gricean pragmatic theory. E.g. the utterance of *John and Mary scrubbed the carpet afresh* engenders the I-implicature that John and Mary scrubbed the carpet afresh together.

miscommunication A misunderstanding between participants in a communication. The failure may result from differences in their ways of using language. This problem is particularly acute when communication takes place cross-culturally and/or cross-linguistically. Miscommunication is a topic of enquiry in pragmatics including *cross-cultural pragmatics.

misexecution A term used by the British philosopher J. L. Austin for a category of *speech act infelicity in which a speech act is damaged by mistakes, etc. In a misexecution, the intended speech act fails to come off. E.g. the use of a wrong name in a marriage ceremony. *See also* misinvocation; misfire; abuse.

misfire A term initiated by the British philosopher J. L. Austin for a category of *speech act infelicity or unhappiness. A misfire stems from a failure to satisfy the *felicity conditions that require (i) a conventional procedure having a conventional effect with appropriate circumstances and persons participating in the procedure, and (ii) that the procedure be carried out correctly and completely. If a misfire takes place, the relevant speech act is not performed successfully. E.g. a bridegroom not saying the exact words that are conventionally required at a marriage ceremony. Also known as **pragmatic misfire (1)**. *See also* misexcution; misinvocation; abuse.

misinvocation A term deployed by the British philosopher J. L. *Austin to refer to a category of *speech act infelicity or unhappiness, in which a speech act is disallowed. E.g. a wrong person conducting a marriage ceremony. *See also* misexecution; misfire; abuse.

mitigation A discursive process which functions primarily to minimize vulnerability. Mitigation has two orientations: self and other. By **self-oriented mitigation** is meant downplay of one's own vulnerability and by **other-oriented mitigation**, downplay of others' vulnerability. It can be realized by a variety of linguistic and non-linguistic devices such as disclaimers, indirectly performed speech acts, and gestures. These are called **mitigators**. E.g. the use of *I guess I need a white board marker* to mitigate or soften the force of a request. Mitigation is closely related to e.g. indirectness, politeness, and reduced commitments and has been extensively studied in pragmatics.

mixed logophoric language *See* semi-logophoric language.

mixed minimalist principle *See* minimalist principle.

mock impoliteness Behaviours including verbal ones that appear to be superficially but not truly impolite. In other words, mock impoliteness constitutes a polite behaviour in a particular context. It often reflects the shared knowledge and values of a social group and reinforces solidarity among its members. *Banter, for instance, is frequently used in the expression of mock impoliteness. Contrasts with **mock politeness**.

mock politeness *Politeness that is clearly insincere. In other words, mock politeness appears to be polite, i.e. to positively constitute, maintain, or enhance an addressee's *face at a superficial level, but actually is impolite, i.e. it threatens, attacks, or damages his or her face at a deeper level. Sarcasm (*see* irony) is a common strategy to convey mock politeness. Contrasts with **mock impoliteness**.

model-theoretic semantics A theory of *formal semantics based on the notion of *truth-conditions. In a model-theoretic semantic account, a sentence is interpreted in terms of a model of an actual or possible world.

moderate contextualism, moderate contextualist A form or version of *contextualism that endeavours to take a middle path between *radical contextualism and *semantic minimalism. It acknowledges limited pragmatic influences on semantic content but rejects semantically unconstrained *pragmatic intrusions. *See also* syncretic view.

modern pragmatics In opposition to **classical pragmatics**, the term is used with reference to pragmatics in contemporary linguistics and the philosophy of language. Modern pragmatics covers *neo-Gricean pragmatics, *relevance theory, and research carried out in *contextualism in the philosophy of language. See Chapman (2011).

modesty maxim One of a set of *maxims of politeness put forward by the British linguist Geoffrey Leech which is speaker-oriented. What the maxim basically states is: minimize praise but maximize dispraise of self. More recently, Leech has preferred the term 'pragmatic constraint' over the term 'maxim'. Contrasted with the **approbation maxim**. See Leech (2007).

modified maxim of Quality A modified version of the British philosopher H. P. Grice's *maxim of Quality. It requires one to say only that which one thinks one knows.

modified Occam's razor (MOR) A particular version of *Occam's razor proposed by the British philosopher H. P. Grice, which dictates that the senses ascribed to a word or dictionary entries must not proliferate. Also called **Occam's eraser**.

modular pragmatics An area of research in pragmatics which considers the question whether or not there is a **pragmatic module**—a specialized cognitive system for pragmatics—in the human mind. It is generally accepted that pragmatics does not constitute a modular system. However, there are scholars such as the Israeli philosopher Asa Kasher who are of the view that certain parts of pragmatics are modular. On his view, modular pragmatics consists of a **pragmatic central system** of pragmatic knowledge, by which e.g. conversational implicature is generated. It also has pragmatic modules. One such module is claimed to be the cognitive system which governs both the production and understanding of speech acts, and especially indirect speech acts. Kasher called this cognitive system the **modular speech act theory**. See Cummings (2005). *See also* modularity; pragmatic central system; pragmatic interface.

modular view (of context effects) The model of pragmatic processing that runs in contrast to the **direct access view**. Unlike the direct access model, the modular view maintains that distinct mechanisms do not interact with each other initially. Lexical access, which is modular, is sensitive only to its domain-specific, lexical information. By contrast, non-modular context affects comprehension only post-lexically, thus playing a rather limited role. For some scholars, the Gricean model is compatible with this view. See Peleg, Giora, and Fein (2004).

modularity, modular A term inspired by computer programs to refer to the property of the human mind being structured into separate components. According to an influential theory proposed by the American cognitive scientist Jerry Fodor in the 1980s, the human mental architect is divided roughly into a central processor and a number of distinct cognitive systems. These independent, innate, and computational cognitive mechanisms, called **(Darwinian) modules**, are characterized by a number of relatively well-defined properties:

(i) domain specificity, (ii) information capsulation, (iii) mandatoriness, (iv) inaccessibility, (v) rapidity, (vi) shallowness, (vii) neural localization, (viii) breakdown, and (ix) development. In other words, these modules are each governed by their own principles and operate independently of each other. From a developmental point of view, a distinction is made between **synchronic** and **diachronic modularity**. For some linguists, certain aspects of language are considered to be 'modular' in that they are largely independent of general intelligence and distinct from general cognitive abilities. In pragmatics, relevance theory, for example, espouses to a large extent the modularity of mind thesis. Also called **cognitive modularity**, **Fodorian modularity**, or the **modularity of mind thesis**. A particular version of cognitive modularity is the **massive modularity of mind thesis**. See Huang (2007); Meini (2010). *See also* connectionism.

modus ponens Latin for 'method of affirming'. A rule in *logic by which if *q* follows from *p*, and *p* is true, then *q* is also true. *See also modus tollens.*

modus tollens Latin for 'method of denying'. A rule in *logic by which if *q* follows from *p*, and *q* is false, then *p* is also false. *See also modus ponens.*

monism of meaning *See* semantic reductionism.

monism of use *See* pragmatic reductionism.

monotone decreasing *See* downward entailment.

monotone increasing *See* upward entailment.

monotonicity, monotonic A term borrowed from mathematics for the property that in an *inference or *reasoning system, no inference or argument (when the inference or reasoning system is instantiated in an argument) can be defeated by the addition of extra premises. In other words, monotonicity refers to the preservation of the truth of a property into a larger (upwards) or smaller (downwards) set. Such an inference or reasoning (system) is said to be **monotonic**. A typical example of a monotonic system is *deduction. Contrasts with **non-monotonicity**.

Montague semantics Named after the American linguist Richard Montague, a theory of *formal semantics that assigns interpretations to a set of syntactically well-formed expressions specified by a formal system of syntax, which is a type of categorial grammar. The semantic interpretations are formulated in terms of a system of intentional logic in conjunction with *possible-world semantics. There is thus a one-to-one correspondence between categories postulated at the syntactic and semantic levels.

Moore's paradox Noted by and named after the British philosopher George Moore by the Austrian-born British philosopher Ludwig Wittgenstein. It refers to an inconsistency that arises when a speaker says '*p* but I don't believe that *p*'. Thus, if John says *Princess Diana died in a car crash in Paris, but I don't believe it*, he is denying that he believes something he has just asserted. This paradox is not due to the semantic content of what is said, because what is said is not contradictory, given that both parts of the sentence could be true. But John nevertheless has violated the epistemic commitment of what a speaker asserts, namely a speaker asserts something only if he or she believes it. Therefore it is a *pragmatic contradiction: what a speaker has violated is the British philosopher H. P. Grice's *maxim of Quality. See Huang (2007).

MOR = modified Occam's razor.

morphopragmatics A research domain at the intersection between morphology and pragmatics. It studies how, given a context, regular pragmatic meanings are derived via the application of morphological rules. In other words, morphology is relevant to pragmatics insofar as word structure can be considered an indication of a speech situation or speech event. Typical examples include case marking in Polish, inflectional suffixes in Hungarian used to encode stylistic meaning, and inflectional suffixes in Japanese deployed for expressing honorifics. Those are in the area of inflection. In terms of the interplay between derivational morphology and pragmatics, there are e.g. beautificational prefixes in Japanese, depreciatives in Australian English, and diminutives in Italian. Morphopragmatics can be distinguished from *lexical pragmatics on the one hand, and *syntactic pragmatics on the other. See Barbaresi and Dressler (2010).

Morris, Charles William (1901–1979) American philosopher and semiotician. He was educated at Northwestern University and the University of Chicago. He was an instructor in philosophy at the Rice Institute in Texas (1925–31), an associate professor of philosophy (1931–47) and a lecturer (1948–58) at the University of Chicago, and a research professor at the University of Florida (1958–71). He died in 1979. Morris was well known for his threefold division of the study of signs into syntax, semantics, and pragmatics. He was also credited with having coined the term 'pragmatics'.

Moses illusion *See* semantic illusion.

mother-in-law language *See* avoidance style.

multiple incomparability *See* incompatibility.

mutual belief Whatever belief is shared by a speaker and an addressee at a given point in communication. The definition of mutual belief usually leads to an infinite regress. *See also* mutual knowledge.

mutual cognitive environment *See* manifestness.

mutual contextual belief Roughly salient contextual information shared by a speaker and an addressee. Also called **common background belief**. *See* mutual knowledge.

mutual implication A logical relation in which each *proposition implies the other. Commonly written as $p \leftrightarrow q$.

mutual knowledge Whatever knowledge, including attitudes, beliefs, and views, is shared by a speaker and an addressee at a given point in a communication. The definition of mutual knowledge usually leads to an infinite regress. Also called **shared knowledge**. *See also* background assumption.

mutual knowledge context *See* general knowledge context.

mutual manifestness *See* manifestness.

mutually manifest *See* manifestness.

N

N400 A term that is encountered in *neuro- and *experimental pragmatics for a dependent variable of *event-related potentials (ERPs). A negative-going brain wave evident between 200 and 700 msec after a word is presented in its spoken, written, or signed form, the amplitude or size of the N400 can be used to measure processing effects. From a pragmatic point of view, given that the N400 is proven to be sensitive to contextual factors, it is particularly suitable for the investigation of the pragmatic aspects of language comprehension. See Coulson (2004).

naïve optimism A term in relevance theory for the lowest level of pragmatic development. On this level, an addressee interprets an utterance in such a way as if he or she did not know that a speaker is not always competent—e.g. sometimes he or she may express unclearly, or benevolent—e.g. sometimes he or she may tell a lie. A very young child may be a naïve optimist. *See also* cautious optimism; sophisticated understanding. See Allott (2010).

narrow context A notion put forward by the American philosopher Kent Bach. It denotes any contextual information that is relevant to the determination of the content of, or the assignment of the semantic values to, variables such as those concerning who speaks to whom, when, and where. Construed thus, narrow context is taken to be semantic in nature. Contrasts with a **broad context**.

narrowing *See* lexical narrowing.

natural gender In opposition to **grammatical gender**, natural gender is determined by the 'natural' feature of the entity referred to. E.g. masculine for *père* (father) and feminine for *mère* (mother) in French. Also called **conventional gender**. Often distinguished from **grammatical gender**.

natural language philosophy *See* ordinary language philosophy.

natural meaning *See* meaning$_{\text{-nn}}$.

natural semantic metalanguage (NSM) A componential semantic approach to meaning originated by the Polish scholar Andrzej Bogusławski in the 1960s and developed and elaborated later by the Polish-born linguist Anna Wierzbicka and her colleagues. The central claim of natural semantic metalanguage is that the description of all aspects of meaning can be reduced to a small but universal set of **semantic primes** or **primitives**—a set of simple, culture-shared, semantically minimal 'core' meanings or expressions which cannot be divided any further. E.g. I, THINK, and NOW. The analysis or description is represented in terms of a **semantic** or **reductive paraphrase**

explication, i.e. a paraphrase composed in the simplest possible terms, which is both exhaustive and translatable across languages. Natural semantic metalanguage is also called **reductive paraphrase**. More recently, it has been developed into *ethnopragmatics. See Wierzbicka (2003).

near-implicature *See* audience-implicature.

near-side pragmatics A term used by the American philosopher John Perry and the Basque philosopher Kepa Korta for pragmatics on the near side of what is said, i.e. pragmatics that determines, together with the semantic properties of the words used, what is said. Contrasted with **far-side pragmatics**. *See also* pre-semantic pragmatics.

near-synonymy, near-synonym A sense relation in which two or more lexical items have more or less similar, but not identical, propositional meanings. E.g. the meaning relation between *murder*, *execute*, and *assassinate*. Also known as **plesionymy**. *See also* synonymy.

negation as failure A term borrowed from computer science and artificial intelligence (AI) to refer to the property of **non-monotonicity** that is characteristic of certain *inference. One such inference is *default inference. E.g. from the 'failure' of the airport departure board to list a late-night flight to London Heathrow, one may infer that the flight has been cancelled. Pragmatic inference like *conversational implicature has this property.

negative face In opposition to **positive face**, negative face refers to an individual's desire that his or her right to freedom of action should not be impeded by others. In other words, it has to do with an individual's maintaining his or her freedom from imposition by others.

negative face goal *See* positive face goal.

negative Horn scale Named after the American linguist Laurence Horn. For each well-formed *positive Horn scale of the form $<x_1, x_2, \ldots, x_n>$, there is a corresponding negative Horn scale of the form $<\sim x_n, \ldots, \sim x_2, \sim x_1>$. In other words, a negative Horn scale contains a set of negative linguistic alternates such that the semantically strong negative linguistic expression unilaterally entails the semantically weak negative ones. All the negative linguistic alternates in the set should be of the same word class, from the same register, and about the same semantic relation. E.g. <not some, not many, not most, not all>. The use of a lower-ranked or semantically weak negative linguistic expression in a negative Horn scale gives rise to a *$Q_{\text{-scalar}}$ implicature. See e.g. Levinson (2000); Huang (2010f). Contrasts with a **positive Horn scale**.

negative impoliteness A way of being impolite which aims at attacking the addressee's negative face wants, i.e. his or her desire for freedom of action. The strategies used include condescending to, scorning, or ridiculing the addressee, associating him or her with a negative aspect, and frightening him or her. Contrasted with **positive impoliteness**.

negative politeness A way of being polite which aims at maintaining, restoring, and enhancing the negative face of addressees and others. When one employs negative politeness, one tends to opt for the speech strategies that express one's reluctance to impose one's desires on, and emphasize deference for, the addressee. Typical examples are performing indirect speech acts, using hedges, and giving deference to the addressee. Contrasted with **positive politeness**. *See also* neg-politeness.

negative pragmatic transfer *See* pragmatic transfer.

negative proposition *See* affirmative proposition.

neg(ative) raising (NR) The movement of a negative element from a lower subordinate clause to a higher main clause, hence the term 'raising'. The negative main clause tends typically to be interpreted as a negation of the subordinate clause. This reading is explained by the *I-principle within *neo-Gricean pragmatics. E.g. the use of *I don't think that the government has responded quickly* gives rise to the I-implicature that the speaker thinks that the government hasn't responded quickly. See Huang (2007); Horn (2009). Also known as **negative transportation**. *See also* negative strengthening.

negative strengthening The strengthening of a negative statement from a contradictory to a contrary understanding via *litotes. E.g. the use of *Maria doesn't like the English weather very much* generates the *I-implicature that Maria positively dislikes the English weather. See Huang (2007); Horn (2009). *See also* neg(ative) raising.

negotiability A term used in the European Continental tradition of pragmatics for the language property that explains why choices are made on the basis of highly flexible principles and strategies, rather than mechanically or in accordance with strict form–function relationships. See Verschueren (1999). *See also* adaptability; variability.

neg-politeness Negative *politeness defined by the British linguist Geoffrey Leech in terms of illocutionary and social goals. E.g. in making a criticism, one's illocutionary goal is to communicate one's low estimation of the addressee. This is at odds with one's social goal, namely saying something polite to maintain or enhance good social relations. The notion is slightly different from the American linguist Penelope Brown and the British linguist Stephen Levinson's notion of *negative politeness. Contrasts with **pos-politeness**. See Leech (2007).

neither subject-prominent nor topic-prominent language A term used by the American linguists Charles Li and Sandra Thompson for a language in which the basic syntactic elements of a sentence are neither a subject and a predicate nor a topic and a comment. Cebuano, Tagalog, and Waray are considered to be among such languages.

Contrasts with a **subject-prominent and topic-prominent language**. *See also* subject- prominent language; topic-prominent language.

neo-Gricean analysis (of presupposition) An analysis of presupposition derived ultimately from the British philosopher H. P. Grice. The central tenet is that presuppositions of a positive sentence are reduced to an entailment, and those of a negative sentence to a conversational implicature. A current advance of this analysis can be found in the work of the American philosopher Jay Atlas. See Atlas (2004). *See also* filtering-satisfaction analysis (of presupposition); cancellation analysis (of presupposition); accommodation analysis (of presupposition).

neo-Gricean pragmatic theory of anaphora A theory of *anaphora developed by the British linguist Stephen Levinson and the British Chinese linguist Yan Huang. The central idea underlying this theory is that the interpretation of certain patterns of anaphora (including binding) can be made utilizing pragmatically enriched meaning such as *conversational implicatures, dependent on the language user's knowledge of the range of options available in the grammar and of the systematic use or avoidance of particular anaphoric expressions or structures on particular occasions. See Huang (2000); Levinson (2000).

neo-Gricean pragmatics A school of thought in pragmatics associated particularly with, and developing, the insights of the British philosopher H. P. Grice. These include Grice's theory of meaning in terms of intentions, co-operation, and rationality, and his theory of conversational implicature. The new developments include the following: (i) individual types of classical Gricean conversational implicature have been systematized, (ii) more complex mechanisms such as the constraints on Horn scales have been devised, (iii) the classical Gricean maxims of conversation have been reinterpreted, and (iv) the whole Gricean mechanism of the co-operative principle and its attendant maxims have been reduced, giving rise to a number of neo-Gricean typologies of conversational implicature such as the Q-, I-, and M-implicatures. The main figures of neo-Gricean pragmatics include the American philosopher Jay Atlas, the American linguist Laurence Horn, and the British linguist Stephen Levinson. See Huang (2010a). *See also* Gricean pragmatics; post-Gricean pragmatics.

neo-pragmatism In opposition to **classical pragmatism**, the term is used for a form of contemporary pragmatism represented by the later work of the philosopher Richard Rorty, who is of the view that there is no truth or objectivity to be had, but only solidarity, or agreement within a community, or what our peers will let us get away with saying. For some philosophers, neo-pragmatism can be distinguished from **new pragmatism**. The latter refers to a revisionist movement in contemporary pragmatism, emerging from the work of such philosophers as Simon Blackburn, Robert Brandom, and Donald Davidson. In the philosophy of language, work by neo-pragmatists like Richard Rorty, Hilary Putnam, and Ian Hacking has aroused a great interest in ***pragmatism** and the pragmatic approach to language. See Misak (2007).

neural network model *See* connectionism.

neuropragmatics A recently emerged branch in pragmatics that examines the neuro-anatomical basis of language in use. It is concerned with the relationship between the human brain/mind and pragmatics. It investigates how the human brain/mind uses language, i.e. how it produces and comprehends pragmatic phenomena in healthy as well as neurologically impaired language users. Pragmatic phenomena that have been studied include *speech acts, *implicature, discourse, *metaphor, and sarcasm. Most neuropragmatic research has focused on aspects of pragmatics in adults with identifiable clinical disorders and brain pathology. The brain-damaged populations include patients with left- and right-hemisphere damage, traumatic brain injury, neuro-degenerative disorders like Parkinson's disease and dementia, and schizophrenia. The field of enquiry overlaps in particular with *clinical and *experimental pragmatics. See Stemmer and Schönle (2000); Cummings (2010).

neutral (speech act) verb A term used by the British linguist Geoffrey Leech for the type of *speech act verb that is neutral between a content-descriptive and a phonically descriptive verb. E.g. *say*, *repeat*, and *reply*. *See also* content-descriptive verb; phonically descriptive verb.

new *See* given; discourse-old; hearer-old.

new philology *See* historical pragmatics.

new pragmatism *See* neo-pragmatism.

next speaker selection A term in conversation analysis for the selection of the next speaker by a current speaker in a conversation. E.g. the uttering of *What do you think of it, John?* by a current speaker selects John to be the next speaker to take the floor, i.e. to speak.

next turn repair initiator (NTRI) A term in conversation analysis for a linguistic expression that is used to invite or initiate a *repair of an utterance in the prior turn in the next turn. E.g. *what* in the following conversation A: *You were at the Halloween thing*. B: *What?* A: *The Halloween party*.

Nixon diamond Named after the former US president Richard Nixon, the term is used in artificial intelligence and computational linguistics and *computational pragmatics for a problem associated with potentially conflicting abnormality conditions that lead to a contradiction. E.g. if one knows that in general Quakers are pacifists and Republicans are not, then what conclusion can one draw when one learns that Nixon is both a Quaker and a Republican?

nominal demonstrative *See* demonstrative.

non-calendrical usage (of a time unit) *See* calendrical usage (of a time unit).

nonce implicature *See* particularized conversational implicature.

nonce inference A once-off *inference, i.e. an inference that is made on a specific occasion. E.g. a *particularized conversational implicature (PCI) is treated as a nonce inference in relevance theory.

nonce scalar implicature A once-off *scalar implicature, i.e. a scalar implicature that is engendered in a specific context. E.g. the use of *Hillary Clinton* in *I've shaken hands with Hillary Clinton* as a reply to the question *Have you shaken hands with Barack Obama?* may give rise to the nonce scalar implicature that the speaker hasn't shaken hands with Barack Obama.

non-central speech act *See* ground-floor speech act.

non-cognitive meaning *See* non-propositional meaning.

non-conceptual meaning *See* non-propositional meaning.

non-conceptual pragmatic marker A *pragmatic marker that does not encode any conceptual information. E.g. *but* does not encode any concept. Three types of non-conceptual pragmatic marker are usually identified: **contrastive**, **elaborative**, and **inferential**. Contrasts with a **conceptual pragmatic marker**.

non-controversiality *See* axioms of non-controversiality.

non-conventional implicature *See* conventional implicature.

non-conventional indirectness An indirect strategy that is not constrained by convention. In other words, non-conventional indirectness is open-ended both in terms of the propositional content (or sentence meaning) and in terms of the linguistic form of a sentence and the pragmatic force of the sentence uttered. A representative example is hints. E.g. the utterance of *I didn't take any notes for the last lecture* to perform the speech act of indirectly requesting the addressee to lend the speaker his or her lecture notes. Contrasts with **conventional indirectness**.

non-conventional pragmatics A term used by the American linguist Adele Goldberg to designate pragmatics that is concerned with the effects of the production or comprehension of a sentence in a particular context of use by a language user. *Gricean pragmatics, for instance, is a typical example of non-conventional pragmatics. Contrasted with **conventional pragmatics**. See Goldberg (2004).

non-conventionality A property of *conversational implicature. Non-conventionality means that a conversational implicature, though dependent on the saying of what is said or coded, is not by nature coded. See Huang (2007). *See also* calculability; defeasibility; indeterminacy; non-detachability; reinforceability; universality.

non-coreference, non-coreferential *See* coreference, coreferential.

non-coreferential anaphora, non-coreferential anaphor An anaphoric relation in which an anaphoric expression and its antecedent do not have the same reference. E.g. *one* and *an iPod* form such a relationship in *John bought an iPod and Bill bought one too*. Often contrasted with **coreferential anaphora**.

non-deictic expression *See* deictic expression.

non-descriptive meaning *See* non-propositional meaning.

non-detachability, non-detachable A property of *conversational implicature. Non-detachability means that the use of any linguistic expression with the same semantic content tends to give rise to the same conversational implicature. E.g. the use of both *almost* and *nearly* in *The film almost/nearly won an Oscar* triggers the same conversational implicature that the film didn't quite win an Oscar. A principled exception is *M-implicature. See Levinson (2000); Huang (2007). *See also* calculability; defeasibility; indeterminacy; non-conventionality; reinforceability; universality.

none (direction of fit of a speech act) There is no relationship between words and world in the performance of a speech act. This is the case for the type of speech act termed *expressives. Also called the **empty** (direction of fit of a speech act). *See also* direction of fit (of a speech act); words-to-world (direction of fit of a speech act); world-to-words (direction of fit of a speech act); both words-to-world and world-to-words (directions of fit of a speech act).

'non-evident' felicity condition A term used for one of the two preparatory conditions for the performance of the speech act of promising, namely, it is clear to both the speaker and the addressee that what is promised will not happen in the normal course of action. *See also* 'hearer preference' felicity condition; 'obligation' felicity condition; felicity condition.

non-indexical contextualism A term used in the philosophy of language and linguistics for the view that contrary to the *indexicalists, context-sensitivity called for by the *contextualists lies in the circumstances of evaluation rather than in a truly indexical content for a sentence. *See also* semantic relativism. See McFarlane (2007).

non-literal illocutionary act *See* literal illocutionary act.

non-logophoric language *See* full logophoric language.

non-long-distance reflexivization language *See* long-distance reflexivization language.

non-monotonicity, non-monotonic A term borrowed from mathematics for the property that in an *inference or *reasoning system, an inference or argument (when the inference or reasoning system is instantiated in an argument) can be defeated by the addition of extra premises, even though none of the original premises is retracted. Such an inference or reasoning (system) is said to be **non-monotonic**. E.g. in artificial intelligence, *abduction is viewed as a species of non-monotonic logic, and in pragmatics, a *conversational implicature, being defeasible, is seen as non-monotonic in nature. Given that much of everyday human reasoning is non-monotonic and much of pragmatic meaning is defeasible, the study of non-monotonicity has attracted a lot of attention in artificial intelligence and *computational pragmatics. Contrasts with **monotonicity**.

non-natural meaning *See* $\text{meaning}_{\text{-nn}}$.

non-positional calendrical time unit *See* calendrical usage (of a time unit).

non-propositional meaning *Meaning that is not propositional. One important type of non-propositional meaning is *expressive meaning. Also called variously **non-descriptive**, **non-conceptual**, **non-cognitive**, and **non-referential meaning**.

non-rigid designator *See* rigid designator.

non-scalar contextual operator *See* scalar contextual operator.

non-specific indefinite reference *See* indefinite reference.

non-speech act An act that is not performed by speaking. An example of a physical act provided by the American linguist Jerry Morgan is this: if upon being asked his opinion of a spinach soufflé he has been served, he shovels the contents of his plate into a dog's dish, then he has made a non-speech act of judging the spinach soufflé as clearly as if he had made the same *speech act by saying *It's awful.*

non-truth-conditional meaning *See* truth-conditional meaning.

non-verbal communication Communication by other means than by words. Two types can be identified: **vocal** or **paralinguistic communication** and **non-vocal communication**. The former includes prosodic features such as loudness, pitch, and stress as well as more general features such as giggles, snorts, grunts, and sighs. The latter comprises what is more commonly referred to as **body language**, including gestures, facial expressions, posture, and eye movement. Both types of non-verbal communication are of relevance to pragmatics.

normative face A term that is used for a person's desire to act correctly in accordance with the set of refined and standardized social norms or conventions in a given context. Sometimes in contrast to **displaying face**, namely, a person's desire to show that he or she is superior to the addressee. Displaying face is satisfied when one performs e.g. the *speech act of approving.

normative pragmatics A form of pragmatics that assumes that language is a kind of game, and as such has rules. These rules are of crucial importance for the use of language, and should be the primary pursuit of pragmatics. This view of pragmatics was put forward especially by the American philosopher Wilfrid Sellars and advanced by the American philosopher Robert Brandom. See Peregrin (2010). *See also* language game.

North American functionalism *See* functionalism.

no truth theory (of truth) *See* deflationist theory (of truth).

novelty-familiarity condition A condition proposed by the American linguist Irene Heim which states that an *indefinite description is associated with novelty, i.e. it introduces a new entity into a discourse; a *definite description is linked to familiarity, i.e. it refers to the entity that has already existed. E.g. *A man came into the office. He/The man greeted everyone.*

NR = negative raising.

NSCO = non-*scalar contextual operator.

NSM = natural semantic metalanguage.

NTRI = next turn repair initiator.

null anaphora, null anaphor See zero anaphora.

number A grammatical category that distinguishes reference to one individual from reference to more than one. Some of the world's languages (e.g. Piraha) have no number category. Others (e.g. English) have a two-term system, namely, **singular** vs. **plural**, which is the simplest system. Still others (e.g. Arabic) exhibit a three-term system, singular vs. **dual** vs. plural. There are also languages (e.g. Lihir) which display a singular/dual/**trial**/**paucal**/plural system. Number marking on personal pronouns is an important deictic aspect of *person deixis. See Huang (2007). *See also* person; gender.

O

object honorific A type of *referent honorific in which deference is shown to the referent by the object of a sentence. E.g. in a Japanese sentence meaning 'Yamada helped Professor Tanaka', the sentence can be marked to show the speaker's deference to the referent of the object Professor Tanaka. *See also* subject honorific.

object language *See* metalinguistic.

object pragmatics *See* metapragmatics.

objectivist semantics *See* formal semantics.

'obligation' felicity condition A term that is used to refer to the essential condition for the performance of the speech act of promising, namely that the speaker's relevant utterance counts as the undertaking of an obligation to do what he or she has promised. *See also* 'non-evident' felicity condition; 'hearer preference' felicity condition.

OBV = obviation, obviative, obviate.

obviation, obviative, obviate (OBV) A distinctive third- or fourth-person form used to distinguish a further entity from a third-person entity that has already been referred to in a sentence or discourse. Contrasts with **proximative** or **proximate**. In a system of obviation, proximatives and obviatives are assigned to different third-person entities on the basis of their relative salience in a sentence or discourse. In general, contextually and/or rhetorically more prominent entities are encoded by means of a proximative form. By contrast, contextually and/or rhetorically less central entities are placed in obviative form. Consequently only proximatives can be read as coreferential with proximatives, and obviatives as coreferential with obviatives. Obviation can thus be seen as representing a natural extension of the *gender or class system to the category of *person, with proximatives marking an unmarked third-person category, and obviatives a subsidiary 'fourth-person' category. It is found in a number of American Indian languages. See Huang (2000).

Occam's eraser *See* modified Occam's razor.

Occam's razor A philosophical and metatheoretical principle which dictates that entities are not to be multiplied beyond necessity (Latin 'entia non sunt multiplicanda praeter necessitatem'). One particular form of the principle is that 'plurality is never to be posited without need'. This **'simplicity' principle** is intended as an overall constraint on theory construction. Also called **Ockham's razor**, **pragmatic minimalism**, or the **law of parsimony**. 'Occam' is a learned spelling of the home village of the medieval English scholastic philosopher known as William of Ockham. See Urmson and Ree (1989). *See also* modified Occam's razor.

off-record A term used in the American linguist Penelope Brown and the British linguist Stephen Levinson's 'face-saving' model of politeness for one of a set of five strategies a speaker can adopt to avoid or weaken a *face-threatening act (FTA). By 'off-record' is meant that the speaker performs the face-threatening act indirectly, for example, by dropping a hint. E.g. the performance of the speech act of requesting a fellow student to lend the speaker his lecture notes by uttering *I didn't take any notes for the last lecture*. *See also* on-record.

off-record impoliteness *Impoliteness where the threat to an addressee's face is expressed indirectly by way of a *conversational implicature, which is cancellable. E.g. *well honestly I left my books here*. Contrasts with **on-record impoliteness**.

old *See* given; discourse-old; hearer-old.

on-record A term encounted in the American linguist Penelope Brown and the British linguist Stephen Levinson's 'face-saving' model of politeness for one of a set of five strategies a speaker can use to avoid or soften a face-threatening act (FTA). By 'on record' is meant that the speaker performs the face-threatening act directly. E.g. the performance of the speech act of requesting a fellow student to lend the speaker his lecture notes by uttering *Lend me your lecture notes*. The face-threatening act can then be performed either baldly, i.e. without redress, or with redress. *See also* off-record.

on-record baldly *See* on-record without redress.

on-record impoliteness *Impoliteness where there is an explicit, direct, and unambiguous attack on an addressee's face. E.g. the use of *Get out, Marshall! You bastard*. Also called **bald on-record impoliteness**. Contrasts with **off-record impoliteness**.

on-record with redress A term used in the American linguist Penelope Brown and the British linguist Stephen Levinson's 'face-saving' model of politeness for one of a set of five strategies a speaker can adopt to avoid or weaken a *face-threatening act (FTA). The term means that the speaker performs the face-threatening act directly but with some compensatory actions. Furthermore, there are two choices: first, a face-threatening act can be carried out with a face-saving act using *positive politeness strategies such as emphasizing solidarity with the addressee to minimize the face-threatening act, e.g. the performance of the speech act of requesting a fellow student to lend the speaker his lecture notes by uttering *How about letting me have a look at your lecture notes?* Secondly, it can be performed using *negative politeness strategies such as showing respect to the addressee's territory and freedom of action, as in *Could you please lend me your lecture notes?*

on-record without redress A term used in the American linguist Penelope Brown and the British linguist Stephen Levinson's 'face-saving' model of politeness for one of a set of five strategies a speaker can take to avoid or weaken a face-threatening act (FTA). The term means that the speaker performs the face-threatening act directly without using any *positive or *negative politeness to weaken it. In other words, by choosing the strategy of on-record without redress, the face-threatening act is realized in the most direct and unambiguous way. E.g. the performance of the speech act of requesting a fellow student to lend the speaker his lecture notes by uttering *Lend me your lecture notes.* Also called **bald on-record** or **on-record baldly**.

one-component model (of presupposition) *See* two-component model (of presupposition).

ontological assumption A term used by the British linguist Sir John Lyons for assumptions about the world. *See also* world knowledge.

opaque context A context in which **Leibniz's Law**—a law of intersubstitutability *salva veritate* (Latin for 'with the truth unchanged') does not hold. This rule states that the substitution of an expression with the same *extension does not affect the truth-conditions of the sentences. E.g. at the time of writing, the expressions *Barack Obama* and *the first black President of the United States of America* have the same extension, i.e. they refer to the same person. According to Leibniz's Law, if *Barack Obama is a wise man* expresses a true *proposition, then so does *The first black President of the United States of America is a wise man.* However, in a referentially opaque context, truth cannot be preserved when the coreferential expressions are substituted for each other. Thus, *I wanted to dine with Obama* and *I wanted to dine with the first black President of the United States of America* will have different truth conditions. This is because the expression *the first black President of the United States of America* is given an *intensional reading, i.e. the reading that the speaker wanted to dine with whoever happened to be the first black President of the United States of America, and did not care and might not have known who that was. *Propositional attitude or intensional verbs typically constitute one type of referentially opaque contexts. Other words that create a referentially opaque context include adjectives like *alleged*, prepositions like *about*, connectives like *because*, and modal words of various categories like *must, may, probably, obviously,* and *permissible*. Also referred to as an **intensional context**. See Lyons (1995).

open proposition A proposition that contains an unspecified or open constituent. E.g. a question like *When is the lecture?* gives rise to the open proposition that the lecture is (at) *x* [time].

operator *See* truth function; logical constant; pragmatic operator.

opposite direction A type of *directional oppositeness. It denotes potential orientations or paths of movement in opposite directions.

E.g. the sense relation between *up* and *down*, *left* and *right*, and *clockwise* and *anticlockwise*. *See also* antipodal; converseness; counterpart; reversive.

opt out, opting-out A term used in the British philosopher H. P. Grice's theory of *conversational implicature to refer to the choice made by a language user not to follow a particular maxim of conversation. Consequently the maxim of conversation is suspended. An opting-out is frequently accomplished by the use of an **opting-out hedge**. E.g. the use of *I'm not sure if this is true, but*... to indicate the opting-out of the *maxim of Quality. *See also* flout.

optimality-theoretic pragmatics (OT pragmatics) A recently emerged *formal pragmatic theory of pragmatic competence combining the insights from both optimality theory (OT) and *neo-Gricean pragmatics. From the perspective of optimality theory, pragmatics is taken to be characterized by defaults and preferences, and utterance interpretation, to present an optimization problem. Although the concept of optimization was developed in pragmatics right from the very beginning, the application of optimality theory to pragmatics makes it possible for pragmatics to be formalized utilizing a system of ranked constraints to achieve both **expressive** and **interpretive optimality**. A particular version of optimality-theoretic pragmatics is **bidirectional optimality-theoretic pragmatics**, or **bidirectional optimality-theory pragmatics**. Optimality-theoretic pragmatics is linked with **game- and decision-theoretic pragmatics**. Also called **optimality-theory pragmatics**. See Blutner and Zeevat (2004).

oratio obliqua Latin name for '*indirect speech'.

oratio recta Latin name for '*direct speech'.

ordinary language philosophy A loosely structured school of thought or movement within *analytic(al) philosophy. Within the tradition of ordinary language philosophy, the philosophers paid a particular attention to natural language, particularly to language use, seeking to analyse everyday linguistic usages as a means of resolving problems created when they were adopted as philosophical terms. The school of ordinary language philosophy flourished principally in Oxford in the 1950s and 1960s. Leading thinkers of the school included the British philosophers Gilbert Ryle, J. L. Austin, H. P. Grice, and Peter Strawson, the Austrian-born British philosopher Ludwig Wittgenstein, and the American philosopher John Searle. It was within the tradition of ordinary language philosophy that Austin developed his theory of speech acts, and Grice his theory of conversational implicature. Both theories have since become landmarks on the path towards the development of a systematic, philosophically inspired pragmatic theory of language use. Also called **natural language philosophy** and the **use of language movement**. Often contrasts with **ideal language philosophy**. *See also* use perspective.

organizational level (of pragmatic analysis) *See* pragmatic analysis level.

ostensive-inferential communication A term used in relevance theory for communication that involves a stimulus or behaviour which makes it mutually manifest to both the communicator and audience that the communicator intends, by means of this stimulus, to make a set of assumptions (more) manifest to the audience.

OT pragmatics = optimality-theoretic pragmatics (and optimality-theory pragmatics).

other-initiated other-repair A correction or clarification of an utterance in a conversation that is prompted and carried out by one or more of the speaker's interlocutors. E.g. *Quails I think* in B's turn in A: *Pigeons*. B: *Quails I think*. *See also* self-initiated self-repair; other-initiated self-repair; self-initiated other-repair.

other-initiated self-repair A correction or clarification of an utterance in a conversation that is carried out by the speaker him- or herself but is prompted by his or her interlocutor. E.g. *What* in B's turn (other-initiation); *Wellington* in A's second turn (self-repair) in A: *Auckland is the capital of New Zealand*. B: *What?* A: *Wellington, sorry*. *See also* self-initiated self-repair; self-initiated other-repair; other-initiated other-repair.

other-oriented mitigation *See* mitigation.

overhearer A speech event participant who hears, by accident, a conversation in which he or she is not involved. *See also* addresser; addressee; bystander; eavesdropper; speech event participant; ratified participant.

overlapping antonymy, overlapping antonym A variety of *antonym (2). E.g. the sense relation between *good* and *bad*. Unlike *gradable antonyms, overlapping antonyms typically display an evaluative polarity. E.g. *good* is the positive term and *bad* is the negative term. Like *equipollent antonyms, overlapping antonyms also operate on their own scales, but unlike in equipollent antonyms, the scales partially overlap in overlapping antonyms. Another characteristic of overlapping antonyms is the feature of 'inheritance'. In talking about things that are inherently bad, such as crimes, illness, and natural disasters, *good* cannot be used. *See also* privative antonym.

overstater A type of *upgrader, which is used to overrepresent the state of affairs denoted in the proposition of a sentence uttered. E.g. *absolutely* in *I'm absolutely disgusted that you lied to your father.*

overt denial (of presupposition). The cancellation of a *presupposition by denying it outright in a co-ordinate clause that follows. E.g. in *John doesn't regret going out with Susan, because in fact he never did so!* the potential presupposition, generated in the first clause, that John went out with Susan is cancelled by the speaker's overt denial of it in the *because* clause. In general, overt denial of presupposition is possible only with negative but not positive sentences. *See also* explicit suspension (of presupposition).

Oxford philosophy *See* analytic(al) philosophy; linguistic philosophy.

oxymoron A phrase or linguistic expression that combines two contradictory words to create a special meaning. E.g. *sweet sorrow* in Juliet: *Good night, good night! Parting is such sweet sorrow . . .* (William Shakespeare, *Romeo and Juliet*).

P

P-literal meaning = primary-*literal meaning.

p-process = primary pragmatic process.

paradigmatic economy *See* speaker's economy.

paradigmatic sense relation *See* sense relation.

paradoxical negation *See* metalinguistic negation.

paralinguistic feature An aspect of vocal behaviour that is meaningful but is not taken to be part of the language system. It includes tone of voice, loudness, and rhythm. Sometimes, the term is also used to refer to such non-vocal phenomena as head and eye movements, facial expressions and hand gestures. Paralinguistic features often accompany speech and sometimes replace it. The study of paralinguistic features is relevant to pragmatics. Also known as **paralanguage**.

parallel distributed processing *See* connectionism.

parallel function principle *See* principle of parallelism (1).

parallel marker A type of *pragmatic marker (1) which conveys another message in addition to the propositional content of the sentence that holds it. E.g. *daddy* in *Hey Daddy, a spider in the corner!*

parallelism *See* principle of parallelism (1), (2).

parametric underdetermination A term, due to the American philosopher Kent Bach, that refers to a mixed type of semantic *underdetermination such as *The encyclopedia is expensive* [relative to what], *Our new secretary is talented* [in what respect], and *Even his little son knows how to send an email* [in addition to who].

parenthetical An expression that is interpolated into a sentence or a sequence of sentences. E.g. *I think*, *say*, and *let's face it*. Parentheticals have been a topic of enquiry in pragmatics. Also called **parenthesis**.

parenthetical phrase *See* pragmatic marker (1).

parody A term taken from literary criticism to refer to an exaggerated copying of someone or something in order to be amusing. It is a variety of *figure of speech.

parole A term borrowed from French and introduced by the Swiss linguist Ferdinand de Saussure. It refers to the individual use of the abstract language system Saussure called ***langue*** in an actual situation. *Parole* is manifested in the concrete psycho-physiological and social reality of particular acts of speaking. *See also langue*; performance.

partial blocking *See* full blocking.

partial homonymy, partial homonym *See* homonymy, homonym.

partial synonymy, partial synonym *See* synonymy, synonym.

partially ordered set (poset) A notion used in Boolean algebra and *algebra semantics. A partially ordered set consists of a domain of entities on which is defined a binary relation, termed a **partial order relation**. The relation is reflexive, transitive and antisymmetric. The concept is adapted in *neo-Gricean pragmatics to recast *Horn scales and *Hirschberg scales as partially ordered sets. Given that the partial ordered relation allows an is-a-kind-of relation and a have-parts relation, one can also obtain sets such as <{apple, banana}, fruit> and <book,{chapter 1, chapter 2,. . . }>.

participant deixis See person deixis.

particularized conversational implicature (PCI) A term used by the British philosopher H. P. Grice for a *conversational implicature whose generation requires particular contextual conditions. E.g. in the following conversation John: *Where's Peter?* Mary: *The light in his office is on*. Mary's utterance gives rise to the conversational implicature that Peter is in his office. The generation of this conversational implicature depends on specific contextual assumptions. Occasionally also called **nonce implicature**, especially in relevance theory. See Grice (1989); Huang (2007). Contrasts with a **generalized conversational implicature (GCI)**.

particularized conversational implicature scale (PCI scale) A pragmatic scale from which a particularized conversational implicature arises. Some *Hirschberg scales belong to this type. E.g. <Barack Obama's autograph, Hillary Clinton's autograph>. Contrasts with a **generalized conversational implicature scale (GCI scale)**.

partonymic anaphora A type of *metonymic anaphora, the anaphoric relation of which is based on the cognitive relation of part–whole continuity. E.g. in *Steve has a car. He washed it yesterday*, *it* refers to the exterior of the car rather than the whole car. Also called **partonymic reference**. *See also* toponymic anaphora.

partonymy See meronymy.

past tense *See* tense.

pause A temporary and brief break in the flow of speech, which is often classified into **filled pause** and **unfilled** or **silent pause**. The former is one taken up or filled by a hesitation form like *ah*, *er*, and *um*. In contrast, the latter is not filled by a hesitation form. In other words, a silent pause is one where there is no vocalization. The study of pause plays an important role in *conversation analysis and is thus clearly relevant for pragmatics.

PC = pragmatic compositionality (view).

PCI = particularized conversational implicature.

PCI scale = particularized conversational implicature scale.

PDP = parallel distributed processing (*see* connectionism).

pep = possible enrichment pair.

perceptual deixis A term coined by the American linguist George Lakoff for such a type of *deixis as used in examples like *There's Mark.*

performadox A term used by the American linguists Steven Boër and William Lycan to refer to the dilemma in which the various attempts to reduce the *illocutionary force of a *performative to ordinary syntax and semantics find themselves.

performance Related to the Swiss linguist Ferdinand de Saussure's notion of *parole* and introduced by the American linguist Noam Chomsky in the 1960s, performance refers to the actual use of language in concrete situations. It manifests **competeance**, but not in a pure form. This is because performance also displays other cognitive systems such as attention, memory, and the physiology of speech. Recently, Chomsky has replaced 'performance' partially with the term 'E [xternalized]-language'. Also referred to as **linguistic performance**. Constrasts with **competence**. *See also parole*; E-language.

performance module A *module that functions as a computational mechanism. In other words, performance modules are devices that process mental representations. Also called a **computational module**. Contrasted with a **competence module**. See Carston (2010a).

performative A concept developed by the British philosopher J. L. Austin for an utterance that is used not only to say things, but actively to do things or perform acts as well. In other words, such an utterance has both a descriptive and an effective aspect. E.g. *I now pronounce you man and wife*. Performatives can further be divided into two types: **explict performatives** and **implicit performatives**. See Austin (1962); Huang (2007). Often distinguished from **constative (1)**. See also collaborative performative; group performative; metalinguistic performative.

performative adverb An adverb that can be used to modify (only) a *performative verb. E.g. *hereby*.

performative analysis *See* performative hypothesis.

performative contradiction An inconsistency that arises from the performance of a *speech act due especially to the violation of its *felicity conditions. E.g. a performative contradiction is committed when someone says *I promise to give up smoking, but I don't have the slightest intention of doing it*.

performative fallacy A term used to refer to the view that a performative is the canonical form of an utterance, against which the forces of other utterances are to be explained. Construed in this way, the **performative hypothesis** is a special case of the performative fallacy. See Leech (1983). *See also* performative hypothesis.

performative hedge A *hedge that is used to modify the illocutionary force of a *performative. E.g. *I am sorry to have to tell you that your house has been destroyed by the bushfire.*

performative hypothesis The assumption that underlying every sentence, there is a 'hidden' matrix perfomative clause. The performative verb of the clause will make explicit what act is being performed. Thus, according to this hypothesis, *Put the chicken in the oven* would be derived from an underlying syntactic structure roughly like *I request you to put the chicken in the oven.* The analysis was later extended from direct performatives or speech acts (as in the above) to indirect ones. Thus, *Can you put the chicken in the oven?* would be derived from the same underlying structure. The latter version, developed by the American linguist Jerrold Sadock, is called the **extended performative hypothesis**. The performative hypothesis was fashionable in the 1970s. However, faced with a variety of syntactic, semantic, and pragmatic problems, it has generally been abandoned. Also known as the **performative analysis**. See Sadock (2004).

performative pragmatics An approach to pragmatics that is associated particularly with the American philosopher Douglas Robinson, inspired by work of the British philosophers J. L. Austin and H. P. Grice. As an action-oriented linguistic approach, performative pragmatics pays more attention to actual performed interactions in groups. What people do with the dramatic aspects of verbal communication such as context, the possibility of misunderstanding, and the sequence of turns taken by conversational participants has figured prominently in performative pragmatics. Contrasts with **constative pragmatics**. See Robinson (2005).

performative prefix A sentence-initial phrase in an explicit performatve such as *I request you to* in *I request you to leave the room.*

performative theory (of truth) A theory of truth, due to the British philosopher Peter Strawson, based on the insights of both the British philosopher and mathematician Frank Ramsey's *deflationist theory of truth and the British philosopher J. L. Austin's *speech act theory. On Strawson's view, to say of a sentence that it is true is to endorse or approve it. *See also* correspondence theory (of truth); coherence theory (of truth); pragmatist theory (of truth).

performative verb A verb that names the act or action it performs. E.g. *name*, *promise*, *request*, *sentence*, and *warn*. Performative verbs constitute a subcategory of the wider range of *speech act verbs.

performative verb of denegation A performative verb that names the act or action it performs to deny the illocutionary force carried by its opposite performative verb. E.g. *refuse* is the denegation of *accept*, *permit* is the denegation of *forbid/prohibit*, and *disclaim* is the denegation of *claim*. See Searle and Vanderveken (1985). *See also* illocutionary denegation; performative verb.

peripheral discourse topic *See* topic (1).

perlocutionary act A concept developed by the British philosopher J. L. Austin for one of the three types of *speech act simultaneously performed by a speaker when he or she says something.
A perlocutionary act is an act which produces a certain effect in or exerts a certain influence on the addressee through the uttering of a linguistic expression, such consequences being special to the circumstances of the utterance. In other words, a perlocutionary act represents a by-product of speaking, whether intentional or not. It is therefore an act performed by speaking. E.g. on hearing John's utterance *Pass me the glasses, please*, Mary may comply with or ignore the request. The consequence that an utterance may have on the addressee is also generally known as the **perlocutionary effect**. Also called **perlocution**. See Austin (1962); Huang (2007). *See also* locutionary act; illocutionary act.

perlocutionary verb A type of *content-descriptive speech act verb that describes the perlocutional act it performs. E.g. *amuse*, *frighten*, and *persuade*. *See also* illocutionary verb; locutionary verb.

person A grammatical category that exhibits a three-way distinction of **first**, **second**, and **third person**. The category first person is the grammaticalization of a speaker's reference to him- or herself or a group of persons including him- or herself. For non-singular first-person pronouns, many of the world's languages make a distinction between **inclusive** and **exclusive person**. Second person is the encoding of a speaker's reference to one or more addressees. For non-singular second-person pronouns, some languages also distinguish between inclusive and exclusive person. Third person is the grammaticalization of reference to persons or entities which are neither speakers nor addressees in a speech event. Person marking on personal pronouns is an important deictic aspect of *person deixis. See Huang (2007). *See also* number; gender.

person deixis The identification of the interlocutors or participant roles in a speech event. E.g. in *I like broccoli*, the person deictic expression *I* refers to whoever is speaking on some specific occasion. Person deixis is commonly expressed by (i) the traditional grammatical category of person, as reflected in personal pronouns, and if relevant, their associated predicate agreements, and (ii) vocatives. Occasionally also called **participant deixis**. *See also* space deixis; time deixis; discourse deixis; social deixis.

person-oriented three-term system (of space deixis) A system in which the middle or medial term refers to a location that is close to an addressee. Basque, Korean, and Tagalog, for instance, belong to this category. See Huang (2007). Contrasts with the **distance-oriented three-term system** (of space deixis).

personal common ground *See* common ground.

perspectivalism *See* point of view.

perspective *See* point of view.

perspective view (of pragmatics) *See* Continental tradition (of pragmatics).

phatic act *See* locutionary act.

phatic communication A term introduced by the Polish-born British anthropologist Bronisław Malinowski in the 1920s to refers to the function of language to establish, maintain, and develop good social relations between speakers and addressees without necessarily communicating any information. A typical example is talking about weather by the British.

phatic connective *See* pragmatic marker (1).

phatic function *See* functions (of language).

phatic maxim A principle of politeness proposed by the British linguist Geoffrey Leech which says that an interlocutor should avoid silence or keep talking in order not to opt out of communication. See Leech (1983).

philosophical linguistics A term that is usually used by a linguist to refer to the branch of linguistics that is devoted to the study of (i) the role played by language in the understanding and elucidation of philosophical concepts, hence = the **philosophy of language** or **linguistic philosophy (1)**, and (ii) the philosophical status of linguistic theories, methods and observations, hence = the **philosophy of linguistics**.

philosophical pragmatics A term used for pragmatic theories such as Gricean and neo-Gricean pragmatics which examines a speaker's communicative intentions, the use of language which requires such intentions, context of use, the relation between a user of a linguistic form, and the act of using that form, and other factors affecting the production and interpretation of language as used. Most of the topics of enquiry in philosophical pragmatics emerged from the traditional concerns of *analytic(al) philosophy.

philosophical semantics A branch of semantics that studies topics such as the relations between linguistic expressions and the entities in the external world they denote or refer to, the validity of propositions, and the conditions under which a linguistic expression can be said to be true or false.

philosophy of language The systematic study of language and the workings of language, in particular linguistic meaning and language use from a philosophical point of view. The philosophy of language attempts to provide a philosophically illuminating analysis of certain general features of language. Current central topics include the theory of meaning, the theory of reference, the theory of truth, philosophical pragmatics, and the philosophy of linguistics. Viewed in this way, almost all philosophical studies in the 20th century and many before have been in one form or another concerned with language. *See also* linguistic philosophy; philosophy of linguistics.

philosophy of linguistics The philosophical study of the academic discipline of linguistics, especially theoretical linguistics as a science or purported science. The investigation includes an examination of the fundamental assumptions in and methodologies of theoretical linguistics. The philosophy of linguistics also attempts to incorporate the findings of theoretical linguistics into the rest of the philosophy of language. *See also* philosophy of language; linguistic philosophy.

philosophy of mind The arena of philosophy devoted to the study of the nature of mental states. The philosophy of mind includes the philosophy of psychology, philosophical psychology, and part of metaphysics. Traditionally, one of its central concerns is the relationship between mind and body. The main relevance of the philosophy of mind to pragmatics is that in addition to questions about how material things can engender consciousness or meaningfulness, it also investigates the extent to which material things give rise to *rationality and *reasoning, the structure of minds and concepts including claims about the *modularity of mind thesis, and the *theory of mind. Consequently, it shares a number of topics with the philosophy of language and pragmatics. These include the relationship between the meaningfulness of thought and the meaningfulness of language, intention, meaning, reference, and propositional attitudes. *See also* philosophy of language.

phonetic act *See* locutionary act.

phonically descriptive (speech act) verb A term used by the British linguist Geoffrey Leech for the type of *speech act verb that has to do with the manner rather than the matter of an utterance. E.g. *mumble*, *shout*, and *whisper*. *See also* content-descriptive (speech act) verb; neutral (speech act) verb.

phrasal pragmatics A term introduced by the Spanish philosopher Esther Romero and the Spanish linguist Belén Soria for a subfield of pragmatics within the framework of relevance theory that investigates the pragmatic adjustments of complex concepts typically expressed by phrases.

phrasal underdetermination A term used by the American philosopher Kent Bach to refer to a case of semantic *underdetermination whose source or locus is a 'phrase'. E.g. *Willie almost robbed the bank* could be understood as Willie refrained from robbing a bank, he decided against robbing a bank, he was prevented from robbing a bank, etc. These undeterminations are the result of using the word *almost*.

physical context One of the main types of *context. Physical context refers to the immediate physical setting of an utterance. E.g. the interpretation of the two instances of *he* in *He's not the CEO; he is* depends crucially on the knowledge computable from the spatio-temporal location of the utterance. *See also* linguistic context; social context; general knowledge context.

physical inertia *See* speaker's economy.

place deixis *See* space deixis.

plan-based (inference) model (of speech act interpretation) A *computational pragmatic model of *speech act interpretation. It is built on the basis of belief logics and utilizes *abductive inference to reason about a speaker's intension, and is hence a version of the **inferential model** of indirect speech act interpretation. The plan-based model contains three components: (i) an axiomatization of belief, desire, action, and planning, (ii) a set of plan inference rules, and (iii) a theorem prover. Also called the **belief, desire, and intention (BDI) model**. See Jurafsky (2004). *See also* cue-based model (of speech act interpretation).

plesionymy *See* near-synonymy, near-synonym.

PLI = pragmatic language impairment (*see* pragmatic disorder).

plug A term used by the Finnish linguist Lauri Karttunnen which refers to a *presupposition operator which blocks off all the presuppositions of an embedded or lower clause. E.g. verbs of saying like *say*, and of *propositional attitude like *think*. *See also* hole; filter.

'plus' committer A type of *upgrader which is deployed to increase a speaker's degree of commitment to the state of affairs referred to in the proposition of a sentence uttered. E.g. *I'm sure* in *I'm sure that France will win the grand slam this year*. Contrasts with a **'minus' committer**.

poetic effect A term used in relevance theory to refer to the effect of a kind that is typically engendered by literary texts, especially poetry. A poetic effect is considered to be achieved through the communication of a wide array of weak *r-implicatures of an utterance.

poetic function See functions (of language).

point of view (POV) A particular way of describing, considering, or judging something. The default *deictic centre for point of view is that of the speaker. Point of view is closely linked to pragmatics. Also called **perspective**, **perspectivalism**, **viewpoint**, or **vantage point**. *See also* logophoricity; *de se*.

polar antonymy, polar antonym *See* gradable antonymy, gradable antonym.

polite form Any form of address that is used to encode respect and social distance to an addressee. A typical example is the use of V pronouns (*see tu/vous* distinction) such as *nin* in Chinese, *vous* in French, and *vy* in Russian. Sometimes also called a **formal form**. *See also* familiar form.

politeness Broadly defined as encompassing both polite friendliness and polite formality, politeness is concerned with the actions people take to maintain their *face and that of the people they are interacting with. Defined in this way, politeness functions as a precondition of human communication. It is one of the central topics in *sociopragmatics. Also called **linguistic politeness**. *See also* absolute politeness; expressive politeness; mock politeness; positive politeness; negative politeness; solidarity politeness; pos-politeness; neg-politeness; withhold politeness.

politeness 1 *See* first-order politeness.

politeness 2 *See* second-order politeness.

politeness implicature A term used by the Australian lingiuist Michael Haugh for a *conversational implicature that engenders *politeness. In other words, by virtue of implying something, a speaker expresses politeness. Contrasted with **impoliteness implicature**. See Haugh (2011).

politeness marker A type of *downgrader used to show respect to an addressee. E.g. *please* in *Give this form to the secretary, please*.

politeness phenomenon In *sociopragmatics, a term which characterizes linguistic features which are used to communicate courtesy, deference, rapport, and distance.

politeness principle (PP) A general principle proposed by the British linguist Geoffrey Leech which dictates that one should minimize the expression of impolite beliefs and maximize that of polite ones. On Leech's view, the politeness principle is on a par with the British philosopher H. P. Grice's *co-operative principle.

politeness strategy hedge A *hedge that is addressed to politeness strategies. It indicates that there will be a violation of *face want. E.g. *I hate to say this, but . . .*

politeness theory Any systematic study of *politeness in linguistic exchanges. A politeness theory aims to develop an account of meaning that puts the use of language fully in its social context. Two classical pragmatic theories have been heavily used in politeness studies: the British philosopher H. P. Grice's theory of *conversational implicature and the British philosopher J. L. Austin's and the American philosopher John Searle's *speech act theory. There are a variety of different versions of politeness theory. Contrasts with **impoliteness theory**.

Pollyanna principle A principle proposed by the British linguist Geoffrey Leech based on the Pollyanna hypothesis in psychology. The principle states that interlocutors in a communication prefer pleasant topics over unpleasant ones and tend to use the best possible words to express what they have to say. It underlies the use and development of *euphemisms. Pollyanna was the eponymous heroine of Eleanor H. Porter's novel published in 1913, a child who always preferred to look on the bright rather than gloomy side of life.

polysemy, polysemous, polysemic The phenomenon of a single lexical item having more than one related meaning. E.g. *face* is polysemous, because it can be used variously of a human or animal face, a clock face, etc. It is commonly accepted that although there are clear cases, polysemy and *homonymy cannot in principle be distinguished from a theoretical point of view. *See also* homophony.

polysemy fallacy A term coined by the Belgian linguist Dominiek Sandra to refer to the view that each contextually derived, distinct sense of a particular lexical item should be analysed as an instance of polysemy. Such a view clearly underestimates the role played by context in determining lexical meaning.

poset = partially ordered set.

positional calendrical time unit *See* calendrical usage (of a time unit).

positive face An individual's desire that his or her ideas, views, and achievements be accepted and liked by others. In other words, it is concerned with an individual's presenting a good or positive self-image of him- or herself and securing the approval of others. Contrasts with **negative face**.

positive face goal A term used by the British linguist Geoffrey Leech to refer to the goal of enhancing *face. By contrast, ***negative face goal** is the term for avoiding loss of face. See Leech (2007).

positive Horn-scale Named after the American linguist Laurence Horn. A positive Horn scale contains a set of linguistic alternates $<x_1, x_2, \ldots, x_n>$ such that the semantically strong linguistic expression unilaterally entails the semantically weak ones. All the linguistic alternates in the set should be of the same word class, from the same register, and about the same semantic relation. In addition, they should be lexicalized to a similar degree. E.g. <all, most, many, some>, <adore, love, like>, and <identical, similar>. The use of a semantically weak linguistic expression in a positive Horn scale gives rise to a *Q_{scalar} implicature. See Levinson (2000). Contrasted with a **negative Horn scale**.

positive impoliteness A way of being impolite which aims to damage the addressee's *positive face goals, i.e. his or her desire to be approved of. The strategies used include ignoring the addressee, excluding him or her from an activity and making him or her feel uncomfortable. Contrasts with **negative impoliteness**.

positive politeness A way of being polite which aims at preserving, restoring, and enhancing the *positive face of addressees and others. When one uses positive politeness, one tends to choose the speech strategies that emphasize one's solidarity with the addressee. These strategies include claiming common ground, emphasizing co-operation with the addressee, and fulfilling the addressee's wants. Distinguished from **negative politeness**.

positive pragmatic transfer *See* pragmatic transfer.

pos-politeness Positive politeness defined by the British linguist Geoffrey Leech in terms of illocutionary and social goals. E.g. in paying a compliment, one's illocutionary goal is to communicate one's high estimation of the addressee. This is consistent with one's social goal, namely saying something polite to maintain or enhance good social relations. The notion here is not quite the same as the American linguist Penelope Brown and the British linguist Stephen Levinson's notion of *positive politeness. Contrasts with **neg-politeness**. See Leech (2007).

possible enrichment pair A term used in optimality-theoretic pragmatics to refer to a pair <f, m>, in which a range of pragmatic enrichments *m* can be generated from an unspecified representation *f* via a *common ground.

possible world(s) A complete and total way that the world could be. In other words, according to this notion, our **actual world**—the world as it is—is only one of an infinite number of conceivable alternative worlds. Some possible worlds may be similar to our actual world; others may be very different. Also known as **possible situation(s)**.

possible-world(s) semantics A formal approach to semantics based on the concept of a possible world. It recognizes that things could be other than they actually are, and postulates a number of possible worlds, or states of affairs, other than what is actually the case. The truth-condition of a sentence may therefore be true in some possible worlds but false in others. *See also* truth-conditional semantics; model-theoretic semantics.

postcedent A linguistic expression that determines in one way or another the interpretation of an *anaphoric expression, and comes later than the anaphoric expression. E.g. in *Before she left, Helen pinned a note on the cork panel on the door, Helen* is the postcedent for *she*. Contrasts with an **antecedent (2)**. *See also* cataphora.

postcolonial pragmatics A sub-branch of intercultural pragmatics (*see* cross-cultural pragmatics) which studies the use of the language of the colonizers in a postcolonial society or postcolonial societies. In a postcolonial society, a second (as opposed to foreign) language is sometimes used in interaction. E.g. the use of English in contemporary India. See Anchimbe and Janney (2011).

post-Gricean pragmatics **(1)** In its broad sense, any school of thought or research paradigm in pragmatics that develops ideas and insights derived from the British philosopher H. P. Grice, especially his theory of meaning in terms of speaker's intentions, and his account of rational communicative behaviour. This includes various versions of neo-Gricean pragmatics, relevance theory, and default semantics. **(2)** In its narrow sense, the term is sometimes used to refer to relevance theory. *See also* neo-Gricean pragmatics.

post-semantic pragmatics *Gricean pragmatics that yields conversational implicatures in a post-semantic way. Often contrasted with **pre-semantic pragmatics**. Also called **Gricean pragmatics 2**. *See also* far-side pragmatics.

potential implicature *See* im-plicature.

potential presupposition *See* pre-supposition.

POV = point of view.

PP = politeness principle.

pract *See* instantiated pragmatic act.

practical rationality *See* rationality.

pragma-dialectics Partly a normative approach to the study of argumentation developed by the Dutch linguists Frans van Eemeren and Rob Grootendorst. It incorporates the British philosopher J. L. Austin's and the American philosopher John Searle's speech act theory and the British philosopher H. P. Grice's theory of conversational implicature. In the pragma-dialectical framework, Grice's co-operative principle is recast as a wider communication principle that subsumes a set of sub-principles such as the **clarity**, **honesty**, **efficiency**, and **relevance principle**. Each of the sub-principles is implemented by certain rules of language use which serve as speech act alternatives to Grice's maxims. See van Eemeren and Grootendorst (2004); Cummings (2010).

pragma-historical linguistics A research trend in *historical pragmatics which represents a 'micro-approach' to looking at pragmatic change through time. Closely related to **discourse-oriented historical linguistics** in **historical discourse analysis**.

pragmalinguistic ability *See* pragmatic ability.

pragmalinguistic development Development by young children of linguistic forms that can be used to perform the appropriate pragmatic functions. *See also* pragmatic development.

pragmalinguistic diachronic pragmatics *See* diachronic pragmatics (2).

pragmalinguistics **1.** = pragmatics. **2.** A term used by the British linguist Geoffrey Leech which refers to the study of the particular structural resources that a given language provides for conveying pragmatic meaning. In other words, pragmalinguistics is concerned with the study of the more linguistic end of pragmatics, as opposed to *sociopragmatics, which is concerned with the more socio-cultural end of pragmatics. See Leech (1983).

pragmantax A blended term coined by the American linguist J. R. Ross to refer to a hybrid approach to the pragmatics–syntax interface, under which pragmatic constraints during the syntactic derivation of a sentence can be taken into account.

pragmantics *See* reductionism.

pragmaphilology A research trend in *historical pragmatics. It represents primarily a 'macro-approach' to the study of the pragmatics of historical texts at a particular point of time. The focus is on the wider changing social and cognitive contexts of the texts in which pragmatic change occurs. Closely related to **historical discourse analysis proper** in **historical discourse analysis**. See Traugott (2004); Culpeper (2010). *See also* diachronic pragmatics; pragma-historical linguistics.

pragmasemantics A term used especially in Continental Europe to refer to a hybrid approach to the pragmatics–semantics interface.

pragmastylistics *See* pragmatic stylistics.

pragmatic ability A term used in applied, interlanguage, instructional, and second and foreign language pragmatics for both knowledge about pragmatics and the ability to use it. Pragmatic ability includes **pragmalinguistic ability**—a learner's receptive and productive pragmatic ability with an emphasis on linguistic forms; **sociopragmatic ability**—his or her pragmatic ability in relation to the social and cultural aspects of pragmatic use of language; and **metapragmatic ability**—his or her pragmatic ability to analyse the pragmatics of the second and foreign languages he or she is learning. Furthermore, pragmatic ability is characterized in terms of situational competence rather than native or non-nativeness. See Ishihara and Cohen (2010). *See also* pragmatic competence.

pragmatic act A term used by the Danish linguist Jacob Mey for any exercise of societal empowerment through language within the European Continental tradition of pragmatics. An example of pragmatic act is implicit denial, which does not depend on what is said but relies on what is not said. Pragmatic acts do not necessarily include any specific speech acts. Indeed, there are pragmatic acts that cannot be reduced to or pinpointed as any specific speech acts. See Mey (2001). *See also* instantiated pragmatic act; allopract; pragmeme.

pragmatic adequacy A term deployed by the British linguist Louise Cummings to refer to a language user's ability to grasp the two essential features characteristic of any act of pragmatic interpretation. First, a pragmatic interpretation is inferential in nature. Secondly, the inferential process involved in a pragmatic interpretation is global in character.

pragmatic adverbial An adverbial that specifies the way of how a speaker is saying what he or she is saying. In other words, such an adverbial serves to indicate the style or manner of saying rather than modifying the propositional content of what is said. E.g. *Frankly/speaking frankly/to speak frankly* in *Frankly/speaking frankly/to speak frankly, you are good-for-nothing.* Alternative terms include a **speech-act adverbial**, **speech-act predicational**, **style disjunct**, and **utterance modifier**.

pragmatic ambiguity A term introduced by the American philosopher Keith Donnellan. It refers to the ambiguity that arises from the built-in duality of language in use. E.g. *Some of John's colleagues have been to an oxygen bar* is pragmatically ambiguous between the non-implicated, one-sided, lower-bounded reading 'At least some/if not all of John's colleagues have been to an oxygen bar' and the implicated, two-sided, upper and lower bounded interpretation 'Some but not all of John's colleagues have been to an oxygen bar'. See Horn (1989).

pragmatic ambivalence A term used by the British linguist Jenny Thomas for the phenomenon whereby the intended *pragmatic force of an utterance is deliberately indeterminate. E.g. sometimes it is unclear whether the utterance of the sentence *If I were you, I would leave this country immediately* performs a speech act of advising, warning, or threatening.

pragmatic analysis level A level on which a pragmatic analysis can be made. Five levels of pragmatic analysis have been proposed: (i) the **formal level**, (ii) the **actional level**, (iii) the **interactional level**, (iv) the **topic level**, and (v) the **organizational level**. On the formal level, a linguistic form is taken as the point of departure. The pragmatic analysis endeavours to determine the communicative functions of that linguistic form in interaction, and thus the mapping is from form to function. By contrast, the actional level is concerned with the function-to-form mapping. The analysis starts with an illocutionary speech act such as a request and establishes the formal or linguistic realizations available to perform the relevant speech act. The interactional level is the one on which interactional units such as adjacency pairs, speech act sequences, and the structure of a complete speech event are analysed. The topic level involves an analysis of propositions and sequences of propositions, and topic selection, maintenance, and development. Finally, on the organizational level, discourse-organizational mechanisms such as the turn-taking system in a conversation are examined.

pragmatic approach (to incomplete definite description) *See* incomplete definite description.

pragmatic central system A controversial view put forward by the Israeli philosopher Asa Kasher according to which there is a pragmatic component in the mind's central system. The pragmatic central system is needed for *conversational implicature and *politeness. See Kasher (1984); Cummings (2005). *See also* modular pragmatics; modularity; pragmatic interface.

pragmatic circle The Basque philosopher Kepa Korta and the American philosopher John Perry's term for *Grice's circle. It refers to the phenomenon that Gricean reasoning requires what is said to get started and is needed to get to what is said.

pragmatic competence One of the aspects of linguistic competence, pragmatic competence refers to a system of knowledge that a language user has in order to be able to use linguistic means (such as a sentence) for attaining linguistic ends (such as performing a speech act). The major components of pragmatic competence include systems of knowledge that govern the production and comprehension of speech acts and conversational implicatures. Defined thus, pragmatic competence is part of linguistic competence and should be contrasted with **pragmatic performance**. See Kasher (2010b).

pragmatic compositionality (view) (PC) A view advocated by the French philosopher François Recanati and others that compositionality should be associated with utterance rather than sentence meaning, and operate at the pragmatic rather than semantic/syntactic level, i.e. the level of pragmatically modulated propositions. In other words, composition of meaning is not determined by the semantics and syntax of a sentence uttered but rather by the intended meaning of a speaker. Such a position, if correct, can form the foundation on which **compositional pragmatics** is built. Pragmatic compositionality is considered to be on the *contextualist side. See Recanati (2005).

pragmatic connective *See* pragmatic marker (1).

pragmatic constraint Any condition that pertains to a principle, process, or representation in a pragmatic theory. It can be taken as an integral part of a pragmatic theory or an external restriction on the application of a pragmatic principle.

pragmatic contradiction An inconsistency that arises from pragmatic rather than semantic or logical implications. In other words, it is engendered by the saying of *what is said rather than the logical or semantic content of what is said. A typical example is *Moore's paradox.

pragmatic crime A type of language or linguistic crime which is committed partially or entirely by means of using language, in particular performing certain speech acts. Representative examples are perjury, solicitation, and threat.

pragmatic deficit *See* pragmatic disorder.

pragmatic definite *See* incomplete definite description.

pragmatic delay hypothesis A hypothesis found in *developmental and *experimental pragmatics which states that, while children have semantic knowledge, they lack a basic piece of pragmatic knowledge, namely Grice's maxim of Quantity, in the computation of scalar implicatures. See Chierchia et al. (2004).

pragmatic design features *See* pragmatic universals.

pragmatic development Development of pragmatic skills by young children to use language appropriately and effectively in social interaction. It includes the development of communicative intentions, conversational skills, and politeness principles. Pragmatic development is the key research topic in *developmental pragmatics.

pragmatic disability *See* pragmatic disorder.

pragmatic disorder Any impairment that lies primarily with the pragmatic use of language rather than with the processing of the structure of language. The deficit ranges from difficulties in the understanding of language in context through the interpretation of non-literal meaning to the use of pragmatic cues in conversation. On one dimension, a distinction can be drawn between **acquired** and **developmental pragmatic disorders**, and on another dimension, pragmatic disorders can be divided into **primary** and **secondary** ones. The diagnosis, assessment, and treatment of pragmatic disorders are a major concern in *clinical pragmatics. Alternative terms include **pragmatic deficit**, **pragmatic disability**, **pragmatic (language) impairment (PLI)**, **semantic-pragmatic disorder (SPD)**, **semantic-pragmatic deficit (syndrome)**, **semantic-pragmatic impairment**, **semantic-pragmatic difficulties**.

pragmatic division of labour *See* division of pragmatic labour.

pragmatic duality A term used by the Israeli linguist Shoshana Blum-Kulka for the feature of *conventional indirectness, namely, a conventionally indirect strategy can normally be interpreted at two levels, the literal and the non-literal level. E.g. *Can you help me with my pragmatics essay?* can be interpreted either as a question or as a request or as both.

pragmatic ellipsis A term used by the American psycholinguist Merrill Garrett and philosopher Robert Harnish for the ellipsis in which what has been omitted can be recovered pragmatically. E.g. in an appropriate context, one can say *I will, if you will*. The resolution of the ellipsis in this example has to be made contextually.

pragmatic entailment A term used by the French linguist Gilles Fauconnier and the American linguist Michael Israel, meaning an *inference that is on the one hand *default and on the other, *defeasible. According to this view, the sentence or the proposition expressed by the sentence *John can run 100m in 9.9 seconds* pragmatically entails the sentence or the proposition expressed by the sentence *John can run a slower 100m*. The latter is an entailment of the former because the inference is default, i.e. automatically valid; it is pragmatic because the inferences can be defeated. See Israel (2004). *See also* entailment.

pragmatic expression *See* pragmatic marker (1).

pragmatic fact A term used by the philosopher Steven Davis for phenomena such as the relation between the sentence *I'll go to Japan* and the range of speech acts such as promising, declaring one's intention, and predicting one's behaviour the sentence can be used to perform.

pragmatic failure Any lack of success in pragmatic use of language, especially by a second or foreign language learner. E.g. a divergence in a native-like pragmatic norm in the performance of a speech act such as complaining. Pragmatic failure can result from a number of factors including negative *pragmatic transfer, and the overgeneralization of pragmatic norms. See Ishihara and Cohen (2010).

pragmatic fallacy A fallacy that arises from a reasoning which does not meet criteria of reasonable argumentative discourse from propositions expressing opinions.

pragmatic force A term used by the British linguist Geoffrey Leech for the aspect of meaning that consists of both the *illocutionary force and the *rhetorical force of an utterance.

pragmatic formula *See* formula.

pragmatic function word *See* pragmatic marker (1).

pragmatic halo A term coined by the American linguist Peter Lasersohn for a set of entities or objects that are associated loosely with or around the denotation of a lexical item or proposition in a context. E.g. the pragmatic halo of the linguistic expression *one hundred kilometres* in *My home town is one hundred kilometres from New York* is a set of lengths clustered around one hundred kilometres. Lexical items such as *exactly*, *precisely*, and *perfectly* that can function to shrink a pragmatic halo are called **pragmatic slack regulators**.

pragmatic indeterminacy *See* indeterminacy (1).

pragmatic inference An *inference that is non-logical or pragmatic in nature in the sense that it is either non-monotonic, i.e. defeasible, or makes no contribution to truth-conditions. *Conversational implicatue is considered by some scholars as an instance of pragmatic inference. Contrasts with **logical inference**.

pragmatic information Any information about a speaker's communicative intentions, the use of language that requires such intentions, contexts of use, the relation between the user of a linguistic form and the act of using the form, the strategies an addressee employs to work out what the intentions and acts are, etc. Pragmatic information is not carried out by a linguistic form but by the uttering of the linguistic form.

pragmatic interface A controversial view proposed by the Israel philosopher Asa Kasher according to which there is an interface between the pragmatic module and the pragmatic component of the mind's central system. The pragmatic interface is claimed to be evidenced by indexicals and lexical pragmatic presuppostions. See Kasher (1984); Cummings (2005). *See also* modular pragmatics; modularity; pragmatic central system.

pragmatic interpretation An interpretation that is *hermeneutic in nature. The hermeneutic character has three properties: (i) **charity**—a pragmatic interpretation is possible only if one presupposes that the interlocutors are rational, (ii) **non-monotonicity**—a pragmatic interpretation is defeasible; (iii) **holism**—given defeasibility of a pragmatic interpretation, there is virtually no limit to the amount of contextual information that can affect such an interpretation. E.g. a conversational implicature of a sentence uttered constitutes a pragmatic interpretation. Sometimes also called **pragmatic reading**. Contrasts sharply with a **semantic interpretation**, which is algorithmic and mechanic in nature. See Recanati (2004).

pragmatic intrusion The phenomenon whereby the pragmatically enriched or inferred content enters into the conventional, truth-conditional content of what is said. E.g. the assignment of reference for the anaphoric pronoun *they* in *The authorities barred the anti-globalization demonstrators because they advocated violence* and *The authorities barred the anti-globalization demonstrators because they feared violence* is dependent crucially on our real-world knowledge about who would most likely be advocating or fearing violence. There is thus pragmatic intrusion into what is said. See Huang (2007). *See also* intrusive construction.

pragmatic intrusionism The view that pragmatics enters semantics, or that pragmatics contributes to what is said.

pragmatic knowledge There are two varieties of pragmatic knowledge. **Primary pragmatic knowledge** is deeply held, default, and perhaps non-representational background information or knowledge. This knowledge is shared so widely between interlocutors as to seem indiscernible. It constitutes an essential part of one's pragmatic understanding of the world. It contributes to the interpretation of what a speaker says. By contrast, **secondary pragmatic knowledge** is information or knowledge that is derived from the local context of an utterance. It contributes to the interpretation of what a speaker implicates. See Gibbs (2004).

pragmatic language A term used by the British Chinese linguist Yan Huang for the class of languages such as Chinese, Japanese, and Korean in which pragmatics plays the central role that in European languages such as English, French, and German is alleged to be played by grammar. In these prototypical pragmatic languages, for example, many of the constraints on *anaphora (1) are primarily due to principles of language use rather than rules of syntactic structure. By contrast, languages such as English, French, and German are taken to be **syntactic languages**. See Huang (1994; 2000).

pragmatic (language) assessment Assessment of pragmatic language skills and *pragmatic disorders in children and adults by clinicians, principally speech and language pathologists in *clinical and *neuropragmatics. Pragmatic language assessments are normally the first step necessary for the diagnosis, management, and treatment of pragmatic disorders. They make use of a large range of techniques such as standardized tests, checklists of pragmatic skills, and conversation and/or discourse analyses of spontaneous outputs from children and adults. Pragmatic concepts such as speech acts, conversational implicatures, conversational structures, and discourse cohesion and coherence in clients across a variety of different clinical groups have been assessed. Patients include those with aphasia, epilepsy and autistic features, left- and right-hemisphere damage, and schizophrenia.

pragmatic language impairment *See* pragmatic disorder.

pragmatic language intervention Remediation of pragmatic skills in children and adults using a range of techniques. These techniques include activities designed to target specific areas of pragmatic deficits such as the performance of certain speech acts, conversational skill training, and pragmatic skills in certain social settings. *See also* pragmatic (language) therapy.

pragmatic (language) therapy A term used in *clinical pragmatics for any therapy that is designed to treat patients with *pragmatic disorders. Sometimes also called **pragmatics-based therapy**. *See also* pragmatic language intervention.

pragmatic linguistics = pragmatics. The term is used especially in conjunction with other branches, trends, and school of linguistics, as in the phrase 'cognitive linguistics, functional linguistics, and pragmatic linguistics'.

pragmatic marker **1.** In its broad sense, the term is used as an overarching one to cover any linguistic expression that does not make any contribution to the propositional content of a sentence uttered but conveys a speaker's potential communicative intentions. E.g. *frankly*, *Professor Davies*, and *however*. Four subtypes can be distinguished: (i) **basic markers**, (ii) **commentary markers**, (iii) **parallel markers**, and (iv) **discourse markers (2)**. The term 'pragmatic marker' in its broad sense is largely interchangeable with the term 'discourse marker' also in its broad sense. See Fraser (1996). Also called variously a **pragmatic connective**, **pragmatic expression**, **pragmatic function word**, **pragmatic particle**, **discourse operator**, **phatic connective**, and **parenthetical phrase**. **2.** In its narrow sense, the term refers to any linguistic expression that conveys a speaker's comments on the propositional content of a sentence uttered but does not contribute to the truth-condition of the sentence that holds it. A pragmatic marker in this sense has a number of distinctive properties: (i) it does not affect the truth-condition of the proposition of the sentence uttered, (ii) it operates on or takes scope over the proposition rather than the syntactic constituents of the sentence uttered, (iii) it is syntactically optional, and (iv) it is semantically parasitic on the proposition of the sentence uttered. E.g. *amazingly*, *I believe*, and *perhaps*. Pragmatic markers in this sense are categorized into two types: **conceptual** and **non-conceptual pragmatic markers**. See Feng (2010).

pragmatic minimalism *See* Occam's razor.

pragmatic misfire **1.** In its narrow sense, = misfire. **2.** In its broad sense, the term refers to any use of language that is not felt to be appropriate in relation to a particular *context. Construed thus, pragmatic misfires are instances of **pragmatic failure**.

pragmatic mode (of communication) A term used by the American linguist Talmy Givón to make reference to communication that is characterized by (i) topic–comment constructions, (ii) loose conjunctions, (iii) slow rate of delivery, (iv) word-order governed by flow of pragmatic information, (v) roughly one-to-one ratio of verbs to nouns in discourse, with verbs being semantically simple, and (vi) no use of grammatical morphology. Contrasts with the **syntactic mode** (of communication).

pragmatic module *See* modular pragmatics.

pragmatic negation *See* metalinguistic negation.

pragmatic norm A term encountered in applied, interlanguage, instructional, and second and foreign language pragmatics to refer to a range of conventions or tendencies for pragmatic language use, which are stereotypical or generally preferred in a speech community.

pragmatic obligatory control A term introduced by the British Chinese linguist Yan Huang for the obligatory control construction that can be interpreted only in pragmatic terms. Pragmatic obligatory control is extensively used in *pragmatic languages like Chinese, Japanese, and Korean. See Huang (1994; 2000).

pragmatic operator An **operator** is a linguistic expression that modifies other linguistic units under its scope. A pragmatic operator is one that makes a pragmatic contribution to a sentence or discourse. E.g. *because*, *but*, and *so* in English.

pragmatic paradox (of politeness) A term used by the British linguist Geoffrey Leech for the contradiction arising from the asymmetry of politeness: what is polite for a speaker (a speaker pays a compliment to an addressee) may be impolite for an addressee (the addressee makes ritual denials of the compliment). If both the speaker and the addressee were equally determined to be polite and not to give way, then this asymmetry would never be resolved, hence the paradox. More recently Leech called the paradox the **battles for politeness**. Also called the **pragmatic quasi-paradox**. See Leech (2007).

pragmatic particle *See* pragmatic marker (1).

pragmatic performance The actual manifestation of *pragmatic competence. In addition, it also manifests a variety of other cognitive systems involved in the physiological and psychological processing of natural language in the human brain/mind. See Kasher (2010b).

pragmatic politeness *See* absolute politeness.

pragmatic preservation A term used in clinical pragmatics for the preservation of pragmatic abilities or pragmatic functioning in patients with *pragmatic disorders.

pragmatic presupposition The conception that *presupposition is a belief a speaker takes for granted in making an assertion. In other words, it is speakers rather than sentences or statements that have presuppositions. If the belief is false, then the utterance will be somewhat inappropriate. But the sentence uttered does not lack a *truth value, and consequently, no truth value gaps are needed. On this characterization of presupposition, if someone says *The king of France is bald*, then since there is no king of France, the utterance is simply infelicitous. Also called **utterance** or **speaker presupposition**. Contrasted with **semantic presupposition**.

pragmatic principle A general, broad statement of how language is used which is hypothetically valid for all languages. A typical example is the *co-operative principle and its attendant *maxims of conversation postulated by the British philosopher H. P. Grice.

pragmatic processing model *See* direct access view (of context effects); modular view (of context effects); graded salience hypothesis.

Pragmatic Protocol One of the most prominent pragmatic assessment instruments used in *clinical pragmatics to assess children's pragmatic skills. It consists of 30 pragmatic parameters categorized into three groups: (i) verbal aspects like speech acts, (ii) paralinguistic aspects like verbal quality, and (iii) non-verbal aspects like physical proximity. The assessment tool has been used to assess the pragmatic abilities, skills, and performances of child and adult patients with e.g. aphasia, brain injuries, chronic schizophrenia, Parkinson's disease, and AIDs.

pragmatic quasi-paradox *See* pragmatic paradox (of politeness).

pragmatic reading *See* pragmatic interpretation.

pragmatic reductionism The view that semantics is wholly included in pragmatics. Also called **pragmaticism** and **monism of use**. Often distinguished from **semantic reductionism**.

pragmatic scale A scale that is given by real world knowledge, context, and/or other pragmatic factors. It is essentially a *nonce scale, i.e. a contextually given *ad hoc* scale. Such a scale can be based on any partially ordered informational contrast sets in a contextual salient way. Stock examples are of the type known as *Hirschberg scales. E.g. the scale of football superstars <David Beckham, Michael Owen>. Contrasts with a **semantic** or **lexical scale**. Also referred to as a **context-dependent scale**.

pragmatic scale model (of politeness) An approach to *politeness proposed by the British linguist Helen Spencer-Oatey in which politeness is accounted for in terms of three pragmatic scales or dimensions: (i) the need for consideration, (ii) the need for being valued, and (iii) the need for relational identity. Interlocutors will select the relevant point on the relevant scale in accordance with their sociocultural values and the *speech event in which they find themselves. *See also* conversational contract model (of politeness); face-saving model (of politeness); conversational maxim model (of politeness); social norm model (of politeness).

pragmatic semantics A term used to refer to a positon in the philosophy of language, according to which the understanding of actions is the point of departure for a theory of meaning. Defined thus, semantics is regarded as a special part of pragmatics (action theory or action logic). Pragmatic semantics can further be divided into two categories: **rule-based** and **intention-based**. According to the former, in order to know the meaning of a sign, one has just to know the rules one has to follow to use the sign correctly. By contrast for the latter, the crucial question is what in a particular situation the sign is being used for. This distinction corresponds roughly to the two possible interpretations of the famous equation 'meaning = use' put forward by the Austrian-born British philosopher Ludwig Wittgenstein. See Kompa and Meggle (2011).

pragmatic slack regulator *See* pragmatic halo.

pragmatic space *See* pragmatic universals.

pragmatic stylistics The application of the findings and methodologies of theoretical pragmatics to the study of the concept of **style** in language, i.e. systematic variations in usage in written or spoken language including those in literary texts among individual writers, genres, and periods. Also termed **pragmastylistics**. See Black (2006). *See also* literary pragmatics.

pragmatic theory (of truth) *See* pragmatist theory (of truth).

pragmatic therapy *See* pragmatic language intervention.

pragmatic tone A term that is encountered especially in applied, interlanguage, instructional, and second and foreign language pragmatics to refer to the affect expressed indirectly by linguistic and/

or non-linguistic means. Metaphorically, a pragmatic tone is taken to be the 'colour' of emotion and attitude on language. Pragmatic appropriateness is regulated not only by way of linguistic devices but also by virtue of pragmatic tone. An utterance may differ in meaning depending on pragmatic tones. This is because effect can be encoded in a pragmatic tone through linguistic structures, intonation, and non-verbal cues such as gesture, posture, and facial expression. See Ishihara and Cohen (2010).

pragmatic topic construction *See* Chinese-style topic construction.

pragmatic transfer A term used in acquisitional, applied, interlanguage, instructional, and second and foreign language pragmatics to refer to the influence of a language learner's first language pragmatic knowledge on the use of his or her second or foreign language. Pragmatic transfer can be positive or negative. In **positive pragmatic transfer**, a learner's first language pragmatic norms are similar and applicable to his or her second or foreign language. Consequently, pragmatic transfer will yield positive results. By contrast, in **negative pragmatic transfer**, the pragmatic norms in a learner's second or foreign language are quite different. As a consequence, the transfer of his or her first language pragmatic norms will generate negative results such as awkwardness, misinterpretation, or even a breakdown in communication. See Ishihara and Cohen (2010).

pragmatic unit A unit for pragmatic analysis. E.g. a statement is considered to be a pragmatic unit by some pragmaticists.

pragmatic universals Statements relating to the pragmatic dimension of language that are true of all languages. A stock example of pragmatic universals is **pragmatic design features**, namely all human languages have pragmatics. A second example is **pragmatic space**, namely the directionality of contextualization. A third is the co-operative principle and its attendant maxims of conversation proposed by the British philosopher H. P. Grice.

pragmatic vagueness Sometimes a convenient cover term for a variety of cases under *vagueness (1) such as approximation, generality, and loose talk. E.g. *John is bald.*

pragmatic wastebasket A catchy label invented by the Israeli philosopher Yehoshua Bar-Hillel in the early 1970s for the then commonly held view that pragmatics functions essentially as a temporary grab-bag for everything that cannot be tackled by certain core branches of linguistics such as syntax, semantics, and perhaps even phonology, and hence cannot be taken seriously. The development of pragmatics has shown that such a view is wrong. In other words, the pragmatic wastebasket has been largely emptied.

pragmatic zero anaphor A term used by the British Chinese linguist Yan Huang to refer to the class of *zero anaphor that is syntactically ambiguous in the Chomskyan sense; i.e. it can fit in simultaneously with more than one type of empty category proposed by the American linguist Noam Chomsky. Pragmatic zero anaphors cannot be determined syntactically but only pragmatically. They are extensively used in *pragmatic languages like Chinese, Japanese, and Korean. Also called an **empty pragmatic category**. See Huang (1994; 2000).

pragmaticalization A term used in *historical pragmatics by some pragmaticists to refer to the process by which, in the history of a language, an autonomous lexical item develops into one with pragmatic meaning. E.g. the process of how *well* changes into a *pragmatic marker. A special case of grammaticalization or grammaticization. See Culpeper (2010).

pragmatically disordered A term used in *clinical pragmatics to refer to children and adults whose impairments lie primarily with the use of language rather than being related to any deficits in the processing of linguistic structures. Also called **pragmatically impaired**.

pragmatically enriched proposition A *proposition that contains not only ingredients that are semantically called for by any constituent of a sentence but also ingredients that have to be supplied by pragmatic processes such as *free enrichment. E.g. the pragmatically enriched proposition of the sentence *I have brushed my teeth* may be that the speaker has brushed his or her teeth this morning. Often contrasts with a **minimal proposition**.

pragmatically enriched said A term coined by the French philosopher François Recanati for those aspects of what is said that must be pragmatically enriched. E.g. 'Elizabeth is cleverer than Naomi' may be the pragmatically enriched said of *Elizabeth is cleverer*.

pragmatically impaired *See* pragmatically disordered.

pragmatician *See* pragmaticist.

pragmaticism (1) *See* pragmatic reductionism.

pragmaticism (2) An unsuccessful term used by the American semiotician Charles Peirce for the philosophical movement known as ***pragmatism**, in the hope that the term would distinguish his version of pragmatism from the versions put forward by the American philosopher William James and other contemporaries.

pragmaticist Usually in the philosophy of language and linguistics, of someone who specializes in, professes, or practises pragmatics. Also termed a **pragmatist** or **pragmatician**.

pragmatico-centrism A term, due to the Japanese linguist S. Fukuohima, that is used in the pragmatics–syntax interface for the view that pragmatics plays a central role in syntax. In contrast, by **syntactico-centrism** is meant the view of centrality of syntax. The position that lies between the two centrisms is called the **syntax–pragmatics alliance**.

pragmatics See the introduction. The systematic study of meaning dependent on language in use. Central topics of enquiry of pragmatics include a speaker's communicative intentions, the use of language that requires such intentions, contexts of use, the relation between the user of a linguistic form and the act of using the form, and the strategies an addressee employs to work out what the intentions and acts are. Currently there are two main schools of thought in pragmatics: the **Anglo-American**, **'component' view** and the **(European) Continental**, **'perspective' view**. With respect to its scope, pragmatics can be divided into **micro-** and **macropragmatics**. Sometimes also called **linguistic pragmatics**. Often contrasted with **semantics** within linguistics.

pragmatics based therapy *See* pragmatic (language) therapy.

Pragmatics Profile One of the most important pragmatic assessment tools used in *clinical pragmatics to assess children's everyday linguistic and communicative behaviours. The central focus of the profile is on pragmatic aspects of these behaviours. Based on a structured interview with a child's parent, teacher, or other carers, an assessor investigates his or her *pragmatic ability in areas such as communicative functions, conversation and interaction, and contextual variation. Pragmatics Profile has been used with a range of clinical groups of children including those with delayed language development, specific language impairment, and autism.

pragmatism (1) A philosophical movement initiated by the American philosopher Charles Peirce in the early 1870s, revived by the American philosopher William James in 1898, and further developed by the American philosopher John Dewey. The central tenet of pragmatism is the belief that one's philosophical concepts must be connected to his or her practices. Put slightly differently, on a **pragmatist**'s view, the meaning of a doctrine is the same as the practical effects of taking it up. On this basis, pragmatism makes use of techniques and methods derived from the natural sciences to address questions of meaning and truth. The relevance of pragmatism to pragmatics is that some philosophers of language, especially those working in the tradition of *ordinary language philosophy are taken to hold views closely akin to those of pragmatism. Also called **American pragmatism** and **classical pragmatism**. *See also* neo-pragmatism.

pragmatism (2) *See* contextualism.

pragmatist (1) *See* pragmaticist.

pragmatist (2) *See* contextualism.

pragmatist (3) Of someone who specializes in, professes, or practises the doctrines of the philosophical movement known as **pragmatism (1)**.

pragmatist theory (of truth) A theory of truth proposed and defended by philosophers in the tradition of the *American pragmatism. According to this theory, truth is that which effectively works. Put in slogan form, a belief is true if and only if it is useful in practice. Also known as the **pragmatic** or **utility theory** of truth. *See also* coherence theory (of truth); correspondence theory (of truth); deflationist theory (of truth); performative theory of (truth).

pragmeme A generalized *pragmatic act or a contextualized or situated speech act, i.e. a speech act that both depends on and gives rise to a situation in which it is realized. E.g. the uttering of *Can I help you?* by a shop assistant in a service encounter situation. See Mey (2001); Capone (2010).

pre-announcement A type of *pre-sequence that serves as preliminary to an announcement in a conversation. The main function of pre-announcement is to check on newsworthiness of a potential announcement. E.g. *Have you heard the news?*

pre-arrangement A variety of *pre-sequence that functions as preliminary to an arrangement in a conversation. Its main function is to check an addressee's availability before making arrangements. E.g. the use of *What are you doing tomorrow afternoon?* to precede and foreshadow an arrangement for future contact. *See also* pre-invitation.

precative Signifying, marking, or constituting a direct request. E.g. *Please stop whining* is precative.

precisification A type of sentence non-literality defined by the American philosopher Kent Bach in which a sentence contains a precisification that is not expressed explicitly. E.g. The precisification that is not expressed explicitly of *John has two sons* is something like [exactly].

pre-closing A type of *pre-sequence that serves as preliminary to the closure of a conversation. The main function of pre-closing is to forewarn an addressee that the speaker wants to close the conversation. E.g. *Okay*. Linguistic expressions like *okay*, *all right*, and *so* used in a pre-closing sequence are called **pre-closing items**.

pre-delicate A variety of *pre-sequence that acts as preliminary to the raising of a delicate issue in a conversation. The main function of pre-delicate is to warn an addressee that a potentially sensitive topic is coming up. E.g. *Do you mind if I ask you something personal?*

predicate A term originally used in logic. **(1)** A part of a sentence traditionally seen as representing what is said, or predicated, of the subject. E.g. in *John smiled*, *smiled* is the predicate. **(2)** A verb or other unit which takes a set of arguments within a sentence. E.g. in *John loves Mary*, *loves* is a two-place predicate which takes *John* and *Mary* as its *arguments.

predicate calculus A branch of mathematical logic, and one of the two main systems of logic used in *formal semantics and pragmatics.

It examines the logical relations that hold within a sentence and attends to propositions containing predicates, arguments and quantifiers. Also known as **predicate logic**. Often contrasts with **propositional calculus**.

predicationary metonymy *See* metonymy.

pre-disagreement A type of *pre-sequence that functions as preliminary to a disagreement in a conversation. Its main purpose is to mitigate disagreement. This is often achieved by exaggerating agreement or expressing partial agreement. E.g. B's *Yes, interesting as a whole* in the conversational exchange A: *The detective story is very interesting.* B: *Yes, interesting as a whole, but there are rather boring sections.*

preference organization A term found in *conversation analysis for the structural allocation of *preferred and dispreferred turn types in response to different speech acts such as summoning, greeting, and requesting. E.g. acceptance is the preferred and refusal the dispreferred response to an invitation. Whether a particular turn type is preferred or dispreferred is sometimes culturally specific. E.g. in reply to a compliment, while acceptance is preferred in some cultures like Western and languages like English, ritual denial is preferred in other cultures such as East Asian or languages such as Chinese.

preferred = preferred second turn.

preferred interpretation (of a phrase, sentence, utterance, etc.) An interpretation that is the most favoured one out of a number of other possible interpretations in or out of a specific context. E.g. the preferred interpretation of *John heard from Professor Smith that he had passed the examination* is that John heard from Professor Smith that John had passed the examination rather than that John heard from Professor Smith that Professor Smith had passed the examination, given real-world knowledge.

preferred second turn (preferred) A second pair part of an *adjacency pair in a conversation that is most likely to occur in response to its first pair part from a structural point of view. E.g. acceptance is the preferred second turn with respect to an invitation, as illustrated in B's turn. A: *Why don't you come up and see me some time?* B: *I would like to.* Also called an **unmarked second turn**.

preferred sequence Any sequence in a conversation that is preferred.

preferred turn *See* preferred second turn; preference organization.

pre-invitation A type of *pre-sequence that serves as preliminary to an invitation in a conversation. The main function of pre-invitation is to check an addressee's availability before issuing an invitation. E.g. *Are you free next Saturday?*

pre-offer A variety of *pre-sequence that acts as preliminary to an offer in a conversation. Its main function is to check whether an offer or help is needed. E.g. *Did you come by car?*

preparatory condition A kind of *felicity condition which states the real-world prerequisites for a *speech act. E.g. in the case of a request (such as A asking B to close the window), the preparatory conditions are (i) the speaker has reason to believe that the addressee has the ability to carry out the action requested (i.e. A believes that B is able to close the window), and (ii) if the addressee is not asked, he or she will not perform the action (i.e. B is not going to close the window of his or her own accord). If the preparatory conditions are not met, especially in the context of performing an *institutionalized speech act, the speech act is not performed successfully because, in the British philosopher J. L. Austin's term, it has *misfired. See Searle (1969).

pre-pre-sequence A term used in *conversation analysis for a *turn or sequence of turns that precedes another turn or sequence of turns which itself prefaces another specific turn or sequence of turns. E.g. the use of *I'd like to ask you something* in A's turn to function as a pre-pre-question in A: *I'd like to ask you something.* B: *M-hm.* A: *I've sent an email to the principal.* B: *M-hm.* A: *telling her what I thought of her plan.* B: *M-hm.* A: *Will I get an answer from her d'you think?* B: *I think so.*

pre-request A type of *pre-sequence that serves as preliminary to a request in a conversation. Its main function is to check on an addressee's willingness or ability to fulfil the request. E.g. *Do you know how to use this printer?*.

pre-s *See* pre-sequence.

pre-self-identification A variety of *pre-sequence that functions as preliminary to a self-identification usually in a telephone conversation. E.g. *Hello Jane?*.

pre-semantic pragmatics *Gricean pragmatics that plays a systematic role in presemantics, i.e. to help determine the *truth-conditional, propositional content of a sentence uttered. Also called **Gricean pragmatics 1**. Often contrasted with **post-semantic pragmatics**. *See also* near-side pragmatics; restricted pre-semantic pragmatics.

present tense *See* tense.

pre-sequence A term used in *conversation analysis for a *turn or sequence of turns that prefigures other specific turns or sequences of turns. E.g. the turn *Do you have any jam?* that prefaces a turn in which the speech act of requesting is performed. For some scholars, this term is reserved for the sequence type only. In that case, the term **pre-s** is used to refer to the turn type.

presumption of optimal relevance An assumption in relevance theory which states that an ostensive stimulus (i.e. an utterance) is relevant enough for it to be worth an audience's processing effort and is the most relevant one compatible with a communicator's abilities and preferences.

presumptive meaning = *default meaning.

presuppose *See* presupposition.

presupposition A concept (re)introduced by the German philosopher, mathematician, and logician Gottlob Frege in modern time, though the notion may go back at least as far as the medieval philosopher Petrus Hispanus. A presupposition is a proposition whose truth is taken for granted in the utterance of a sentence. The main function of presupposition is to act as a precondition or presumption of some kind for the appropriate use of the sentence. E.g. the uttering of the sentence *John regrets that he became temperamental* **presupposes** that John became temperamental. There are two conceptions of presupposition: (i) **semantic**, **sentence**, or **statement presupposition**, and (ii) **pragmatic**, **utterance**, or **speaker presupposition**. Presuppositions in general exhibit two distinctive properties: *constancy under negation and *defeasibility or cancellability. Currently, most linguists and philosophers of language are of the view that presupposition is largely a pragmatic phenomenon. See Huang (2007). *See also* conversational implicature; entailment; cleft presupposition; existential presupposition; factive presupposition.

pre-supposition The British linguist Gerald Gazdar's technical term for a **potential presupposition**, i.e. a presupposition to which the uttering of a sentence could possibly give rise prior to cancellation. E.g. the uttering of the first sentence in *The king of France isn't bald—there is no king of France* would pre-suppose, i.e. engender the potential presupposition, that the king of France exists. But this potential presupposition is then overtly denied by the second sentence. If a potential presupposition is not defeated, it will then survive to become an **actual presupposition**.

presupposition failure One of the main issues in the study of presupposition: if a statement presupposes something which does not exist, what are the consequences for that statement? A much-quoted example of a statement of this kind is *The king of France is bald*. On the British philosopher Bertrand Russell's view, the sentence asserts both that there is a king of France and that he is bald. If the king of France does not exist, the sentence is false. By contrast, according to the British philosopher Peter Strawson, in using the sentence, a speaker does not assert but merely presupposes that there is a king of France. If there is no king of France, then there is a presupposition failure. Consequently the sentence is neither true nor false: there is simply a *truth value gap.

presupposition projection problem The problem of stating and explaining the presuppositions of complex sentences (as 'wholes') in terms of the presuppositions of their component simple sentences (as 'parts').

presupposition trigger A linguistic expression or construction whose use engenders a presupposition. There are two types of presupposition trigger: **lexical presupposition trigger** and **constructional** or **structural presupposition trigger**.

primary deixis A term used by the British linguist Sir John Lyons for both *gestural and symbolic deixis. Often distinct from **secondary deixis**.

primary illocution A term used by the American philosopher John Searle for the most likely intention a speaker has when he or she performs an illocutionary act. The primary illocution usually derives from the **secondary illocution**, which is not the speaker's most likely intention. Thus, when someone asks *Can you pass the soy sauce?* the primary illocution of the utterance is a request and the secondary illocution is a question. *See also* direct illocution.

primary illocution indicator A linguistic expression that has purely non-propositional meaning and is used to indicate the illocutionary act it performs. E.g. *hello* (greeting), *bravo* (congratulating or expressing admiration), *hooray* (expressing (exuberant) approval). Sometimes also called a **verbal gesture**. See Hurford, Heasley, and Smith (2007).

primary-literal meaning *See* literal meaning.

primary performative *See* implicit performative.

primary pragmatic disorder A type of *pragmatic disorder that does not have its source in structural language deficits, i.e. deficits in syntax and/or semantics. An adult with a traumatic brain injury, for instance, can have relatively intact structural language and can pass standardized language tests but can still present with significant impairment of pragmatics. Contrasts with a **secondary pragmatic disorder**.

primary pragmatic knowledge *See* pragmatic knowledge.

primary pragmatic process (p-process) A term used by the French philosopher François Recanati for any pragmatic process that plays a role in the very constitution of *what is said. In other words, such a process pragmatically enriches what is said. E.g. the pragmatic process involved in the enrichment from *Mary was early* to 'Mary was early for the lecture'. *Saturation and *free enrichment are two instances of a primary pragmatic process. See Recanati (1993). Contrasted with a **secondary pragmatic process**.

primitive speech act A term used by the Danish linguist Anna Trosborg for a *speech act that is performed by a child before it develops into a **full-fledged adult speech act**. Primitive speech acts are often performed by means of incomplete linguistic expressions with rudimentary propositions. Their illocutionary force frequently has to be worked out inferentially from the context in which the linguistic forms are used. E.g. the utterance of *red pencil* by a three-year-old child to perform the indirect speech act of requesting.

principle of bivalence *See* law of bivalence.

principle of charity (1) A methodological constraint on interpretation, proposed by the British philosopher Donald Davidson, which states that in the process of interpretation we assume that our interlocutors' belief systems are very much like our own. In other words, on this view, charity is a condition of possibility of interpretation because interpretation must be charitable in order to be meaningful. See Medina (2005).

principle of charity (2) A pragmatic, interpretive principle used extensively in *Argumentation Theory. It demands the addition to the stated premises of the most plausible proposition needed to make the whole set of premises relevant to the conclusion, provided that the added statement is consistent with what is already in the discourse.

principle of clarity A principle in the pragma-dialectical approach to the study of argumentation, which states that one should not perform any speech act that is incomprehensible.

principle of compositionality A principle which dictates that the meaning of a complex expression is a compositional function (i.e. combination) of the meanings of its parts and their syntactic mode of combination. Thus, the meaning of *young people* is derivable from the meaning of *young* and the meaning of *people*. The appropriate way of adding meanings up is provided by syntactic rules. Expressions that conform to the principle (such as *young people* above) are called **compositional expressions**. In other words, these expressions have **compositional meaning**. Expressions that do not (such as the idiom *kick the bucket*) are said to be **non-compositional** or **semantically opaque**. Compositionality in this sense is also known as **semantic compositionality**. The notion of (semantic) compositionality is referred to as the '**building block metaphor**' by some cognitive linguists such as the American linguist Ronald Langacker. Also called the **principle of semantic compositionality** or the **Fregean principle (of compositionality of meaning)**. *See also* pragmatic compositionality (view).

principle of contrast A general pragmatic principle proposed by the American linguist Eve Clark which states that speakers will take any difference in form to signal a difference in meaning. Consequently, innovative expressions must contrast in meaning with conventional ones. See Clark (2004). Distinguished from the **principle of conventionality**.

principle of conventionality A general pragmatic principle postulated by the American linguist Eve Clark which says that if there is a conventional expression for a certain meaning, speakers are expected to use that form to express that meaning. See Clark (2004). Contrasts with the **principle of contrast**.

principle of economic versatility A principle proposed by the American linguist George Zipf which posits a direct correlation between a lexical item's semantic versatility and its frequency of use: the more semantically general, the more use. Contrasts with his **law of abbreviation**.

principle of economy *See* principle of least effort.

principle of effective means A principle put forward by the Israeli philosopher Asa Kasher which proposes an optimal trade-off between effect and effort: 'Given a desired end, one is to choose that action which most effectively, and at least cost, attains that end.' Also known as the **principle of rationality**. *See also* minimax principle.

principle of efficiency (1) *See* principle of least effort.

principle of efficiency (2) A principle in *pragma-dialectics which states that one should not perform any speech acts that are redundant or meaningless. *See also* principle of honesty; principle of relevance.

principle of effort minimization *See* E-principle.

principle of honesty A principle in *pragma-dialectics which states that one should not perform any speech acts that are insincere. *See also* principle of efficiency (2); principle of relevance.

principle of least effort A principle which states that speakers do no more than is necessary to achieve successful communication.

principle of parallelism (1) An utterance interpretation strategy: 'Unless there is evidence to the contrary, parallel constructions or functions tend to be interpreted in a parallel fashion.' E.g. people tend to interpret *He* and *him* in *John saw Peter this morning. He told him about the incident* as being linked to *John* and *Peter*, respectively. Also called the **parallel function principle**. See Huang (1994).

principle of parallelism (2) A term used by the French philosopher François Recanati for the view that if a sentence can be used in different contexts to express different propositions, then the explanation for this contextual variation of the propositional content of the sentence is that the sentence has different linguistic meanings. In other words, it is semantically ambiguous.

principle of rationality *See* rationality; principle of effective means.

principle of relevance A principle in *pragma-dialectics which states that one should not perform any speech acts that are not in an appropriate way connected with previous speech acts or communicative situations. *See also* principle of efficiency (2); principle of honesty.

principle of relevance maximization *See* R-principle (2).

principle of semantic compositionality *See* principle of compositionality.

principle of semantic innocence *See* semantic innocence.

privative antonym A type of *overlapping antonym. E.g. the sense relation between *clean* and *dirty*. A distinct feature of privative antonyms is that the positive term implies the absence of some undesirable property, and the negative term, the presence of some undesirable property. *See also* gradable antonymy; equipollent antonymy.

privileged ground In opposition to the notion of **common ground**, the notion of privileged ground refers to the information that is available only to one of the participants of a speech event, usually the speaker.

probabilistic model (of speech act interpretation) *See* cue-based model (of speech act interpretation).

problem-solver pragmatics, problem-solver *See* big-tent pragmatics.

procedural meaning A term used in *relevance theory for any meaning that does not contribute any concept to the logical form of a sentence or utterance, but rather provides a constraint on, or indication of, the ways in which certain aspects of pragmatic inference should proceed. This applies to the derivation of both the explicit content (*see* explicature) and the implicit content (*see* r-implicature). In other words, in procedural encoding, linguistic forms indicate computational processes. *After all*, *but*, and *so* are examples of lexical items that encode procedural information. These lexical items are called **procedural markers**. Contrasts with **conceptual meaning**.

procedural semantics (1) A term encountered in relevance theory for the category of linguistic semantics whose domain contains linguistic forms whose encoded meaning does not contribute concepts to the logical form of a sentence or utterance, but rather provides a constraint on, or indication of, the ways in which some aspects of pragmatic inference should proceed. Contrasted with **conceptual semantics**.

procedural semantics (2) An approach in psycholinguistics which takes the sense of a word as a set of mental operations for deciding upon the applicability of a word to an entity or state of affairs.

processing effort *See* relevance.

projected deixis *Deixis whose default centre is shifted from the speaker to some other participant in a speech event.

projective pair A conversational pair in which one person proposes a joint project to another, and the other person takes up that proposal. E.g. John: *Let's paint the wall*. Mary: *Okay*.

promissive Signifying, marking or constituting a promise. E.g. *will* in *I will certainly come* is promissive.

Promoting Aphasics Communicative Effectiveness A functional pragmatic treatment used in *clinical pragmatics for aphasics. As a progressive exercise set within the context of naturally occurring conversation, it improves aphasic patients' communicative skills with the help of a therapist.

pronoun of laziness So-called because the pronoun is neither a referential one nor a bound-variable one, but seems to function as a shorthand for repetition of its antecedent. In other words, it is a device for a repeated occurrence of the linguistic form, rather than the truth-conditional content, of its antecedent. E.g. *it* in *The man who gave his pay cheque to his wife was wiser than the man who gave it to his mistress.* A sentence of the above type is called a **paycheque sentence**. *See also* E-type anaphora; Bach–Peters sentence; donkey sentence.

proper name *See* proper noun.

proper name broadening A type of *lexical broadening. It refers to the use of a salient proper name to denote a broader category. E.g. the proper name *Castro* in the utterance *Oh my god, they have elected another Castro!* may be understood to represent a broader category of a particular type of communist politicians. See Wilson and Carston (2007). Contrasts with **proper name narrowing**.

proper name narrowing A type of *lexical narrowing. It refers to the use of a proper name to pick up a particular, socially or culturally salient referent. E.g. in the utterance *Have you been to Shakespeare's birthplace?*, *Shakespeare* is used to refer to 'William Shakespeare, the English dramatist and poet'. See Huang (2007). Contrasted with **proper name broadening**.

proper noun A noun which is used as the name of individual people, places, dates and periods of time, works of literature, music, art, etc., distinguished only by their having that name. E.g. *John*, *London*, *July*, *Pride and Prejudice*, and *Swan Lake*. Proper nouns have been a central topic of inquiry in the *philosophy of language. One view is that proper nouns are *definite descriptions. Another is that they are directly referring *rigid designators or indexicals. Also called a **proper name**.

property In semantics and pragmatics, the term is sometimes used to refer to the sort of thing denoted by a predicate which is an incomplete or unsaturated proposition. E.g. the property of being something which sleeps peacefully.

proposition What is expressed by a declarative sentence when that sentence is used to make a statement, i.e. to say something, true or false, about some state of affairs in the external world. A proposition usually consists of a single *predicate and one or more *arguments. E.g. THE EDITOR IGNORED THE BAN is the proposition underlying both the active sentence *The editor ignored the ban* and the passive sentence *The ban was ignored by the editor*. *See also a priori* proposition; *a posteriori* proposition; affirmative proposition; foregrounded proposition; generic proposition; open proposition; simple proposition; complex proposition; timeless proposition.

proposition expressed = the content of *what is said.

propositional act A term used by the American philosopher John Searle for the third sub-act of a *locutionary act. A propositional act consists of an act of referring or reference and an act of predicating or predication. In the former, a speaker picks up a particular entity through the use of a referring expression, as in the utterance of *The opposition leader fired a broadside to the government*. In the latter, a speaker couples a predicate to a referring expression, as in *John had a crew-cut*.

propositional attitude A mental state or attitude such as belief, knowledge, desire, doubt, expectation, and fear one has with respect to a content that can be expressed in a particular proposition. E.g. the sentence *John believes that the Berlin Wall came down on 9 November 1989* is said to express or report John's belief that the proposition that the Berlin Wall came down on 9 November 1989 is the case. Such a sentence constitutes one type of referentially *opaque context.

propositional attitude verb A verb that is used to report an attitude of someone to a particular proposition. E.g. *believe*, *know*, *doubt*, *help*, *want*, *hope*, *fear*, *look*, *seem*, and *seek*. The use of a propositional attitude verb typically creates a referentially opaque context.

propositional calculus A branch of mathematical *logic, and one of the two main systems of logic used in formal semantics and pragmatics. It treats propositions as unanalysed atomic wholes, and examines systematic logical relations among them in terms of *truth tables. Truth tables list all the possible combinations of truth values. Also known as **propositional logic**. Often contrasts with **predicate calculus**.

propositional concept A term used in the philosophy of language, formal semantics and formal pragmatics to refer to a function from possible worlds to propositions. Given that a proposition itself is treated as a function from possible worlds to *truth values, a propositional concept can then be defined as a function from possible worlds to a function from possible worlds to truth values.

propositional content (of a sentence) The part of the meaning of a sentence that can be reduced to a proposition. E.g. in some analyses, the declarative sentence *The editor ignored the ban* and the interrogative sentence *Did the editor ignore the ban?* are said to have the same propositional content THE EDITOR IGNORED THE BAN. This notion allows one to claim that different (type of) sentences may share the same propositional content, even though they differ in other aspects of meaning. Thus the difference between the declarative sentence and the interrogative sentence above is that while in saying the former, the speaker commits him- or herself to the truth of the proposition, in uttering the latter, he or she questions its truth.

propositional content condition A kind of *felicity condition which relates in essence to what a *speech act is about. It has to do with specifying the restrictions on the content of what remains as the 'core' of the utterance after the *illocutionary act part is removed. For a promise, the propositional content is to predicate some future act of the speaker, whereas in the case of a request, it is to predicate some future act of the addressee. See Searle (1969).

propositional fragment *See* propositional radical.

propositional hyperbole *See* hyperbole.

propositional logic = propositional calculus.

propositional meaning Meaning that is identified with the proposition asserted or expressed in a statement. E.g. the propositional meaning of the sentence *John was attacked by a dog* is that a dog attacked John. Also called variously **descriptive**, **conceptual**, **cognitive**, and **referential meaning**.

propositional radical A term used by the American philosopher Kent Bach to refer to a propositional fragment that does not express a complete proposition and therefore needs to be filled in or completed contextually to become fully propositional. E.g. the proposition expressed by the sentence *John is ready* is a propositional radical, which needs to be completed to become a minimal but full proposition such as 'John is ready for the job interview'. Sometimes also called a **propositional fragment** or **propositional skeleton**. See Bach (2004).

propositional synonymy, propositional synonym *See* synonymy, synonym.

propositionalism The view that a declarative sentence has to express a proposition. If it does not, it has to be completed to become fully propositional with the help of either context or speaker's intention, to be evaluable by means of truth-conditions. Propositionism is said to be associated with *contextualism.

prosodic contour *See* prosody.

prosodic feature *See* prosody.

prosodic hedge A *hedge that is encoded by prosodic means. E.g. the presence of high pitch is frequently associated with the expression of tentativeness. It may suggest that the speaker is not committing him- or herself to the truth of what he or she says. See Brown and Levinson (1987). Often distinct from a **verbal hedge**. *See also* kinesic hedge.

prosodic pragmatics The study of how *prosody like intonation can affect the interpretation of a variety of linguistic phenomena in relation to context. See Hirschberg (2004).

prosody Also known as **prosodic features.** Variation in intonation, stress, rhythm, loudness, tempo, etc. encountered at the utterance level in speech, thus subsuming the traditional sense of meter in verse. E.g. a pattern of intonation such as rising, falling, etc. constitutes a **prosodic contour**. Prosody can signal different speech acts. It can also display a speaker's emotions. E.g. the sentence *John won't come to the meeting tomorrow* can be pronounced or read out aloud in different ways, indicating, for example, boredom, certainty, or surprise.

prospective anaphora *See* cataphora.

protasis *See* conditional.

proto-literalism A term used by the French philosopher François Recanati for the view that like ambiguity, context-sensitivity, or dependency is a defect of natural language. Consequently, the fact that a natural language sentence is indexical and has content only when it is uttered in a context should be ignored in theorizing about language. See Recanati (2005).

proto-speech act A term introduced by the British philosopher Stephen Barker for the act of uttering a linguistic expression such as a word, phrase, and sentence and advertising certain intentions to denote, represent, or communicate.

protrepic utterance *See* exhibitive utterance.

proverb A generally recognized phrase or sentence that is recurrent, pithy, fairly stable, and frequently *formulaic and/or *figurative. It is often used to state truths and give advice. E.g. *Slow and steady wins the race.*

proximal A term used in the description of *distance in *space deixis. It indicates that the entity referred to is close or closer to the speaker. E.g. *zheli* in Chinese, *here* in English, and *itt* in Hungarian. Also described as **proximate**. Contrasts with **distal**. *See also* medial.

proximate (1) *See* proximal.

proximate (2) *See* obviation.

proximative *See* obviation.

pseudo-cleft presupposition *See* cleft presupposition.

psycholinguistic pragmatics See psychopragmatics.

psychological focus *See* focus.

psychopragmatics The psycholinguistic study of aspects of language in use and mind. It is primarily concerned with the issue of how human beings acquire, store, produce, and understand the use of language from the vantage point of psychology. Within psychopragmatics, two main subfields are indentified: **developmental pragmatics** and **experimental pragmatics**. The importance of psychopragmatics is that it has a crucial role to play not only in the formulation and development of pragmatic theories but also in the testing and revision of these theories.

pun Typically the humorous use of a word that has more than one meaning, or of different words that have the same or similar pronunciation. E.g. *If we don't hang together, we'll hang separately* (Benjamin Franklin).

pure conversation analysis (pure CA) A term that is employed with reference to the type of *conversation analysis (CA) that collects data from naturally occurring conversations. In other words, in pure conversation analysis the data is not arranged or provoked by the analyst, as in a psycholinguistic experiment or a sociolinguistic interview. Used in contrast to **applied conversation analysis (applied CA)**, by which is meant the type of conversation analysis that studies (the audio and/or video recordings of) specific types of conversational situation. See ten Have (2010).

pure deixis A term used by the British linguist Sir John Lyons for a linguistic expression whose meaning can be explained fully in terms of the concept of deixis. E.g. *that* in *Who's that?* Contrasts with **impure deixis**. *See also* deictic expression.

pure indexical A term used in the *philosophy of language for *indexicals such as *I*, *here*, and *now*. Unlike demonstratives, pure indexicals do not need a demonstration or directing intention to establish reference. Also called an **essential indexical**.

pure logophoric language *See* full logophoric language.

pure pragmatics = *theoretical pragmatics especially using methodologies of intuition and argument, as practiced in the *philosophy of language and theoretical linguistics. Sometimes used in contrast to **experimental pragmatics**.

pure textual deixis *See* impure textual deixis.

Q

Q-$_{\text{alternate}}$ implicature Also called a **Quantity-$_{\text{alternate}}$ implicature**. A term introduced by the British Chinese linguist Yan Huang to refer to a neo-Gricean *conversational implicature that is derived from the operation of the *Q-principle. There are two subtypes of Q-$_{\text{alternate}}$ implicatures: (i) **Quantity-$_{\text{ordered alternate}}$** or **Q-$_{\text{ordered alternate}}$ implicatures**, and (ii) **Quantity-$_{\text{unordered alternate}}$** or **Q-$_{\text{unordered alternate}}$ implicatures**. The former comes from a semantically or informationally ranked contrast set. E.g. given the contrast set <succeed, try>, the uttering of *John tried to mislead the committee* engenders the Q-$_{\text{ordered alternate}}$ implicature that John didn't succeed in misleading the committee. By contrast, the latter is derived from a semantically or informationally non-ranked contrastive set. E.g. given the contrast set <French, German, Russian, Spanish, Italian ...>, the uttering of the sentence *They teach French, German and Russian there* generates the weak Q-$_{\text{unordered alternate}}$ implicature that they don't teach, for example, Spanish and Italian there. See Huang (2007).

Q-$_{\text{clausal}}$ implicature Also known as **Quantity-$_{\text{clausal}}$ implicature**. The term is due to the British linguist Gerald Gazdar. It refers to a neo-Gricean *conversational implicature that is derived via the operation of the *Q-principle. Given a semantic contrastive set of a constructional kind usually involving a coordinate or subordinate clause, the use of a semantically weaker expression gives rise to a Q-$_{\text{clausal}}$ implicature of epistemic uncertainty, i.e. the speaker does not know whether the embedded proposition is true or false. Q-$_{\text{clausal}}$ implicatures are commonly involved with *disjunction, *conditional, model, and verbal doublet. E.g. given the **verbal doublet scale** <(know that *p*), (believe that *p*)>, the uttering of the sentence *John believes that the war is over* generates the Q-$_{\text{clausal}}$ implicature that the war may be over, it may not be over, the speaker doesn't know which. See Huang (2007).

Q-heuristic *See* Q-principle.

Q-implicature Also known as **Quanity-implicature**. A neo-Gricean *conversational implicature derived via the operation of the *Q-principle. Three types of Q-implicature can be identified: (i) **Q-$_{\text{scalar}}$ implicature**, (ii) **Q-$_{\text{clausal}}$ implicature**, and (iii) **Q-$_{\text{alternate}}$ implicature**. Sometimes also called a **Q-inference**. *See also* I-implicature; M-implicature.

Q-$_{\text{ordered alternate}}$ implicature *See* Q-$_{\text{alternate}}$ implicature.

Q-principle Also known as the **Quantity-principle. 1.** One of the two neo-Gricean pragmatic principles put forward by the American linguist Laurence Horn. Q stands for 'quantity'. Collecting the British philosopher H. P. Grice's first sub-*maxim of Quantity and first and second sub-*maxims of Manner, what the Q-principle basically says is that a speaker should give as much information as he or she can. Consequently, the operation of the lower-bounding Q-principle generates an upper-bounding *conversational implicature: a speaker, in saying '. . . *p* . . .', implicates that (for all he or she knows) . . . at most *p* . . . Contrasts with Horn's **R-principle**. See Horn (2004); Huang (2007). **2.** One of the three neo-Gricean pragmatic principles proposed by the British linguist Stephen Levinson. Q stands for 'quantity'. The Q-principle operates in terms of a semantically contrast set. It has two sides: a speaker's maxim, by which a speaker is expected not to say less than is required, and a recipient's corollary, which allows an addressee to infer that what is not said is not the case. In other words, the basic idea of the Q-principle is that the use of a semantically weaker linguistic expression from a set of contrastive semantic alternates Q-implicates the negation of the interpretation associated with the use of the semantically stronger linguistic expression(s) in the same set. Seen the other way round, from the absence of a semantically stronger expression, one infers that the interpretation associated with the use of that expression does not hold. Hence, the Q-principle is essentially negative in nature. E.g. the uttering of the sentence *Some of the candidates are ready for the test* engenders the Q-implicature that not many/most/all of the candidates are ready for the test. A simplified version of the Q-principle is sometimes called the **Q-heuristic** in the form of 'Speaker: Don't say less than is required. Addressee: What isn't said isn't the case.' See Levinson (2000); Huang (2007). Contrasted with Levinson's **I-principle** and **M-principle**.

Q-$_{\text{scalar}}$ implicature *See* scalar implicature.

Q-$_{\text{scalar}}$ scale *See* Horn scale.

Q-scale *See* Horn scale.

quadruple hedge *See* compound hedge.

qualia structure An approach to *lexical semantics developed by the American linguist James Pustejovsky. It is based on the assumption that the semantic or conceptual content of a lexical item can be divided into a small number of types (i.e. qulia (*sg* quale)), and that different types are evoked in different contexts. Four types of **qualia roles** have been proposed: (i) **formal** (a lexical item's place in a taxonomy), (ii) **constitutive** (a lexical item's part–whole relation), (iii) **telic** (how a lexical item is typifcally used), and (iv) **agentive** (a lexical item's life history). In some cases, the qualia structure approach can provide an explanation of how different senses of a lexical item can arise in different contexts, as 'school' can be used to refer to both an institution and a building.

qualitative corpus pragmatics *See* corpus pragmatics.

Quality *See* maxim of Quality.

quality face A term used by the British linguist Helen Spencer-Oatey to refer to one's desire to be evaluated positively in terms of personal qualities. In other words, quality face reflects one's desire to be liked and admired by others. The concept is similar to the American linguist Penelope Brown and the British linguist Stephen Levinson's notion of *positive face. Also called **individual** or **individualistic face**. Contrasts with **social identity face**.

Quality hedge A *hedge that is addressed to the British philosopher H. P. Grice's *maxim of Quality. It may serve to strengthen a speaker's commitment to the truth of what he or she says, as in *With complete honesty, I can say that . . .*, or indicate that the speaker cannot take the full responsibility for the truth of his or her utterance, as in *I am not sure if this is true, but . . . . See also* Manner hedge; Quantity hedge; Relation hedge.

quantifier 1. Any lexical item that expresses a relative or indefinite notion of quantity. E.g. *all*, *every*, and *some*. **2.** In logic, an operator that is used to make a statement over a set of entities. Two most common quantifiers are **existential quantifiers**(∃); **universal quantifiers** (∀). The existential quantifier (∃x) can be read as 'there is at least one *x* such that *x* . . . ', and the universal quantifier (∀x) can be interpreted as 'for all *x*/of every *x* it holds that *x* . . . '.

quantitative corpus pragmatics *See* corpus pragmatics.

Quantity *See* maxim of Quantity.

Quantity-$_{\text{alternate}}$ implicature *See* Q-$_{\text{alternate}}$ implicature.

Quantity hedge A *hedge that is oriented to the British philosopher H. P. Grice's *maxim of Quantity. It may suggest that the speaker is *opting out of the maxim, i.e. he or she is providing too much or too little information. E.g. *I can't tell you any more than this. See also* Quality hedge; Manner hedge; Relation hedge.

Quantity-heuristic *See* Q-principle.

Quantity-implicature *See* Q-implicature

Quantity-$_{\text{ordered alternate implicature}}$ *See* Q-$_{\text{alternate}}$ implicature.

Quantity-principle *See* Q-principle.

Quantity-$_{\text{unordered alternate}}$ implicature *See* Q-$_{\text{alternate}}$ implicature.

quasi-contextualism, quasi-contextualist A term used by the French philosopher François Recanati for the position that crosscuts the *literalist/*contextualist divide in the contemporary *philosophy of language and linguistics, according to which there is no role for the minimal proposition that is literally expressed by a sentence to play in the process of communication. See Recanati (2004).

quasi-indicator A term introduced by the Guatemalan philosopher Héctor-Neri Castañeda to refer to a linguistic expression that can be used to attribute a **de se* belief to an attributee from a third-person perspective. Such a linguistic expression is typically marked by an asterisk (*). E.g. **he himself* in *John says that *he himself is healthy* used to represent John as saying 'I am healthy'.

queclarative A blended term coined in the 1970s which refers to a sentence having the form of an interrogative but with the *illocutionary force of a statement. E.g. the use of *What use is this projector?* to mean that this projector is no use. It is an instance of *indirect speech act.

quessertion A blended term invented to refer to something that lies somewhere in between an assertion and a question or a speech act of asserting something but at the same time emphasizing that it is questionable.

Q-$_{\text{unordered alternate}}$ implicature *See* Q-$_{\text{alternate}}$ implicature.

R

r-implicature Also termed **relevance-theoretic implicature**. A term coined by the British Chinese linguist Yan Huang to refer to a *conversational implicature in the sense of relevance theory. An r-implicature is a communicated assumption derivable solely via the process of pragmatic inference. It corresponds therefore to what is implicated (i.e. the implicit content). It is largely equivalent to a *particularized conversational implicature (PCI) in Gricean and neo-Gricean pragmatics. Two types of r-implicature can be identified: **implicated premises** and **implicated conclusions**. The former is a contextual assumption intended by the speaker and supplied by the addressee, and the latter is a contextual implication communicated by the speaker. E.g. in the following conversation John: *Let's go and watch* The Last Emperor. Mary: *Period epics are tedious*, Mary's reply may yield two r-implicatures: (i) *The Last Emperor* is a period epic, and (ii) Mary does not want to go and see *The Last Emperor*. The first r-implicature is an implicated premise, and the second, an implicated conclusion. Finally, r-implicatures may vary in strength along a continuum. A **strong r-implicature** is one whose recovery is essential to understand a speaker's intended meaning. By contrast, a **weak r-implicature** is one whose recovery is not essential, because it may be one of a wide array of equally possible r-implicatures engendered by an utterance. E.g. in the following conversation John: *Did Bill pay back the money he owed you?* Mary: *No, he forgot to go to the bank*, Mary's reply may give rise to a range of r-implicatures such as (i) Bill was unable to repay Mary the money he owed because he forgot to go to the financial institution, and (ii) Bill may repay Mary the money he owes when he next goes to the financial institution. Of these two r-implicatures, the first is a strong one and the second a weak one. The concept of weak r-implicature plays an important role in the relevance-theoretic analysis of *metaphors and other tropes, and in the idea of *poetic effect as well. See Huang (2007). Contrasts with an **explicature**. *See also* implicature.

R-implicature Also called a **relation-implicature**. A neo-Gricean *conversational implicature derived via the operation of the *R-principle (1). E.g. the uttering of the sentence *John cut a finger yesterday* engenders the R-implicature that John cut a finger of his own yesterday. See Horn (2004).

r-intention Also known as **reflexive intention**. The American philosophers Kent Bach and Robert Harnish's term for *m-intention.

R-principle (1) Also known as the **relation principle**. One of the two neo-Gricean pragmatic principles put forward by the American linguist Laurence Horn, following a proposal by the American philosopher Jay

Atlas and the British linguist Stephen Levinson. 'R' stands for 'relation'. Subsuming the British philosopher H. P. Grice's second sub-*maxim of Quantity, *maxim of Relation, and third and fourth sub-*maxims of Manner, what the R-principle basically says is that a speaker should not give more information than is needed. Consequently, the operation of the upper-bounding R-principle generates a lower-bounding conversational implicature: a speaker, in saying '...*p*...', implicates that (for all he or she knows)... more than *p*... See Horn (2004). *See also* Q-principle (1); I-principle; M-principle.

R-principle (2) A principle in *bidirectional optimality-theoretic pragmatics put forward by the Dutch linguist Robert van Rooij. 'R' stands for 'relevance maximization'. Given this pragmatic principle, a speaker is expected to optimize relevance. Also called the **relevance maximization principle**. Contrasts with the **E-principle**.

radical construction grammar (RCG) A version of *construction grammar (1) developed by the American linguist William Croft. It has two distinctive characteristics. In the first place, using insights from linguistic typology, it takes grammatical diversity rather than grammatical universals as a starting point, and endeavours to build a model of grammar which can give an adequate account of typological variations. Secondly, it is 'radical' in the sense that in this model, only constructions are taken as the primitive theoretical construct. See Evans (2007).

radical contextualism, radical contextualist A form or version of *contexualism that holds the view that pragmatic processes such as *free enrichment play a central role in explaining *context variations in semantic content. The work of the French philosopher François Recanati, the American philosopher Charles Travis, and the relevance theorists belongs to this camp.

radical pragmatics The view that as much of the study of meaning as possible should be assimilated to pragmatics and the role played by semantics should be reduced to a minimum. This view is to some extent represented by e.g. philosophers in the tradition of *ordinary language philosophy and linguists in *neo-Gricean pragmatics and *relevance theory. The term 'radical pragmatics' is in general considered to appear first in a collection of articles edited by the American linguist Peter Cole in 1981. See Huang (2007). Contrasts with **radical semantics**.

radical semantic minimalism A form or version of *semantic minimalism, which holds the view that the semantic properties of a sentence should be taken as on a par with the sentence's syntactic and phonological properties. Some of the American philosopher Kent Bach's work falls in this camp.

radical semantics The view that much of the study of meaning should be attributed to *semantics and the role played by pragmatics should be reduced to a minimum. This view is represented by e.g. philosophers in the tradition of *ideal language philosophy and generative semanticists in the 1970s. See Huang (2007). Contrasted with **radical pragmatics**.

range topic A Chinese-style or pragmatic topic that delimits the range of a variable of which the predication is made. In other words, a range topic restricts the range of values that a variable in the subsequent predication can take. E.g. 'fish' in the Japanese topic–comment construction 'Fish, red snapper (is) good'. In this example, the topic specifies the range of variable *x* in '*x* is good' to a type of fish and states that of the fishes in that range, it is red snappers for which '*x* is good' is true. *See also* instance topic; frame topic.

rank order A term used by the American lingust Laurence Horn to refer to a set of linguistic alternates such that the informationally strong linguistic expression unilaterally entails the negation of the interpretation associated with the informationally weak ones. E.g. <<full professor, associate professor, assistant professor>>. *See also* Horn scale; Hirschberg scale.

rapport management A framework developed by the British linguist Helen Spencer-Oatey for the study of *politeness and *impoliteness, among other things. According to this approach, our understanding and interpretation of interactions are dependent on two components: **face** and **sociality rights**. Face is further divided into **quality face** and **social identity face**, and sociality rights into **equity rights** and **association rights**. Under this approach, emphases are placed on people's interactional rather than individual wants. The framework is in many respects akin to the *relational work approach.

ratified participant A speech event participant not directly addressed, but expected to attend to what is said.

rational reconstruction *See* formal pragmatics (2).

rationalistic pragmatics *See* empirical pragmatics.

rationality The capacity of identifying a particular action, belief, or desire as making sense, appropriate, justified, required, or in accordance with some acknowledged goal etc. A distinction is made between **theoretical** and **practical rationality**. Theoretical rationality applies to belief. By contrast, practical rationality is concerned with action. For some philosophers, practical rationality is identical to **instrumental rationality**. According to the **principle of rationality**, acting rationally simply means that, given a desired goal and a variety of means, one should choose that action which most effectively and at least cost attains that goal. Considerations of rationality play an important role in pragmatics. For example, rationality is an essential ingredient of Gricean and neo-Gricean pragmatics.

RCG = radical construction grammar.

RDRP = revised disjoint reference presumption.

real-world knowledge = world knowledge.

real-world knowledge context *See* general knowledge context.

realist theory (of truth) *See* correspondence theory (of truth).

reasoning A systematic mental process in which implications among propositions are evaluated, and a conclusion is drawn from a set of premises. One of the basic forms of reasoning is *inference.

receiving time (RT) The moment an utterance is received. Contrasts with **coding time**.

recipient's corollary *See* speaker('s) maxim

reductionism The view in the pragmatics–semantics interface that the putative distinction between semantics and pragmatics should be abolished—a position the British linguist Stephen Levinson dubbed **pragmantics**. Within reductionism, a further distinction can be made between **semantic reductionism** and **pragmatic reductionism**. See Huang (2007). Contrasts with **complementarism**.

reductive paraphrase *See* natural semantic metalanguage.

reductive paraphrase explication *See* natural semantic metalanguage.

redundancy theory (of truth) *See* deflationist theory (of truth).

reference The relationship between a linguistic expression and an entity, activity, property, relationship, etc. or a clearly delimited set of entities, activities, properties, relationships, etc. in the external world, to which it is used to refer. In other words, referring is an act of a speaker picking out a particular entity or set of entities, denoted by a linguistic expression, in the external world. Reference is performed through the speaker's utterance of that linguistic expression on some occasion of use. E.g. if John says *The United Nations is a talking shop*, he uses the *referring expression *The United Nations* to pick out a particular international organization. Thus, reference is essentially a context-dependent aspect of utterance meaning and therefore it falls largely in the domain of pragmatics. See Lyons (1995); Abbott (2010). *See also* constant reference; variable reference; circumscriptive reference; definite reference; indefinite reference; deictic reference; demonstrative reference; indexical reference; generic reference; specific reference; gestural reference; metaphoric reference; discourse reference.

reference assignment The process of assigning a *referent to a referring or anaphoric expression. Given that reference assignment is usually context-sensitive and involves the working out of a speaker's *referential intention, it is largely a pragmatic process. In neo-Gricean pragmatics, it is achieved via a conversational implicature, and in relevance theory, it is accomplished in terms of an explicature.

reference frame *See* frame of (spatial) reference.

reference tracking Keeping track of the various entities referred to in an ongoing discourse. Linguistic mechanisms that are deployed for such a purpose are called **reference-tracking systems**. Cross-linguistically, four main types of reference-tracking systems can be identified: (i) **gender** or **class systems**, (ii) **switch-reference systems**, (iii) **switch-function systems**, and (iv) **inference systems**.

reference transfer Also called **referential transfer**. A term for a *proper name or *definite description that is used to refer to an entity that is in some way pragmatically associated with the *default referent of the proper name or definite description. E.g. the use of *Chomsky* in *Chomsky is in both the linguistics and politics section* to refer to the linguistics and politics books written by him. The terms **'reference shift'**, **'referential shift'**, and **'deferred reference'** are also used. *See also* meaning transfer; metonymy.

referent What is referred to by the use of a *referring expression. E.g. Barack Obama is the referent of the *definite description *the President of the United States of America* at the time of writing (2010).

referent-controlled honorific *See* subject honorific; object honorific.

referent honorific A variety of *relational social deixis that holds between speaker and referent. Referent honorifics are forms used by a speaker to show respect towards a referent. In this type of honorific, respect or honour can only be conveyed by referring to the target of the respect. E.g. the use of an honorified noun such as *arta* 'money' in Javanese. Referent honorifics are the most basic form of the **honorific system**. *See also* addressee honorific; bystander honorific.

referential ambiguity *Ambiguity through the assignment of two or more interpretations to a referring or anaphoric expression in a sentence or discourse. Thus, *John told Bill that he had won a scholarship* is referentially ambiguous; the anaphoric expression *he* has at least two possible interpretations, referring to John and Bill, respectively. Also called **anaphoric ambiguity**.

referential anaphora An anaphoric relation in which an anaphoric expression refers to some entity in the external world either directly or via its antecedent in the same sentence or discourse. E.g. *Barack Obama* and *the President* form such a relation in *Barack Obama said that the President would visit Afghanistan.*

referential-attributive ambiguity *See* referential use.

referential-attributive distinction *See* referential use.

referential conflict A term that is used to refer to the case whereby there is more than one possible candidate competing for the referent of a referring or an anaphoric expression. E.g. *John* and *Peter* in *John told Peter that he had won an award* are both possible antecedents for the anaphoric expression *he*.

referential deixis A term used by the American anthropological linguist William Hanks to refer to *deixis whose primary function is to individuate objects of reference such as things, events, and concepts. Referential deixis is commonly encoded by (i) demonstratives, (ii) person markers, (iii) locative, directional, and temporal markers, and (iv) sociolinguistic markers. See Hanks (2011).

referential expression *See* referring expression.

referential function *See* functions (of language).

referential givenness/newness distinction A distinction made by the American linguist Jeanette Gundel for the relation between a linguistic expression, especially a *referring expression, and a corresponding non-linguistic entity that is assumed to reside in a speaker's and/or addressee's mind, a discourse, or some real or possible world. A typical example is *existential presupposition. Contrasts with the **relational givenness/newness distinction**. *See also* given.

referential intention What a speaker intends the semantic referent of a linguistic expression whose referent is not determined by the convention of a language to be. E.g. a speaker's intention to fix the semantic referent of an *indexical like *I*, a demonstrative like *this*, and an *incomplete definite description like *the house*.

referential meaning *See* *propositional meaning.

referential metonymy *See* metonymy.

referential pragmatics A term used by the British linguist Geoffrey Leech which is applied to the study of the assignment of reference to referring expressions in communication.

referential presupposition The American philosopher Jay Atlas's term for the German philosopher, mathematician, and logician Gottlob Frege's notion of *presupposition in relation to the Fregean sentence *After Schleswig-Holstein was separated from Denmark/After the separation of Schleswig-Holstein from Denmark, Prussia and Austria quarrelled.*

referential theory (of meaning) A theory which states that the meaning of a linguistic expression is what it refers to, denotes, or stands for in the external world. E.g. *lion* means the class of all lions in the external world or the essential property of lion-hood. Also known as the **denotational theory** (of meaning). See Lyons (1995). *See also* behaviourist theory (of meaning); meaning-is-use theory (of meaning); mentalistic theory (of meaning); truth-conditional theory (of meaning); verificationist theory (of meaning).

referential underdetermination A term, due to the American philosopher Kent Bach, that refers to a variety of cases of semantic *underdetermination that are due to reference in its broad sense. E.g. in *Peter asked Rod to turn on his heater*, what is underdetermined, i.e. [Peter's or Rod's heater], arises from the indeterminacy of the anaphoric expession *his*.

referential use (of referring expressions) The use of a *referring expression to pick out a particular entity that a speaker chooses to describe in a particular way, as opposed to the **attributive use**, on which the referring expression is employed to attribute the predicated property to whatever satisfies the description. Thus, the classic example *Smith's murderer is insane* is ambiguous between the reading 'that person, who murdered Smith, is insane' (the referential use) and the reading 'whoever murdered Smith is insane' (the attributive use). This **referential-attributive ambiguity** or **distinction** was introduced by the American philosopher Keith Donnellan.

referential versatility A term for a referring expression that can be used to refer to a wide range of entities. E.g. *he* is **referentially versatile**. See Hurford, Heasley, and Smith (2007).

referentially opaque context *See* opaque context.

referring expression Any linguistic expression that can be used in an utterance to refer to a particular entity or set of entities in the external world. The major types of referring expressions are (i) **definite NPs** including (a) **proper names** (e.g. *Nelson Mandela*), (b) **definite descriptions** (e.g. *the British Prime Minister*), and (c) **definite pronouns** (e.g. *she*); (ii) **demonstrative NPs** (e.g. **demonstrative descriptions** like *this city*) including **demonstrative pronouns** (*that*); (iii) **indefinite NPs** (e.g. **indefinite descriptions** like *a beautiful girl*) including **indefinite pronouns** (e.g. *someone*); and (iv) **quantificational NPs** (e.g. *many tigers*) including **quantificational pronouns** (e.g. *all*). Also known as a **referential expression**.

reflectiveness *See* metapragmatics.

reflexive intention *See* r-intention.

reflexiveness *See* metapragmatics.

reflexivity *See* metapragmatics.

refusal A *face-threatening speech act in which an unwillingness to go along with a proposal like a request, offer, and invitation is expressed. Refusals are frequently structured with three components: (i) responding positively, (ii) expressing regrets, and (iii) providing an excuse. In terms of refusal strategies, three types are identified: (i) **direct refusals** (with or without *hedges or intensifiers), (ii) **indirect refusals** (e.g. asking for more information, challenging certain aspects of the proposal, and offering an alternative), and (iii) **avoidance** (e.g. saying nothing, postponing a response, and changing the topic). There is ample evidence that both the structure and strategies of refusals vary cross-culturally and/or linguistically and in different contexts. Refusals have been extensively studied especially in cultural, cross-cultural, and interlanguage pragmatics.

register A variety of language as it is used in various social situations. For example, a register of legal English has a set of features which is characteristic of that type of linguistic activity, and which is different from that of religious English. In pragmatics, one of the types of *social deixis is the speaker–setting axis. The speaker–setting axis is concerned with the relation between the speaker (and perhaps other participants) and the speech setting or event.

regular negation *See* descriptive negation.

regulative rule (of a speech act) A norm that antecedently controls the performance of a *speech act. It is involved with what is optimal and desirable in a speech act. The violation of a regulative rule will normally lead to deficits or infelicities of a speech act. Often contrasts with the **constitutive rule** (of a speech act). See Searle (1969).

regulative speech act One of the three types of speech act proposed by the German philosopher Jürgen Habermas. A regulative speech act is one that purports to set up normative expectations which regulate actions. E.g. the speech act of commanding. *See also* constative speech act; expressive speech act (2).

reinforceability, reinforceable A property of *conversational implicature according to which a conversational implicature can be made explicit without producing too much of a sense of redundancy. This is because a conversational implicature is not part of the conventional import of an utterance. E.g. the uttering of the sentence *The tea is warm* engenders the conversational implicature that the tea is not hot. This conversational implcature can be made explicit in *The tea is warm, but not hot*, and the sentence is not felt to be semantically redundant. See Huang (2007). *See also* calculability; defeasibility; indeterminacy (1); non-conventionality; non-detachability; universality.

Relation *See* maxim of Relation.

Relation hedge A *hedge that is addressed to the British philosopher H. P. Grice's *maxim of Relation. It questions if the maxim is met or serves notice that it is not satisfied. E.g. *I'm not sure this is relevant, but ...* Also called a **Relevance hedge**. *See also* Quality hedge; Quantity hedge; Manner hedge.

Relation-implicature *See* R-implicature.

Relation-principle *See* R-principle (1); (2).

relational givenness/newness distinction A distinction postulated by the American linguist Jeanette Gundel for a division of the semantic or conceptual representation of a sentence into two complementary parts. Defined thus, relational givenness/newness is typically associated with the construction known as the topic–comment and topic–focus construction. Therefore, it provides a main dimension of thematic meaning. Contrasts with the **referential givenenness/newness distinction**. *See also* given.

relational opposite *See* converseness, converse.

relational practice *See* relational work.

relational social deixis The codification of the social status of the speaker, the addressee, or a third person or entity referred to, as well as the social relationships holding between them by forms that are not reserved for authorized speakers, addressees or other recipients. E.g. the use of generalized *forms of address such as *bankilal* 'elder brother' in Tzeltal to show respect to strangers. Four types of relational *social deixis can be identified, i.e. the relational information is between (i) **speaker and referent** (e.g. *referent honorifics), (ii) **speaker and addressee** (e.g. *addressee honorifics), (iii) **speaker and bystander** (e.g. *bystander honorifics), and (iv) **speaker and setting** (e.g. levels of formality). Contrasts with **absolute social deixis**.

relational work An approach advocated by the Swiss linguists Miriam Locher and Richard Watts which endeavours to cover a broad spectrum of language behaviour including *politeness and *impoliteness. Relational work refers to all aspects of the work interlocutors carry out in constructing, maintaining, and transforming their relationships in interaction. It is based on the idea that any communicative act has both an informational and an interpersonal function. In this framework, significance is placed on interpersonal relations in social practice rather than individuals performing politeness. Relational work is similar in many aspects to **rapport management**. Also called **relational practice** and **face work (2)**.

relative frame (of spatial reference) A linguistic frame of reference to express a spatial relation between a figure and a ground. A relative frame is an egocentric coordinate system that expresses a ternary spatial relation between a viewpoint, a figure, and a ground that are distinct from the viewpoint. It uses the coordinates fixed on the viewpoint to assign directions to the figure and the ground. The *deictic use of this frame is prototypical. E.g. in *The dog is to the left of the car*, the viewpoint is the speaker, which is employed to specify the spatial relation between the figure (the dog) and the ground (the car). See Levinson (2003). *See also* intrinsic frame (of spatial reference); absolute frame (of spatial reference).

relative politeness *See* absolute politeness.

relativity *See* maxim of relativity.

relevance Established as a technical term in relevance theory, relevance is a function or measure of two factors: (i) **cognitive** or **contextual effects** and (ii) **processing effort**. The first factor refers to the fruitful outcome of an interaction between a newly impinging stimulus and a subset of the assumptions already in a cognitive system. The second is the effort a cognitive system has to expend in order to yield a satisfactory interpretation of any incoming information processed. Defined thus, relevance is a matter of degree. It is claimed to be of fundamental importance for both cognition and communication. *See* Sperber and Wilson (1995); Huang (2007).

Relevance hedge *See* Relation hedge.

relevance maximization principle *See* R-principle (2).

relevance principle *See* principle of relevance.

relevance principles *See* cognitive principle of relevance; communicative principle of relevance.

relevance-theoretic comprehension strategy A procedure in relevance theory which requires an addressee to follow a path of least effort in constructing an interpretation, and to stop when his or her expectations of relevance are satisfied or abandoned. The strategy is taken to be a *heuristic.

relevance-theoretic implicature. *See* r-implicature.

relevance theory (RT) A cognitive pragmatic theory of cognition and communication developed by the French scholar Dan Sperber and the British linguist Deirdre Wilson. Grounded in a general view of human cognition, the central thesis of the theory is that the human cognitive system works in such a way as to tend to maximize *relevance with respect to communication. Relevance theory can best be regarded as both a reaction against and a development of classical Gricean pragmatics. Occasionally also called **relevance-theoretic pragmatics** or **relevance-theoretic semantics**. See Sperber and Wilson (1995).

remote conditional *See* counterfactual conditional.

repair A term used in *conversation analysis for any type of 'mending' of misunderstanding or unclarities. Two important distinctions are usually made. First, there is the contrast between self-initiated and other-initiated repair—repair initiated by a speaker without querying or prompting vs. repair made in response to querying or prompting by an addressee or a third party. Secondly, we have the opposition between self-repair and other repair—repair carried out by a speaker him- or herself vs. repair made by an addressee or a third party. Consequently, there are four types of repair: (i) **self-initiated self-repair**, (ii) **self-initiated other-repair**, (iii) **other-initiated self-repair**, and (iv) **other-initiated other-repair**. Also called **conversational repair**.

repair sequence A term taken from *conversation analysis for any part of a *turn, any turn, or any succession of turns by which a repair is carried out. E.g. B's turn in A: *Rosemary said . . .*' B: *Philip?* A: *Yeah, Rosemary Philip*.

reported speech *See* indirect speech.

representation A term used in relevance theory for anything that can be used to be about something else. This 'aboutness' may be truth- or resemblance-based. In the former case, the representation describes a state of affairs that makes it true. E.g. an assertion like *In 1966, Mao* *lauched his brutal Cultural Revolution in China*. This is called a **descriptively used representation** or **descriptive use**. By contrast, in the latter case, the representation represents another representation such as another utterance or thought and resembles it in content. E.g. B's utterance in A: *What did the President say about Libya?* B: *Gaddafi must go*. In this example, B reports what the President said rather than expressing his or her opinion. This is termed an **interpretively used representation** or **interpretive use**.

representation by resemblance A term used in relevance theory for the representation of one thing by another. This 'aboutness' is based on a relation of similarity or resemblance rather than a relation of truth between what represents and what is represented.

representation function *See* functions (of language).

representational meaning *See* conceptual meaning (2).

representationality *See* intentionality.

representative A type of *speech act proposed by the American philosopher John Searle by which a speaker commits him- or herself to the truth of the expressed proposition. Paradigmatic cases include asserting, claiming, concluding, reporting, and stating. Also called **representative speech act** or **assertive**. E.g. *Mohandas Gandhi inspired Martin Luther King Jr and Nelson Mandela*. See Searle (1975). *See also* commissive; directive; expressive; declaration.

request A *face-threatening act of asking for something or asking someone to do something usually in a polite or formal way. In other words, in performing the speech act of requesting, a speaker intends to regulate his or her interactant's behaviour. Requests can be **direct** or **indirect**. They can also be **canonical** (i.e. made by a single speaker to a single addressee) or **collective** (i.e. made by a single speaker to more than one addressee). Strategies of requests vary cross-culturally and/or linguistically and in different contexts. This speech act has been extensively studied especially in socio-, cultural, cross-cultural, interlanguage, and clinical pragmatics.

resolution schema (for the interaction of the Q-, I-, and M-principles) A neo-Gricean resolution mechanism proposed by the British linguist Stephen Levinson, inspired in part by the American linguist Laurence Horn's *division of pragmatic labour. What it basically says is that *Q-implicatures (where *$Q_{clausal}$ implicatures cancel rival *Q_{scalar} implicatures) precede inconsistent *I-implicatures, but otherwise I-implicatures take precedence until the use of a marked linguistic expression triggers a complementary *M-implicature to the negation of the applicability of the pertinent I-implicature. E.g. in *It is not unlikely that Oxford will win the next boat race, and indeed I think it is likely*, given the scale <(know that *p*), (think that *p*)>, the use of the semantically weaker <(think that *p*)> gives rise to the $Q_{clausal}$ implicature that it is possible and likely that Oxford will win the next boat race. On the other hand, there is also a potential M-implicature associated with the use of the marked double negation *not unlikely*, namely, it is less than fully likely that Oxford will win the next boat race. Since the M-implicature is less powerful than the Q-implicature, it is blocked. See Levinson (2000). *See also* division of pragmatic labour.

respective style *See* avoidance style.

restricted pre-semantic pragmatics A term used by the British linguist Stephen Levinson to refer to the position that only pragmatics of a special, limited kind such as *explicature in relevance theory plays a role in determining the truth-conditional, propositional content of a sentence uttered prior to its semantic interpretation. *See also* pre-semantic pragmatics.

retrospective anaphora *See* anaphora (2).

return pop A term taken from *conversation analysis for the phenomenon whereby return of current discussion to an utterance other than the linearly most recent utterance in the preceding conversation. The returned utterance is called the **popped-back utterance**, and the returning utterance is referred to as the **popping utterance**.

reversive A type of *directional oppositeness. It denotes (cause of) movement or (non-spatial) change in opposite directions between two states. E.g. the sense relation between *rise* and *fall*, *advance* and *retreat*, and *lighten* and *darken*. *See also* antipodal; converseness; counterpart; opposite direction.

revised disjoint reference presumption (RDRP) A revised version of the *disjoint reference presumption (DRP) postulated by the British Chinese linguist Yan Huang, which states that the co-arguments of a predicate are intended to be disjoint in reference, unless one of them is reflexive-marked. See Huang (2000).

rheme The part of a sentence that provides the large amount of information relative to what is expressed by the theme. E.g. *Mary wants to marry a park ranger* in *The thing is that Mary wants to marry a park ranger.* Contrasts with **theme**. *See also* comment.

rhetic act *See* locutionary act.

rhetoric The art of using language effectively in communication including making public speeches elaborated by stylistic techniques such as *figures of speech to persuade and influence people. Conceived of in this way, part of rhetoric can be seen as a form of pragmatics. Work in rhetoric has inspired some central pragmatic notions such as the British philosopher H. P. Grice's *maxims of conversation.

rhetorical force A term used by the British linguist Geoffrey Leech to refer to the meaning an utterance conveys in relation to a speaker's compliance with certain rhetorical principles such as the politeness principle.

rhetorical principle The British linguist Geoffrey Leech's term for the co-operative principle, the politeness principle, and the irony principle, which are situated in his interpersonal rhetoric.

rhetorical question A question that functions as a challenging statement to convey a speaker's firm commitment to its implicit answer in order to induce the addressee's acceptance of the validity of the answer. Some of the other pragmatic functions of a rhetorical question are to make an ironic or sarcastic comment, to issue a warning, and to make a criticism. E.g. the question uttered by Rosemary in John: *Are you going to marry Bill?* Rosemary: *Have you seen pigs flying?*

right dislocation *See* antitopic.

Right Hemisphere Language Battery (RHLB) A test deployed in *clinical pragmatics to assess among other things the pragmatic skills of patients with language disorders in right-hemisphere damage. Such patients are known to have difficulties identifying a speaker's communicative intentions, using contextual information to derive meaning, and appreciating humour. The battery covers areas such as inference comprehension, metaphor comprehension, and verbal humour comprehension.

rigid designator A *referring expression that designates the same entity in all *possible worlds in which that entity exists. Proper names such as *Confucius* are in general taken to be rigid designators because they refer to the same entity, no matter what world is being talked about. By contrast, a **non-rigid designator** is a referring expression that picks up different entities in different worlds without change of meaning. Definite descriptions such as *the King of England* are in general held to be non-rigid designators, because whom they refer to is dependent on what world is being discussed. The **rigid/non-rigid designator distinction** was introduced by the American philosopher Paul Kripke. See Green (1996). *See also* referential/attributive distinction.

ritual performative *See* institutionalized speech act.

ritualized performative *See* institutionalized speech act.

rogative verb A term used by the British linguist Geoffrey Leech for a subtype of *directive speech act verb that introduces a question. E.g. *ask, inquire, and query.*

RT = (1) relevance theory, (2) receiving time.

rudeness *See* impoliteness.

rule-based pragmatic semantics *See* pragmatic semantics.

rule of politeness A principle of *politeness put forward by the American linguist Robin Lakoff in the early 1970s which requires a speaker to behave politely in a linguistic interaction. Under this general principle of politeness, there are three sub-principles. The first asks a speaker to refrain from making demands on his or her addressees. By the second sub-principle of politeness, a speaker is expected to offer options to his or her addressees. Finally, the third sub-principle enjoins a speaker to be friendly to his or her addressees and to make them feel good.

Russellian singular proposition *See* singular proposition.

S

s-process = secondary pragmatic process.

Sacks, Harvey (1935–1975) American sociologist. Educated at Columbia College, Yale Law School, and the University of California at Berkeley, he taught first at the University of California at Los Angeles as an acting assistant professor of sociology (1963–4) and an assistant professor (1964–8), and then at the University of California at Irvine as an associate professor (1968–74) and a full professor (1974–5). He died in a car accident in 1975. His great influence on pragmatics is the development of a new field of research, known as *conversation analysis. His main work, put together in *Lectures on Conversation* (1992), was published posthumously.

salva veritate *See* opaque context; transparent context; slingshot.

sarcasm *See* irony.

SAS = speech act schema.

satire The use of derision, ridicule, irony, humour, etc. to expose faults, folly, and vice in a person, an idea, an institution, a system, etc. As an instance of non-literal use of language, satire is of interest to pragmatics.

satisfaction A term used in the philosophy of language according to which a set of sentences is satisfied in a domain if it can be provided with an interpretation in that domain in which it is true. See Blackburn (2005).

satisfaction condition A cover term used by the Canadian philosopher Steven Davis to refer to *truth conditions for a declarative sentence, *answer conditions for an interrogative sentence, and *compliance conditions for an imperative sentence.

saturation A type of *primary pragmatic process (p-process) postulated by the French philosopher François Recanati whereby a given slot, position, or variable in the linguistically decoded logical form of a sentence is contextually filled in or completed. Saturation is a typical linguistically mandated, 'bottom-up' process, i.e. a process which is triggered by a linguistic expression in the sentence itself. E.g. the slot [than whom] in the logical form of the sentence *Elizabeth is cleverer* may be contextually saturated into 'Elizabeth is cleverer than Naomi' for the sentence to express a complete proposition. See Recanati (2004). *See also* completion; free enrichment.

SAV = speech act verb.

SCA = socio-cognitive approach (to pragmatics).

scalar contextual operator (SCO) An operator whose interpretation is made in a contextually situated scalar way. E.g. *at least*, *even*, and *let alone*. By contrast, a **non-scalar contextual operator (NSCO)** is one that does not require that any sentence in which it is used be interpreted in a scalar way. E.g. *respective(ly)*.

scalar entailment An *entailment that arises from the use of a *scalar expression. There are two types of scalar entailment: **semantic entailment** and **pragmatic entailment**. In a Horn-scale such as <freezing, cold, cool>, *freezing* semantically entails *cold*, which in turn semantically entails *cool*. By contrast, the sentence or the proposition expressed by the sentence *John can run 100m in 9.9 seconds* pragmatically entails the sentence or the proposition expressed by the sentence *John can run a slower 100m*.

scalar expression A linguistic expression that can form a point on a **scale**—an ordering among certain linguistic expressions based on semantic or informational strength. E.g. *most*, *often*, and *love*. The scalar expression *often*, for example, can form a scale with the scalar expressions *always* and *sometimes*, i.e. <always, often, sometimes>. Also called a **scalar term** and **scalar item**. *See also* Horn scale.

scalar implicature A *conversational implicature derived from a set of salient contrastive alternates ordered in semantic or informational strength such as a *Horn scale. The derivation of a scalar implicature is due to the British philosopher H. P. Grice's first sub-*maxim of Quantity or the American linguist Laurence Horn's and the British linguist Stephen Levinson's *Q-principle, hence a scalar implicature is also called a **Q-$_{\text{scalar}}$ implicature** or a **scalar Q-implicature**. E.g. given the contrast set <beautiful, pretty, attractive>, the uttering of the sentence *Maria is pretty* gives rise to the scalar implicature that Maria is not beautiful. See Levinson (2000); Huang (2010f).

scalar implicature trigger Any scalar expression whose use generates a scalar implicature. E.g. the use of *some* in *Some students enjoy going to John's lectures* triggers the scalar implicature that not many/most/all students enjoy going to John's lectures.

scalar inference An *inference that arises from the use of a scalar expression. There are two types of scalar inference: **scalar implicature** and **scalar entailment**.

scalar item *See* scalar expression.

scalar pragmatics Pragmatics that handles *scalar expressions and via which *scalar implicatures or scalar inference are engendered.

scalar Q-implicature *See* scalar implicature.

scalar scale *See* Horn scale.

scalar term *See* scalar expression.

scale *See* scalar expression.

SCI = short-circuited implicature.

scientific empiricism = logical positivism.

SCO = scalar contextual operator.

scope ambiguity *See* semantic scope ambiguity.

scope principle A principle proposed by the British philosopher Jonathan Cohen and the French philosopher François Recanati which states that a pragmatically determined aspect of utterance meaning is part of what is said (and, therefore, not a *conversational implicature) if—and perhaps only if—it falls within the scope of logical operators (*see* truth function). Also called the **scope embedding test** and the **Cohen–Recanati principle**. See Recanati (1993); Huang (2007).

scope underdetermination A term used by the American philosopher Kent Bach to refer to a case of semantic *underdetermination which is due to semantic scope. E.g. in *A few arsonists destroyed many buildings*, what is underdetermined, i.e. [each/together], arises from the relation between *a few* and *many*. *See also* semantic scope ambiguity.

SDRT = segmented DRT (*see* Discourse Representation Theory).

second and foreign language pragmatics *See* applied pragmatics.

second-order concept *See* first-order concept.

second-order face In contrast to **first-order face**, this is the scientific notion of *face, i.e. a theoretical construct defined within a theory of *politeness. Also described as **face 2**.

second-order impoliteness The scientific concept of *impoliteness. In other words, second-order impoliteness is a theoretical construct defined within a theory of impoliteness. Also called **impoliteness 2**. Contrasts **with first-order impoliteness**.

second-order politeness The scientific concept of *politeness, i.e. second-order politeness, is a theoretical construct defined within a theory of politeness. Also known as **politeness 2**. Contrasted with **first-order politeness**.

second pair part (SPP) *See* adjacency pair.

second person *See* person.

second principle of relevance *See* communicative principle of relevance.

secondary deixis A term used by the British linguist Sir John Lyons for any *deixis that involves the displacement or reinterpretation of the spatio-temporal parameter of the primary deictic context. E.g. *emphatic deixis is an example of secondary dexis. Distinct from **primary deixis**.

secondary illocution *See* primary illocution.

secondary pragmatic disorder A type of *pragmatic disorder that is related to or caused by deficits in structural language. E.g. an adult with non-fluent aphasia has poor expressive syntax and may not be able to achieve the inversion of a subject pronoun and auxiliary verb that is required to form an indirect request like *Can you turn on the heater?* Contrasts with a **primary pragmatic disorder**.

secondary pragmatic knowledge *See* pragmatic knowledge.

secondary pragmatic process (SPP or **s-process)** A term used by the French philosopher François Recanati for any pragmatic process that presupposes that something has been said or some proposition has been expressed. An example of a secondary pragmatic process is provided by a *particularized conversational implicature (PCI) in the Gricean sense. E.g. the particularized conversational implicature that Lucy may have a boyfriend in London these days, stemming from the uttering of *She's been paying a lot of visits to London recently* as a comment on *Lucy doesn't seem to a have a boyfriend these days*. See Recanati (1993). Contrasted with a **primary pragmatic process**.

self-antonym *See* antagonym.

self-initiated other-repair A correction or clarification of an utterance in a conversation that is prompted by the speaker but carried out by one or more of his or her interlocutors. E.g. *What's his name* (self-initiation) in A's turn and *Martin* (other-repair) in B's turn in A: *The guy who has just resigned. What's his name?* B: *Martin*. *See also* self-initiated self-repair; other-initiated self-repair; other-initiated other-repair.

self-initiated self-repair A correction or clarification of an utterance in a conversation that is carried out by the speaker him- or herself without prompting. E.g. *Alex Marsh I mean* in A: *Uh Alex you know the boy*. B: (pause). A: *Alex Marsh I mean*. Self-initiated self-repair is by far the most common type of conversational repair. *See also* other-initiated self-repair; self-initiated other-repair; other-initiated other-repair.

self-oriented mitigation *See* mitigation.

self-refuting utterance An utterance that is proven to be false in the very fact of its being said. E.g. someone says *I'm not now talking*.

semantic approach (to incomplete definite description) *See* incomplete definite description.

semantic autonomy The view that semantics can operate independently of context of use to establish a truth-conditional proposition, even a basic or minimal one, without *pragmatic intrusion being necessary.

semantic component *See* componential analysis.

semantic compositionality *See* principle of compositionality.

semantic economy *See* semantic minimization.

semantic entailment See entailment.

semantic explication *See* natural semantic metalanguage.

semantic externalism, semantic externalist The view in the *philosophy of language and the *philosophy of mind which denies that the semantic content of an individual's utterances or thoughts is determined by his or her internal mental states. Put in slogan form, 'Meanings ain't in the head', as famously proclaimed by the American philosopher Hilary Putman. The three main reasons are (i) factors of a person's environment and his or her history constitute the content of mental states, (ii) the very possibility of an individual's thoughts referring to the external world relies on the world partly constituting his or her mental states, and (iii) the existence of proper names, natural kind terms, and indexical expressions whose semantic content has to be determined by features outside a person. Contrasts with **semantic internalism**.

semantic feature *See* componential analysis.

semantic feature theory *See* componential analysis.

semantic field theory *See* structural semantics.

semantic focus *See* focus.

semantic frame *See* frame semantics.

semantic gender *See* grammatical gender.

semantic generality *See* semantic minimization.

semantic guilt *See* semantic innocence.

semantic holism *See* holism, holistic.

semantic illusion A term referring to the phenomenon whereby the answer to the question 'How many animals of each type did Moses take into the ark?' is normally two. But the fact is that it was not Moses but Noah who led the animals into the ark. This shows that in order to provide an answer, the utterer failed to interpret the question fully, hence a pragmatic rather than semantic illusion. Also called **Moses illusion**.

semantic innocence The view that a linguistic expression makes the same contribution to meaning in every linguistic environment including in an intensional or metarepresentational context such as a belief report. In other words, according to this view, a linguistic expression does not change its meaning from one linguistic context to another. Any principle expressing such a view is called the **principle of semantic innocence**. The principle of semantic innocence is a principle of metatheoretical and methodological economy, similar to what is called *modified Occam's razor. It was introduced by the British philosopher Donald Davidson and promoted by the American philosophers Jon Barwise and John Perry. By contrast, semantic non-innocence is sometimes called **semantic guilt**.

semantic internalism, semantic internalist The view in the *philosophy of language and the *philosophy of mind that the semantic content of an individual's utterances or thoughts is determined by his or her internal mental states. Contrasts with **semantic externalism**.

semantic interpretation *See* pragmatic interpretation.

semantic minimalism, semantic minimalist A school of thought in the contemporary *philosophy of language and linguistics, the central thesis of which is that context is allowed to have a very limited, or minimal, effect on the semantic content of an utterance. In addition, semantic minimalism holds that semantic content is entirely determined by syntax, semantic context sensitivity is grammatically triggered, and it is not the job of semantic content to capture one's intuitive judgement of what a speaker says when he or she utters a sentence. Consequently, the object of study of semantics should be separated strictly from *pragmatic intrusion. Currently, there are a number of variants of semantic minimalism such as the British philosopher Emma Borg's **minimal semantics**, the Norwegian philosopher Herman Cappelen and the American philosopher Ernest Lepore's **insensitive semantics**, and the American philosopher Kent Bach's **radical semantic minimalism**. Also called **minimal(ist) semantics** or **minimalism** for short. Contrasts with **contextualism**. See Borg (2007; 2010).

semantic minimization Opposed to **expression minimization**, the term is used by the British linguist Stephen Levinson to refer to the thesis that semantically general linguistic expressions are preferred to semantically specific ones. E.g. the use of *egg* instead of *hen's egg*. Also referred to as **semantic economy** or **semantic generality**. See Levinson (2000).

semantic network theory *See* structural semantics.

semantic opacity A term used to refer to the phenomenon whereby the meaning of a complex expression is not apparent from the meaning of its component parts. E.g. *dentist* in English is **semantically opaque**. Contrasts with **semantic transparency**. *See also* principle of compositionality.

semantic politeness *See* absolute politeness.

semantic-pragmatic deficit (syndrome) *See* pragmatic disorder; semantic-pragmatic disorder.

semantic-pragmatic difficulties *See* pragmatic disorder; semantic-pragmatic disorder.

semantic-pragmatic disorder (SPD) A term used in the 1980s to refer to a *pragmatic disorder. Children with semantic-pragmatic disorder have relatively intact syntax and phonology but display disordered semantics and pragmatics. In recent years, there has been much diagnostic debate about semantic-pragmatic disorder. For instance, is semantic-pragmatic disorder a subtype of specific language impairment, a disorder on the autistic spectrum, or a separate diagnostic entity? Alternative terms include **semantic-pragmatic deficit (syndrome)**, **semantic-pragmatic impairment**, **semantic-pragmatic difficulties**.

semantic-pragmatic impairment *See* pragmatic disorder; semantic-pragmatic disorder.

semantic presupposition The conception, introduced by the British philosopher Peter Strawson, that *presupposition is a relation between sentences or statements. On this view, presupposition is defined in terms of, but distinct from, entailment. Thus, if someone says *The king of France is bald*, then there will be a *presupposition failure. Since there is no king of France, the sentence is taken to be neither true nor false: there is simply a *truth value gap. Also called **sentence** or **statement presupposition**. Contrasts with **pragmatic presupposition**.

semantic prime *See* natural semantic metalanguage.

semantic primitive *See* natural semantic metalanguage.

semantic reductionism The view that in the pragmatics-semantics interface, pragmatics should be entirely reduced to semantics. Also termed **semanticism** and **monism of meaning**. Contrasts with **pragmatic reductionism**.

semantic reference *See* speaker('s) reference.

semantic referent *See* speaker('s) reference.

semantic relativism, semantic relativist A school of thought in the contemporary *philosophy of language and linguistics that falls largely in the *semantic minimalist camp. While acknowledging that varying standards have a semantic role to play, proponents of semantic relativism reject the contextualist claim that the role in question is relevant to the determination of what is said by an utterance. Rather, the role played by varying standards is relevant to determining whether what is said is true or false. Some semantic relativists distinguish a context of use from a context of assessment, and insist that epistemic standards, for example, are features of the context of assessment. E.g. according to semantic relativism, the proposition expressed by the sentence *John knows that there was a network outage yesterday* does not vary across different contexts (specifically in relation to the meaning of *know*), but its truth value is relative to, or varies with, a standard of knowledge. See Garcia-Carpintero and Kölbel (2008). *See also* contextualism.

semantic representation A description or representation of the meaning of a sentence in the abstraction of any context in which the sentence might be used. *See also* logical form.

semantic scale A scale that is given by the lexicon without requiring any specific context. It can be based on different structures of the lexicon such as taxonomies, metonymies, and helices. A representative example is a *Horn scale. E.g. <boiling, hot, warm>. Also called a **lexical scale** or **context-independent scale**. Contrasts with a **pragmatic scale**.

semantic scope ambiguity Ambiguity arising from the use of certain logical operators (such as quantifiers, negative forms, and tense markers) that may have different semantic scopes. E.g. *Every secretary hates some boss.* While this sentence is not grammatically ambiguous, it expresses two different propositions—either that every secretary hates a different boss or that every secretary hates the same boss. This ambiguity is a result of the ambiguity of the semantic relation between the two quantifiers *every* and *some*. Also called **scope ambiguity** for short.

semantic theory (of truth) A theory of truth which says that if a language is given a truth definition, i.e. a definition of the *truth predicate '... is true' for the sentences of that language, there is no need to philosophize further about truth itself or truth as shared across different languages. There are some similarities between this view and the *deflationist theory (of truth). *See also* coherence theory (of truth); correspondence theory (of truth); pragmatist theory (of truth); performative theory (of truth).

semantic transfer *See* meaning transfer.

semantic transparency A term used to refer to the phenomenon whereby the meaning of a complex expression is apparent from the meaning of its component parts. E.g. *yayi* 'tooth doctor' in Chinese is **semantically transparent**, and so is *tannlege* 'tooth doctor' in Norwegian. Contrasts with **semantic opacity**.

semantic underdeterminacy *See* underdetermination.

semantic underdetermination *See* underdetermination.

semantic underspecification *See* underspecification.

semantically opaque *See* semantic opacity.

semanticism *See* semantic reductionism.

semanticist Usually in the philosophy of language and linguistics, of someone who specializes in, professes, or practises semantics. *See also* pragmaticist.

semantics The study of *meaning in abstraction from speakers' intentions, their psychological states, the cultural and social aspects of and the contexts in which linguistic expressions are used. It includes the investigation of meaning as between linguistic expressions and what these expressions refer to, and of the relationship between compositionally constructed sentences and the thoughts these sentences express. Sometimes also called **linguistic semantics**. Contrasted with **pragmatics** within linguistics.

semasiology *See* semiology.

semeiology *See* semiology.

semeiotic *See* semiotics.

semeiotics *See* semiotics.

semi-logophoric language Any language which allows either *logophoric expressions to be used for non-logophoric purposes or the extended use of reflexives in logophoric contexts. Igbo, Icelandic and Northern Pomo are such languages. Also called a **mixed logophoric language**.

semiology Also known as **semeiology.** A general science that investigates 'the role of signs in social life', of which linguistics including pragmatics is a part. 'Semiology' (*sémiologie* in French) is the term in a European Continental tradition associated with the work of the Swiss linguist Ferdinand de Saussure. Also called **semasiology** and **significs**. *See also* semiotics.

semiotic pragmatics The tripartite model of *semiotics put forward by the American philosopher Charles Morris, the last component of which is pragmatics.

semiotics Also referred to as **semeiotics**, from Greek *sêmeiotikos* ('observant of signs'). A general science of signs, signals, and their use, of which linguistics including pragmatics is a part. Within semiotics, the American philosopher Charles Morris presented a threefold division into syntax, semantics, and pragmatics. But unlike **semiology**, the term 'semiotics' is primarily linked to an Anglo-American tradition originating in the work of the American philosophers Charles Peirce and Charles Morris. It can be argued that since semiotics constitutes essentially a *code model of communication, *inferential pragmatics does not fall entirely within its domain. Also called **semiotic** or **semeiotic**. *See also* semiology.

sense (1) A meaning of a word that is distinguishable from other meanings the word has, as e.g. in a dictionary. Such a word is usually a *polysemous or *homonymous one. E.g. *ear* has several senses. In one sense, it is used to refer to a human or animal organ, and in another, it is used to refer to the top part of a grain plant.

sense (2) The place of a word in a system or network of semantic relationships with other words in the same language. E.g. the sense of *dog* is constituted by the meaning or **sense relations** that contrast it with, for instance, *animal*, *spaniel*, and *cat*.

sense (3) In certain semantic and pragmatic theories derived from or influenced by the work of the German philosopher, mathematician, and logician Gottlob Frege, the term refers to the meaning of a word as distinct from its **reference**. Thus, to take a famous example of Frege's, *the morning star* and *the evening star* have the same referent, i.e. the planet Venus, but they have different senses. The sense of the former is paraphrasable as 'the star that is seen in the morning', that of the latter as 'the star that is seen in the evening'. In other words, the sense of a word is a 'mode of presentation' of the word's referent. The meaning of the term in this usage is equivalent to that of *intension.

sense component *See* componential analysis.

sense generality A term used by the American philosopher Jay Atlas which is largely synonymous with the term **underdetermination**, but the emphasis is on the epistemological commitment to *pragmatic intrusion into *truth-conditional meaning. E.g. a sentence such as *John is not old enough* is considered to be sense general and needs to be pragmatically completed to become fully propositional.

sense modulation *See* contextual modulation.

sense relation Any meaning relation that holds between lexemes or lexical units within a semantic system of a language. E.g. the meaning relation between *old* and *young*. Also called the **lexical relation**. Two main types of sense relation can be identified: **paradigmatic** and **syntagmatic sense relations**. Paradigmatic sense relations hold between lexical items which can occupy the same position in a syntactic structure. E.g. the meaning relation between *bird* and *robin* in *John caught a bird/robin*. Syntagmatic sense relations hold between lexical items which occur in the same syntactic structure. E.g. the meaning relation between *dental* and *toothache* in *?John has a dental toothache.*

sense transfer *See* meaning transfer.

sentence A well-formed string of words put together according to the grammatical rules of a language. As a unit of the language system, and the largest unit of grammar, a sentence is an abstract entity or construct defined within a theory of grammar. E.g. *Love conquers all* is a sentence in English. Ofen contrasts with an **utterance**.

sentence implicature A term used by the American philosopher Wayne Davis to refer to a *conversational implicature that involves conventionality rather than speaker intentions. Contrasts with his notion of **speaker implicature**—a conversational implicature that depends on the recognition of speaker intentions. The **sentence/speaker implicature distinction** may explain cases where a sentence may implicate something that the speaker who utters it does not implicate.

sentence meaning In opposition to **utterance meaning**, the term refers to those aspects of meaning that are ascribed to a sentence in the abstract, i.e. a sentence independent of its realization in any concrete form. Sentence meaning is often considered to be the *semantic representation or *logical form of a sentence determined by a grammar.

E.g. the meaning of the English sentence *Mathematics is fascinating* is that mathematics is very interesting. Consequently, the study of sentence meaning falls largely under *semantics. Sometimes also called **sentence-type meaning** or **statement meaning**.

sentence non-literality A term used by the American philosopher Kent Bach to refer to the phenomenon whereby a sentence can be used non-literally without any of its constituents being employed in such a way. While a sentence of this kind expresses a complete or full proposition, a speaker may intend it to be used to express a more specific or elaborate proposition. The difference between the two propositions is not due to any particular constituent of the sentence. E.g. a speaker may intend to use *Only John knows that a kiwi can't fly* to mean only John [among those in his class] knows that a kiwi can't fly. By contrast, **constituent non-literality** can be attributed to a constituent of a sentence. A typical example of constituent non-literality is a metaphor. See Bach (1994).

sentence presupposition *See* semantic presupposition.

sentence topic *See* topic (2); (3).

sentence-type meaning *See* sentence meaning.

sentential logophoric domain *See* logophoric domain.

set expression *See* formula.

shared belief *See* mutual belief.

shared knowledge *See* mutual knowledge.

shifter Another term for *deixis used by linguists.

short-circuited implicature (SCI) A term coined by the American linguist Jerry Morgan for a *conversational implicature that can be worked out by jumping to it by means of the convention of usage (see convention of language) without an actual calculation of the inference involved. E.g. from the uttering of the sentence *Sorry I am not wearing a watch* one obtains the short-circuited implicature that the speaker is not in a position to tell the time.

side A *deictic parameter used in the description of *space deixis, which involves the side of an entity. E.g. in Aleut, *ukan* is used to indicate an entity that is 'inside the house', and *sadan* is employed to mark a referent that is 'outside the house'. There are languages that distinguish side-proximal from side-distal. See Huang (2007). *See also* distance; visibility; elevation; stance.

sign **1.** In its broad sense, the term refers to anything that stands for something other than itself, as in **semiotics**. **2.** In its narrower, linguistic sense, the term makes reference to any linguistic expression such as a morpheme, word, and sentence that is used to stand for an entity, concept and/or state of affairs. Also known as a **linguistic** or **language sign**. This relationship between linguistic signs and things, or linguistic signs and concepts, is traditionally called **signification**. In Saussurean and European structural linguistics, a distinction was drawn between a **signifier** (French *signifiant*); the **concept signified** (French *signifié*), and the arbitrariness of the relationship between the form and meaning of signs was emphasized.

signal A term taken from information theory for an encoded version of a messsage transmitted by the sender to the receiver.

significs *See* semiology.

signifier *See* sign.

signifying Arguably a *speech act that is associated with speakers of African American Vernacular English, in which criticism is directed at another person indirectly.

silent pause *See* pause.

simile A *figure of speech in which the comparison between two things is made explicit by the use of words such as *as*, *like*, and *as if* in English. E.g. *I wandered lonely as a cloud* (William Wordsworth). As a variety of *figurative (non-literal) use of language, simile has been a subject of extensive study in pragmatics. *See also* metaphor; hyperbole.

simple indirect = conventional indirectness.

simple proposition A proposition that contains a single predicate and a number of arguments. E.g. the proposition expressed by the sentence *People tore down the Berlin Wall*. Contrasts with a **complex proposition**.

simple theory (of truth) *See* correspondence theory (of truth).

sincerity condition A kind of *felicity condition, which requires a speaker to be sincere so that the *speech act can be performed sincerely. E.g. when carrying out an act of promising, the speaker must genuinely intend to keep the promise. If the sincerity condition is not satisfied, the act is still performed, but there is what the British philosopher J. L. Austin called an *abuse.

single hedge *See* compound hedge.

singular proposition A proposition that contains one or more of actual entities such as people. E.g. the proposition <Confucius, the property of being wise> of the sentence *Confucius was wise*. Also named a **Russellian singular proposition** after the British philosopher Bertrand Russell by the American philosopher Barbara Abbott.

singular reference *See* singular term.

singular term A label found in the philosophy of language for any linguistic expression that can be used to refer to an object or objects including an individual or individuals. Singular terms include *indexicals, *definite descriptions, and *proper nouns. Reference to an object or objects including an individual or individuals through the use of a singular term is called **singular reference**. By contrast, a **general term** is a linguistic expression such as a *predicate that when added to singular terms, constructs a sentence. See Abbott (2010).

Sinn German for *sense (3). Appeared in the title of the German philosopher, mathematician, and logician Gottlob Frege's famous paper *Über Sinn und Bedeutung* (On sense and reference) published in 1892. Contrasted with ***Bedeutung***.

SIP = sociopragmatic interactional principle.

situated speech act *See* pragmeme.

situation *See* situation semantics.

situation of interaction A speech event in which the participants can interact with each other in a reciprocal way. E.g. a conversation. Contrasts with a **situation of reception**.

situation of reception A speech event in which the participants can only receive what is communicated to them but cannot interact reciprocally. E.g. listening to a radio programme. Often distinct from a **situation of interaction**.

situation semantics A *formal semantic account of meaning developed by the American philosophers Jon Barwise and John Perry in the early 1980s as a reaction to *model-theoretic semantics. In this framework, a sentence is taken as a picture of reality, describing a **situation**—a set of facts that consists of individuals, properties, relations, and spatio-temporal locations in a specific context—rather than denoting *truth or falsity. A particular version of situation semantics, which does make use of truth or falsity, is called **Austinian semantics**, inspired by the work of the British philosopher J. L. Austin. In this account, whenever there is a representation, two semantic dimensions are postulated: a linguistic or mental representation and the situation relative to which the linguistic or mental representation is represented as true or false.

situational anaphora *See* exophora, exophoric.

situational context **1.** In its broad sense, the term refers to the total non-linguistic factors involved in the use of a linguistic unit, and is therefore approximately equivalent to *context. **2.** In its narrow sense, the term means roughly *physical context. *See also* context of situation.

skeletal proposition *See* minimal proposition.

slingshot Sometimes also known as the **Frege–Church argument** after the German philosopher, mathematician, and logician Gottlob Frege and the American philosopher Alonzo Church. The argument goes roughly thus: if a context is such that coreferential expressions can be substituted for each other *salva veritate* (Latin for 'with the truth unchanged), sentences that share the same truth-value can also be substituted. *See also* opaque context; transparent context.

slur A linguistic expression that is used to harm a person's or a group of people's reputation by making unfair or false statements about them on the basis of ethnicity, race, nationality, gender, occupation, religion, sexual orientation, and/or other culturally and socially significant categories. E.g. *kike*, *nigger*, and *queer*. Slurs are a subject of study in the philosophy of language and pragmatics. Also called a **slurring term**.

social context One of the main types of *context. Social context refers to the totality of features in a social situation, which may involve the social status of speech event participants such as speakers and addressees, the social relationship between them, and the social setting in which the speech event takes place. For some scholars, social context is primarily established in social interactions. *See also* cultural context; physical context; linguistic context; general knowledge context.

social, cultural, and world-knowledge default A term used in *default semantics for a default meaning or interpretation that is based on the way in which society and culture operate. E.g. the default interpretation of the sentence *John has recently bought a Picasso* uttered, namely John has recently bought a painting by Picasso, is a social, cultural, and world knowledge default. Contrasts with **cognitive default**.

social deixis The codification of the social status of a speaker, an addressee, or a third person or entity referred to, as well as the social relationships holding between them. The information encoded in social deixis includes social class, kin relationship, age, sex, profession, and ethnic groups. E.g. the use of a respectful pronoun or V form (*see tu/vous* distinction) to indicate that the addressee is socially superior to or distant from the speaker in a language like French. There are two categories of social deixis: (i) **absolute** and **relational**. Social deixis can be accomplished by a wide range of linguistic devices including personal pronouns, *forms of address, honorific affixes, clitics, and particles, and the choice of vocabulary. It is a central topic of inquiry in *sociopragmatics. Also called **attitudinal deixis**.

social identity face A term used by the British linguist Helen Spencer-Oatey to refer to a person's desire for acknowledgment of his or her social identities or roles such as a close friend, a leader, and a valued client. Social identity face is group-oriented. Also referred to as **collective** or **collectivistic face**. Contrasts with **quality face**.

social norm model (of politeness) An approach to *politeness outlined by the American linguist Bruce Fraser which reflects the historical, lay conceptualization of politeness. According to this view, politeness is seen as arising from the need for a member of a society to have correct personal conduct prescribed by a set of social norms or convention. It shapes politeness as **social politeness**. It is also linked with a variety of politeness called **wakimae* (discernment) in Japanese.

social politeness *See* social norm model (of politeness).

social pragmatics *See* sociopragmatics.

societal pragmatics A term used by the Danish linguist Jacob Mey to refer to *sociopragmatics from the perspective of the Continental tradition of pragmatics. From a macro point of view, the hand of societal pragmatics can be detected in any area that pertains in any way at all to society, dealing with topics as diverse as language in education, pragmatics and social struggle, and what is called **critical pragmatics (1)**. See Mey (2010).

societalism A term encountered in the Continental tradition of pragmatics which refers to the societal strand of pragmatic theorizing, represented by societal pragmatics.

socio-cognitive approach (SCA) (to pragmatics) An approach to language in use associated particularly with the Hungarian-born American linguist Istvan Kecskes. It is based on two assumptions. First, the communicative process is shaped by the interplay of both societal and individual factors. In such a process, communicators act as individuals on their own right and speakers and addressees are equal participants. Given the differences between speakers and addressees, a pragmatic theory should be both speaker- and addressee-centred (**speaker-hearer pragmatics**) to be able to account for both production and comprehension. Secondly, the process of communication is rough rather than smooth. Four characteristics, called 'traits', have been put forward in the framework to link individual and societal feature: attention–intention, private experience–actual situational experience, egocentrism–co-operation, and salience–relevance.

socio-person deixis A term used by the Greek linguist Sophia Marmaridou for *deixis that serves to identify the participants and codify their social roles in a speech event simultaneously. E.g. the use of **tu/vous* in French.

sociopragmatic ability *See* pragmatic ability.

sociopragmatic competence One of the aspects of *communicative competence, the term refers to a system of knowledge that a language user has in order to be able to use language appropriately in a social situation.

sociopragmatic diachronic pragmatics *See* diachronic pragmatics (2).

sociopragmatic interactional principle (SIP) A set of socioculturally based principles proposed by the British linguist Helen Spencer-Oatey and her colleagues. These principles are said to guide or influence interlocutors' productive and interpretive use of language. The fundamental sociopragmatic interactional principles are responsible for interlocutors' basic interactional motivations, covering their concerns of *face, rights and obligations, and task achievement. The secondary ones are concerned with interlocutors' stylistic strategies such as directness vs. indirectness, cordiality vs. restraint, modesty vs. approbation, and routinization vs. novelty. See Cheng (2010).

sociopragmatics A research domain at the intersection of pragmatics and sociolinguistics. In other words, sociopragmatics provides a systematic study of the use of language in relation to society. One topic that has long been the focus of sociopragmatic research is *politeness. Other topics that have attracted attention in this branch of pragmatics include *social deixis, social conventions relating to the performance of speech acts, and social factors which constrain language in use. *See also* societal pragmatics.

soft pragmatics *See* hard pragmatics.

solidarity politeness The American linguists Ronald and Suzanne Scollon's term for positive politeness.

sophisticated understanding A term used in relevance theory for the highest level of pragmatic development. On this level, an addressee interprets an utterance in such a way that he or she knows that a speaker is not always competent (e.g. sometimes the speaker may express him- or herself unclearly) or benevolent (for instance, sometimes the speaker may tell a lie). See Allott (2010). *See also* cautious optimism; naïve optimism.

sortal crossing *See* zeugma.

source-in-target metonymy *See* metonymy.

space deixis The specification of location in space relative to that of the participants at utterance time in a speech event. E.g. *Take this there; bring that here!* Space deixis is commonly expressed by the use of (i) **demonstratives**, (ii) **deictic adverbs of space**. (iii) **deictically marked third-person personal pronouns**, and (iv) **verbal affixes of motion and verbs of motion**. Other terms include **place**, **spatial**, **local**, and **locational deixis**. *See also* person deixis; time deixis; social deixis; discourse deixis.

spatial relation A relationship, based on spatio-geometric properties, that holds between a *figure and a ground. E.g. the spatial relation between the figure 'the dog' and the ground 'the car' denoted by *behind* in *The dog is behind the car*. A number of linguistic frames have been proposed to account for spatial reference.

SPD = semantic-pragmatic disorder.

speaker *See* addresser.

speaker-hearer pragmatics *See* socio-cognitive approach (to pragmatics).

speaker implicature *See* sentence implicature.

speaker meaning *See* utterance meaning.

speaker orientation A property of a meaning, proposition and inference that is or tends to be oriented to the speaker of a sentence. Speaker orientation, for example, is considered to be a property of *conventional implicature. E.g. the conventional implicature brought in by *surprisingly* in *Surprisingly, John found that the city council handled the situation well* is a contribution made by the current, external speaker, rather than the internal protagonist, to the meaning of the sentence.

speaker presupposition *See* pragmatic presupposition.

speaker('s) maxim A speaker-oriented *maxim of conversation. It is normally concerned with production, and is a prohibition. E.g. the first part of the British linguist Stephen Levinson's *Q-principle: do not say less than is required. By contrast, a **recipient's corollary** or **an addressee('s)** or **hearer('s) maxim** is an addressee-oriented conversational maxim. It is usually concerned with comprehension, and is an obligation. E.g. the second part of Levinson's *Q-principle: what is not said is not the case. See Atlas (2004).

speaker('s) reference Reference to an entity which a speaker wishes to talk about in the use of a particular *referring expression on a particular occasion. In other words, a **speaker('s) referent** of a referring expression is fixed by what the speaker intends to refer to on a given occasion. E.g. suppose two people A and B see John in the distance and mistake him for Bill. A asks *What's Bill doing?* B replies *Walking a dog*. In this case of misidentification, although both A and B use the referring expression *Bill*, what they have clearly referred to is John. Therefore, John is the speaker('s) referent. By contrast, **semantic reference** is reference to what is denoted by a referring expression. That is to say, a semantic referent of a referring expression is the referent the referring expression has in a particular language and is determined by the conventions of that language. In the example above, Bill, the man named by *Bill*, is the semantic referent. This **speaker('s)/semantic reference distinction** was introduced by the American philosopher Paul Kripke.

speaker's economy A principle of economy put forward by the American linguist George Zipf. It posits a tendency toward a vocabulary of one word which has many distinct meanings, thus minimizing a speaker's effort. Speaker's economy is further distinguishable between **mental inertia** or **paradigmatic economy** and **articulatory** or **physical inertia** or **syntagmatic economy**, hence internally dialectic in its operation. The former is concerned with the reduction in the inventory of mental lexicon, the latter with the reduction in the number of linguistic units. Speaker's economy is related to the American linguist Laurence Horn's *R-principle (1). It contrasts with Zipf's **auditor's economy**. Also called the **force of unification**. See Horn (2007); Huang (2007).

speaker–setting axis *See* register.

speaker's meaning *See* utterance meaning.

specific indefinite reference *See* indefinite reference.

speech act The uttering of a linguistic expression whose function is not just to say things, but actively to do things or to perform acts as well. Thus, if someone says: *Could you please close the door?* he or she is performing the speech act of requesting. A threefold distinction is made among the speech acts a speaker simultaneously performs when saying something: **locutionary act**, **illocutionary act**, and **perlocutionary act**. Speech acts can also be divided into **direct speech acts** and **indirect speech acts**. See Austin (1962); Searle (1969); Huang (2007). See also canonical speech act; collective speech act; constative speech act; expressive speech act (1); ground-floor speech act; primitive speech act; regulative speech act.

speech act adverbial *See* pragmatic adverbial.

speech act empathy hierarchy A scale which states that a speaker cannot empathize with someone else more than with him- or herself. In other words, E (speaker) > E (others). *See also* humanness empathy hierarchy; topic empathy hierarchy; surface structure empathy hierarchy. See Kuno (2004).

speech act fallacy A term used by the American philosopher John Searle to refer to the view that the meaning of a (philosophically important) word can be explained in terms of the fact that it typically functions to perform a certain speech act. In other words, the speech act fallacy identifies what a word is typically used to do with its semantic content. Thus, on this account, since *true* is used to endorse or concede a statement, *good* to make a commendation, *know* to give a guarantee, and *probably* to qualify a commitment, those uses constitute the meanings of those words. This analysis is fallacious because saying *The iPod is good* is not equivalent to saying *I commend the iPod*. See Bach (2004).

speech act monism A term used by the Norwegian philosopher Herman Cappelen and the American philosopher Ernest Lepore for the belief that every utterance in a particular context can only express one particular *proposition or perform one particular *speech act. Contrasts with **speech act pluralism**.

speech act paradox An inconsistency in which the (primary) speech act of an utterance is frequently realized in terms of a conventional interpretation of that utterance rather than by its literal interpretation.

speech act pluralism A position in the contemporary *philosophy of language and linguistics which holds the view that what is said may express more than one proposition or an utterance in its context may carry out more than one speech act. In other words, each minimal representation may correspond to a wide variety of speech acts which it is capable of conveying, hence the name. What is said depends on a wide range of factors other than the proposition semantically expressed. It depends on a potential infinitude of features of the context of utterance and of the context of those who report on or think about what was said. Speech act pluralism is needed to supplement *semantic minimalism. The major advocates of this view are the Norwegian philosopher Herman Cappelen and the American philosopher Ernest Lepore. See Cappelen and Lepore (2005). *See also* speech act monism.

speech act predicational *See* pragmatic adverbial.

speech act schema (SAS) An *inference mechanism proposed by the American philosophers Kent Bach and Robert Harnish which shows how an addressee, on the basis of what a speaker utters, mutual contextual beliefs, *linguistic presumptions, and *communicative presumptions, can work out the force and content of the speaker's illocutionary act.

speech act set A combination of individual speech act strategies which, put together, can be used to perform a complete speech act or acts. E.g. the speech act set for apologizing contains at least five distinct speech act strategies: (i) expression of an apology, (ii) acknowledgement of responsibility, (iii) explanation, (iv) offer of repair, and (v) promise of non-recurrence. See Ishihara and Cohen (2010).

speech act theory A theory originally proposed by the British philosopher J. L. Austin in the 1930s, and after his death in 1960 refined, systematized, and advanced especially by his Oxford pupil, the American philosopher John Searle, though somewhat foreshadowed by the Austrian-born British philosopher Ludwig Wittgenstein's views about language games. Speech act theory was expounded in a series of lectures Austin gave at Oxford in 1952–4 and later in the William James Lectures he delivered at Harvard in 1955. These lectures were subsequently published posthumously as *How to Do Things with Words* in 1962. The central tenet of speech act theory is that the uttering of a sentence is (part of) an action within the framework of social institutions and conventions. Put in slogan form, saying is (part of) doing, or words are (part of) deeds. The most important components of the theory include a division of speech acts into locutionary, illocutionary, and perlocutionary acts and a set of felicity conditions listed for each speech act.

speech act type The class in which a *speech act is placed. There have been two approaches to **speech act typology**: (i) a classification of illocutionary verbs, as exemplified by the British philosopher J. L. Austin's taxonomy, and (ii) a classification of acts, as illustrated by the American philosopher John Searle's typology. Under Searle's taxonomy, speech acts are universally divided into five types along a number of dimensions such as (i) illocutionary point, (ii) *direction of fit, (iii) expressed psychological states, and (iv) the strength with which an illocutionary point is presented. The five types of speech acts are *representatives, *directives, *commissives, *expressives, and *declarations. Also called an **illocutionary type**.

speech act verb (SAV) **1.** In its broad sense, the term refers to any verb that can be used to describe and sometimes perform types or aspects of linguistic action. E.g. *broadcast*, *mutter*, and *write*. Also called a **linguistic action verb**. **2.** In its narrow sense, the term refers to any verb that can be used for the description and sometimes performance of speech acts. E.g. *promise*, *sentence*, and *threaten*. Defined thus, speech act verbs constitute a wider category than **performative verbs**. Put the other way round, performative verbs form a subcategory of speech act verbs. E.g. while *threaten* is a speech act verb, it is not a performative verb. For some scholars, speech act verbs can be divided into **content-descriptive**, **neutral**, and **phonically descriptive verbs**. Furthermore, content-descriptive verbs can be grouped into locutionary, illocutionary, and perlocutionary verbs. See Leech (1983); Verschueren (1999). *See also* performative verb.

speech community A group of speakers of any size such as a family, village, town, region, and country who share, or believe that they share, the same language or language variety including the same norm of language behaviour and language use. Sometimes also called a **linguistic community**.

speech event An instance of speech which consists of one or more speech acts. Examples include a single utterance, a conversation, and a lecture.

speech event participant Anyone involved in a speech event such as a speaker or utterer, addressee, or hearer or interpreter, bystander, overhearer, or eavesdropper.

speech exchange system In *conversation analysis, the term refers to a mechanism of organizing spoken interaction, in which various parameters of *turn-taking such as the number of participants, the content and order of turns, and turn types are constrained.

speech genre *See* genre.

SPP = **1.** second pair part; **2.** secondary pragmatic process.

Square of Opposition A square of the following form, which was formulated by Boethius on the basis of Aristotelian logic two millennia ago.

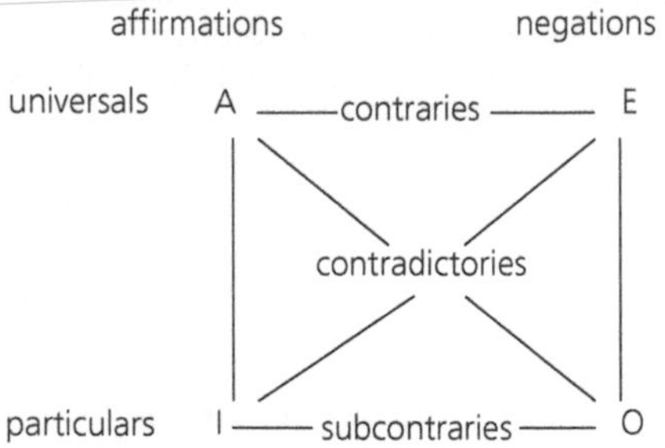

Regarding the lexicalization of the logical operators (*see* truth function) on the square, there is an asymmetry: whereas the A, E, and I corners can all be lexicalized, the O vertex cannot. What is relevant to pragmatics, then, is that this puzzle can partially be accounted for in terms of *neo-Gricean pragmatics. The I and O corners are related by a *Q_{scalar} implicature, and what is Q-implicated on the square (if it is a negative term) is not lexicalized.

stance A term used in the description of *space deixis which indicates the stance or motion of an entity—whether it is standing, sitting, lying, coming, or going. A typical example involves the use of demonstratives in languages of the Waikuruan family.

standard conversational implicature *See* conversational implicature.

standardized non-literality *See* short-circuited implicature.

statement presupposition *See* semantic presupposition.

static semantics Any semantic theory that is not dynamic in nature. E.g. *truth-conditional semantics. Often contrasts with **dynamic semantics**.

Strawson, Peter Frederick (1919–2006) British philosopher. He was educated at the University of Oxford. After a distinguished period in the British army, he spent a year (1946–7) as an assistant lecturer in philosophy at the University College of North Wales, Bangor. He returned to Oxford in 1947, becoming a Fellow in Philosophy at University College, Oxford, in 1948 and succeeding the British philosopher Gibert Ryle to the Waynflete Chair in Metaphysical Philosophy at Oxford in 1968. He was knighted in 1977 and retired in 1987. A prominent figure of the postwar school of 'ordinary language philosophy', one of Strawson's most important contributions to the philosophy of language and pragmatics was his celebrated challenge to the British philosopher Bertrand Russell's theory of definite descriptions and his related work on presupposition.

strengthened belief *See* maxim of strengthened belief.

strengthened evidence *See* maxim of strengthened evidence.

strengthened maxim of Quality A term introduced by the British Chinese linguist Yan Huang for a strengthened version of the Gricean *maxim of Quality proposed by the British linguist Gerald Gazdar, which demands that a speaker asserts only what he or she knows.

strengthening A type of *free enrichment. Strengthening takes a completed proposition resulting from *saturation as input, and yields as output a richer proposition which entails the original input proposition. E.g. the proposition expressed by the sentence *Mary has a brain* will be strengthened into a richer proposition that Mary has a high-functioning brain, which entails the original proposition. By contrast, in *expansion, a contextually provided conceptual constituent needs to be added to the proposition of a sentence uttered, but the output proposition yielded by the input one does not need to entail the original input proposition. E.g. the proposition expressed by the sentence *The windows are bullet-proof* may be expanded into a proposition that the windows of the president's limousine are bullet-proof. But the enriched proposition does not entail the original one. Strengthening is also called **logical enrichment**. See Recanati (2004).

strong massive modularity of mind thesis *See* massive modularity of mind thesis.

strong r-implicature *See* r-implicature.

structural ambiguity *See* syntactic ambiguity.

structural inference theory (of scalar implicature) The view that the working out of the meaning of *scalar implicatures relies heavily on structural or grammatical factors. This position is represented by the Italian linguist Gennaro Chierchia. *See also* contextual inference theory (of scalar implicature); default inference theory (of scalar implicature).

structural meaning *See* grammatical meaning.

structural presupposition trigger *See* constructional presupposition trigger.

structural semantics A branch of structural linguistics that is devoted to the study of meaning. The central idea is that the meaning of a word is accountable in terms of the notion of *sense relations and the concept of lexical or *semantic fields. According to this semantic theory, a word's meaning is determined by its position in a network of lexical or semantic relations with other words in the same lexical or semantic field. A **lexical** or **semantic field** is a distinct, coherent subset of the lexicon defined by some general term or concept. Sometimes also known as the **lexical field theory**, **semantic field theory,** and **semantic network theory**.

style *See* pragmatic stylistics.

style disjunct *See* pragmatic adverbial.

sub-atomic semantics A term introduced by the American philosopher Terence Parsons for an approach to meaning which includes the study of aspects of meaning below the level of the word. E.g. event is a component of sub-atomic semantics.

subject honorific A type of *referent honorific in which deference is shown to the referent by the subject of the sentence. E.g. in a Japanese sentence meaning 'Professor Tanaka came', the verb can change its form to show the speaker's respect toward the referent of the subject, i.e. Professor Tanaka. Often contrasts with **object honorific**.

subject-prominent and topic-prominent language A term used by the American linguists Charles Li and Sandra Thompson for a language in which the basic syntactic elements of a sentence are both a subject and a predicate and a *topic and a *comment. E.g. Japanese and Korean are considered to be such languages. Contrasted with a **neither**

subject-prominent nor topic-prominent language. *See also* subject-prominent language; topic-prominent language.

subject-prominent language A term used by the American linguists Charles Li and Sandra Thompson to refer to a language in which the basic syntactic elements of a sentence are a subject and a predicate. E.g. English, Malagasy, and Twi are considered to be such languages. Distinct from a **topic-prominent language**. *See also* subject-prominent and topic-prominent language; neither subject-prominent nor topic-prominent language.

subjectification A term deployed in *historical pragmatics for the process in which a lexical item has gradually been used as a discourse marker to reflect a speaker's *point of view. E.g. *in fact* is such a lexical expression.

subjectivity, subjective The property of being either a subject of consciousness such as cognition, feeling, and perception or a subject of an action. By **locutionary subjectivity** or **subjectivity of utterance** is meant a speaker's expression of him- or herself in the act of uttering a linguistic expression. In other words, subjectivity refers to a speaker's expression of his or her own attitudes, beliefs, emotions, views, and perceptions of the world, as well as his or her own will, authority, and self-concept such as identity, values, and morals in dynamic relation to others. If the expression is based on evidence shared between a speaker and others, it is called **intersubjectivity**. The concept of subjectivity was crucial to the *French approach to pragmatics. It is considered central to pragmatics including the theory of speech acts by many functional linguists. See Lyons (1995).

subjectivizer A marker of subjectivity that a speaker can use to express subjective opinions about the proposition of an utterance. E.g. *I think*.

subordinate-level concept *See* basic-level concept.

sub-sense A term used by the British linguist Alan Cruse for a *sense (1) of a word that is motivated by the specific *context of situation in which the word is used. E.g. the meaning of *knife* in A: *Do you need a knife?* B: [sitting at the meal table about to eat his beef steak, with a penknife in his right hand] *Yes, please*. Also called **micro-sense**.

subtractive implicature A *conversational implicature that removes, modifies, or replaces the semantic content of a sentence uttered. E.g. the implicature that philosophy is deadly boring arising from the ironic uttering of the sentence *Philosophy is fascinating*. See Levinson (2000). Contrasts with an **additive implicature**.

summons *See* call.

superordinate *See* hyponymy, hyponym.

superordinate-level concept *See* basic-level concept.

surface anaphora A term initiated by the American linguists J. Hankamer and Ivan Sag for *anaphora that requires a linguistic antecedent and therefore cannot be pragmatically constrained. A typical example is VP ellipsis in English. E.g. in the context in which John attempts to open a safe, one cannot say to him *Are you able to?* Instead, one has to ask, *Are you able to open it?* This indicates that VP ellipsis needs a linguistic antecedent, and is hence a case of surface anaphora. Contrasts with **deep anaphora**.

surface structure empathy hierarchy A scale which states that it is easier for a speaker to empathize with the referent of the subject of a sentence than with that of any other NP in the sentence. In other words, E (subject) > E (non-subject). *See also* humanness empathy hierarchy; speech act empathy hierarchy; topic empathy hierarchy. See Kuno (2004).

surface structure syntactic ambiguity *See* syntactic ambiguity.

switch-function system (of reference tracking) One of the four main types of *reference-tracking systems. By switch function is meant the mechanism which tracks the reference of an NP across clauses in a discourse by means of verbal morphology indicating the semantic function of that NP in each clause. The switch-function system is found in a wide range of languages in the world. *See also* gender system (of reference tracking); switch-reference system (of reference tracking); inference system (of reference tracking).

switch-reference system (of reference tracking) One of the four main types of *reference-tracking systems. In this system, the verb of a dependent clause is morphologically marked to indicate whether or not the subject of that clause is the same as the subject of its linearly adjacent, structurally related independent clause. If both subjects are coreferential, a 'same subject' (SS) marker is used; otherwise, a 'different subject' (DS) marker is employed. Switch reference is found in many of the native Indian languages spoken in North America, of the non-Austronesian languages spoken in Papua New Guinea, and of the aboriginal languages spoken in Australia. It has been given a pragmatic analysis within the *neo-Gricean pragmatic theory of anaphora. See Huang (2010b). *See also* gender system (of reference tracking); inference system (of reference tracking); switch-function system (of reference tracking).

syllepsis *See* zeugma.

symbolic deixis *See* gestural deixis.

symbolic field *See* deictic field.

symbolic use (of a deictic expression) The extended use of a *deictic expression. The interpretation of symbolic use does not require a direct, moment-by-moment monitoring of any physical aspects of the speech event by the addressee, but involves only knowing the basic spatio-temporal parameter of the speech event. E.g. if one knows the general location of the speaker, one can interpret *This* in *This town is famous for its small antiques shops* without any problem. Contrasts with the **gestural use** (of a deictic expression).

symmetric conjunction A conjunction in which '*p* and *q*' and '*q* and *p*' are understood as equivalent. E.g. *Beijing is the capital of China and Tokyo is the capital of Japan*. The reversal of the order of the two conjuncts here does not affect the truth-conditional meaning of the conjunction as a whole. Contrasted with **asymmetric conjunction**.

sympathy maxim One of a set of *maxims of politeness proposed by the British linguist Geoffrey Leech, which is addressee-oriented. What the maxim basically says is: maximize sympathy but minimize antipathy to the addressee and others. More recently, Leech has preferred the term 'pragmatic constraint' over the term 'maxim'.
See Leech (2007).

synchronic historical sociopragmatics *See* historical sociopragmatics.

synchronic modularity *See* diachronic modularity.

synchronic pragmatics A subfield of pragmatics that studies language use in general or in a particular language as it is, or was, at a particular point in time, with 'synchronic' meaning 'at a single point in time'. In other words, synchronic pragmatics is concerned with the pragmatics of what the Swiss linguist Ferdinand de Saussure called an '***état de langue***', i.e. the pragmatics of the state of language at a particular point in time, regardless of its previous or subsequent history. Contrasts with **diachronic pragmatics**.

syncretic view A term used by the French philosopher François Recanati for the approach in the contemporary *philosophy of language and linguistics that falls between *literalism and *contextualism. It allows pragmatic processes to play a role in the determination of what is said, but limits their effects to what is said in the intuitive sense, as opposed to what is strictly and literally said. Also called **syncreticism**.
See Recanati (2004). *See also* moderate contextualism.

synecdoche A *figure of speech in which a linguistic expression denoting a part is used to refer to a whole or vice versa. Synecdoche is one kind of non-literal language. E.g. the use of *faces* in *There were two or three new faces at the meeting* to refer to the people. Often treated as a special case of **metonymy**.

synonymy, synonym A *sense relation in which two or more lexical items have the same propositional or descriptive meaning, hence also called **propositional** or **descriptive synonymy**. E.g. the meaning relation between *hide* and *conceal*. **Absolute synonyms**, if they exist at all, are synonyms that share the identical meaning in all respects and contexts. In other words, to use the British linguist Sir John Lyon's terminology, they are **fully**, **totally**, and **completely synonymous**. By contrast, **partial synonyms** are synonymous, but not absolutely so. Absolute synonyms are extremely rare, almost nonexistent. As a result, most synonyms are partial synonyms. See Lyons (1995). *See also* near-synonymy; lexical oppositeness.

synonymy blocking Blocking of a lexical expression by another synonymous but distinct lexical expression. E.g. *hospitalize* (v) blocks **hospital* (v). *See also* homonymy blocking.

syntactic ambiguity *Ambiguity through the assignment of two or more different syntactic structures to a single string of words in a sentence. Thus *Visiting relatives can be boring* is ambiguous, because the phrase *Visiting relatives* has two possible grammatical structures: the first with the meaning of 'the act of visiting relatives' and the second with the meaning of 'relatives who are visiting'. Syntactic ambiguity can further be divided into two types: **surface structure syntactic ambiguity** and **deep structure syntactic ambiguity**. The former occurs when the words can be syntactically grouped in different ways, as in the above example. The latter occurs when the structural source of the ambiguity is less easily identifiable. E.g. *The chicken was ready to eat*, which may mean either 'the chicken was about to eat the feed' or 'the chicken was about to be eaten'. Also called **grammatical** or **structural ambiguity**. *See also* lexical ambiguity; semantic scope ambiguity; pragmatic ambiguity; lexico-syntactic ambigutiy.

syntactic correlation constraint (on what is said) A criterion proposed by the American philosopher Kent Bach for what is said, according to which what is said should be closely linked with both the conventional, semantic content and the syntactic structure of a sentence uttered.

syntactic language *See* pragmatic language.

syntactic mode (of communication) A term used by the American linguist Talmy Givón to refer to communication that is characterized by (i) subject–predicate constructions, (ii) tight subordination, (iii) fast rate of delivery, (iv) word order used to signal semantic case functions, (iv) a large ratio of nouns over verbs in discourse, with verbs being semantically complex, and (v) elaborate use of grammatical morphology. Contrasts with the **pragmatic mode** (of communication).

syntactic pragmatics A term used by the Hungarian linguist Ferenc Kiefer to refer to syntactically relevant morphological categories that make a contribution to pragmatics. The contribution is made via the syntactic structure in which such a category appears. E.g. plural marking.

syntactic topic construction *See* English-style topic construction.

syntactico-centralism *See* pragmatico-centrism.

syntagmatic economy *See* speaker's economy.

syntagmatic sense relation *See* sense relation.

syntax–pragmatics alliance *See* pragmatico-centrism.

synthetic *See* analytic/synthetic distinction.

synthetic proposition *See* analytic/synthetic distinction.

system perspective (in the philosophy of language) A term used by the Canadian philosopher Robert Stainton for one of the two main schools of thought in the 20th-century Anglo-American *philosophy of language, which is largely equivalent to *ideal language philosophy. Contrasts with the **use perspective**.

system sentence The British linguist Sir John Lyons' term for a sentence in the sense of an element posited as a unit of the language system. Contrasts with his notion of a **text sentence**.

T

T form *See tu/vous* distinction.

T-literal meaning = type-*literal meaning.

T pronoun *See tu/vous* distinction.

T-sentence A sentence that states the *truth condition for an object language sentence and has the Tarskian formula: *S* is true if and only if *p*. E.g. *Snow is white* is true if and only if snow is white. Another example: the French sentence *La neige est blanche* is true if and only if snow is white.

taboo language *See* avoidance style.

tacit knowledge The subconscious knowledge a native speaker is assumed to possess of his or her language.

tact maxim One of a set of *maxims of politeness proposed by the British linguist Geoffrey Leech, which is addressee-oriented. What the maxim basically says is: minimize cost but maximize benefit to the addressee and others. This maxim is particularly applicable to speech acts like directives and commissives. More recently Leech has preferred to use the term 'pragmatic constraint' over the term 'maxim'. See Leech (2007). Contrasts with the **generosity maxim**.

target-to source metonymy *See* metonymy.

tautology A term used in logic which refers to a proposition that is necessarily true. A tautological utterance can take a variety of syntactic forms such as (i) **equatives**: *a* is *a*, (ii) **conditionals**: if *p*, then *p*, and (iii) **disjunctions**: either *p* or not *p*, (iv) **coordinations**: *a* is *a* and *b* is *b*, (v) **subordinate sentences**: *p* because *p*; when *p*, *p* and (vi) **relative sentences**: whatever *p*, *p*; *p*, what *p*. E.g. *War is war*. Tautology has been extensively studied in pragmatics. See Meibauer (2008).

taxonymy, taxonym A special type of **hyponymy** that constitutes the vertical *sense relation in a classificatory or taxonomic hierarchy. The sense relation can be expressed by '*x* is a kind/type of *y*', in which *x* is a taxonym. E.g. the meaning relation between *mango/apple/grape* and *fruit*. The horizontal sense relation between sister taxonyms or **co-taxonyms**, e.g. *apple*, *grape*, and *mango*, is that of **co-taxonymy**, which is a variety of *incompatibility. Taxonymy can be distinguished from hyponymy. E.g. while *kitten* is a hyponym of *cat*, it is not a taxonym of it, because it is rather odd to say *A kitten is a type of cat*.

TCP = truth-conditional pragmatics.

TCU = turn constructional unit.

Teaching Pragmatics An online teacher's resource guide for teaching various features of pragmatics, especially second and foreign language pragmatics (*see* applied pragmatics). It was written by the American linguists Kathleen Bardovi-Harlig and Rebbeca Mahan-Taylor and published by the Office of English Language Programs, US Department of State. The guide covers topics such as pragmatic awareness, pragmatic variation, conversational implicature, conversational management, politeness, and speech acts. URL:

SEE WEB LINKS

- http://draft.eca.state.gov/education/engteaching/pragmatics.html

temporal adverb *See* deictic adverb of time.

temporal deixis *See* time deixis.

tense The linguistic expression of the time of an event described in a proposition in relation to the moment of speaking. It is done typically through verbal inflection, but also in the form of other periphrastic constructions. Tense is divided traditionally into **past** (earlier than the moment of speaking), **present** (at the time of speaking), and **future** (later than the time of speaking). Also called **linguistic** or **L-tense** as opposed to **metalinguistic** or **M-tense**—the theoretical category of tense. Tense is a common means to encode *time deixis.

terms of address *See* forms of address.

Test of Pragmatic Language (TOPL) A reliable test used in *clinical pragmatics to assess pragmatic language skills and disorders in children, adolescents, and adults. It covers six core components of language use. The test is administered by professionals such as speech and language pathologists, psychologists, and mental health workers. It has been used with a wide range of clinical population including children and adolescents with language delays and learning disabilities, adults with aphasia, and children with autism spectrum disorders.

text deixis *See* discourse deixis.

text pragmatics The study of the formal structure of the linguistic unit larger than a sentence, especially within writing from the perspective of pragmatics. The label is given to a number of theories of the functions of a spoken or especially written text in communication rather than to a well-established discipline in pragmatics. Sometimes also called **discourse pragmatics**.

text sentence The British linguist Sir John Lyons' term for a sentence that may be uttered or written as part of a text or discourse. Contrasts with his notion of a **system sentence**. *See also* utterance.

textual deixis *See* discourse deixis.

texuality Also called **texture**. The term refers to the property by which successive sentences form a coherent text. *See also* cohesion; coherence.

thematization The process of putting a constituent to the front of a sentence to function as a **theme**. E.g. *Nick, please don't leave him out*. Also called **thematic fronting**. *See also* topicalization.

theme The first major constituent of a sentence. E.g. *Tomorrow* in *Tomorrow you need to feed the hamster*. Contrasts with a **rheme**. *See also* topic (3).

theoretical pragmatics The study of language in use with a view of constructing a general theory or theories of pragmatics without regard to practical applications the investigation might have. Often contrasts with **applied pragmatics**. *See also* descriptive pragmatics; pure pragmatics.

theoretical rationality *See* rationality.

theory of mind (ToM) A term introduced by the American psychologists David Premack and Guy Woodruff for a more general cognitive ability to attribute inferentially certain mental states such as belief, knowledge, and intention to others on the basis of their behaviour. In other words, theory of mind refers to a person's capacity to understand a situation from another person's *viewpoint. A system that describes this ability is called the **theory of mind mechanism (ToMM)**. **Mind blindness** is the label given to a person who does not have a theory of mind. Theory of mind plays an important role in *cognitive pragmatics (1). Also called **mind-reading**.

theory of satisfaction A theory that aims to specify a set of, and provide an account of the set of, *satisfaction conditions of sentences, i.e. the *truth conditions for declarative sentences, the *answer conditions for interrogative sentences, and the *compliance conditions for imperative sentences, in a language. These include the satisfaction conditions for the sentences whose interpretation is dependent on a particular context of use. The theory should also take a speaker's communicative intentions into account. Defined thus, a theory of satisfaction is in part pragmatic in nature. The term is due to the Canadian philosopher Steven Davis.

theory-theory A term that is used to refer to the idea that daily attributions of beliefs, knowledge, and intentions to others operate through the tacit use of a theory that empowers us to formulate these interpretations as explanations. *See also* theory of mind.

thick term A label introduced by the British philosopher Bernard Williams for a linguistic expression that contains two parts: a descriptive part and an evaluative part. E.g. a sexist *epithet such as *bitch*. *See also* definite description.

third person *See* person; obviation.

three-levelled theory (of communication and meaning) A theory proposed by the British linguist Stephen Levinson, as opposed to the traditional, standard **two-levelled theory** of communication and meaning. Levinson proposed that a third, intermediate level—*utterance-type meaning—be added to the two generally accepted levels of *sentence-type meaning and *utterance-token meaning. While sentence-type meaning falls under the province of semantics, both utterance-type meaning and utterance-token meaning belong to pragmatics. See Levinson (2000); Huang (2007). Often contrasts with the **two-levelled theory** (of communication and meaning).

time deixis The encoding of temporal points and spans relative to the time at which an utterance is produced in a speech event. E.g. the use of *now* in *Send the email now* relates to such a time point. Time deixis is commonly expressed by (i) **deictic adverbs of time** and (ii) **tense**. Also called **temporal deixis**. *See also* person deixis; space deixis; social deixis; discourse deixis.

timeless meaning The British philosopher H. P. Grice's term for roughly linguistic meaning or linguistically encoded meaning, i.e. the meaning of a sentence or 'utterance type' abstracting away from any context of use. E.g. the meaning of the sentence or utterance type *John and Mary make a pleasant couple*. By **applied timeless meaning** is meant timeless meaning of an applied sentence or utterance-type on a particular occasion. A sentence may have more than one timeless meaning, as in the case of ambiguity. E.g. in a sentence such as *The coach has left the stadium*, there are two timeless meanings: the trainer of a sports team has left the stadium and the bus has left the stadium. On a particular occasion, we have to select one of the two timeless meanings, e.g. the trainer has left the stadium. That is applied timeless meaning. See Grice (1989).

timeless proposition A proposition that does not make any reference to a specific time or times for which it holds. E.g. the proposition expressed by the sentence *Raised cholesterol level increases the risk of heart disease*.

time-zone sentence A sentence like '*It's two o'clock*, as thought by a young child who does not yet have the concept of a time zone' discussed by the American philosopher John Perry. Given that a young child does not have the notion of a particular time being true or false relative to a time zone, this example raises the issue of whether such a sentence contains an *unarticulated constituent or not. *See also* Z-land sentence.

token An individual instance of a unit, as opposed to the unit as variously instantiated, which is the token's **type**. E.g. in the sentence *A life without books is a life without life*, there are nine word tokens, but since three of the words—the second, the seventh, and the ninth (*life*)—are identical, i.e. they are different instances or tokens of the same type, there are only seven word types. Such an ambiguity is known as the **type/token ambiguity**. In addition, the **type/token distinction** also gives rise to potential ambiguity by level. E.g. the *a* in the sentence *John built a wall around the garden* can be taken as a letter or a word (form). The terms 'type' and 'token' were introduced into semantics and pragmatics by the American philosopher Charles Peirce. See Lyons (1995).

token reflexive *See* indexical.

ToM = theory of mind.

ToMM = theory of mind (mechanism).

tone German *Beleuchtung*. A non-propositional aspect of meaning of an utterance isolated by the German philosopher, mathematician, and logician Gottlob Frege, for the effect etc. expressed by a linguistic form on e.g. the emotions of an addressee. *See also* pragmatic tone.

top-down pragmatic process Usually discussed in opposition to the notion of **bottom-up pragmatic process**. A top-down pragmatic process is one that is not under linguistic control. In other words, the context-sensitivity or dependency shown is not triggered by any linguistic expression in a sentence. E.g. free enrichment from *The blonde has a brain* to 'the blonde has a highly functioning brain'.

topic 1. What a stretch of language is about. Also called a **discourse topic**. Discourse topics can further be divided into **central** and **peripheral discourse topics**. The former is usually the most important topic of the discourse. By contrast, the latter constitutes topics that are subordinate to the former. **2.** What a sentence is about. Also referred to as a **sentence topic**. E.g. in an appropriate context, the topic of the sentence *You shouldn't question that dogma of the Church* may be *that dogma of the Church*. **3.** A syntactic constituent placed typically at the beginning of a sentence to function as a sentence topic. E.g. *The potatoes* in *The potatoes, Sue hasn't peeled yet* or 'Flower' in the Korean sentence 'Flower, chrysanthemum last(s) long'. Also known as a **sentence topic**. Topic is largely a pragmatic concept. *See also* theme.

topic chain A series of two or more topic–comment constructions put together. E.g. *Linguistics, I like; statistics, I hate.*

topic–comment construction A construction that contains two parts: a topic, which typically occurs first, and a comment or focus, i.e. a clause which follows the topic and says something about it, hence also called a **topic–focus construction**. E.g. *John, Mary loves*. The **topic/comment distinction** provides a main dimension of thematic meaning. Also known as a **topic–comment sentence** or **topic–comment structure.**

topic drop The phenomenon whereby the topic of a non-initial topic–comment construction is freely omitted, with the effect that an empty topic chain is formulated. E.g. in the Chinese topic–comment construction 'China, territory is vast; population is large; history is long; and civilization is brilliant', the topic established in the first topic–comment construction, 'China', serves as the antecedent of the linguistically unrealized topics in the chain of topic–comment constructions following it.

topic empathy hierarchy A scale which states that it is easier for a speaker to empathize with the referent of the topic of a sentence or discourse than with the referent that is not the topic. In other words, E (topic) > E (non-topic). *See also* humanness empathy hierarchy; speech act empathy hierarchy; surface structure empathy hierarchy. See Kuno (2004).

topic–focus construction See topic–comment construction.

topic level (of pragmatic analysis) *See* pragmatic analysis level.

topic marker Any linguistic expression that marks a topic in a topic–comment construction. E.g. *wa* in Japanese.

topic-neutral A term encountered in the philosophy of language, introduced by the British philosopher Gilbert Ryle, for a form that occurs in sentences about any kind of subject matter. E.g.*logical constants such as those for conjunction (&), negation (~), and the existential quantifier (∃).

topic–prominent language A term used by the American linguists Charles Li and Sandra Thompson for a language in which the basic syntactic elements of a sentence are a topic and a comment. E.g. Chinese, Lahu, and Lisu are considered to be such languages. Contrasts with a **subject-prominent language**. *See also* subject-prominent and topic-prominent language; neither subject-prominent nor topic-prominent language.

topicalization The process of putting a constituent to the topic position at the front of a sentence to act as a *topic (3). It may involve syntactic movement, as in an *English-style or syntactic topic–comment construction *The piano sonata, John likes very much*. It may not involve syntactic movement but the comment is related to the topic semantically and/or pragmatically, as in a *Chinese-style or pragmatic topic–comment construction. E.g. 'Beijing, historical sites are many'.

TOPL = Test of Pragmatic Language.

toponymic anaphora A variety of *metonymic anaphora whose anaphoric relation is based on the cognitive relation of spatio-locational continuity such as container–content. E.g. in *I tried the bowl to find it not tasty, it* refers to the food in the bowl rather than the bowl itself. Also called **toponymic reference**. *See also* partonymic anaphora.

total synonymy, total synonym A term coined by the British linguist Sir John Lyons for *synonyms that are synonymous in all contexs. In other words, according to this view, two or more lexical items are total synonyms if and only if they are identical in meaning in all contexts. Total synonyms are very rare. *See also* full synonymy; complete synonymy.

transition relevance place (TRP) A term used in *conversation analysis for any point in a speaker's turn in conversation at which another participant may start speaking. E.g. the end of a sentence. A transition relevance place usually begins slightly before the end of a *turn constructional unit (TCU), when possible completion becomes projectable.

translation holism *See* holism.

transparent context A context in which **Leibniz's law**—a law of intersubstitutability *salva veritate* (Latin, 'with the truth unchanged')—holds. According to this law, the substitution of an expression by another one with the same *extension or *reference does not affect the truth-condition of the sentence involved. In other words, a context is referentially transparent if any two expressions referring to the same entity can be substituted in it without the truth value of the sentence uttered being altered. Contrasted with a (referentially) **opaque context**.

triple hedge *See* compound hedge.

trope A *figure of speech, especially one involving a figurative use of language. E.g. *metaphors, *hyperboles, and *similes are tropes.

TRP = transition relevance place.

truth One of the most important issues in philosophy. Concerned with the central question of how truth can be defined, i.e. what it is to say that a sentence, statement, or proposition is true. The question is closely linked to many of the major issues in the philosophy of language, semantics, and pragmatics. A number of philosophical theories of truth have been developed, attempting to provide an answer to the question. These include the **correspondence theory, coherence theory, deflationalist theory, performative theory**, and **pragmatist theory**. There has been a tendency in recent research, especially with the development of the deflationalist theory of truth, to take truth as an undefined primitive concept governed by maxims. The opposite of truth is **falsity**. See Rajagopalan (2009); Burgess and Burgess (2011).

truth apt (of a sentence) A term found in the philosophy of language. A sentence is truth apt if there is a certain *context in which it could be uttered and express a true or false *proposition. E.g. *Yan Huang did his PhD in linguistics at Cambridge.*

truth condition A set of conditions under which a declarative sentence is true. In other words, these conditions specify the state of affairs which would have to hold for a sentence to be true. E.g. the sentence *You have blue eyes* is true under the condition that the addressee has in fact blue eyes. *See also* truth value.

truth-conditional meaning Aspects of meaning that make a contribution to the *truth conditions of a sentence uttered. In contrast, by **non-truth-conditional meaning** is meant those aspects of meaning that do not affect the truth conditions of a sentence uttered. E.g. the meaning of contrast carried by *but* does not make any contribution to the truth condition of the sentence that contains it, because *John is poor but honest* and *John is poor and honest* have exactly the same truth condition.

truth-conditional pragmatics (TCP) The view that various pragmatic processes influence and determine the *truth condition of an utterance. Truth-conditional pragmatics is closely associated with the position known as *contextualism or contextualist semantics in the *philosophy of language. *See also* truth-conditional semantics. See Recanati (2010).

truth-conditional semantics A version of *formal semantics originated in logic and the philosophy of language. The central tenet is that knowing the meaning of a sentence is equivalent to knowing the conditions under which the sentence would be true or false.

truth-conditional theory (of meaning) A theory which states that the meaning of a linguistic expression is the contribution it makes to the truth condition of the sentence that contains the linguistic expression. See Lyons (1995). *See also* behaviourist theory (of meaning); meaning-is-use theory (of meaning); mentalistic theory (of meaning); referential theory (of meaning); verificationist theory (of meaning).

truth definition *See* truth predicate.

truth function, truth-functional Any logical connective which has the property of making the *truth value of the compound proposition it creates computable from the truth values of the simple propositions it combines is said to be **truth-functional**. This is because the truth value of the compound proposition is a function of the truth values of its component simple propositions. The logical connectives involved are known as **logical** or **truth-functional operators** or **operators** for short. E.g. *and*, *or*, and *not*.

truth predicate The *predicate '. . . is true' for the sentences of a language. E.g. '. . . is true' in: The Chinese sentence *xue shi bai de* is true if and only if snow is white. A definition of the truth predicate that meets the material adequacy condition put forward by the Polish logician Alfred Tarski is called a **truth definition**. Any theory that gives the truth definition for a language is referred to as **truth theory**. *See also* truth-condition; T-sentence.

truth table A table in *propositional calculus that provides a full account of a contribution that a connective makes to the truth or falsity of a complex proposition. E.g. the truth table for the connective &.

p	**q**	**p & q**
t	t	t
t	f	f
f	t	f
f	f	f

In the table, *p* and *q* are variables standing for any proposition. The rows in the left-hand columns display all the possible combinations of the truth values (t for **true** and f for **false**) that can be assigned to a pair of propositions. The corresponding values listed in the right-hand column are the truth values of the formula *p* & *q* for those combinations.

truthmaker principle A principle encountered in the philosophy of language which states that *propositions cannot be 'barely' true. There must be something such as a fact, a state of affairs, or a substantial complex that makes them true. The term is due to the Australian philosopher David Armstrong. See Blackburn (2005).

truth-theoretic meaning = sentence meaning.

truth theory *See* truth predicate.

truth value In logic, the philosophy of language, formal semantics, and pragmatics, a truth value is a property of a proposition. In a standard, bivalent logic, only two possible truth values are identified: **true** and **false**. The truth value 'true' is assigned to a true proposition and the truth value 'false' is assigned to a false proposition. Note that a sentence such as *The tiger killed the keeper* does not in itself have a truth value, though it does have a *truth condition. But when the sentence is used on a particular occasion in a particular context to express a particular proposition, this proposition will have a particular truth value, and the truth value is either true or false. In other types of logic, there may be more than two truth values, such as true, false, and possible, or there may be a **truth value gap**, i.e. a proposition may not have any truth value. One of the reasons why the notion of a truth value gap is posited is due to *presupposition failure.

try marker A term taken from *conversation analysis for a linguistic expression that is modified with an upward or rising intonation contour and a slight or brief *pause, thus 'marked' as a 'try'. A try marker is frequently used, for example, when a speaker presents a name he or she is uncertain about the recognition of its referent from the addressee. E.g. *Fords* in A: . . . *well I was the only one other than than tch Fords uh Mrs Holmes Ford?*.

***tu/vous distinction* (T/V distinction)** A distinction in *second-person singular pronouns that is found in many of the world's languages. The T (so-called from the first letter of French *tu*) or **familiar form** or **pronoun** is typically singular and marks familiarity; the V (so-called from the first letter of French *vous*) or **formal** or **polite form** or **pronoun** is typically plural and encodes politeness. There are also languages like Oriya, which in addition to T and V forms, have a third, **neutral form**. The V pronoun is derived from a variety of sources, including second-person plural pronouns, as in French; third-person singular and plural pronouns, as in Italian and German, respectively; first-person plural pronouns, as in Ainu; second-person demonstrative pronouns, as in Sinhalese; reflexive pronouns, as in Hungarian; and status terms, as in Spanish. When the T form is used reciprocally, it indicates intimacy and social closeness. By contrast, the mutual use of the V form shows respect and social distance. Asymmetric usage encodes an imbalance of power and social status between the speaker and addressee. The *tu/vous* distinction is an important topic of research in *sociopragmatics, and in particular *social deixis. See Huang (2007).

turn A term used in *conversation analysis to refer to an uninterrupted contribution made by one speaker to a conversation, preceded, followed, or both by a turn of another speaker, unless it represents the beginning or end of a conversation. A conversation is made of a series of turns. In some analyses, the turn is considered to be the basic unit of a conversation. Also called a **conversational turn**.

turn constructional unit (TCU) A term encountered in *conversation analysis for a unit from which turns at talk in conversation are constructed. Turn constructional units can be made of a word, a phrase, a clause, a sentence etc. They are also marked in part by prosodic, especially intonational, means. The end of a turn constructional unit constitutes a *transition relevance place (TRP) at which the *floor is open.

turn-taking The basic mechanism in terms of which conversation is organized. In a conversation, only one speaker talks at any one time barring overlap, and changes of speaker occur in a way that is coordinated and rule-governed. The specific mechanism that regulates speakers taking turns to speak in conversation is called the **turn-taking system**. Turn-taking is thus one of the most essential characteristics of the structure of conversation. It appears to be innate in humans but is rare among animals, though it is found in the so-called antiphonal singing of some bird species.

T/V distinction = *tu/vous* distinction

two-component model (of presupposition) An approach to *presupposition that views presupposition as having a special status. According to this approach, a sentence has two types of content, an ordinary semantic content and a secondary, presuppositional content which is pragmatic in nature. This position is represented by the work of the Finnish linguist Lauri Karttunen, the American linguist Stanley Peters, and the British linguist Gerald Gazdar. The two-component model contrasts with the **one-component model** of presupposition, which treats presupposition as an admittance condition for a sentence to be introduced into a context. This pragmatic presupposition position is represented by the American philosopher Robert Stalnaker and the American linguist Irene Heim.

two-levelled theory (of communication and meaning) The traditional, standard view which holds that there are only two levels of meaning to a theory of communication: a level of sentence meaning vs. a level of utterance or speaker meaning, or to make use of the British linguist Sir John Lyons' distinction between type and token, a level of *sentence-type meaning (*see* sentence meaning) vs. a level of *utterance-token meaning. While the former is the pursuit of semantics, the latter falls under the province of pragmatics. See Levinson (2000); Huang (2007). Often contrasts with the three-levelled theory (of communication and meaning).

type *See* token.

type-literal meaning *See* literal meaning.

type/token ambiguity *See* token.

U

UC = unarticulated constituent.

UM = underspecification model.

unarticulated constituent (UC) A term introduced by the American philosopher John Perry to refer to a propositional or conceptual constituent of a sentence that is not linguistically expressed explicitly in the sentence. E.g. [for the seminar] may be an unarticulated constituent of the proposition expressed by the sentence *John was late*. The opposite term is an **articulated constituent**.

under-articulation, under-articulated A term employed in the philosophy of language and pragmatics and semantics to refer to the phenomenon whereby in uttering a sentence a speaker does not put into words all that is needed in order to obtain the truth conditions of the sentence uttered. E.g. the utterance of *It's snowing* to mean it is snowing in Paris, with the salient location 'Paris' not explicitly uttered. In other words, a sentence like *It's snowing* is **under-articulated**. *See also* unarticulated constituent; incomplete predicate.

underdetermination A representation of the meaning of a sentence that contains a *propositional radical that needs to be filled in pragmatically. E.g. the propositional radical expressed by the sentence *You won't die* can mean either 'the addressee is immortal' or 'the addressee is not going to die from that cut' in an appropriate context. The semantic representation of the sentence is not determined to the extent that it can distinguish between these two meanings. In other words, a sentence is semantically underdetermined if and only if its meaning does not determine the truth conditions or truth values of its utterances. The term tends to be used for the analysis of the interpretation of an utterance by an addressee. Also variously called **indeterminacy, underdeterminacy, semantic underdetermination**, or **semantic underdeterminacy**. See Bach (1994). *See also* argumental underdetermination; lexical underdetermination (2); parametric underdetermination; phrasal underdetermination; referential underdetermination; scope underdetermination; underspecification.

underspecification = underdetermination, but the term tends to be deployed with reference to the logical form of a sentence. Also known as **semantic underspecification**.

underspecification model (UM) A term used especially in *experimental pragmatics (2) to refer to the pragmatic processing model that is equivalent to what is labelled the **contextual inference theory**, or **global theory** (of scalar implicature). Contrasted with the **default model**.

understatement *See* meiosis.

understater A variety of *downgrader which is deployed to underrepresent the state of affairs denoted in the proposition of a sentence uttered. E.g. *a little bit* in *Your father is a little bit disappointed in your behaviour.*

unfilled pause *See* pause.

universal pragmatics *See* formal pragmatics (2).

universal(ist) pragmatics A term used by proponents of *ethnopragmatics for any pragmatic theory that views human communication as governed largely by a rich inventory of universal pragmatic principles, with variations between cultures being accounted for in terms of local adjustments to and local construals of these universals.

universal quantifier *See* quantifier.

universality A property of *conversational implicature according to which, a conversational implicature tends to be universal, being motivated rather than arbitrary. See Huang (2007). *See also* calculability; defeasibility; indeterminacy; non-conventionality; non-detachability; reinforceability.

universe of discourse A particular domain, world, or universe a speaker assumes that he or she is talking about at the time of utterance, hence also called the **domain of discourse**. Put slightly differently, the universe of discourse contains a range of situations, topics, etc. within which a discourse is placed. E.g. the universe of discourse for the uttering of the sentence *The Berlin Wall was knocked down in 1989* is the actual or real world.

unmarked *See* marked, markedness.

unmarked second part *See* preferred second turn.

unreal conditional = counterfactual conditional.

update semantics A type of *dynamic semantics which offers an intuitive way of updating the dynamics of interpretation. In update semantics, an information state is modelled as a set of *possible worlds. It is used to define the **information change potential** of a linguistic expression—the change brought about by the uttering of a sentence.

upgrader A type of modality marker, which is used to strengthen the impact an utterance is likely to have on the addressee. E.g. *bloody* in *That's bloody rude of you*. Many linguistic devices can be employed as an upgrader. These include **overstaters**, **intensifiers**, **'plus' committers**, and **aggressive interrogatives**. Considerable use of this notion is found in the study of the illocutionary force of a speech act. Contrasted with a **downgrader**.

uptake A term introduced by the British philosopher J. L. Austin for an addressee's acceptance of the validity of the performance of a speech act. Thus, in making a bet, the bet is not 'on' unless *You are on* or something with the same effect is uttered by the addressee. This response on the part of the addressee counts as an acknowledgement of a satisfactory uptake, i.e. a fully successful performance of a speech act, the absence of which will cause a *misfire.

upward entailment An *entailment from a subset to a set. In other words, the direction of upward entailment is from more specific to less specific. E.g. the sentence or the proposition expressed by the sentence *Every woman is roasting beef* entails the sentence or the proposition expressed by the sentence *Every woman is cooking*. Also called **upward entailing** or **monotone increasing**. Contrasts with **downward entailment**.

usage event *See* utterance.

use (1) *See* mention.

use (2) Two distinct senses of use of language are identified. First, by use of language is meant anything done with words. E.g. one's system of knowledge that regulates rhyming in writing poems is a system of knowledge that governs a use of language. A speaker who does not possess that system of knowledge can still be a competent speaker of his or her native language. This is the broad sense of use of language. In the second, narrower sense, the term refers to use of utterances in various contexts. According to the Israeli philosopher Asa Kasher, use of language in the latter sense constitutes a speaker's *pragmatic competence. See Kasher (2010b).

use/mention distinction *See* mention.

'use of language' movement *See* ordinary language philosophy.

use perspective (in the philosophy of language) A term used by the Canadian philosopher Robert Stainton for one of the two dominant schools of thought in the 20th-century Anglo-American *philosophy of language, which is broadly equivalent to *ordinary language philosophy. Contrasts with the **system perspective** (in the philosophy of language).

use-theoretic meaning = utterance meaning.

use theory (of meaning) *See* meaning-is-use theory (of meaning).

utility theory (of truth) *See* pragmatist theory (of truth).

utterance Any particular piece of language—be it a word, a phrase, a sentence or a sequence of sentences—spoken or written by a particular speaker or writer in a particular context on a particular occasion. In other words, an utterance is a situated instance of language use which is partially contextually, culturally, and/or socially conditioned. It constitutes an occurrence of language behaviour on the part of a speaker. E.g. *The juice spilled over the table* is an utterance in English. This utterance is an issuance or use of the English sentence *The juice spilled* *over the table*. Occasionally also called a **usage event**. Contrasts with a **sentence**. *See also* self-refuting utterance.

utterance act *See* locutionary act.

utterance cluster A coherent, organized conglomerate of utterances such as a conversation, novel, or letter.

utterance$_E$ Also referred to as an **embedded utterance**. An utterance that is embedded in another utterance or utterance cluster. E.g. a quotation in a newspaper report.

utterance cluster$_E$ Also called an **embedded utterance cluster**. An utterance cluster that is embedded in another utterance cluster. E.g. a conversation contained in a detective story.

utterance interpretation The assignment of meaning to an utterance. Utterance interpretation is a central topic of enquiry in pragmatics.

utterance meaning Aspects of meaning that are ascribed to an utterance or what a speaker intends to convey in a particular context on a particular occasion. Therefore utterance meaning is also called **speaker meaning**, **speaker's meaning**, or **contextual meaning**. E.g. the utterance meaning intended by a speaker in saying the English sentence *Mathematics is fascinating* may be ironically that mathematics is very boring, depending on context. In the British linguist Stephen Levinson's analysis, utterance meaning is further divided into ***utterance-type meaning** and ***utterance-token meaning**. The study of utterance meaning falls under pragmatics. Contrasted with **sentence meaning**.

utterance modifier *See* pragmatic adverbial.

utterance presupposition *See* pragmatic presupposition.

utterance schema A term invented by the American developmental psychologist Michael Tomasello to refer to a multi-word utterance in early child language. An utterance schema contains a functionally salient and stable element and a slot that can be filled by other words. E.g. *Here is the* X, where X can be lexically filled. An utterance schema manifests children's *communicative intention (1). *See also* holophrase.

utterance-token meaning One of the two types of utterance meaning proposed by the British linguist Stephen Levinson. Utterance-token meaning is not a *default meaning. It requires direct computations about speaker intentions. *Particularized conversational implicatures (PCIs) are a typical example of utterance-token meaning. See Levinson (2000); Huang (2007). Contrasts with **utterance-type meaning**.

utterance-type meaning One of the two types of utterance meaning postulated by the British linguist Stephen Levinson. Utterance-type meaning is a generalized, preferred, or *default meaning, which is dependent not upon direct computations about speaker-intentions but rather upon expectations about how language is characteristically used. *Generalized conversational implicatures (GCIs) are a typical example of utterance-type meaning. See Levinson (2000); Huang (2007). Contrasted with **utterance-token meaning**.

utterance-type occasion-meaning The British philosopher H. P. Grice's term for the meaning an utterer or speaker intends the sentence or utterance type to have on a particular occasion. It is characterized by Grice as '*U* meant by *x* "*p*"'. Contrasts with **utterer's occasion-meaning**.

utterer A person who utters a linguistic expression. *See also* addresser; addressee; bystander; hearer; overhearer; eavesdropper; speech event participant; ratified participant.

utterer-implicature *See* audience implicature.

utterer's occasion-meaning The British philosopher H. P. Grice's term for what an utterance means or what an utterer or speaker means by an utterance. It is characterized by Grice as '*U* meant by uttering *x* that . . . '. Contrasts with **utterance-type occasion-meaning**.

V

V form *See tu/vous* distinction.

V pronoun *See tu/vous* distinction.

vagueness, vague 1. In its broad sense, the term refers to any meaning that is inherently and intentionally unclear or imprecise. It includes **ambiguity, ambivalence, fuzziness, generality, imprecision, in-** or **underderterminacy, loose talk, vague expressions**, and **vague language**. E.g. the meanings expressed by *some* and *things* in *John has bought some apples, carrots, and things* are vague. The same can be said of *child* that is unspecified or vague for gender. **2.** In its narrow sense, it is distinguished technically from ambiguity. Vagueness occurs in a variety of contexts and serves a variety of functions. Its interpretation is typically dependent on e.g. context, real-world knowledge, and pragmatic inference. The ability to use and understand vague language is an important aspect of *communicative competence. *See also* ambiguity; underdetermination.

values-pragmatics theory *See* ecological pragmatics.

vantage point *See* point of view.

variability A term used in the European Continental tradition of pragmatics for the property of language that defines the range of possibilities from which choices can be made. See Verschueren (1999). *See also* negotiability; adaptability.

variable A fundamental concept in logic. It refers to an element in a logical formula that can take any of a range of values. A variable that is bound by a quantifier is known as a **bound variable**. A variable that is not bound is called a **free variable**.

variable reference *Reference in which a referring expression refers to different entities in the external world depending on context, i.e. the referent of the referring expression varies according to the circumstances in which it is used. E.g. the referring expressions *the President of the United States, their house*, and *it* have variable reference. Contrasts with **constant reference**.

variational pragmatics (VP) A newly emerged branch of pragmatics that has a close affinity with *sociopragmatics and *cross-cultural pragmatics. It endeavours to study and determine the influence or impact of macro-social factors such as region, social class, ethnicity, gender, and age, and the interplay of these factors on language use, especially pragmatic variation, in interaction. Construed thus, variational pragmatics represents a research domain at the intersection of pragmatics and sociolinguistics, in particular dialectology. See Barron and Schneider (2009).

verba dicendi Verbs or verb-like expressions that are used to describe forms of language in use. The range of such verbs or verb-like expressions includes performative verbs, speech act verbs, and verbs or verb-like expressions denoting other aspects of verbal behaviour. See Verschueren (1999).

verbal communication *See* communication.

verbal demonstrative *See* demonstrative.

verbal doublet scale *See* $Q_{clausal}$ implicature.

verbal gesture *See* primary illocution indicator.

verbal hedge *See* hedge.

verbal irony *See* irony.

verdictive A type of *speech act defined by the British philosopher J. L. Austin by which a speaker gives a verdict or delivers a finding. It is a **judicial act**. Paradigmatic cases include acquitting, convicting, finding, calling (by an umpire or referee), and assessing. E.g. *I find the accused guilty*. See Austin (1962). *See also* commissive; exercitive; behabitive; expositive.

verification principle The most characteristic doctrine of *logical positivism for determining meaningful sentences or propositions. For any sentence or proposition which is neither analytically true nor belonging to logic or mathematics to be meaningful, it must be capable of being verified, i.e. tested for its truth or falsity, through the senses. Hence, a sentence or proposition which cannot be so verified is strictly speaking meaningless. Also known as the **verifiability principle**.

verificationist theory (of meaning) A theory which states that the meaning of a linguistic expression is determined by the verifiability of the sentence or proposition that contains the linguistic expression. Also known as the **verificationist thesis** or **verificationism**. See Lyons (1995). *See also* behaviourist theory (of meaning); meaning-is-use theory (of meaning); mentalistic theory (of meaning); referential theory (of meaning); truth-conditional theory (of meaning).

viewpoint *See* point of view.

visibility A term used in the description of *space deixis, which is in general concerned with whether an entity referred to is within sight of the *deictic centre, typically the speaker or not. If it is, a **visibility marker** is used; if it is not, an **invisibility marker** may or may not be used. The term used to describe the latter is called **invisibility**. Three types of invisibility have been identified in the literature: (i) **invisible-remote** (ii) **invisible-occlusion**, and (iii) **invisible-periphery**.

visibility marker Any linguistic expression that is used to mark visibility in the description of *space deixis. E.g. the suffix *-t/m* in Daga. Contrasts with **invisibility marker**.

VOCA = voice output *communication aid.

vocative A linguistic expression used in calling someone or getting his or her attention. Vocatives can be encoded in, for example, kinship terms, titles, proper names, and in combination of these. Syntactically, they do not form any part of the arguments of a predicate. Prosodically, they are separated from the body of an utterance that may company them. E.g. *Doctor Williams, do you think I need a blood test?* Vocatives are in general socially marked. They are grouped into two types: **calls** or **summonses** and **addresses**. In a language like Latin, nouns used as vocatives are marked in the vocative case. Vocatives are commonly used to express *person deixis and *social deixis. See Huang (2007).

voice output communication aid *See* communication aid.

VP = variational pragmatics.

W

wakimae Japanese for 'discernment'. The term refers to polite behaviour or practice of it according to social norms or conventions.

weak massive modularity of mind thesis *See* massive modularity of mind thesis.

weak minimalist thesis *See* Occam's razor.

weak r-implicature *See* r-implicature.

weightiness (of a face-threatening act) A term introduced by the American linguist Penelope Brown and the British linguist Stephen Levinson for the seriousness of a face-threatening act (FTA). The following equation for its calculation is proposed: $W_x = D(S, H) + P(H, S) + R_x$ where 'W' stands for weightiness, 'x' for any particular face-threatening act, 'S' for speaker. and 'H' for hearer. 'D' is the sociological variable for the social distance between speaker and hearer, 'P', for the power that hearer has over speaker, and 'R', for the ranking of imposition involved in performing the face-threatening act within a particular culture/language. Given the equation above, the weightiness of a particular face-threatening act can be determined by the adding up of the extent of the social distance between speaker and hearer, the degree of power the hearer has over the speaker, and the extent to which the face-threatening act is deemed to be an imposition in a particular culture and/or language. See Brown and Levinson (1987).

well-formedness, well-formed *See* acceptability, acceptable.

WF = wrong format view.

what is communicated The sum of *what is said and what is implicated (*see* implicature). E.g. when someone says *Many of John's friends saw the Berlin Wall collapse*, strictly speaking, 'many of John's friends saw the Berlin Wall collapse' is what is said, 'not all' is what is implicated, and 'not all of John's friends saw the Berlin Wall collapse' is what is communicated. Also called **what is meant**.

what is conventionally implicated *See* conventional implicature.

what is conversationally implicated *See* conversational implicature.

what is implicated *See* implicature.

what is meant *See* what is communicated.

what is meant$_{-n}$ = what is naturally meant. *See* meaning$_{-nn}$.

what is meant$_{-nn}$ = what is non-naturally meant *See* meaning$_{-nn}$.

what is said A technical concept developed by the British philosopher H. P. Grice in opposition to **what is implicated**. What is said is generally taken to be (i) the conventional meaning of a sentence uttered with the exclusion of any *conventional implicature, and (ii) the truth-conditional propositional content of the sentence uttered. Recently, the domain of what is said has been both narrowed, as in the work of the American philosopher Kent Bach, and broadened, as in relevance theory, the work of the French philosopher François Recanati and that of the British linguist Stephen Levinson. E.g. in Recanati's account, what is said has a semantic part, i.e. semantic representation or sentence meaning, and a pragmatic part, i.e. the *pragmatically enriched said. Recanati dubs the semantic part **i-content** (intuitive truth-conditional content of utterance) or **what is said**$_{min}$, as opposed to **c-content** (compositionally articulated content of utterance) or **what is said**$_{max}$ for the pragmatic part. See Huang (2010h). Contrasts with **what is implicated**.

whimperative A blended term coined in the 1970s which refers to a sentence having the form of an interrogative but the illocutionary force of an order. E.g. the use of *Why don't you stop nagging?* to mean 'Stop nagging!' It is an instance of *indirect speech act.

whinge *See* complaint.

withhold politeness The absence of communicated *politeness where it would normally be expected. E.g. failure to thank someone who has helped find your relative's house.

Wittgenstein, Ludwig (1889–1951) Austrian-born British philosopher. He was educated in Berlin, and at the universities of Manchester and Cambridge. He became a Fellow of Trinity College, Cambridge in 1929 and Professor of Philosophy at Cambridge in succession to the British philosopher G. E. Moore in 1939. In 1947, he resigned his Chair in order to devote himself entirely to research, but soon his health declined. He died of cancer in 1951. Wittgenstein's work as a philosopher is usually divided into two periods, often labelled the **early** and the **later Wittgenstein**. The principle text of the early period is the *Tractatus Logico-Philosophicus*, published in German in 1921 and in English in 1922. The definitive account of his later views is contained in *Philosophical Investigations*, published posthumously in 1953. Wittgenstein was one of the most original and challenging philosophers of the 20th century, especially after the Second World War. He was a major influence, perhaps only second to the German philosopher, mathematician, and logician Gottlob Frege, on the study of language. From an early date he was largely convinced by the idea that philosophical problems can be resolved by studying the workings of language. Both of Wittgenstein's periods were dominated by a concern with the nature of language and meaning. But from the perspective of pragmatics, the contributions made by the later Wittgenstein are much more substantial than those made by the early one. As a prominent member of the school of *ordinary language philosophy, his insistence on meaning being constituted by use ('Don't look for the meaning, look for the use'), his view of language as a collection of 'games' (language games), and his account of rule-following have become a profound influence on the development of pragmatics.

words-to-world (direction of fit of a speech act) A type of relationship between words and world in which a speaker represents the world as he or she believes it is, thus making the words match the world of belief. This is the case of the performance of the speech act of *representatives. E.g. *Many intellectuals were politically persecuted during Mao's Cultural Revolution in China. See also* direction of fit (of a speech act); world-to-words (direction of fit of a speech act); both words-to-world and world-to-words (direction of fit of a speech act); none (direction of fit of a speech act); words-to-world and world-to-words (direction of fit of a speech act).

world knowledge A structured body of knowledge of the world distinguishable from knowledge of the language system to which a linguistic unit such as a lexical item potentially provides access. E.g. knowledge that a surgeon normally operates on a patient rather than vice versa. World knowledge plays an important role in pragmatics. Also known as **real-world knowledge, general world knowledge**, or **encyclopedic knowledge**. *See also* background assumption; ontological assumption.

world-to-words (direction of fit of a speech act) A type of relationship between words and world in which the world is adapted to the words by either the speaker or the addressee. This is the case with the performance of the speech act of *directives (via the addressee); that of the speech act of *commissives (through the speaker). E.g. *Don't speak too fast. See also* direction of fit (of a speech act); both words-to-world and world-to-words (directions of fit of a speech act); none (direction of fit of a speech act); words-to-world (direction of fit of a speech act).

wrong format view (WF) A term used by the French philosopher François Recanati for the view that the meanings of an individual word do not have the proper or right format for them to go directly into interpretation. This is because they are either too abstract and schematic or too rich. In the former case, elaboration is needed to flesh out the meanings in order to arrive at a determinate content. In the latter case, cancellation or some other screening process is needed. The wrong format view is considered to represent a radical position in *contextualism in the philosophy of language. See Recanati (2005).

Z

zero anaphora, zero anaphor An anaphoric relation in which the anaphoric expression is phonetically or phonologically null. In other words, a zero anaphor is an anaphoric expression that is not explicitly expressed linguistically. E.g. in the Italian sentence *Pavarotti dice che Ø mangia gli spaghetti* 'Pavarotti says that (he) eats spaghetti', what is represented by Ø is a zero anaphor, which is anaphorically linked to its antecedent *Pavarotti*. Also called **null anaphora**, **null anaphor**.

zeugma A *figure of speech in which a single linguistic expression has to be interpreted in two distinct ways simultaneously, which often gives rise to a type of semantic and/or pragmatic anomaly. E.g. *Mary came in, wearing a skirt and a smile*. Also referred to as **sortal crossing** or **syllepsis**, especially when its formulation is deliberate.

Zipfian theory of economy Named after the American linguist George Zipf, the term refers to the theory of economy proposed by him in the 1940s, which includes his *auditor's and *speaker's economy, *principle of economy versatility and *law of abbreviation. The Zipfian theory of economy has been influential in the development of certain pragmatic theories.

Z-land sentence An example like '*It's raining*, as thought by a Z-lander' discussed by the American philosopher John Perry. Z-landers are a community of primitive thinkers imagined by Perry, who, when hearing a meteorological sentence like the above, do not have the conception of when it rains (at a given time), it usually rains at a particular place, typically where the speaker is. This raises the issue of whether a Z-land sentence contains an *unarticulated constituent or not. *See also* time-zones sentence.

References

Abbott, B. (2010). *Reference.* Oxford: Oxford University Press.
Achiba, M. (2003). *Learning to Request in a Second Language: A Study of Child Interlanguage Pragmatics.* Clevedon: Multilingual Matters.
Agha, A. (2010). Honorific language. In Cummings (2010: 195–9).
Aitchison, J. (2003). *A Glossary of Language and Mind.* Oxford: Oxford University Press.
Allott, N. (2010). *Key Terms in Pragmatics.* London: Continuum.
Alston, W. (1994). Illocutionary acts and linguistic meaning. In S. L. Tsohatzidis (ed.), *Foundations of Speech Act Theory: Philosophical and Linguistic Perspectives.* London: Routledge, 29–49.
Anchimbe, E. A., and Janney, R. W. (eds) (2011). *Journal of Pragmatics* 43.6, Special Issue on Postcolonial Pragmatics.
Andersen, G. (2011). Corpus-based pragmatics I: qualitative studies. In Bublitz and Norrick (2011: 587–628).
Anscombre, J. C., and Ducrot, O. (1989). Argumentativity and informativity. In M. Meyer (ed.), *From Metaphysics to Rhetoric.* Dordrecht: Kluwer, 71–87.
Ariel, M. (2010). *Defining Pragmatics.* Cambridge: Cambridge University Press.
Asher, R. E. (ed.) (1994). *The Encyclopedia of Language and Linguistics.* Oxford: Pergamon Press.
Atlas, J. (2004). Presupposition. In Horn and Ward (2004: 29–52).
Audi, R. (1999). *The Cambridge Dictionary of Philosophy,* 2nd edn. Cambridge: Cambridge University Press.
Austin, J. L. (1962). *How to Do Things with Words.* Oxford: Oxford University Press.
Bach, K. (1994). Conversational impliciture. *Mind and Language* 9: 124–62.
— (2004). Pragmatics and the philosophy of language. In Horn and Ward (2004: 463–87).
Bara, B. G. (2010). *Cognitive Pragmatics: The Mental Processes of Communication.* Cambridge, Mass.: MIT Press.
— and Tirassa, M. (2000). Neuropragmatics: brain and communication. *Brain and Language* 71: 10–14.
Barbaresi, L. M., and Dressler, W. (2010). Morphopragmatics. In Cummings (2010: 278–80).
Barber, A. (2009). Holism. In Chapman and Routledge (2009: 81–4).
— and Stainton, R. J. (eds) (2010). *Concise Encyclopedia of Philosophy of Language and Linguistics.* Oxford: Elsevier.
Barron, A. (2003). *Acquisition in Interlanguage Pragmatics.* Amsterdam: Benjamins.
— and Schneider, K. P. (2009). Variational pragmatics: studying the impact of social factors on language use in interaction. *Intercultural Pragmatics* 6.4, Special Issue on Variational Pragmatics.
Benz, A., Jäger, G., and van Rooij, R. (2006). *Game Theory and Pragmatics.* London: Palgrave Macmillan.
Bezuidenhout, A. (2010). Primary pragmatic processes. In Cummings (2010: 353–7).
Black, E. (2006). *Pragmatic Stylistics.* Edinburgh: Edinburgh University Press.
Blackburn, S. (2005). *The Oxford Dictionary of Philosophy,* 2nd edn. Oxford: Oxford University Press.
Blum-Kulka, S., House, J., and Kasper, G. (eds) (1989). *Cross-Cultural Pragmatics: Requests and Apologies.* Norwood, NJ: Ablex.

Blutner, R. (2004). Pragmatics and the lexicon. In Horn and Ward (2004: 488–514).
— and Zeevat, H. (eds) (2004). *Optimality Theory and Pragmatics*. New York: Palgrave Macmillan.
Borg, E. (2004). *Minimal Semantics*. Oxford: Clarendon Press.
— (2007). Minimalism vs. contextualism in semantics. In Preyer and Peters (2007: 339–59).
— (2010). Semantic minimalism. In Cummings (2010: 423–5).
Bousfield, D. (2008). *Impoliteness in Interaction*. Amsterdam: Benjamins.
— and Locher, M. A. (eds) (2008). *Impoliteness in Language*. Berlin: Mouton de Gruyter.
Bright, W. (ed.) (1992). *International Encyclopedia of Linguistics*. 4 vols. Oxford: Oxford University Press.
Brinton, L. J. (2001). Historical discourse analysis. In D. Schiffrin, D. Tannen, and H. E. Hamilton (eds), *The Handbook of Discourse Analysis*. Oxford: Blackwell, 138–60.
Brown, K. (ed.) (2006). *The Encyclopaedia of Language and Linguistics*, 2nd edn. 14 vols. New York: Elsevier Science.
Brown, P., and Levinson, S. C. (1987). *Politeness: Some Universals in Language Usage*. Cambridge: Cambridge University Press.
Bublitz, W., and Norrick, N. (eds) (2010). *Foundations of Pragmatics*. Berlin: Mouton de Gruyter.
Bucciarelli, M., Colle, L., and Bara, B. G. (2003). How children comprehend speech acts and communicative gestures. *Journal of Pragmatics* 35: 207–41.
Bunt, H., and Black, W. (2000). The ABC of computational pragmatics. In H. Bunt and W. Black (eds), *Abduction, Belief and Context in Dialogue: Studies in Computational Pragmatics*. Amsterdam: Benjamins.
Burgess, A. G., and Burgess, J. P. (2011). *Truth*. Princeton, NJ: Princeton University Press.
Butler, C. S. (2010). Functionalist theories of language. In Barber and Stainton (2010: 268–75).
Capone, A. (ed.) (2010). *Journal of Pragmatics* 42.11, Special Issue on Pragmemes.
Cappelen, H., and Lepore, E. (2005). *Insensitive Semantics: A Defence of Semantic Minimalism and Speech Act Pluralism*. Oxford: Blackwell.
Carlson, G. (2004). Reference. In Horn and Ward (2004: 74–96).
Carston, R. (2002). *Thoughts and Utterances*. Oxford: Blackwell.
— (2010a). Modularity. In Barber (2010: 480–81).
— (2010b). Explicit communication and 'free' pragmatic enrichment. In B. Soria and E. Romero (eds), *Explicit Communication*. Basingstoke: Palgrave Macmillan, 217–85.
Chapman, S. (2000). *Philosophy for Linguists: An Introduction*. London: Routledge.
— (2011). *Pragmatics*. Basingstoke: Palgrave Macmillan.
— and Routledge, C. (eds) (2005). *Key Thinkers in Linguistics and the Philosophy of Language*. Edinburgh: Edinburgh University Press.
— — (eds) (2009). *Key Ideas in Linguistics and the Philosophy of Language*. Edinburgh: Edinburgh University Press.
Cheng, W. (2010). Cross-cultural pragmatics. In Cummings (2010: 89–92).
Chierchia, G., Guasti, M., Gualmini, L., Crain, S., and Foppolo, F. (2004). Semantic and pragmatic competence in children's and adults' comprehension of *or*. In Noveck and Sperber (2004: 283–300).
Chiou, M., and Huang, Y. (2010). NP-anaphora in Modern Greek: a partial neo-Gricean pragmatic approach. *Journal of Pragmatics* 42: 2036–57.
Christie, C. (2000). *Gender and Language: Towards a Feminist Pragmatics*. Edinburgh: Edinburgh University Press.

Clark, E. V. (2004). Pragmatics and language acquisition. In Horn and Ward (2004: 562–77).
— (2007). Conventionality and contrast in language and language acquistion. *New Directions in Child and Adolescent Development* 115: 11–23.
Coulson, S. (2004). Electrophysiology and pragmatic language comprehension. In Noveck and Sperber (2004: 187–206).
Cruse, A. (2006). *A Glossary of Semantics and Pragmatics*. Edinburgh: Edinburgh University Press.
Crystal, D. (2008). *A Dictionary of Linguistics and Phonetics*, 6th edn. Oxford: Blackwell.
Culpeper, J. (ed.) (2009). *Journal of Historical Pragmatics* 10.2, Special Issue on Historical Sociopragmatics.
— (2010). Historical pragmatics. In Cummings (2010: 188–92).
— (2011). *Impoliteness: Using Language to Cause Offence*. Cambridge: Cambridge University Press.
Cummings, L. (2005). *Pragmatics: A Multidisciplinary Perspective.* Edinburgh: Edinburgh University Press.
— (2009). *Clinical Pragmatics.* Cambridge: Cambridge University Press.
— (ed.) (2010). *The Pragmatics Encyclopedia*. Routledge.
Evans, V. (2007). *A Glossary of Cognitive Linguistics*. Edinburgh: Edinburgh University Press.
Felix-Brasdefer, J. C. (2008). *Politeness in Mexico and the United States*. Amsterdam: Benjamins.
Feng, G. W. (2010). *A Theory of Conventional Implicature and Pragmatic Markers in Chinese*. Bingley: Emerald.
Fodor, J. (1983). *The Modularity of Mind*. Cambridge, Mass.: MIT Press.
Fraser, B. (1996). Pragmatic markers. *Pragmatics* 6: 167–90.
— (2010). Discourse markers. In Cummings (2010: 125–9).
Frawley, W. J. (ed.) (2003). *International Encyclopedia of Linguistics*. 4 vols. Oxford: Oxford: Oxford University Press.
Garcia-Carpintero, M., and Kölbel, M. (2008). *Relative Truth*. Oxford: Oxford University Press.
Garfinkle, H. (1972). Remarks on ethnomethodology. In J. J. Gumperz and D. Hymes (eds), *Directions in Sociolinguistics.* New York: Holt, Rinehart & Winston.
Gibbs, R. W. (2004). Psycholinguistic experiments and linguistic-pragmatics. In Noveck and Sperber (2004: 50–71).
Goddard, C. (ed.) (2006). *Ethnopragmatics: Understanding Discourse in Cultural Context.* Berlin: Mouton de Gruyter.
— and Wierzbicka, A. (eds) (2004). *Intercultural Pragmatics* 1, Special Issue on Cultural Scripts.
Goldberg, A. E. (2004). Pragmatics and argument structure. In Horn and Ward (2004: 427–41).
Green, G. M. (1996). *Pragmatics and Natural Language Understanding*, 2nd edn. Mahwah, NJ: Erlbaum.
— (2010). Discourse particles. In Cummings (2010: 130–33).
Grice, H. P. (1989). *Studies in the Way of Words.* Cambridge, Mass.: Harvard University Press.
Grundy, P. (2000). *Doing Pragmatics*, 2nd edn. London: Arnold.
Gundel, J. (2010). Focus. In Cummings (2010: 166–7).
Hanks, W. F. (2010). Deixis and indexicality. In Bublitz and Norrick (2010: 315–46).
— Ide, S., and Katagiri, Y. (eds) (2009). *Journal of Pragmatics* 41.1, Special Issue on Towards an Emancipatory Pragmatics.
Haugh, M. (2011). *(Im)politeness Implicatures*. Berlin: Mouton.

Hirschberg, J. (2004). Pragmatics and intonation. In Horn and Ward (2004: 515–37).

Hobbs, J. R. (2004). Abduction in natural language understanding. In Horn and Ward (2004: 724–41).

Hodges, B. (2009). Ecological pragmatics: values, dialogical arrays, complexity, and caring. *Pragmatics and Cognition* 17: 628–52.

Horn, L. R. (1989). *A Natural History of Negation*. Chicago: University of Chicago Press.

— (2004). Implicature. In Horn and Ward (2004: 3–28).

— (2007). Neo-Gricean pragmatics: a Manichaean manifesto. In N. Burton-Roberts (ed.), *Pragmatics*. London: Palgrave Macmillan, 158–83.

— (2009). WJ-40: implicature, truth, and meaning. *International Review of Pragmatics* 1: 3–34.

— and Ward, G. (eds) (2004). *The Handbook of Pragmatics*. Oxford: Blackwell.

Huang, Y. (1991). A neo-Gricean pragmatic theory of anaphora. *Journal of Linguistics* 27: 301–35.

— (1994/2007). *The Syntax and Pragmatics of Anaphora*. Cambridge: Cambridge University Press.

— (2000a). *Anaphora: A Cross-Linguistic Study*. Oxford: Oxford University Press.

— (2000b). Discourse anaphora: four theoretical models. *Journal of Pragmatics* 32: 151–76.

— (2004). Anaphora and the pragmatics–syntax interface. In Horn and Ward (2004: 288–314).

— (2006a/2009/2010). Speech acts. In K. Brown (ed.), *The Encyclopedia of Languages and Linguistics*, 2nd edn, vol. 11. New York: Elsevier Science. Reprinted in Mey (2009: 1000–1009), and in Barber and Stainton (2010: 705–14).

— (2006b/2009). Anaphora, cataphora, exophora, logophoricity. In K. Brown (ed.), *The Encyclopedia of Languages and Linguistics*, 2nd edn, vol. 1. New York: Elsevier Science. Reprinted in A. Keith (ed.), *Concise Encyclopaedia of Semantics*. New York: Elsevier Science, 18–25.

— (2006c/2009). Neo-Gricean pragmatics. In Mey (2009: 676–9).

— (2007). *Pragmatics*. Oxford: Oxford University Press.

— (2009). Neo-Gricean pragmatics and the lexicon. *International Review of Pragmatics* 1: 118–53.

— (2010a). Neo-Gricean pragmatic theory of conversational implicature. In B. Heine and H. Narrog (eds), *The Oxford Handbook of Linguistic Analysis*. Oxford: Oxford University Press, 607–31.

— (2010b). Switch-reference in Amele and logophoric verbal suffix in Gokana: a generalized neo-Gricean pragmatic analysis. In D. F. Shu and K. Turner (eds), *Contrasting Meaning in Languages of the East and West*. Berlin: Lang, 75–101.

— (2010c). Pragmatics: Anglo-American and European Continental traditions. In Cummings (2010: 37–40).

— (2010d). Implicature. In Cummings (2010: 234–8).

— (2010e). Impliciture. In Cummings (2010: 238–40).

— (2010f). Scalar implicature. In Cummings (2010: 441–4).

— (2010g). The pragmatics of anaphora. In Cummings (2010: 33–7).

— (2010h). What is said. In Cummings (2010: 520–22).

— (2010i). Types of inference: entailment, presupposition, and implicature. In Bublitz and Norrick (2010: 397–421).

— (2012). Relevance and neo-Gricean pragmatic principles. In H.-J. Schmid (ed.), *Cognitive Pragmatics*. Berlin: Mouton de Gruyter.

Hurford, J. R., Heasley, B., and Smith, M. B. (2007). *Semantics: A Coursebook*. Cambridge: Cambridge University Press.

Hutchby, I., and Wooffitt, R. (2008). *Conversation Analysis: Principles, Practices and Applications*, 2nd edn. Cambridge: Polity.

Iglesias, M. H. (2007). Meaning 'literal'. In M. J. Frapolli (ed.), *Saying, Meaning and Referring*. Basingstoke: Palgrave Macmillan, 128–40.

Ishihara, N., and Cohen, A. D. (2010). *Teaching and Learning Pragmatics*. London: Pearson Education.

Israel, M. (2004). The pragmatics of polarity. In Horn and Ward (2004: 701–23).

Jacobs, A., and Jucker, A. H. (1995). The historical perspective in pragmatics. In A. H. Jucker (ed.), *Historical Pragmatics: Pragmatics Developments in the History of English*. Amsterdam: Benjamins.

Jaszczolt, K. M. (2010). Default semantics. In B. Heine and H. Narrog (eds), *The Oxford Handbook of Linguistic Analysis*. Oxford: Oxford University Press, 193–221.

Jucker, A. H., and Taavitsainen, I. (eds) (2010). *Historical Pragmatics*. Berlin: Mouton de Gruyter.

Jurafsky, D. (2004). Pragmatics and computational linguistics. In Horn and Ward (2004: 578–604).

Kallia, A. (2004). Linguistic politeness: the implicature approach. *Multilingua* 23: 145–9.

Kaplan, D. (1989). Demonstratives: an essay on the semantics, logic, metaphysics, and epistemology of demonstratives and other indexicals. In J. Almog et al. (eds), *Themes from Kaplan*. Oxford: Oxford University Press, 481–563.

Kasher, A. (1984). Pragmatics and the modularity of mind. *Journal of Pragmatics* 8: 539–57.

— (2010a). Modular pragmatics. In Cummings (2010: 275).

— (2010b). Pragmatic competence. In Cummings (2010: 67–8).

Kasper, G. (2010). Interlanguage pragmatics. In Cummings (2010: 231–4).

— and Blum-Kulka, S. (eds) (1993). *Interlanguage Pragmatics*. Oxford: Oxford University Press.

Kehler, A. (2004). Discourse coherence. In Horn and Ward (2004: 241–65).

Kompa, N., and Meggle, G. (2010). Pragmatics in modern philosophy of language. In Bublitz and Norrick (2010: 203–28).

Kopytko, R. (1995). Against rationalistic pragmatics. *Journal of Pragmatics* 23: 475–91.

Korta, K., and Perry, J. (2008). The pragmatic circle. *Synthese* 165: 347–57.

— — (2011). *Critical Pragmatics*. Cambridge: Cambridge University Press.

Kraft, B., and Geluykens, R. (eds) (2007). *Cross-Cultural Pragmatics and Interlanguage English*. Munich: Lincom Europa.

Kuno, S. (2004). Empathy and direct discourse perspectives. In Horn and Ward (2004: 315–43).

Kurzon, D. (2010). Legal pragmatics. In Cummings (2010: 245–7).

Leech, G. N. (1983). *Principles of Pragmatics*. London: Longman.

— (2007). Politeness: is there an East–West divide? *Journal of Politeness Research* 3: 167–206.

Leezenberg, M. (2010). Gricean and Confucian pragmatics: a contrastive analysis. In D. F. Shu and K. Turner (eds), *Contrasting Meaning in Languages of the East and West*. Berlin: Lang, 3–32.

Levinson, S. C. (1983). *Pragmatics*. Cambridge: Cambridge University Press.

— (2000). *Presumptive Meanings: The Theory of Generalized Conversational Implicature*. Cambridge, Mass.: MIT Press.

— (2003). *Space in Language and Cognition: Explorations in Cognitive Diversity.* Cambridge: Cambridge University Press.

Locher, M. A., and Graham, S. I. (eds) (2010). *Interpersonal Pragmatics*. Berlin: Mouton de Gruyter.

Lyons, J. (1977). *Semantics*. 2 vols. Cambridge: Cambridge University Press.

— (1995). *Linguistic Semantics.* Cambridge: Cambridge University Press.

Matthews, P. (2007). *The Concise Oxford Dictionary of Linguistics*, 2nd edn. Oxford: Oxford University Press.

McFarlane, J. (2007). Semantic minimalism and nonindexical contextualism. In Preyer and Peter (2007).

Medina, J. (2005). *Language: Key Concepts in Philosophy*. London: Continuum.

Meibauer, J. (2008). Tautology as presumptive meaning. *Pragmatics and Cognition* 16: 439–70.

— and Steinbach, M. (eds) (2011). *Experimental Pragmatics/Semantics*. Amsterdam: Benjamins.

Meini, C. (2010). Modularity of mind thesis. In Cummings (2010: 275–8).

Mey, J. L. (2001). *Pragmatics: An Introduction*, 2nd edn. Oxford: Blackwell.

— (ed.) (2009). *Concise Encyclopaedia of Pragmatics*, 2nd edn. New York: Elsevier Science.

— (2010). Societal pragmatics. In Cummings (2010: 444–6).

Misak, C. (ed.) (2007). *New Pragmatists*. Oxford: Oxford University Press.

Nerlich, B. (2010). History of pragmatics. In Cummings (2010: 192–5).

Noveck, I. A., and Sperber, D. (eds) (2004). *Experimental Pragmatics.* New York: Palgrave Macmillan.

Nunberg, G. (2004). The pragmatics of deferred interpretation. In Horn and Ward (2004: 344–64).

Overstreet, M. (2010). Metapragmatics. In Cummings (2010: 266–8).

Panther, K.-U., and Rodden, G. (2005). Metonymy. In J. O. Östman and J. Verschueren (eds), *Handbook of Pragmatics*, 2003–2005 Instalment. Amsterdam: Benjamins.

Peleg, O., Giora, R., and Fein, O. (2004). Contextual strength: the whens and hows of context effects. In Noveck and Sperber (2004: 172–86).

Peregrin, J. (2010). Normative pragmatics. In Cummings (2010: 275–8).

Perkins, M. R. (2007). *Pragmatic Impairment*. Cambridge: Cambridge University Press.

Pilkington, A. (2010). Literary pragmatics. In Cummings (2010: 297–300).

Portner, P. (2005). *What is Meaning? Fundamentals of Formal Pragmatics.* Oxford: Blackwell.

Preyer, G., and Peter, G. (eds) (2005). *Contextualism in Philosophy*. Oxford: Oxford University Press.

— — (eds) (2007). *Context-Sensitivity and Semantic Minimalism: New Essays on Semantics and Pragmatics.* Oxford: Oxford University Press.

Rajagopalan, K. (2009). Truth theories. In Chapman and Routledge (2009: 238–44).

Reboul, A. (2004). Conversational implicatures: nonce or generalized? In Noveck and Sperber (2004: 322–32).

Recanati, F. (1993). *Direct Reference: From Language to Thought.* Oxford. Blackwell.

— (2004). *Literal Meaning.* Cambridge: Cambridge University Press.

— (2005). Literalism and contextualism: some varieties. In Preyer and Peter (2005: 171–96).

— (2010). *Truth-Conditional Pragmatics*. Oxford: Oxford University Press.

Reimer, M. and Bezuidenhout, A. (eds) (2004). *Descriptions and Beyond*. Oxford: Oxford University Press.
Roberts, C. (2010). Institutional and professional discourse. In Cummings (2010: 224–5).
Robinson, D. (2005). *Introducing Performative Pragmatics*. London: Routledge.
Rühlemann, C. (2011). Corpus-based pragmatics II: quantitative studies. In Bublitz and Norrick (2011: 629–56).
Sacks, H. (1992). *Lectures on Conversation*. 2 vols. Oxford: Blackwell.
Sadock, J. M. (2004). Speech acts. In Horn and Ward (2004: 53–73).
Sauerland, U., and Yatsushiro, K. (eds) (2009). *Semantics and Pragmatics: From Experiment to Theory*. London: Palgrave Macmillan.
Saul, J. (2002). Speaker meaning, what is said and what is implicated. *Noûs* 36, 228–48.
Searle, J. R. (1969). *Speech Acts: An Essay in the Philosophy of Language*. Cambridge: Cambridge University Press.
— (1975). A taxonomy of speech acts. In K. Gunderson (ed.), *Language, Mind and Knowledge*. Minneapolis: University of Minnesota Press, 344–69.
— and Vanderveken, D. (1985). *Foundations of Illocutionary Logic*. Cambridge: Cambridge University Press.
Sidnell, J. (2010). *Conversation Analysis*. Oxford: Wiley-Blackwell.
Slobin, D. I. (1996). From 'thought and language' to 'thinking for speaking'. In J. J. Gumperz and S. C. Levinson (eds), *Rethinking Linguistic Relativity*. Cambridge: Cambridge University Press.
Spencer, C. (2010). Character vs. content. In Barber and Stainton (2010: 44–6).
Sperber, D., and Wilson, D. (1995). *Relevance: Communication and Cognition*, 2nd edn. Oxford: Blackwell.
Stanley, J. (2000). Context and logical form. *Linguistics and Philosophy* 23, 391–434.
Stemmer, B., and Schönle, P. W. (2000). Neuropragmatics in the 21st century. *Brain and Language* 71: 233–6.
Taylor, K. (2010). Contextualism. In Cummings (2010: 75–9).
ten Hacken, P. (2010). Formalism/formalist linguistics. In Barber and Stainton (2010: 258–65).
ten Have, P. (2010). Conversation analysis. In Cummings (2010: 84–5).
Traugott, E. C. (2004). Historical pragmatics. In Horn and Ward (2004: 538–61).
Trosborg, A. (ed.) (2010). *Pragmatics across Languages and Cultures*. Berlin: Mouton de Gruyter.
Trudgill, P. (2003). *A Glossary of Sociolinguistics*. Oxford: Oxford University Press.
Urmson, J. O., and Rée, J. (eds) (1989). *The Concise Encyclopedia of Western Philosophy and Philosophers*. London: Routledge.
van Eemeren, F. H., and Grootendorst, R. (2004). *A Systematic Theory of Argumentation: The Pragma-dialectical Approach*. Cambridge: Cambridge University Press.
van Rooij, R. (2004). Relevance in bidirectional Optimality Theory. In Blutner and Zeevat (2004: 173–210).
Verschueren, J. (1995). The pragmatic perspective. In J. Verschueren, J. O. H. Östman, J. Blommaert, and C. Bulcaen (eds), *Handbook of Pragmatics*. Amsterdam: Benjamins.
— (1999). *Understanding Pragmatics*. London: Arnold.
Ward, G., and Birner, B. (2004). Information structure and non-canonical syntax. In Horn and Ward (2004: 153–74).
Watts, R. J., Ide, S., and Ehlich, K. (eds) (2005). *Politeness in Language: Studies in its History, Theory and Practice*, 2nd edn. Berlin: Mouton de Gruyter.

Wierzbicka, A. (2003). *Cross-Cultural Pragmatics*, 2nd edn. Berlin: Mouton de Gruyter.

Wilson, D., and Carston, R. (2007). A unitary approach to lexical pragmatics: relevance, inference and *ad hoc* concepts. In N. Burton-Roberts (ed.), *Pragmatics*. London: Palgrave Macmillan, 230–59.

— and Sperber, D. (2004). Relevance theory. In Horn and Ward (2004: 607–32).

Yus, F. (2011). *Cyberpragmatics: Internet-Mediated Communication in Context*. Amsterdam: Benjamins.